Children Are Born Mathematicians

Supporting Mathematical Development, Birth to Age 8

Eugene Geist

OHIO UNIVERSITY

Merrill
is an imprint of

Upper Saddle River, New Jersey
Columbus, Ohio

Library of Congress Cataloging-in-Publication Data

Geist, Eugene.

Children are born mathematicians: supporting mathematical development, birth to age eight/Eugene Geist.—1st ed.

p. cm.

Includes bibliographical references and index.

ISBN-13: 978-0-13-111677-1 (alk. paper)

ISBN-10: 0-13-111677-0 (alk. paper)

1. Mathematics—Study and teaching (Preschool) 2. Mathematics—Study and teaching (Primary) 3. Education, Preschool. 4. Education, Primary. I. Title.

QA135.6.G45 2009

372.7'044—dc22

2007038910

Vice President and Executive Publisher: Jeffery W. Johnston
Publisher: Kevin M. Davis
Acquisitions Editor: Julie Peters
Editorial Assistant: Tiffany Bitzel
Production Coordination: Erin Melloy, S4Carlisle Editorial Services
Senior Project Manager: Linda Hillis Bayma
Design Coordinator: Diane C. Lorenzo
Photo Coordinator: Valerie Schultz
Cover Designer: Ali Mohrman
Cover Image: Jupiter Images
Operations Specialist: Laura Messerly
Director of Marketing: Quinn Perkson
Marketing Manager: Darcy Betts Prybella
Marketing Coordinator: Brian Mounts

This book was set in Berling Roman by S4Carlisle Publishing Services. It was printed and bound by R.R. Donnelley & Sons Company. The cover was printed by R.R. Donnelley & Sons Company.

Pearson Education Ltd.
Pearson Education Singapore Pte. Ltd.
Pearson Education Canada, Ltd.
Pearson Education–Japan

Pearson Education Australia Pty. Limited
Pearson Education North Asia Ltd.
Pearson Educación de Mexico, S.A. de C.V.
Pearson Education Malaysia Pte. Ltd.

Merrill
is an imprint of

10 9 8 7 6 5 4 3 2
ISBN-13: 978-0-13-111677-1
ISBN-10:   0-13-111677-0

Preface

Children Are Born Mathematicians is a book designed for prospective early childhood practitioners. In a departure from many books for early childhood mathematics, this book begins at birth and goes through the completion of third grade. As early childhood professionals, we need to understand that, much as with literacy, becoming a mathematician begins at birth. That is why this book is entitled *Children Are Born Mathematicians*. The title does not imply that children are born *knowing* mathematics, but that they are born as active thinkers constantly trying to make sense of their world. Their brains are designed to take in information, synthesize it, and grow from the process. These same mechanisms that allow them to interact with and experience the world help them to organize the knowledge they gain from these experiences. Part of that organization takes the form of emergent mathematical abilities.

In my teaching of mathematics to future early childhood professionals, I struggled to find a book that had all the elements that I desired. Therefore I wrote this book to be all of the following:

- **Chronological**—Many books are topically organized. They focus on ways of teaching specific content such as addition, multiplication, division, and other topics. However, I have always wanted to be able to easily find out what each developmental age range was like and what mathematics topics young children are developmentally ready for. I also wanted to know what schools were expecting from each age range and grade. Every state has a set of standards for each grade level that guides teachers. I feel that clearly understanding what is expected from each age is vitally important. The National Council of Teachers of Mathematics recently released their *Curriculum Focal Points for Prekindergarten Through Grade 8 Mathematics*, which also emphasizes a chronological and developmental approach to mathematics. I have relied heavily on this document and refer to it throughout this book.

- **Developmental**—This book focuses on what we know about how children grow and develop. In fact Chapters 5 to 8 begin with sections on what each age range is like physically, emotionally, socially, and cognitively and a section on what mathematical concepts each age range is typically developmentally ready to learn. Teaching mathematics is more than just helping children to learn their numbers. It is a complex process that involves all domains of development. Understanding the child is the first step in teaching mathematics in a developmentally appropriate and interactive way.

- **Constructivist**—Much of the philosophy and ideas presented in this book are based on Dr. Constance Kamii's work on constructivist mathematics done at the University of Alabama at Birmingham. Her excellent *Young Children Reinvent Arithmetic* and *Young Children Continue to Reinvent Arithmetic* were vital resources for the constructivist basis of this book. The videos that accompany these books are available from Teachers College Press and make a wonderful addition to any program on learning how to teach children mathematics. The first paragraph of *Young Children Continue to Reinvent Arithmetic—Second Grade* states the principle I tried to base this book on: "According to common sense, human beings acquire knowledge by *internalizing* it from the environment. Piaget showed with scientific evidence, however, that each child *constructs*, or *creates*, logico-mathematical knowledge from within" (p. 3). This book also relies on Vygotsky and other social-constructivists for concepts such as the *Zone of Proximal Development* and scaffolding.

- **Comprehensive**—This book strives to be the most comprehensive resource for teaching mathematics available. I have included information on different theories of mathematical learning, research on how the brain develops, practical information on preparing your environment and yourself for teaching mathematics to children, information on dealing with diverse populations of students, developmental guidelines for teaching mathematics, sample standards, resources, lesson plans, and many other resources to help prepare teachers for helping children grow mathematically. I tried to include all the things that I need in a textbook in order to effectively and thoroughly teach a course on early childhood mathematics.

The Guiding Principles of This Book's Approach to Mathematics

The first guiding principle of this book is that **there is a Mathematics Acquisition Device that allows us as human beings to develop an understanding of mathematics** (Butterworth, 1999; Geist, 2003). It is as difficult to prevent a child from learning basic mathematical concepts as it is to prevent him from learning to speak. However, children can and must be stimulated and facilitated in a mathematically rich environment, where they are asked to think mathematically and use math as a tool, if they are to move beyond the basic concepts.

The second guiding principle of this book is that **mathematics is an interactive process.** Children learn mathematics by using it to solve problems in their environment, such as collecting lunch money and playing math games. This type of interactive learning requires children to be social, discussing and arguing mathematics with other children and even adults. The adult's role is one of a facilitator rather than a transmitter of knowledge. For example, if two children are working on a problem and neither seems to be moving forward individually, the teacher may suggest that they work together. As they discuss the problem, they should gain new insight that will help them come up with a solution. If not, the teacher can use questioning techniques to help them discuss the problem. The teacher should refrain from offering them solutions, but rather, encourage them to use their own natural thinking ability to come up with an answer.

The third guiding principle of this book is that **teachers should allow children to come up with ways of problem solving based on their own thought process rather than directly teaching methods to achieve a correct answer.** For example, when I was taught how to add, I was taught the standard algorithm. Add the ones column, and carry the 10. However, there is much research that shows that when we teach children adult methods of solving problems rather than allowing them to rely on their own thinking, the child's mathematical thinking abilities are weakened. Instead, they learn how to follow procedures without a deeper conceptual understanding. When children are allowed to come up with their own methods of solving double-column addition, their methods vary greatly, but all demonstrate an understanding of the process that is not evident when they blindly follow rules.

The fourth guiding principle of this book is that *all* **children can learn mathematics.** Males, females, and people of all ethnic, linguistic, and cultural backgrounds are equally able to succeed at mathematics. Myths to the contrary have no basis in research or reality. An examination of diversity issues reveals that there are disparities between these groups especially linked to the effects of poverty. However, these issues are not rooted in the child's ability to learn mathematics, but in the educational pitfalls and assumptions that lead to a self-fulfilling prophecy. Many times the subtle and unconscious signals sent to groups can lead them to believe that they are "not good at mathematics." Luckily, when knowledge and research highlight these prejudices, these misconceptions shrivel. If teachers are aware of the issues, the pitfalls can be avoided.

The fifth and final guiding principle of this book is that **mathematics is integrated into our daily lives and should therefore be integrated throughout the school day.** Mathematics is best learned in the context of real-life situations and activities. During math time, problems should be relevant to the life of the child. During other subjects and activities such as reading, science, art, music, and even recess and lunch, teachers should look for ways to inject mathematics. Using the project approach is a great way to integrate mathematics with other subjects in a meaningful context for the child. An investigation of a school bus can elicit many questions and provide many opportunities for children to integrate mathematics with other subjects, as they learn about what makes the bus go, how it was built, and what it is used for. A simple question such as "How many people can ride on this bus?" can lead to more questions, such as "How many seats are there?", "How many children can sit in each seat?", "Do we count the driver?", and "How big are the people?" not to mention "What shapes do we find in or on a school bus?", all of which can be answered using mathematical principles and processes.

Organization of This Book

The first four chapters cover aspects of becoming a teacher of mathematics to young children. This includes: understanding standards-based education and using standards from the National Council of Teachers of Mathematics and your state; topics on development including the physical, social-emotional, and physical domains, as well as new research on the development and growth of the brain; developmental theory and how it relates to the teaching of mathematics; working with ethnically, culturally, and linguistically diverse students; working with children with special needs and learning disabilities such as dyslexia and dyscalculia; developing an engaging environment for supporting mathematics; and dealing with your own personal development as a teacher and perhaps overcoming your own anxieties about using and teaching mathematics.

Chapters 5 to 8 are devoted to understanding the unique developmental and mathematical needs of specific age ranges and requirements for learning mathematics. Each chapter includes a section on what children are like during this age physically, socially-emotionally, and cognitively; what mathematical concepts they should be learning; incorporating standards into mathematical teaching at each age level; adapting the environment to meet the unique needs of each age level; developmentally appropriate strategies for teaching mathematics to each age level; sample lesson plans; and developmentally appropriate assessment techniques. The old adage "Give a person a fish and he eats for a day, teach him to fish and he eats for a lifetime" applies here. The lesson plans in these chapters are designed to give examples of good lessons and the chapters are meant to guide you to learning how to develop more good lessons. This book is not designed as a collection of lesson plans to be directly implemented, but rather a resource for learning about individual students and groups of students and designing developmentally appropriate, interactive, engaging, and constructivist lessons to meet their needs.

Chapter 9 is my favorite chapter because it shows how math pervades all other content. This chapter includes strategies on integrating math with reading, science, social studies, music, art, and physical activity. Math occurs in the context of daily living. In real life people don't just stop and do math, they use it as a tool in situations such as leaving a tip at a restaurant, balancing a checkbook, building something useful or for amusement, or playing games such as cards or dominoes. Many people who claim to hate math love to play games, which often include some pretty complex mathematics. It is also my favorite chapter because it allows me to discuss the project approach as a method of integrating mathematics into other subjects and bringing the child's real-life context into the classroom. Classroom environments should not be isolated from the outside world, though this is often the case. The project approach allows children and teachers to explore mathematics and other subjects in their community and surroundings through field trips, guest speakers, and in-depth investigations of topics.

For Students: How to Succeed in This Course

This book relies on the PQ4R approach to reading and studying. As you read these chapters there are pedagogical elements to help you use this system. **PQ4R** stands for **Preview, Question, Read, Reflect, Recite, Review.** The first step is to **preview** the chapter. Skim over each chapter and preview the headings and subheadings of each section. You may also use the chapter objectives to preview what the objectives for this chapter are going to be. Next, you will want to decide on some **questions** that you would like to have answered by this chapter. After previewing, decide on some questions based on the objectives and headings. At the end of each chapter are sample questions to help you discuss and apply what you have learned. They may also help you develop questions to answer while you read. The next step is to **read** the chapter in depth. Pay attention to the definitions that are bolded in the text. These are important concepts and vocabulary to know as you study. Read for understanding. If something is not clear, read it again or make a note of it so you can ask your instructor in class. After reading you must **reflect**. This is the step that many overlook. Reflection requires you to think about the information and synthesize new ideas from it. Learning is more than just memorization. It requires analysis, synthesis, and consolidation. Reflect on how this relates to your experiences and what you have seen in classrooms. How does it fit with your preconceived knowledge or beliefs about how mathematics is learned and taught? Most importantly, think about how this information will *change* your practices and beliefs about mathematics. The next step is the one most people dread—**recite**. There are some concepts and vocabulary you will need to memorize and know in order to understand the material. Use the vocabulary and bolded words to help with this. Also use the chapter objectives and discussion questions to help you develop an effective recitation method. Finally, you should **review** your learning. How well do you feel you understand the objectives laid out at the beginning of the chapter? You may want to go back and skim over the chapter again to test your understanding of the material. The discussion questions at the end are designed to help facilitate group review of the material.

As an early childhood teacher, you will guide the first formal experiences with mathematics that most of these children will have. It is important to get these children off on the right foot. Too many have developed negative attitudes toward mathematics by as early as second grade. It is vital that teachers of children birth through third grade understand child development and developmentally appropriate mathematics for young children, in order to promote a love of mathematical learning in all children.

Acknowledgments

I would like to thank everyone who helped me put this book together.

My Editors—Thank you for your support, suggestions, and above all patience in completing this process. Thank you to Julie Peters and Ben Prout, who helped me to take some raw ideas and mold them into a book that will be useful and readable to people other than just myself. I would also like to thank copyeditor Holly Tavel, photo editor Valerie Schultz, and project managers Erin Melloy at S4Carlisle Editorial Services and Linda Bayma at Pearson/Merrill for their help in polishing this first edition.

The Reviewers—Thank you for your time, insights, and suggestions: Thomasenia Lott Adams, University of Florida; Junie Albers-Biddle, University of Central Florida; Alan B. Bates, Illinois State University; Cecelia Benelli, Western Illinois University; Diane Cerreto, Eastern Connecticut State University; Frances Kuwahara Chinn, California State University, Los Angeles; Johnna Darragh, Heartland Community College; Sara M. Davis, University of Arkansas, Fort Smith; Mary Larue, J. Sargeant Reynolds Community College; Joohi Lee, University of Texas, Arlington; Judith Macks, Towson University; Debra Shelt, Bowling Green State University; and Donna Wittmer, University of Colorado.

The Teachers at the Ohio University Child Development Center—Thank you for your willingness to let me come and observe in your classrooms. The chapters on infants, toddlers, and preschoolers would not be the same without your input and cooperation.

My Family—I would especially like to thank my mother, Gloria Joan Geist, who, while holding down a full-time job, still found time to do a great deal of editing when the book needed it. It would never have gotten to this stage without you. Thanks also to my father, who put up with her late-night editing. A special thanks goes to my wife Kamile Geist, a music therapist and music educator, whose help on the sections of this book devoted to integrating music were invaluable. Without your love and support this project never would have reached completion. Thanks also to my stepson Dylan, for providing me with valuable material for this book by agreeing to sit for pictures, answering my questions about math, and even helping to write some of the pages in this book. Your first-grade perspective on learning mathematics was revelatory.

NCTM—Portions of *Curriculum Focal Points for Prekindergarten Through Grade 8 Mathematics: A Quest for Coherence* by the National Council of Teachers of Mathematics were reprinted with permission.

About the Author

Eugene Geist is an Associate Professor of Early Childhood Education at Ohio University where he studies how children construct and learn mathematics. He holds a PhD in Child Development and Early Childhood Education from the University of Alabama at Birmingham and a Masters degree in Education from the University of Cincinnati.

At Ohio University he has been teaching Introduction to Child Development for over eight years. Additionally, he has taught courses in mathematics methods, advanced integrated curriculum, and graduate level developmental theory and child development.

As an active advocate for young children, he has participated in several international conferences in Spain and Mexico speaking on the concepts of emergent mathematics and the idea of a "Mathematics Acquisition Device." Some of his recent presentations include the keynote address at the First International Conference on Logico Mathematical Thinking, the Strategies and Methods of Education Conference, and the First World Preschool and Primary Education Conference as a part of UNESCO's 2007 Universal Forum of Cultures.

Among the numerous articles he has published in NAEYC's *Young Children* journal, an article on using music to enhance mathematics teaching and learning was published in March 2008, which he co-wrote with his wife, Kamile Geist.

References

Butterworth, B. (1999). *What counts: How every brain is hardwired for math*. New York: Free Press.

Geist, E. (2003). Teaching and learning about math: Infants and toddlers exploring mathematics. *Young Children, 58*(1), 10–12.

Brief Contents

Chapter 1 / Children and Mathematics: A Natural Combination   1

Chapter 2 / Building a Knowledge Base and Learning to Reflect   35

Chapter 3 / Diversity, Equity, and Individualized Instruction   65

Chapter 4 / Creating a Constructivist Classroom   103

Chapter 5 / Infants and Toddlers   135

Chapter 6 / Preschool Age   183

Chapter 7 / Kindergarten and First Grade   239

Chapter 8 / Second and Third Grade   291

Chapter 9 / Integrating Mathematics   349

Appendix / Sample State Standards   379

Index   394

Contents

Chapter 1 / Children and Mathematics: A Natural Combination   1

Chapter Objectives   1

Principle 1 – Thinking about the problem, not the answer, is what is most important / Principle 2 – Process is more important than product / Principle 3 – Answers come from a logical certainty, not an authority figure

WHAT IS EMERGENT MATHEMATICS?   4

Promoting Emergent Math

MAKING A DIFFERENCE AS A TEACHER   7

RECENT FINDINGS IN TEACHING MATHEMATICS   9

TREATING CHILDREN AS MATHEMATICIANS   11

Implications for Early Childhood Education / NCTM Principles, Standards, and Curriculum Focal Points / NCTM's Guiding Principles for School Mathematics / NCTM Standards for School Mathematics / NCTM and NAEYC Joint Statement on Mathematics / Curriculum Focal Points for Prekindergarten Through Grade 8

PUTTING THE PIECES TOGETHER: THE "3E" APPROACH   28

SUMMARY   29

WEB SITES   31

DISCUSS AND APPLY WHAT YOU HAVE LEARNED   31

REFERENCES   32

Chapter 2 / Building a Knowledge Base and Learning to Reflect   35

Chapter Objectives   35

UNDERSTANDING YOURSELF   36

The Process of Reflection   /   Dealing with Our Own
Math Anxiety First

TEACHERS ARE DECISION MAKERS   40

A Lesson in Mathematics

UNDERSTANDING CHILD DEVELOPMENT   43

The Behaviorist Approach   /   Behaviorism and Mathematics   /
The Montessori Method   /   Montessori's Materials and Mathematics   /
A Visual Approach to Learning Mathematics   /   The Constructivist
Approach   /   Constructivism and Mathematics   /   NCTM and
Theoretical Basis for Mathematics

UNDERSTANDING YOUR STUDENTS   57

Learning Styles

SUMMARY   60

WEB SITES   61

DISCUSS AND APPLY WHAT YOU HAVE LEARNED   62

REFERENCES   62

Chapter 3 / Diversity, Equity, and Individualized Instruction   65

Chapter Objectives   65

NATURE AND NURTURE IN THE MATHEMATICS CLASSROOM   66

INDIVIDUALIZED INSTRUCTION   67

Holding High Expectations for All Students

SOCIOECONOMIC FACTORS   72

Overcoming SES Obstacles

MINORITY STUDENT ACHIEVEMENT   78

CHILDREN WITH SPECIAL NEEDS   82

Creating Inclusive Environments   /   Gifted Students

ENGLISH LANGUAGE LEARNERS AND LINGUISTIC DIVERSITY   89

Overcoming the Language Barrier

GENDER DIFFERENCES   91

Accommodating Differences in Boys' and Girls' Learning Styles   /
Standardized Testing and Gender Differences

SUMMARY   95

WEB SITES   96

DISCUSS AND APPLY WHAT YOU HAVE LEARNED   97

REFERENCES   98

Chapter 4 / Creating a Constructivist Classroom   **103**

Chapter Objectives   103

THE CHILD-CENTERED CURRICULUM   104

    Teachable Moments   /   Common Objections to the Child-

    Centered Approach

PREPARATION OF THE CHILD-CENTERED

   ENVIRONMENT   115

    Preparing the Environment

MATERIALS   118

    Manipulatives   /   Textbooks and Math Series

WHAT TO DO BEFORE THE FIRST DAY   123

SUMMARY   128

WEB SITES   129

DISCUSS AND APPLY WHAT YOU HAVE LEARNED   130

REFERENCES   131

Chapter 5 / Infants and Toddlers   **135**

Chapter Objectives   135

WHAT ARE INFANTS AND TODDLERS LIKE?   136

WHAT MATHEMATICAL CONCEPTS DO INFANTS

   AND TODDLERS LEARN?   145

    The Concept of "More"   /   The Concept of "One"   /

    Making Relationships

MEETING STANDARDS WITH INFANTS

   AND TODDLERS   152

WHAT DOES AN INFANT AND TODDLER LEARNING

   ENVIRONMENT LOOK LIKE?   157

DEVELOPMENTALLY APPROPRIATE STRATEGIES

   AND ACTIVITIES FOR INFANTS AND TODDLERS   159

    Supporting Emergent Mathematics

SAMPLE INFANT AND TODDLER LESSON PLANS   168

ASSESSMENT   174

  Standardized vs. Authentic Assessment   /   Formal vs. Informal
  Assessment   /   Formative vs. Summative Assessment   /   Using
  Assessment with Infants and Toddlers

SUMMARY   177

WEB SITES   178

DISCUSS AND APPLY WHAT YOU HAVE LEARNED   179

REFERENCES   180

Chapter 6 / Preschool Age   183

Chapter Objectives   183

WHAT ARE PRESCHOOL CHILDREN LIKE?   184

  Physical Development   /   Cognitive Development   /   Symbolic and
  Intuitive Thought   /   Conservation   /   Centration   /   Reversibility of
  Thought   /   Emotional Development   /   Play   /   Developmental
  Milestones for Preschool Mathematics

WHAT MATHEMATICAL CONCEPTS DO PRESCHOOL
  CHILDREN LEARN?   191

  Mathematical Concepts in Preschool   /   Numerical Concepts   /
    Shape, Measurement, and Geometric Concepts

MEETING STANDARDS WITH PRESCHOOL CHILDREN   204

  General Mathematics Standards and Benchmarks
  for Preschool Mathematics

WHAT DOES A PRESCHOOL MATHEMATICS LEARNING
  ENVIRONMENT LOOK LIKE?   205

DEVELOPMENTALLY APPROPRIATE STRATEGIES
  AND ACTIVITIES FOR PRESCHOOL-AGE CHILDREN   208

SAMPLE PRESCHOOL LESSON PLANS   217

ASSESSMENT   230

SUMMARY   233

WEB SITES   234

DISCUSS AND APPLY WHAT YOU HAVE LEARNED   235

REFERENCES   235

Chapter 7 / Kindergarten and First Grade   239

Chapter Objectives   239

WHAT ARE K–1 CHILDREN LIKE?   240

  Physical Development   /   Cognitive Development   /   Linguistic
  Development   /   Social-Emotional Development

WHAT MATHEMATICAL CONCEPTS DO K–1 CHILDREN LEARN?   245
   Encouraging Intellectual Autonomy / Mathematical Concepts
   in Kindergarten / Mathematical Concepts in First Grade
MEETING STANDARDS WITH K–1 CHILDREN   259
   NCTM Focal Points
WHAT DOES A K–1 MATHEMATICS LEARNING
   ENVIRONMENT LOOK LIKE?   262
DEVELOPMENTALLY APPROPRIATE STRATEGIES AND ACTIVITIES FOR
   K–1 CHILDREN   263
   Word Problems / Whole-Class Instruction /
   Math Games / Projects
SAMPLE KINDERGARTEN AND FIRST GRADE LESSON PLANS   269
ASSESSING MATHEMATICS IN K–1   282
SUMMARY   287
WEB SITES   288
DISCUSS AND APPLY WHAT YOU HAVE LEARNED   288
REFERENCES   289

Chapter 8 / **Second and Third Grade**   **291**
   Chapter Objectives   291
WHAT ARE SECOND AND THIRD GRADERS LIKE?   292
   Physical Development / Cognitive Development /
   Social-Emotional Development
WHAT MATHEMATICAL CONCEPTS DO SECOND-
   AND THIRD-GRADE CHILDREN LEARN?   296
   Base 10 and Place Value / Multiplication and Division / Fractions /
   Linear Measurement / Sides and Angles That Make Up Two-Dimensional
   Shapes
LEARNING DISABILITIES—ADHD, DYSLEXIA, AND
   DYSCALCULIA   311
MEETING STANDARDS FOR SECOND- AND THIRD-GRADE
   CHILDREN   314
WHAT DOES A SECOND- AND THIRD-GRADE MATHEMATICS
   LEARNING ENVIRONMENT LOOK LIKE?   317
DEVELOPMENTALLY APPROPRIATE STRATEGIES AND
   ACTIVITIES FOR SECOND- AND THIRD-GRADE CHILDREN   318
   Teaching Lessons and Problem Solving / Technology / Logo /
   Calculators / Timed and Fluency Activities / Worksheets and
   Homework / Hands-On Materials and Manipulative

SAMPLE SECOND- AND THIRD-GRADE LESSON PLANS   326
ASSESSING MATHEMATICS IN SECOND AND THIRD GRADE   338
SUMMARY   341
WEB SITES   342
DISCUSS AND APPLY WHAT YOU HAVE LEARNED   343
REFERENCES   343

Chapter 9 / Integrating Mathematics   **349**
Chapter Objectives   349
THE IMPORTANCE OF INTEGRATION   350
   Integrating Math with Reading   /   Integrating Math with Science   /
   Integrating Math with Social Studies   /   Black History Month   /
   Integrating Math with Music   /   Music Experiences to Promote Emergent
   Mathematics   /   Integrating Math with Art   /   Leonardo DaVinci   /
   Integrating Math with Physical Activity
THE PROJECT APPROACH   370
   Topic Selection   /   Using the Project Approach
SUMMARY   373
WEB SITES   374
DISCUSS AND APPLY WHAT YOU HAVE LEARNED   375
REFERENCES   376

Appendix   /   Sample State Standards   **379**

Index   **394**

Note: Every effort has been made to provide accurate and current Internet information in this book. However, the Internet and information posted on it are constantly changing, and it is inevitable that some of the Internet addresses listed in this textbook will change.

CHAPTER 1

Children and Mathematics:
A Natural Combination

CHAPTER OBJECTIVES

After you have read this chapter, you should be able to:

- Explain some of the basic principles of best practice in teaching mathematics to young children
- Explain how mathematics can be understood as *emergent*
- Describe the benefits of viewing children as young mathematicians
- Analyze the importance of TIMSS findings for teaching mathematics to young children
- Discuss the importance of the *NCTM Principles and Standards for Mathematics* and *Curriculum Focal Points*

A man buys a horse for $40 and sells it for $50. He then realizes he has another buyer that would pay even more for the horse. So he buys the horse back for $60 and sells it again for $70. Did the seller break even, lose, or make money? If he made or lost money, how much? (Burns, 1992)

Siblings ages 5, 8, and 9 have a heated discussion about this problem around the dinner table. The mother weighs in with her take on the matter, and the children begin to argue with her.

"He makes $10 each time he sells it but loses $10 when he buys it back, so he only makes $10."

"But he's only putting down $100 total and taking in $120—that's a $20 profit."

"But he loses $10 of that when he buys it back . . ."

A family discussing a math problem over dinner? Impossible? Not necessarily. What is happening here should be the goal of every mathematics teacher. If children are excited enough about a topic that they want to talk about it outside of the classroom, many of the problems of teaching mathematics will be solved. Truth be told, this situation actually happened. The parent involved was excited to pass the story along to me. And this is not an isolated case; many teachers have reported similar results when mathematics is made engaging for children.

When I introduced this problem to my college students, we followed a few simple rules in our discussion:

1. Each student worked on the problem alone.
2. We started the discussion and then collected all the different answers each student came up with.
3. Students explained how they came to their answers and defended them if another student pointed out a flaw in their method.
4. As the instructor I remained neutral. I did not give evaluative feedback about any given answer.
5. The students were free to disagree with another person's answer.
6. I encouraged them not to give in until they were convinced of a better answer.
7. I never revealed the answer, even though I knew it.

From this exercise, we discovered a few behaviors among college students that are also common among young children. First, students were shy about giving their answers, maybe because they have learned that mathematics is a passive experience, or because they feared being wrong in front of the whole class. Even being told that their answer is incorrect is enough to make most children hesitate to answer a question next time. Second, once an answer was given to the group, all eyes went to the teacher. Perhaps the college students, like many young students, expected the teacher to pass judgment on an answer before entertaining another.

In this case, the teacher may feel uncomfortable because she may not know the answer either. You might be asking, "How can I be a teacher if I don't know the answer myself?" This is a good question. However, what is most important is that teachers understand a set of principles for using best practices to teach mathematics.

Principle 1—Thinking about the problem, not the answer, is what is most important

The teacher is a facilitator, not the person with all the answers. The teacher's job in this scenario is to record the students' solutions, focus the discussion, and follow up with questions. As they discussed this problem, in the example outlined above, the students

The process children go through to get an answer is just as important as the answer they give.

Katelyn Metzger/Merrill

formed into "camps" around certain answers. Usually, with enough discussion, one answer emerges as being the best because everyone agrees on it. Now comes the hard part: You should still not give children the answer. Children need to understand that correct answers do not come from a teacher or a textbook, but rather from logical deduction. As children discuss possible answers among themselves, they discover they are very good at finding errors in a thinking process (Kamii, 1984). In this way, they learn to think for themselves and defend their answers until they are convinced of a better approach. This leads us to the second rule of teaching mathematics.

Principle 2—Process is more important than product

As we will discuss throughout this book, math is not just a series of facts. Math is a series of relationships, concepts, and thought processes. While memorization and skills development help children do some math tasks faster and more efficiently, these methods should not be the central focus of teaching mathematics, especially for young children (Kamii, 1984; Kamii & De Vries, 1973; Wenglinsky, 2004). For example, memorization of addition facts works best after children have been introduced to the concepts of addition and place value through exploration of thought-provoking problems and everyday activities. If children are directly taught addition "facts" before they personally experience addition through play and manipulation, they will learn a set of unrelated facts such as "5 + 4 = 9" with no conceptual understanding of number to link them to. Our goal in teaching young children mathematics should be to help them achieve a deep understanding of the complex numerical relationships that underlie the answers. Kamii (1984) called this process "reinvention of mathematics." Children have to reinvent the concepts of mathematics in their own minds.

Furthermore, when children are trained to expect teachers to have all the answers, they learn to rely upon their own thinking ability less and less (Kamii et al., 2000; Kamii, 2004). As long as the solution is ambiguous, however, children will continue to think about and refine their answers. Perhaps, as in the opening scenario, this might lead to children discussing the problem, exchanging views, and solving the problem in many different ways. We assign so much power to classroom authorities that as soon as that authority, usually a teacher or textbook, confirms an answer, we accept it as a fact. This leads us to the third and final principle.

Principle 3—Answers come from a logical certainty, not an authority figure

Children are natural problem solvers. In infancy and toddlerhood, children explore their world with an amazing zeal. Their problem-solving abilities grow stronger in preschool and kindergarten as they develop symbolic thought, and use numbers to represent quantities of objects, such as holding up three fingers on their third birthday. In the primary grades, children's logic begins to develop, and their ability to perform mathematical functions such as addition and subtraction bloom. The danger along the way is when adults discourage thinking and problem solving in favor of memorization and recitation. Children in these early childhood years adapt quickly to what is expected of them. If they are encouraged to think for themselves and be self-reliant, their natural thinking ability will grow and flourish. If they are told to sit quietly and do repetitive, uninteresting worksheets that have no relevance to their lives and which demand memorization and recitation rather than thinking, they will begin to see math as *that type of activity*.

We should be treating children like young mathematicians from their earliest prenumber explorations. The critical thinking involved in solving a problem such as $12+12$ is similar to that used by adolescents and adults in solving quadratic equations (Kamii, 1984; Kamii & Chemeketa, 1982; Kamii et al., 2000). Children are born mathematicians; it is our job as teachers to facilitate their innate mathematical thinking ability. A meaningful understanding of mathematics is nurtured through a wide variety of critical explorations rather than an emphasis on facts.

WHAT IS EMERGENT MATHEMATICS?

Emergent mathematics is a term we will use to describe how children construct mathematics from birth and continuing throughout the life of the person through a combination of cognitive development and interaction with their environment. The principle is similar to the concept of *emergent literacy*, which has become the standard for teaching children to read and write in early childhood classrooms. Both emergent mathematics and emergent literacy suggest that, young children, whether they are 6 weeks, 6 months, or 6 years old, need to be immersed in mathematics and literacy from the day they are born, through interactions with parents or caregivers.

Educators and researchers are beginning to look at the construction of mathematical concepts the same way that we understand literacy development—as emergent. The idea that literacy learning begins the day that children are born is widely accepted. Noam Chomsky has discovered strong evidence for an innate "language acquisition device" that provides humans with a framework for learning language (Chomsky, 2006; Chomsky, 2002). The internal structure of this "device" allows children to interact with language at a very early age without being directly taught the rules of grammar and syntax (Otto, 2002). Reading to infants, toddlers, and preschoolers is known to be an early predictor of positive literacy because it immerses children in language and gives them an opportunity to interact with it (Feiler & Webster, 1997; Kamii, Manning, & Manning, 1991; Lally et al., 2001; Pickett, 1998).

Mathematical understanding can be viewed in a very similar way. During the first few months of life, children begin to construct the foundations for future mathematical concepts as they interact mentally, physically, and socially with their environment and with others. Even before a child can add or count, he must construct ideas about mathematics that cannot be directly taught. Just as emergent readers learn that letters in the alphabet correspond to spoken sounds, the understanding that numbers have a quantity attached to them is actually a complex relationship that children must construct (Xu, Spelke, & Goddard, 2005). There is evidence for a "mathematics acquisition device" (MAD) that provides a framework for mathematical concepts similar in function to the "language acquisition device" (Butterworth, 1999; Butterworth, 2005). This MAD allows children to:

1. Naturally acquire some mathematical concepts even without direct teaching;
2. Follow a generally standard sequence of gradual development;
3. Construct mathematical concepts from a very early age.

With careful examination of infants, toddlers, preschoolers, and children in primary grades, one can see evidence of all these criteria.

Young children may not be able to add or subtract, but the relationships they are forming and their interactions with a stimulating environment encourage them to construct a foundation and framework for what will eventually become mathematical concepts (Sinclair & Kamii, 1994; Sinclair & Kamii, 1995). If you watch long enough you will see some amazing mathematical thought going on in even the youngest children (Butterworth, 1999). Consider the following example:

> An 18-month-old child playing in a large pit filled with different colored balls drops one ball, then a second ball, and then a third ball over the side of the pit. The child then goes to the opposite side of the pit and drops two balls. He then goes back to the first side, reexamines the grouping of balls, moves to the second side and drops another ball over the side to make a grouping of three.

The coordination and comparison of "threes" on opposite sides of a structure is clear evidence of this 18-month-old child making a mathematical relationship and putting order into his world. It is not yet a numerical relationship because the child is solely using visual perception—what he sees—to make the judgment of "same" or "different." However, the coordination of dropping three balls each time is evidence of an early understanding of "more," "less," and basic equality. This child may not be developmentally ready for number concepts like counting and quantification, but this simple task shows that children as young as 18 months are making relationships and exercising their logical thought processes. Teachers of infants and toddlers need to be aware of these actions and abilities and provide activities to encourage construction of these mathematical concepts. Emergent mathematics continues throughout early childhood. Encouraging children to construct many different relationships between and among objects, to interact with other children and adults, and to mentally and physically act on the objects around them promote the concept of building we refer to in discussions of emergent mathematics.

Promoting Emergent Math

As mentioned earlier, emergent mathematics requires that teachers take advantage of the natural mathematical development in children and the mathematical environment in which the child participates on a daily basis. This interaction will be different depending on the age and developmental level of the child. What is important is that it emerges from within the child, rather than being taught to him by an adult. Many basic mathematical concepts cannot and should not be directly taught to young children. However, using the concept of emergent mathematics, educators of young children can emphasize and encourage children's interaction with the people,

Construction of math concepts begins as early as birth.

Shirely Zeiberg/PH College

experiences, and materials around them as a means of promoting and encouraging emergent math concepts. Children's logic and mathematical thinking develop through mathematical interaction.

However, not all mathematical knowledge develops naturally and math is not best learned in isolation. The role of the teacher in the development and learning of mathematics is very important. Children need to be nurtured and their learning facilitated to enable them to progress to higher levels of mathematics. A teacher's questions, guidance, and facilitation of the problem-solving *process* cannot be underestimated, even when she does not supply answers.

MAKING A DIFFERENCE AS A TEACHER

All children are unique and have different interests, talents, and modes of learning, and all learn at different rates. When they come into the classroom you can expect to see various levels of mathematical understanding among them. Standard or "cookie cutter" curricula may not meet the needs of children in early childhood. Unfortunately, a reality in schools today is that most public school curricula involves lessons from a math textbook series, a math workbook, or another guide that gives exact step-by-step instructions for how and when to teach a certain concept (Clements & Sarama, 2004; Elkind & Piaget, 1979; "JumpStart 2nd grade," 1996; Kamii & Piaget, 1973).

Despite the presence of a commercial curriculum for young children you as the teacher can still mold and customize your teaching to meet the needs of all children in your classroom. The curriculum you deliver must be flexible enough to allow you to use your knowledge of children's prior understanding to create a mathematics program that meets their level. This program must also stimulate the construction of more complex mathematical understanding (Clements & Sarama, 2004; Elkind & Piaget, 1979; Kamii & Piaget, 1973; Loveless, 2001).

Let's use the analogy of a short-order cook and a chef. The job of a short-order cook at a chain restaurant is to follow a set of instructions for making the food exactly as specified. The cook's goal is to make sure that if someone goes into one of the chain's restaurants in California and orders a hamburger, it will be exactly the same as one served anywhere else in the country. The cook can be trained quickly because all he has to do is follow instructions.

A chef, on the other hand, has a much different job. Not only does a chef prepare food, he also develops dishes, based on his knowledge of how ingredients blend and complement each other. Chefs train for years to learn their trade. They are inventive, creative, and each has his or her own style. While a chef knows the basic recipe for a dish, he also experiments, adding his own spin and using his knowledge of locally available foods to make the dish the best it can be. Chefs try new things, think about what will work and what won't work, and make decisions and judgments based on their combination of knowledge and training.

As a teacher of young children you need to be a chef, not a cook. Acting like a chef means that you know your students' abilities, developmental levels, and interests; you know what resources are available in your school, families, and community; and you have a knowledge base of research and experience in pedagogy. All of these resources help you to develop a mathematics program that is interactive and tailored to meet the educational needs of your students. Teachers acting as cooks, however, simply follow directions that were developed by some outside authority such as a textbook, and serve the same mathematics program to every child year after year with no change.

The United States does not have a national curriculum. Therefore, each individual state is responsible for developing a set of standards that the citizens of that state feel are appropriate for their children. This allows for regional variations in what is required of children and greater autonomy for residents in certain regions of the country. Just as a good chef incorporates regional preferences into his cuisine, teachers should use their state's standards as a basis for creating exciting and engaging curricula.

Unfortunately, many textbooks are not individualized for each state and use a more general standards base. Teachers that use a textbook alone may end up following a recipe that was developed by someone who, while knowing how children generally develop, does not have intimate knowledge of the individual children in a teacher's classroom. This approach does not use the knowledge base and understanding of children to develop curriculum, but instead follows instructions laid down by someone else.

Here are a few guidelines for developing your instructional repertoire.

- Understand child development.
- Understand each individual student and his needs and interests.
- Use this understanding to design the best curriculum for your class.
- Take an active role in the development of the curriculum.

- Use the body of resources at your disposal (materials, natural materials from the environment, community resources, museums, parents, etc.).
- Consider the interests that your students have. What would they like to know about a topic? What is going on in the school or community that you could integrate into classroom activities? Develop a curriculum based on best practices to make the learning tangible for the children.
- Consider *your* goals for the mathematics curriculum, and develop a curriculum based on best practices to meet those goals.
- Avoid an overreliance on premade lessons or worksheets; a few are okay, but don't overdo it. Many teachers give worksheets as the lesson and the "brainteaser" as the bonus. Try doing it in the opposite order. Remember that thinking comes first, and skills second.
- Know your state's standards. Use them to guide your curriculum development, and do not blindly adhere to covering all the chapters in a textbook.

Let's begin our journey by looking at the state of mathematics education today. I think you will find that there is a great need for teachers to think about how math is approached in the early childhood classroom.

RECENT FINDINGS IN TEACHING MATHEMATICS

Since the 1980s there has been concern that the United States has been falling behind the rest of the world in mathematics (Greene, Herman, Haury, & ERIC Clearinghouse for Science, Mathematics, and Environmental Education, 2000). In the mid-1990s, the Trends in Mathematics and Science Study (TIMSS) began and continues to this day as the Trends in International Mathematics and Science Study (National Center for Education Statistics, 1997). TIMSS looks at achievement in mathematics and science among students in Grades 4, 8, and 12, and at the many aspects of mathematics teaching and learning. Although this text is about early childhood education, it is still important to know about children's achievement in mathematics in later grades. If the foundations of mathematics are grasped and deeply understood in the early grades, children will perform better down the line.

A startling finding, of interest to any teacher of young children, was that as U.S. students get older, their achievement in mathematics goes down in comparison to other participating nations. Fourth-grade students from the United States scored well above the international average (see Figure 1.1). While the United States outperforms more than half of the participating TIMSS nations in the early grades, fourth-grade students in Japan still scored significantly higher than these U.S. students (National Center for Educational Statistics, 1997 & Trends in Mathematics and Science Study, 1996; Trends in Mathematics and Science Study, 1996, 1997; United States & Office of Educational Research and Improvement, 1997, 1998). Perhaps there is something going on in Japanese early childhood classrooms that we should pay attention to.

Fourth-Grade Achievement Results

Nations with average scores significantly higher than the U.S.		Nations with average scores not significantly different from the U.S.		Nations with average scores significantly lower than the U.S.	
Singapore	625	Slovenia	552	Latvia	525
Korea	611	Ireland	550	Scotland	520
Japan	597	Hungary	548	England	513
Hong Kong	587	Australia	546	Cyprus	502
Netherlands	577	United States	545	Norway	502
Czech Republic	567	Canada	532	New Zealand	499
Austria	559	Israel	531	Greece	492
				Thailand	490
				Portugal	475
				Iceland	474
				Iran, Islamic Rep.	429
				Kuwait	400

Eighth-Grade Achievement Results

Nations with average scores significantly higher than the U.S.		Nations with average scores not significantly different from the U.S.		Nations with average scores significantly lower than the U.S.	
Singapore	643	Thailand	522	Lithuania	477
Korea	607	Israel	522	Cyprus	474
Japan	605	Germany	509	Portugal	454
Hong Kong	588	New Zealand	508	Iran, Islamic Rep.	428
Belgium-Flemish	565	England	506	Kuwait	392
Czech Republic	564	Norway	503	Colombia	385
Slovak Republic	547	Denmark	502	South Africa	354
Switzerland	545	United States	500		
Netherlands	541	Scotland	498		
Slovenia	541	Latvia	493		
Bulgaria	540	Spain	487		
Austria	539	Iceland	487		
France	538	Greece	484		
Hungary	537	Romania	482		
Russian Federation	535				
Australia	530				
Ireland	527				
Canada	527				
Belgium-French	526				
Sweden	519				

NOTE:
Not all countries participated in both grade level assessments, 26 nations participated in the fourth-grade assessment and 41 in the eighth-grade assessment

Figure 1.1   TIMSS Findings.

Source: National Center for Education Statistics. (1997). Pursuing excellence: initial findings from the Trends in Math and Science Study. Washington, DC, United States Dept. of Education, Office of Educational Research and Development, National Center for Education Statistics.

The eighth-grade results, however, show that U.S. scores are dropping compared to the international mean. U.S. eighth graders scored 500, 13 points below the international average of 513. In four years, U.S. students went from being better than over half of the world's nations to worse than over half. What is causing this dramatic change in four short years?

Japan again scored significantly higher than the United States in the eighth-grade achievement test results. Their score of 605 was 92 points above the international average (Greene, Herman, Haury, & ERIC Clearinghouse for Science, Mathematics, and Environmental Education, 2000; Trends in Mathematics and Science Study, 2004a, 2004b). Why is this so? Why, as they get older, do American students perform worse in math as Japanese students improve? The TIMSS study may provide some insight into these questions.

TREATING CHILDREN AS MATHEMATICIANS

The concern that the United States is falling behind in mathematics compared to other countries such as Japan led the directors of TIMSS to look at aspects of mathematics teaching and learning outside of achievement scores. They wanted to know what other factors were behind this seeming disparity between U.S. students and those of other countries. Toward this end, the study included an intensive videotape survey of 231 eighth-grade mathematics lessons in the United States, Japan, and Germany. TIMSS was the first attempt to collect a nationally representative sample of videotaped observations of American classroom instruction. According to TIMSS, "The purpose of gathering this information was to understand better the process of classroom instruction in different cultures to improve student learning in our schools" (Trends in Mathematics and Science Study, 1997; Verzosa, 2001).

By using the videotape study and other TIMSS data, we can begin to examine and compare instructional methods in the United States with those of Japan. One conclusion drawn from the videotape study is that the Japanese do a much better job of treating their students as mathematicians. In U.S. classrooms, however, the tradition is to teach mathematics through memorization and practice (Elkind & Piaget, 1979; Kamii, 1984, 1990; Wenglinsky, 2004; Wood, Nelson, & Warfield, 2001). Ultimately there is little difference in the teaching philosophies that inform how primary, middle grade, and high-school students are taught in the United States (Greene et al., 2000). The study found that the main goal in the U.S. classroom was "teaching children *how* to solve a problem and obtain a correct answer."

> Mr. Gerhig said to his class, "I am going to show you how to figure out the number of degrees in any figure. First you take the number of sides, then you subtract two and multiply by 180. Juan, how many degrees would a square have?" Juan answers, "360?" as more of a question than an answer. "Right," says Mr. Gerhig. "All you have to do is remember this formula and you can compute the answer."

You may ask, "Is it not the same in Japan?" In Japan, students are given the tools to solve problems; the emphasis is on concepts rather than answers. The study found that in Japan the goal is to support conceptual understanding—in other words, less memorizing of formulas and more thinking about concepts.

> Mr. Okawa draws a polygon on the board and says, "Using what we know about the area of a triangle, can you change this 4-sided figure into a 3-sided figure without changing its area?" Students then work in groups and present their solutions to the class. Mr. Okawa asks one student, "Can you tell me how you know the area is

the same?" The student replies, "If the height and the base are the same it *must* be the same area."

When we begin to think of children as competent mathematicians who, while working on age-appropriate problems, are using the same thought processes as advanced mathematicians, it changes the way we think about curriculum development. To do this, we must know what mathematicians do when they are presented with a problem. We can then apply these principles to design mathematics curricula for young children. Throughout this discussion, we will step inside the Japanese and American classrooms of the TIMSS study to examine how these instructional methods can be applied.

Mathematicians Often Work for a Time on a Single Problem. Mathematicians may spend months and years thinking about and working on a proof to one problem. To enhance their problem-solving abilities students need to be offered fewer problems and more time to complete them. In reality, children are often given many problems and a short time limit in which to complete them. They should be allowed ample time to work on a few meaningful problems, or even just one, rather than a worksheet of 20, 50, or even 100 problems (Kamii et al., 2000).

In the video of the U.S. eighth-grade geometry class, over 100 geometry questions were asked and answered in rapid-fire succession. When students were asked to do problems alone in class, they were given over 40 problems to complete in just 20 minutes (Trends in Mathematics and Science Study, 1997). In contrast, the Japanese class worked on only three problems during the entire 50-minute class period. The students were given ample time to think and experiment with many different methods of achieving a solution. They were also given only one problem for homework, which was derived from their discussion during class time.

Mathematicians Collaborate with Their Colleagues and Study the Work of Others. Social interaction is one of the most important aspects of being a mathematician. A mathematics classroom should include many opportunities for social interaction (Kamii & National Association for the Education of Young Children, 1982). Piaget felt that the simple act of one child explaining his problem-solving method to another caused the child to understand his own thought process better. Have you ever had the experience of explaining something to someone and realizing you had made an error halfway through the explanation? Vygotsky, on the other hand, felt that the social interaction needed to be based on a peer-tutoring model—a more experienced peer can help a less experienced peer work to solve a problem more efficiently. Both of these views can be developed into actual classroom practice by having children interact with each other, argue and defend their answers, and tutor their peers when they need help. If children are going to be viewed as young mathematicians, they must be allowed to collaborate, argue, consult, defend, ask, explain, and pose questions to and with other students using mathematical ideas (Kamii, Lewis, & Jones, 1991, 1993).

Traditional U.S. mathematics lessons and homework are designed to be solitary acts. Children are not encouraged to defend solutions or collaborate on solving problems. Instead, they are given individual practice worksheets and asked to

Research suggests taking an active approach to mathematics (Kamii, 1984).

Barbara Schwartz/Merrill

complete them quietly. Without interaction, children simply memorize how to get the correct solution, without developing a greater understanding. While memorization often helps short-term test scores, it harms long-term conceptual understanding. This deficiency is evident in the TIMSS scores (Kamii, 1990; Kamii & Institute for Development of Educational Achievement, 1996).

Mathematicians Must Prove for Themselves That Their Solution Is Correct and So Should Children. Mathematicians must question assumptions and understand the mathematics behind their answers. They must prove to themselves and others that their solutions are correct, and why. If students are taught merely to memorize answers and constantly rely on their teachers to tell them whether or not they are correct then they are denied this important process of proving a solution (Weinstein, 2002).

In the TIMSS videotape study, the U.S. classroom primarily used a *call-and-response* model. The teacher would call out the problem and a student would respond with an answer. If his response was incorrect, the teacher would ask rhetorically, "Are you sure about your answer?" He would then call on another student to give the correct answer and reinforce that answer by repeating it and saying, "Right" or "Correct." By contrast, in the Japanese classroom, after the students had been given time to think and discuss their answers, they were asked to present and defend their solutions to the class. The teacher did not tell them whether they were correct but asked the class if they understood how a student got his answer. They were then required to reason and prove their answers.

The Problems That Mathematicians Work on Are Complex. Complex problems promote problem-solving abilities. Children, like mathematicians, should be immersed in complex problems that require mathematical problem solving and complex numerical thinking. Good problems ask students to find innovative solutions without a time limit being set on their thinking process (Kamii et al., 2000; Kamii et al., 2004; Kamii, Knight, & Teachers College Press, 1990). Problems can and should spark discussion and even disagreement among students.

This does not mean that problems have to be overly complicated or contrived, but they should be designed to spark children's thinking processes, rather than simply promoting rote memorization and repetition. Marilyn Burns (1992) outlined the four criteria to designing a good math problem:

1. It presents a perplexing situation that the student can understand.
2. The student is interested in finding a solution.
3. The student is unable to proceed directly toward a solution.
4. The solution requires application of mathematical ideas.

With these simple criteria, teachers can develop mathematics problems that are engaging and promote the mathematical thinking process. The "horse" problem you were asked to present earlier is a good problem from this perspective. While it may seem that this problem is too advanced for first graders, since there are numerous ways to solve it, they have a great time trying to figure it out.

Mathematicians Get Satisfaction from The Problem-Solving Process and Take Pride in Their Solutions.   Children will understand mathematical concepts and procedures more thoroughly if they are allowed to use their own thinking processes to explore mathematics (Kamii & Lewis, 1991; Kamii & Lewis, 1993a; Kamii & Lewis, 1993b). It allows them to make connections to prior knowledge and real life experiences. In the process of discussing and comparing the different methods they use to reach solutions, children strengthen their understanding of both concepts and procedures.

At the end of the lesson in the Japanese classroom the students discussed the day's problem with the teacher. They asked if the procedures they learned could be applied to other similar situations. The teacher replied by asking them to think about it and try some alternatives at home that evening, and they would discuss them in class the next day. In essence, the students developed their own homework and were excited by both the process and the content of the day's work. They demonstrated a sense of great accomplishment.

Children can get very excited about a mathematics problem and take pleasure in the process of problem solving. If children are allowed to think for themselves and discuss and defend their ideas, mathematics becomes just as fun as trying to solve a video game or diligently working to put a puzzle together.

Mathematicians Use Unsuccessful Attempts as Stepping-Stones to Solutions.   If we really want children to be treated as mathematicians, we need to encourage them to realize that they may have to try many different approaches, some unsuccessfully, before they reach a solution. We need to place an emphasis on the valuable mathematical thinking going on in the child's mind rather than on the production of a correct answer. It should be emphasized and modeled to children that unsuccessful attempts and errors can be stepping-stones to solutions.

In the U.S. classroom, students did not have time to go through this process. They were given one chance to get the solution right and the thinking behind incorrect solutions was never discussed or examined. Incorrect attempts at providing an answer would often silence a student's participation in the lesson. The Japanese lesson, by contrast, was designed in such a way that students could experiment with different solutions and then discuss them with other students or with their teacher. They were given time to use different methods and prove their answers to themselves and others.

Negative responses to answers can have disastrous consequences for the way children interact with mathematics. Math anxiety can develop if failure leads to shame or if students perceive too high a risk factor (Burns, 1998; Kitchens, 1995; Stuart, 2000). Math should be presented as a process where wrong answers are a natural and recurring element, not an end point. Instead of getting a problem "wrong," children should understand that progress is being made toward a correct solution, and they should be encouraged to continue working (Kamii, 1996; Kamii, Joseph, & Livingston, 2003).

Implications for Early Childhood Education

Children have a natural curiosity and zeal for exploration and understanding that applies to learning mathematics. If they are encouraged to act like young mathematicians and use their natural thinking ability to attack and solve problems, as we see in the classrooms of Japan, mathematics becomes not a chore but an engaging challenge to the student.

Excitement about mathematics should be the goal of every teacher of mathematics. This philosophical change is not accomplished by emphasizing "skill and drill" methods or through additional mandatory tests. If children are to be viewed and treated as young mathematicians from the beginning, many of our beliefs and practices will have to be deliberately changed. We can foster children's mathematical thinking skills by offering materials and experiences that will build a strong foundation for future mathematical learning.

Fortunately there is a professional organization, made up of teachers of mathematics, that helps teachers plan and individualize instruction for children. This organization outlines what the mathematics experience for children should be like, as we will discuss. The standards give teachers a set of concrete, measurable goals for children to strive for in each grade, and the curriculum focal points guide teachers toward offering a depth of understanding of the most important concepts for each age or grade.

NCTM Principles, Standards, and Curriculum Focal Points

The National Council of Teachers of Mathematics is the professional organization for those who teach mathematics at all age levels. NCTM is concerned with making sure that the teaching of mathematics in our schools and classrooms conforms to what research says about mathematics and how it can best be taught. This organization has developed several guidelines to help classroom teachers:

1. Principles for School Mathematics
2. Standards for School Mathematics
3. Curriculum Focal Points for Prekindergarten through Grade 8 Mathematics

NCTM's Guiding Principles for School Mathematics

Figure 1.2 shows a brief summary of NCTM's general principles of teaching mathematics. These address overarching themes in teaching math to children. They cover issues dealing with equity, curriculum, teaching, learning, assessment, and technology. Teachers are expected to follow these principles and make sure they are an integral part in planning and carrying out mathematics instruction. When we develop lesson plans, provide play-based activities involving mathematics, use a worksheet, or teach a chapter in a textbook, we should be thinking of these six principles.

NCTM Standards for School Mathematics

NCTM also sets standards for mathematics education. Each state in the United States has its own set of math standards, but all are based on the NCTM standards. These standards guide what children should learn in each grade level, were developed in cooperation with experts and teachers in the field of mathematics, and are based on developmental levels and abilities of children in each age range. This focus on understanding individual children and their mathematical development will help teachers inspire children to think and act as mathematicians. While they identify the Number and Operations and the Geometry Standards as the core of early childhood mathematics programs, NCTM lists instructional objectives for all 10 standards:

- Number & Operations
- Algebra
- Geometry
- Measurement
- Data Analysis & Probability
- Problem Solving
- Reasoning & Proof
- Communication
- Connections
- Representation

There are two types of standards that NCTM addresses. First are the **content standards**. These are the things that children should be learning during a certain grade, such as "number and operations" and "geometry." Each goal, within the larger content standards, encompasses as many as seven specific expectations that children must achieve.

Process standards support and augment the content standards. These encompass the processes that children must use to meet the goals set forth by the content standards. The process standards include problem solving, reasoning and proof, communication, connections, and representation.

The six principles for school mathematics address overarching themes:

- **Equity.** Excellence in mathematics education requires equity—high expectations and strong support for all students.

    - *All students are expected to achieve at high levels and receive support from the teacher that meets their individual needs and helps the child not only to succeed at mathematics, but to have a positive attitude toward mathematics.*

- **Curriculum.** A curriculum is more than a collection of activities: it must be coherent, focused on important mathematics, and well articulated across the grades.

    - *Curriculum planning is of the utmost importance. Teachers need to be taking an active role in developing curriculum to meet the needs of children in their classrooms and facilitating true understanding of mathematics.*

- **Teaching.** Effective mathematics teaching requires understanding what students know and need to learn and then challenging and supporting them to learn it well.

    - *Focusing simply on producing correct answers without true understanding is not sufficient. Teachers need to understand the child's mathematical development, examine their thinking and problem-solving process, and support their inquiry.*

- **Learning.** Students must learn mathematics with understanding, actively building new knowledge from experience and prior knowledge.

    - *Mathematics needs to be linked to the child's life and what they see every day. It needs to be integrated into all that they do and see during their school day so that children don't just learn "facts" but concepts as well.*

- **Assessment.** Assessment should support the learning of important mathematics and furnish useful information to both teachers and students.

    - *Teachers are to use formative as well as summative assessments. Formative assessments help the teacher to modify and adapt the curriculum to each individual child's needs and summative assessments allow the teacher to assess progress. Tests and assessments need not be simple paper-and-pencil tests or "timed tests." There are many forms of authentic assessments that can be used.*

- **Technology.** Technology is essential in teaching and learning mathematics; it influences the mathematics that is taught and enhances students' learning.

    - *Computers and calculators are not the only form of technology that can be used to promote mathematics learning. There are other technological applications that can be used also, such as Global Positioning System (GPS), Internet, email, videoconferencing, personal digital assistants (PDAs). But it should never be forgotten that the learning of mathematics is a mental process and technology is nothing but a tool to promote that construction.*

Figure 1.2   NCTM Principles of Teaching Mathematics.

NCTM and NAEYC Joint Statement on Mathematics

To support the NCTM pre-K standards, NCTM issued a joint statement with the National Association for the Education of Young Children (NAEYC). NAEYC is the early childhood learned society that collects and disseminates research on best practices for children, birth through age eight. NAEYC and NCTM's joint position statement is called *Early Childhood Mathematics: Promoting Good Beginnings* (National Association for the Education of Young Children, 2004), summarized in Figure 1.3.

For children PreK–second grade and third–fifth grade there is a list of standards, linked to developmental level, that outlines what children should be able to do by the end of those grades. A general age range chart is shown in Table 1.1. Many state standards break these down into individual age and grade level indicators. There is a change in expectations between PreK–second and third–fifth grade because it takes the level of the child into account when developing expectations. For example, examine the number and operations standard for PreK–second and third–fifth grade. When comparing the expectations for each of these grades, you can see that not only has the content become more difficult, there is an understanding that the primary-grade students have developed a different way of thinking about mathematics. While the PreK-Second standards contain visual and concrete representation, older children are expected to use more abstract representation.

These standards are general and each grade level has a more refined set of indicators that students should be able to achieve by the end of that grade level. Think of them as guidelines for your instruction. You should check with your state department of education for a more complete and unique set of standards for your individual state.

One of the findings of the TIMSS study was that the U.S. curriculum seemed to be "a mile wide and an inch deep," meaning that teachers were being required to cover many topics, but in little depth (National Center for Education, 1997). In response to this TIMSS finding, NCTM saw the need for an additional document to help individual states deal with the problem of implementing the principles and standards

Standards are a part of every school's math program.

Katelyn Metzger/Merrill

In high-quality mathematics education for 3- to 6-year-old children, teachers and other key professionals should

1. enhance children's natural interest in mathematics and their disposition to use it to make sense of their physical and social worlds
2. build on children's experience and knowledge, including their family, linguistic, cultural, and community backgrounds; their individual approaches to learning; and their informal knowledge
3. base mathematics curriculum and teaching practices on knowledge of young children's cognitive, linguistic, physical, and social-emotional development
4. use curriculum and teaching practices that strengthen children's problem solving and reasoning processes as well as representing, communicating, and connecting mathematical ideas
5. ensure that the curriculum is coherent and compatible with known relationships and sequences of important mathematical ideas
6. provide for children's deep and sustained interaction with key mathematical ideas
7. integrate mathematics with other activities and other activities with mathematics
8. provide ample time, materials, and teacher support for children to engage in play, a context in which they explore and manipulate mathematical ideas with keen interest
9. actively introduce mathematical concepts, methods, and language through a range of appropriate experiences and teaching strategies
10. support children's learning by thoughtfully and continually assessing all children's mathematical knowledge, skills, and strategies.

To support high-quality mathematics education, institutions, program developers, and policymakers should

1. create more effective early childhood teacher preparation and continuing professional development
2. use collaborative processes to develop well-aligned systems of appropriate high-quality standards, curriculum, and assessment
3. design institutional structures and policies that support teachers' ongoing learning, teamwork, and planning
4. provide resources necessary to overcome the barriers to young children's mathematical proficiency at the classroom, community, institutional, and system-wide levels.

Figure 1.3 NAEYC/NCTM Recommendations for Teachers of Children Ages 3–6.

Source: http://www.naeyc.org/about/positions/psmath.asp. National Council of Teachers of Mathematics. (2000). *Principles and Standards for School Mathematics.* E-Standards ver. 1.0.

Table 1.1   NCTM Standards and Indicators for PreK–5th

STANDARDS	INDICATORS	INDICATORS
Instructional programs from prekindergarten through grade 12 should enable all students to—	*In prekindergarten through grade 2 all students should—*	*In grades 3–5 all students should—*
Number and Operations		
understand numbers, ways of representing numbers, relationships among numbers, and number systems	count with understanding and recognize "how many" in sets of objects	understand the place-value structure of the base-10 number system and be able to represent and compare whole numbers and decimals
	use multiple models to develop initial understandings of place value and the base-10 number system	recognize equivalent representations for the same number and generate them by decomposing and composing numbers
	develop understanding of the relative position and magnitude of whole numbers and of ordinal and cardinal numbers and their connections	develop understanding of fractions as parts of unit wholes, as parts of a collection, as locations on number lines, and as divisions of whole numbers
	develop a sense of whole numbers and represent and use them in flexible ways, including relating, composing, and decomposing numbers	use models, benchmarks, and equivalent forms to judge the size of fractions
	connect number words and numerals to the quantities they represent, using various physical models and representations	recognize and generate equivalent forms of commonly used fractions, decimals, and percents
	understand and represent commonly used fractions, such as ½, ⅓, and ¼	explore numbers less than 0 by extending the number line and through familiar applications
		describe classes of numbers according to characteristics such as the nature of their factors
understand meanings of operations and how they relate to one another	understand various meanings of addition and subtraction of whole numbers and the relationship between the two operations	understand various meanings of multiplication and division
	understand the effects of adding and subtracting whole numbers	understand the effects of multiplying and dividing whole numbers

Table 1.1 NCTM Standards and Indicators for PreK–5th		
	understand situations that entail multiplication and division, such as equal groupings of objects and sharing equally	identify and use relationships between operations, such as division as the inverse of multiplication, to solve problems
		understand and use properties of operations, such as the distributivity of multiplication over addition.
compute fluently and make reasonable estimates	develop and use strategies for whole-number computations, with a focus on addition and subtraction	develop fluency with basic number combinations for multiplication and division and use these combinations to mentally compute related problems, such as 30×50
	develop fluency with basic number combinations for addition and subtraction	develop fluency in adding, subtracting, multiplying, and dividing whole numbers
	use a variety of methods and tools to compute, including objects, mental computation, estimation, paper and pencil, and calculators	develop and use strategies to estimate the results of whole-number computations and to judge the reasonableness of such results
		develop and use strategies to estimate computations involving fractions and decimals in situations relevant to students' experience
		use visual models, benchmarks, and equivalent forms to add and subtract commonly used fractions and decimals
		select appropriate methods and tools for computing with whole numbers from among mental computation, estimation, calculators, and paper and pencil according to the context and nature of the computation and use the selected method or tools
Algebra		
understand patterns, relations, and functions	sort, classify, and order objects by size, number, and other properties	describe, extend, and make generalizations about geometric and numeric patterns

Table 1.1 NCTM Standards and Indicators for PreK–5th

	recognize, describe, and extend patterns such as sequences of sounds and shapes or simple numeric patterns and translate from one representation to another	represent and analyze patterns and functions, using words, tables, and graphs
analyze how both repeating and growing patterns are generated		
represent and analyze mathematical situations and structures using algebraic symbols	illustrate general principles and properties of operations, such as commutativity, using specific numbers	identify such properties as commutativity, associativity, and distributivity and use them to compute with whole numbers
	use concrete, pictorial, and verbal representations to develop an understanding of invented and conventional symbolic notations	represent the idea of a variable as an unknown quantity using a letter or a symbol
		express mathematical relationships using equations
use mathematical models to represent and understand quantitative relationships	model situations that involve the addition and subtraction of whole numbers, using objects, photos, and symbols	model problem situations with objects and use representations such as graphs, tables, and equations to draw conclusions
analyze change in various contexts	describe qualitative change, such as a student's growing taller	investigate how a change in one variable relates to a change in a second variable
	describe quantitative change, such as a student's growing two inches in one year	identify and describe situations with constant or varying rates of change and compare them
Geometry		
analyze characteristics and properties of two- and three-dimensional geometric shapes and develop mathematical arguments about geometric relationships	recognize, name, build, draw, compare, and sort two- and three-dimensional shapes	identify, compare, and analyze attributes of two- and three-dimensional shapes and develop vocabulary to describe the attributes
	describe attributes and parts of two- and three-dimensional shapes	classify two- and three-dimensional shapes according to their properties and develop definitions of classes of shapes such as triangles and pyramids
	investigate and predict the results of putting together and taking apart two- and three-dimensional shapes	investigate, describe, and reason about the results of subdividing, combining, and transforming shapes

Table 1.1 NCTM Standards and Indicators for PreK–5th

		explore congruence and similarity
		make and test conjectures about geometric properties and relationships and develop logical arguments to justify conclusions
specify locations and describe spatial relationships using coordinate geometry and other representational systems	describe, name, and interpret relative positions in space and apply ideas about relative position	describe location and movement using common language and geometric vocabulary
	describe, name, and interpret direction and distance in navigating space and apply ideas about direction and distance	make and use coordinate systems to specify locations and to describe paths
	find and name locations with simple relationships such as "near to" and in coordinate systems such as maps	find the distance between points along horizontal and vertical lines of a coordinate system
apply transformations and use symmetry to analyze mathematical situations	recognize and apply slides, flips, and turns	predict and describe the results of sliding, flipping, and turning two-dimensional shapes
	recognize and create shapes that have symmetry	describe a motion or a series of motions that will show that two shapes are congruent
		identify and describe line and rotational symmetry in two- and three-dimensional shapes and designs
use visualization, spatial reasoning, and geometric modeling to solve problems	create mental images of geometric shapes using spatial memory and spatial visualization	build and draw geometric objects
	recognize and represent shapes from different perspectives	create and describe mental images of objects, patterns, and paths
		identify and build a three-dimensional object from two-dimensional representations of that object
		identify and draw a two-dimensional representation of a three-dimensional object
	relate ideas in geometry to ideas in number and measurement	use geometric models to solve problems in other areas of mathematics, such as number and measurement

Table 1.1   NCTM Standards and Indicators for PreK–5th

	recognize geometric shapes and structures in the environment and specify their location	recognize geometric ideas and relationships and apply them to other disciplines and to problems that arise in the classroom or in everyday life
Measurement		
understand measurable attributes of objects and the units, systems, and processes of measurement	recognize the attributes of length, volume, weight, area, and time	understand such attributes as length, area, weight, volume, and size of angle and select the appropriate type of unit for measuring each attribute
	compare and order objects according to these attributes	understand the need for measuring with standard units and become familiar with standard units in the customary and metric systems
	understand how to measure using nonstandard and standard units	carry out simple unit conversions, such as from centimeters to meters, within a system of measurement
	select an appropriate unit and tool for the attribute being measured	understand that measurements are approximations and how differences in units affect precision
		explore what happens to measurements of a two-dimensional shape such as its perimeter and area when the shape is changed in some way
apply appropriate techniques, tools, and formulas to determine measurements	measure with multiple copies of units of the same size, such as paper clips laid end to end	develop strategies for estimating the perimeters, areas, and volumes of irregular shapes
	use repetition of a single unit to measure something larger than the unit, for instance, measuring the length of a room with a single meter stick	select and apply appropriate standard units and tools to measure length, area, volume, weight, time, temperature, and the size of angles
	use tools to measure	select and use benchmarks to estimate measurements
	develop common referents for measures to make comparisons and estimates	develop, understand, and use formulas to find the area of rectangles and related triangles and parallelograms
		develop strategies to determine the surface areas and volumes of rectangular solids

Table 1.1   NCTM Standards and Indicators for PreK–5th

Probability and Analysis

formulate questions that can be addressed with data and collect, organize, and display relevant data to answer them	pose questions and gather data about themselves and their surroundings	design investigations to address a question and consider how data-collection methods affect the nature of the data set
	sort and classify objects according to their attributes and organize data about the objects	collect data using observations, surveys, and experiments
	represent data using concrete objects, pictures, and graphs	represent data using tables and graphs such as line plots, bar graphs, and line graphs
		recognize the differences in representing categorical and numerical data
		describe the shape and important features of a set of data and compare related data sets, with an emphasis on how the data are distributed
select and use appropriate statistical methods to analyze data	describe parts of the data and the set of data as a whole to determine what the data show	use measures of center, focusing on the median, and understand what each does and does not indicate about the data set
		compare different representations of the same data and evaluate how well each representation shows important aspects of the data
develop and evaluate inferences and predictions that are based on data	discuss events related to students' experiences as likely or unlikely	propose and justify conclusions and predictions that are based on data and design studies to further investigate the conclusions or predictions
understand and apply basic concepts of probability		describe events as likely or unlikely and discuss the degree of likelihood using such words as certain, equally likely, and impossible
		predict the probability of outcomes of simple experiments and test the predictions

Table 1.1   NCTM Standards and Indicators for PreK–5th

	understand that the measure of the likelihood of an event can be represented by a number from 0 to 1
Problem Solving	
	build new mathematical knowledge through problem solving solve problems that arise in mathematics and in other contexts apply and adapt a variety of appropriate strategies to solve problems monitor and reflect on the process of mathematical problem solving
Reasoning and Proof	
	recognize reasoning and proof as fundamental aspects of mathematics make and investigate mathematical conjectures develop and evaluate mathematical arguments and proofs select and use various types of reasoning and methods of proof
Communication	
	organize and consolidate their mathematical thinking through communication communicate their mathematical thinking coherently and clearly to peers, teachers, and others analyze and evaluate the mathematical thinking and strategies of others use the language of mathematics to express mathematical ideas precisely
Connections	
	recognize and use connections among mathematical ideas understand how mathematical ideas interconnect and build on one another to produce a coherent whole recognize and apply mathematics in contexts outside of mathematics
Representation	
	create and use representations to organize, record, and communicate mathematical ideas select, apply, and translate among mathematical representations to solve problems use representations to model and interpret physical, social, and mathematical phenomena

into instruction and address the lack of focus in mathematics curriculum. This led to the creation of a document entitled *Curriculum Focal Points for Prekindergarten through Grade 8 Mathematics* (National Council of Teachers of Mathematics, 2006), released in 2006.

As NCTM also recognized, TIMSS data showed that U.S. classrooms did not seem to be implementing the six NCTM guiding principles as well as the Japanese classroom as shown in Figure 1.1. Many teachers were either not familiar with the NCTM Principles and Standards or did not understand what they meant for classroom practice. In the videotape the Japanese classroom example came much closer to what NCTM, current research, and best practice suggest. To help bridge this gap, NCTM created the focal points document. It is even subtitled "A Quest for Coherence."

Curriculum Focal Points for Prekindergarten Through Grade 8

NCTM's *Curriculum Focal Points for Prekindergarten through Grade 8 Mathematics* (NCTM, 2006) gives even more specific guidelines for each grade level. The document was designed to give three to five curriculum *focal points* per grade level. These would then become the main topics that teachers, curriculum designers, and school boards would incorporate into their grade level curriculum plans. Developers of these focal points looked at what is mathematically important at each age and grade level, what research says about learning math, and what methods are effective in classroom practice. In the introduction the authors clarify the difference between the focal points and the NCTM Standards document; see Figure 1.4.

These focal points give us a guide for each individual age and grade, helping teachers to avoid covering too many topics with little depth of understanding. The

An approach that focuses on a small number of significant mathematical "targets" for each grade level offers a way of thinking about what is important in school mathematics that is different from commonly accepted notions of goals, standards, objectives, or learning expectations. These more conventional structures tend to result in lists of very specific items grouped under general headings. By contrast, *Curriculum Focal Points for Prekindergarten through Grade 8 Mathematics* offers more than headings for long lists, providing instead descriptions of the most significant mathematical concepts and skills at each grade level. Organizing a curriculum around these described focal points, with a clear emphasis on the processes that Principles and Standards addresses in the Process Standards—communication, reasoning, representation, connections, and, particularly, problem solving—can provide students with a connected, coherent, ever-expanding body of mathematical knowledge and ways of thinking. Such a comprehensive mathematics experience can prepare students for whatever career or professional path they may choose as well as equip them to solve many problems that they will face in the future.

Figure 1.4 Rationale for Curriculum Focal Points.

three focal points identified for each grade level, together with any other content or processes integrated into the lessons dealing with those three focal points, should encompass the major portion of instruction at that grade level. The focal points for each grade level also identify "Connections to the Focal Points." According to NCTM, these connections serve two purposes:

1. They recognize the need for introductory and continuing experiences related to the focal points in each grade and other grade levels.
2. They identify ways in which a grade level's focal points can support learning in relation to strands that are not focal points at that grade level. In other words, the connections make sure that there is coherence through the grades (NCTM, 2006).

The idea is to build students' strength in the use of mathematical processes. According to the focal points document, instruction in these grade-specific content areas should incorporate:

- the use of the mathematics to solve problems
- an application of logical reasoning to justify procedures and solutions
- an involvement in the design and analysis of multiple representations, in order to learn, make connections among, and communicate ideas within and outside of mathematics. (NCTM, 2006)

The focal points will be an integral part of the ages and grade level sections of this book (Chapters 5–8). The full focal points document is available for download at the NCTM web site. What the principles, standards, and focal points all emphasize is that child development should have an influence on "what" and "how" we teach mathematics in each grade. This also means that teachers should present mathematics differently to children of different ages and developmental levels. In this book, we will call this the "3E" approach.

PUTTING THE PIECES TOGETHER: THE "3E" APPROACH

The **three Es** represent Environment, Experience, and Education. For each age level (infants and toddlers, preschoolers and kindergarteners, and primary grades) one of the Es will be of paramount importance (see Figure 1.5). For infants and toddlers we will discuss how *Environment* is the primary focus of mathematics education. With

Infants and Toddlers	Environment
Preschool and Kindergarten	Experience
1st–3rd Grade	Education

Figure 1.5   The 3 Es and the Ages That They Are Most Prevalent.

these young children, we need to think about structuring the environment so that children can construct important prenumber concepts through interaction with objects, comparisons in their environment, and sensorimotor play.

The focus for preschoolers and kindergarteners will be on *Experiences* for learning mathematics. These children construct mathematical concepts through everyday experience and by using counting, numbers, and shapes in their play and school activities. Teachers need to make sure that when designing experiences for children of this age that mathematics receives ample consideration. In the primary grades we will focus on *Education*. This is where some teacher-directed, yet still child-centered, mathematical instruction takes place. This is also when standards will become especially important. As you design educational programs for primary-grade children in addition, subtraction, multiplication, and division, you will always need to keep the principles and standards in mind. While we will discuss those standards in detail in Chapters 5 to 8, here are a few key points to remember.

- The standards are a goal and you can develop steps to achieve them. You don't have to achieve the indicator in one step.
- Each state has different standards. Know the standards for your state.
- Keep the six NCTM principles in mind when developing curriculum. They are as important as the standards and indicators.
- The standards do not dictate *how* to teach the standard, so be creative. Use a child-centered and constructivist approach.
- Remember that each child and each age level is different not just in *what* they know but also in *how* they learn it. The standards are the same for all children, but how they individually get there is not.
- Be flexible. Textbooks are often very prescriptive and broad in scope. Use the textbook to help you meet the standards for your state. Don't just use a textbook cover to cover.

SUMMARY

When beginning to think about teaching mathematics to young children, consider these three basic principles:

1. Thinking is what is important in mathematics, not producing the correct answer.
2. Fight the urge to correct students; instead, support questioning.
3. "Right" answers come from a logical certainty, not from a teacher or a textbook.

Children use their natural thinking ability to understand and construct mathematical concepts. Mathematical learning comes naturally to children through an emergent process, much like literacy acquisition. They think like young mathematicians and their construction of mathematical concepts begins at birth. Furthermore, many basic mathematical concepts, such as quantity, classification, and conservation, cannot be directly taught. Some concepts are better taught by promoting children's natural thinking ability and encouraging children to construct mathematical knowledge rather than just giving them a set of rules to follow.

As teachers, if we are to make a difference and develop students that can think about mathematics, we need to be chefs—not short-order cooks. We need to plan, develop, adapt, and learn, not simply follow instructions, whether they come from textbooks or directly from standards. Teachers need to understand child development, each individual student and his needs and interests. Then they need to use this understanding to take an active role in planning and developing the best mathematics program for both individual students and the class using all the resources available in the school and community.

TIMSS shows that not only is the United States lagging behind other countries such as Japan in mathematical achievement, but that our methods of teaching mathematics have changed little in the last 150 years. In Japan, where achievement is high, students are taught in a manner that encourages concept construction. By contrast, U.S. students are taught rules and steps to get a correct answer, with little emphasis on conceptual understanding.

If we are to improve the achievement of our students in mathematics, we need to rethink the way we teach math in preschool and the primary grades. We can develop a mathematical program that treats the young child like a young mathematician. Toward this end, teachers need to:

1. Allow children to work for long periods of time on one problem.
2. Allow children to use their own methods for solving a given problem.
3. Understand that children's excitement about mathematics comes from their own thinking ability.
4. Understand that good problems can have multiple solutions and different ways to arrive at those solutions.
5. Encourage social interaction that promotes children to act as young mathematicians by requiring them to prove their answer and all the steps they took to attain the answer.
6. Understand that math is not *a physical part or property of the manipulative;* it is in the child's mind.
7. Allow children to be wrong many times before being right. It is important to encourage children to see "wrong" answers as a natural part of mathematical processes.

If we remember these basic tenets when developing mathematics activities for children, we can provide a mathematical experience that encourages children to think, gets them excited about mathematics, and ultimately improves their achievement. Using the "3E" approach of environment, experience, and education, and recognizing which of these three is dominant in each age range, will help teachers to address NCTM principles and standards as well as the newly developed Curriculum Focal Points.

WEB SITES

Trends in International Mathematics and Science Study (TIMSS)
http://nces.ed.gov/timss/
More information about the Trends in Mathematics and Science Study

NCTM
http://nctm.org
The web site for the National Council for Teachers of Mathematics

NAEYC
http://naeyc.org
The web site for the National Association for the Education of Young Children

National Center for Education Statistics (NCES)
http://nces.ed.gov/
This site contains many statistics about our nation's schools, students, and teachers. Trends in mathematics test scores can be found here in many different formats.

DISCUSS AND APPLY WHAT YOU HAVE LEARNED

Observe

1. Observe children in a preschool setting. What kind of mathematics opportunities do you see being taken advantage of by the teacher?
2. Observe a math lesson in a primary classroom. Are any of the seven guidelines for treating children as young mathematicians (refer to the summary) being implemented? If not, what could be changed in order to implement them?

Apply

1. Interview an early childhood teacher about his mathematics teaching. What opinions does the teacher hold about math and math education? What level of mathematics does the teacher believe his students are capable of?
2. Give the "horse" problem to a first, second, or third grader. How did he react?
3. In groups, discuss ways that teachers can treat children as young mathematicians. What other ideas or guidelines can you come up with?
4. Locate your state's mathematical standards on its Department of Education web site.

Reflect

1. What do you remember about learning math in school, especially the early grades? Did you enjoy math? Why or why not?

2. How do you feel about mathematics now? Do you feel you know enough mathematics to teach young children?

3. How would you feel if answers were not immediately given in a mathematics course you were taking? Think back to the "horse" problem. Are you frustrated or uncomfortable with not having the solution? Why do you think you reacted to the problem in the manner you did?

REFERENCES

Burns, M. (1992). *About teaching mathematics: A K–8 resource.* Sausalito, CA: Marilyn Burns Education Associates.

Burns, M. (1998). *Math facing an American phobia.* Sausalito, CA: Math Solutions Publications.

Butterworth, B. (1999). *What counts: How every brain is hardwired for math.* New York: Free Press.

Chomsky, N. (2002). *On nature and language* (A. Belletti & L. Rizzi, Eds.). Cambridge: Cambridge University Press.

Chomsky, N. (2006). *Language and mind* (3rd ed.). Cambridge: Cambridge University Press.

Clements, D. H., & Sarama, J. (Eds.). (2004). *Engaging young children in mathematics: Standards for early childhood mathematics education.* Mahwah, NJ: Lawrence Erlbaum Associates.

Elkind, D., & Piaget, J. (1979). *Child development and education: A Piagetian perspective.* New York: Oxford University Press.

Feiler, A., & Webster, A. (1997, September). *Teacher predictions of young children's literacy success or failure in four primary schools.* Paper presented at the annual meeting of the British Educational Research Association, York, England.

Greene, B. D., Herman, M., & Haury, D. L. (2000). *TIMSS: What have we learned about math and science teaching?* Columbus, OH: ERIC Clearinghouse for Science, Mathematics, and Environmental Education. *ERIC Document Reproduction Service No. 463948.*

JumpStart 2nd grade. (1996). Glendale, CA: Knowledge Adventure.

Kamii, C. (1984). *Autonomy as the aim of childhood education: A Piagetian approach.* Galesburg, IL: Knox AV.

Kamii, C. (1990). *Achievement testing in the early grades: The games grown-ups play.* Washington, DC: National Association for the Education of Young Children.

Kamii, C., & Chemeketa, C. (1982). *Piagetian research on how children construct number concepts.* Salem, OR: Chemeketa Community College.

Kamii, C., Clark, F. B., Housman, L. B., & Teachers College Press (2000). *First graders dividing 62 by 5: A teacher uses Piaget's theory.* New York: Distributed by Teachers College Press.

Kamii, C., & DeVries, R. (1973). *Piaget-based curriculum for early childhood education: The Kamii-DeVries approach* [Electronic version]. *ERIC Document Reproduction Service No. 080192.*

Kamii, C., & Institute for Development of Educational Achievement (1996). *Piaget's constructivism and elementary mathematics education.* Dayton, OH: IDEA.

Kamii, C., Joseph, L. L., & Livingston, S. J. (2004). *Young children continue to reinvent arithmetic—2nd grade: Implications of Piaget's theory (2nd ed.).* New York: Teachers College Press.

Kamii, C., Knight, M., & Teachers College Press. (1990). *Multiplication of 2 digit numbers: Two teachers using Piaget's theory.* New York: Teachers College Press.

Kamii, C., Manning, M. M., & Manning, G. L. (Eds.)(1991). *Early literacy: A constructivist foundation for whole language.* Washington, DC: NEA Professional Library, National Education Association.

Kamii, C., & Piaget, J. (1973). *The Piagetian based curriculum.*

Kitchens, A. N. (1995). *Defeating math anxiety.* Chicago: Irwin Career Education Division.

Lally, J. R., Butterfield, G., Mangione, P. L., Signer, S. M., et al. (2001). *The next step: Including the infant in the curriculum* [videorecording]. Sacramento, CA: California Dept. of Education.

Loveless, T. (2001). *The great curriculum debate: How should we teach reading and math?* Washington, DC: Brookings Institution Press.

National Association for the Education of Young Children (2004). *Early childhood mathematics: Promoting good beginnings.* A joint position statement of the National Association for the Education of Young Children and the National Council of Teachers of Mathematics. [Electronic version]. Retrieved May 29, 2007, from *http://www.naeyc.org/about/positions/ pdf/psmath.pdf*

National Center for Education Statistics. (1997). *Pursuing excellence: Initial findings from the Trends in Math and Science Study.* Washington, DC: U.S. Dept. of Education, Office of Educational Research and Development, National Center for Education Statistics.

National Council of Teachers of Mathematics. (2006). *Curriculum focal points for prekindergarten through Grade 8 mathematics.* Reston, VA: Author.

National Council of Teachers of Mathematics. (2000). *Principles and standards for school mathematics.* E-Standards ver. 1.0.

Otto, B. (2002). *Language development in early childhood.* Upper Saddle River, NJ: Merrill/Prentice Hall.

Pickett, L. (1998). Literacy learning during block play. *Journal of Research in Childhood Education, 12*(2), 225–230.

Stuart, V. B. (2000). Math curse or math anxiety? *Teaching Children Mathematics, 6*(5), 330.

Weinstein, R. S. (2002). *Reaching higher: The power of expectations in schooling.*

Wenglinsky, H. (2004). Facts or critical thinking skills? What NAEP results say. *Educational Leadership, 62*(1), 32.

Wood, T. L., Nelson, B. S., & Warfield, J. (2001). *Beyond classical pedagogy: Teaching elementary school mathematics.* Mahwah, NJ: Lawrence Erlbaum Associates.

Xu, F., Spelke, E. S., & Goddard, S. (2005). Number sense in human infants. *Developmental Science, 8*(1), 88–101.

CHAPTER 2

Building a Knowledge Base and Learning to Reflect

CHAPTER OBJECTIVES

After you have read this chapter, you should be able to:

- Explain the importance of reflection in teaching mathematics
- Analyze and compare the different theoretical approaches to teaching mathematics
- Identify different theoretical approaches in instructional practices used by teachers, in the classroom and through math textbooks
- Explain how a certain theoretical orientation is reflected in classroom practice in teaching mathematics
- Demonstrate an understanding of the uses and importance of understanding developmental theory to the teaching and learning of mathematics in young children

Watching an effective mathematics lesson or observing a teacher expertly negotiating the diverse needs of the students in her classroom can be an inspiring thing. There is no doubt that teaching requires immense skill, dedication, knowledge, and craft. But how do we best understand what it is we do as educators? Our opinion of this seemingly innocent question can have great implications for our time with students. Before we explore the theories that are critical to mathematics instruction, an answer to the following question might shed some light on this issue: is teaching more of an art . . . or a science?

Teachers who defend teaching as an art will tell you that talent, technique, and passion are the most important aspects of exceptional teaching. To them, teaching is an art because it cannot be reduced to a set of procedures a robot could follow. Teaching is a subjective activity that requires many important attributes: compassion, an ability to synthesize, keen observation skills, and above all else, creativity and imagination.

On the other side of the debate are teachers who see teaching as a science. Their argument is that in order to teach a child, you must understand scientific data and research on how the mind works and how people learn, develop the most effective ways to present information, and have a deep understanding of the core knowledge and concepts of the information. As in most sciences, data is testable and quantifiable; methods are clear, specific, and uniform; and results are observable.

Teaching math cannot be pigeonholed into either an art or a science. Using elements of both approaches is necessary to be an effective teacher. Teachers need a detailed understanding of the sciences of child development, developmental theory, content knowledge, and pedagogy while also having the ability to be creative, imaginative, passionate, and sensitive to the human experience.

Therefore as a teacher of mathematics, you must:

1. Understand yourself.
2. Understand child development as it relates to math and cognitive abilities.
3. Understand individual students and how each learns.

Although all three of these forms of knowledge are interrelated and overlap in the discussions that follow, this chapter will primarily cover the first two items on this list. Understanding the many different students that comprise your class will be covered in more detail in Chapter 4. Since we must understand ourselves first, our discussion begins there.

UNDERSTANDING YOURSELF

I remember my first year as a teacher, fresh from the university and full of enthusiasm. Within the first few weeks, I realized that I was seriously overwhelmed and began to doubt my abilities as a teacher and even my choice of profession. What I didn't know then was that all teachers go through this stage of adjustment. For me, it was vitally important to remember my core beliefs about teaching and children. I had to do a lot of soul searching each night to keep from "burning out."

> In ancient Greece, above the door to the Oracle of Delphi were the words "Know Thyself." This was also the maxim of one of the first great educators, Socrates. As a teacher in our modern world, this maxim still holds true. Before you can help others to learn, you must "know thyself."

The demands and pressures that all new teachers experience can easily cause a teacher to lose his or her own personal beliefs and philosophy. When I became preoccupied with meetings, schedules, tests, standards, and many other everyday teaching chores, it became tempting to revert to a premade textbook curriculum rather than doing what I knew was best for children. I had to remember to trust in what I believed. For the first few "survival years" I engaged in more teacher-directed, premade curricula than I would have liked, but as I developed as a teacher, I began to incorporate more elements of teaching that fit my personal philosophy. It was a difficult, but ultimately rewarding, task that required me to examine all aspects of my teaching closely.

The Process of Reflection

Many of you may have been asked to do reflective journaling for your classes. This kind of reflection entails much more than simply writing down what happens in the classroom, what you do, and what you see. **Reflection** is a kind of problem solving that starts when your basic journaling ends. John Dewey introduced the idea of reflection in the teaching process. He considered it to be a special form of problem solving and thinking used to resolve an issue which involved active **chaining**, a careful ordering of ideas linking each with its predecessors. When teachers reflect, they must think about their own beliefs regarding mathematics or any other topic and the **knowledge base** that supports these beliefs. A knowledge base comprises what you know about the research and theory concerning best practices in mathematics or other topics.

Reflection is an active and deliberative cognitive process, involving sequences of interconnected ideas, which takes account of underlying beliefs and knowledge. Reflective thinking generally addresses practical problems, allowing for doubt, questioning, and perplexity before possible solutions are reached. In other words, it's normal to be confused and not to have all the answers when reflecting (Hatton & Smith, 1995).

Keeping abreast of new research is vital for the reflection process.

Anne Vega/Merrill

Once you have written your observations, you need to think about them in depth and consider what they mean (Dewey, 1933). In some sense, this is similar to the type of problem solving we want to encourage in young children.

This type of thinking produces many potentially valuable questions. Why did the teacher choose to present the lesson in that manner? What theoretical base does the teacher seem to be employing? How would a teacher with a different philosophy teach the same lesson? What kind of questions did the teacher ask her students?

Reflection is one of the most important aspects of teaching. You first must examine your own decisions and abilities in relation to your math teaching tasks. These types of questions often demand honesty and a willingness to challenge yourself and your ideas about teaching. What worked in that lesson? What did not work? Why did the lesson work or not work? Do I feel comfortable with this concept or topic? Do I need more information to teach this concept or topic? What are my feelings toward mathematics? How will I approach the decisions I will have to make as a teacher?

The next step in reflection is to formulate classroom ideas based on your observations and interpretations, for example, "How can I teach that same lesson without using worksheets?" or "How can I teach an interactive lesson and still prepare the children for standardized tests?" This is the essence of reflective practice. Thinking and problem solving lead to a continual reevaluation and improvement of your methods, rather than stagnation. Part of reflective practice is discovering and understanding your strengths and weaknesses as a math teacher as well as coming to grips with your thoughts and feelings about the subject matter you are teaching.

As a first-year teacher, I went home every night and evaluated my process of teaching. The problem-solving method included thinking about everything I did during the day, how it fit with my personal philosophy, and how I could do it better next time. It also involved thinking about practical aspects of my job as a teacher as well and assessing whether I was being true to my personal beliefs. This approach also led me to seek out more information in the form of new research, teaching methods, and innovative practices in the classroom. All of this became part of my reflective process of problem solving. My problems were, "How do I become a better teacher?" and "How do I best incorporate child-centered, constructivist practices in a standards-based setting?"

> Take a moment to reflect on your past experience as a math student. How do these experiences affect how you teach math to our students? How can you best ensure that students approach mathematics with their natural enthusiasm intact?

Dealing with Our Own Math Anxiety First

Many early childhood teachers feel uncomfortable teaching mathematics because they did not and do not like mathematics. Some also feel that they are not good at mathematics, and therefore feel uncomfortable teaching it to their students. Math anxiety is a well-researched topic and current practices perpetuate the problem (Burns, 1998; Kitchens, 1995; Stuart, 2000). Many teachers who have math anxiety themselves inadvertently pass it on to their students. If you have math anxiety, rest assured that you are not alone.

Math anxiety does not come from mathematics itself, but rather from the way math is presented in school and may have been presented to you as a child (Burns, 1998; Kitchens, 1995; Stuart, 2000). Often math is presented to students as a high-stakes memorization process. Think back to your early school years. Do you remember timed math tests? Many students are still subjected to these high-pressure competitions that are intended to help them learn their "math facts." For many young students, these stressful events both create and confirm a general aversion to math (Altermatt & Kim, 2004; Burns, 1998; Kamii, 1990; Kamii, Joseph, & Livingston, 2003; Kitchens, 1995; Levine, 1995; Stuart, 2000).

I can remember a chart posted prominently in my second-grade classroom with the class roster in a column down the right-hand side of the chart. As we progressed through the year, we had daily timed mathematics tests on addition. If you did not finish in time with all the answers correct, you did not earn a star. You would then retake the test the next day and on subsequent days until you passed it. Near the middle of the year, by looking at the chart, everyone could see which students had the most stars and which had the fewest. As you can imagine, those students with the fewest stars began to dislike math and became stressed whenever the time came for a test.

If math anxiety is a common problem, what can we do about it? The first thing is to recognize the signs of mathematics anxiety in ourselves. Take a deep breath and remind yourself that no matter how scared of math you are, you still have enough mathematical content knowledge to teach children in the early childhood classroom. The second thing to do is to make a pact with yourself that, as a teacher, you will do your best to combat math anxiety in the children that you teach. Fighting math anxiety may seem difficult, but by:

- making mathematics about process rather than product
- integrating mathematics into everyday activities
- having children use their natural mathematical ability
- making mathematics relevant to children's lives, and above all,
- minimizing the use of high-stakes and high-stress activities and assessments, such as timed tests, whenever possible

We can eliminate the underlying causes of math anxiety and may never have to hear "I hate math" again. Children are naturally drawn to mathematical and logical thinking. Teachers should allow this natural interest to grow and bloom. Through a reflective process, teachers can develop more effective methods that avoid the problems of math anxiety. To do this, teachers have to take ownership of the curriculum in their classroom by becoming decision makers.

TEACHERS ARE DECISION MAKERS

Teaching is all about making decisions (Fosnot, 1989). Teachers need to be able to assess a situation and make complex decisions based on a vast knowledge base developed during their teacher preparation program. A **knowledge base** includes all the things learned in your teacher preparation program courses such as child development, guidance and discipline, teaching methods, and developmental theory. It includes all your past experiences as both a teacher and a student. This body of knowledge will help guide curricular planning in all your subjects.

Teachers as decision makers are adept at combining what children need to know with what their knowledge base tells them is the best way to present this information, and the needs of individual children, in order to create effective and enjoyable learning experiences. Information about child development, the class at large, individual students, and the teachers themselves all factor into making decisions about what and how to teach. Teachers must develop their knowledge base to answer these questions and make the best decisions possible.

For example, when planning a mathematics lesson, first you will need to think about your objective for the lesson. Is it to teach your students a specific skill, or is it for them to understand a concept? I heard of a trained horse that would stomp its hoof 9 times when it heard someone say "4 plus 5." This certainly doesn't mean the horse understood the concept of addition. But when a first-grade child gives the same answer, we often think of it in the same terms—as a "fact" to be recited. However, this is not just a trained response, but evidence of a complex relationship of number concepts that the child has constructed.

The decisions you make concerning your mathematics curriculum, informed by your understanding of developmental theory and child development, will have a great impact on how you design lessons. To be effective, teachers need to understand different theories of child development and current research on how children develop. An understanding of theories past and present can help us evaluate current practices and improve those practices for the future.

Determining "what" children need to know and when to teach it is a bit more complicated. Each individual state has a different set of standards that must be met, and local school districts often have their own requirements. In many states, textbooks are adopted at a statewide level, while in others it is done at a local level. Remember that choosing "what" to teach needs to be grounded in what you know about children and how they learn mathematics. Decision making goes hand in hand with reflective practice.

During fieldwork or observations in schools, ask yourself, "What decisions has the teacher made to develop this math lesson? What were those decisions based on? What theories can I see behind this lesson? Whose research does this activity represent? What developmental principles is this strategy based on?"

Teachers make complex decisions based on their ever-developing and growing knowledge base and their understanding of their students and the curriculum. One of the first steps is to understand developmental theory and what it says about how children learn mathematics. Every educational practice is based on some theory or assumption about how children learn. The challenge as a teacher is to keep current on this research. Researchers constantly discover new things about how children develop and learn and how their brains develop and function. As we learn more and more about how children construct knowledge, we can develop increasingly better teaching strategies and make better decisions.

Knowing children's individual needs and strengths is another crucial element of being a good decision maker. Every child is different, and knowing how best to present curricular material will enhance both their interest and comprehension of mathematics.

A Lesson in Mathematics

The following problems are designed to help you conceptualize the type of open-ended problems that will be discussed throughout the text. Take your time and discuss possible solutions with as many people as you wish. They are just as useful with first graders as with adults. Giving younger children measuring cups might help them think through the first problem.

- You need 9 cups of water exactly but you only have a 4- and 7-cup measuring bowl. How could you use these to get exactly 9 cups?
- Now consider a problem that has a larger number of solutions. If we assign numerical values to the letters of the alphabet like this, can you come up with a word that adds up to exactly 100?

a	b	c	d	e	f	g	h	i	j	k	l	m	n	o	p	q	r	s	t	u	v	w	x	y	z
1	2	3	4	5	6	7	8	9	10	11	12	13	14	15	16	17	18	19	20	21	22	23	24	25	26

The answers can be found on the next page.

How long did it take you before you decided to check the next page for the answers? Did you really discuss your answers with other people? How many? What if the answers were not in this book? How would that make you feel?

We have come to expect someone to confirm or correct our answers immediately. When I give this exercise to classes of future teachers, the following *invariably* happens: I present the problem, allow the class to discuss it for a while alone or in groups, and then have them present their answers. After presentation of the answers and some initial discussion, the class stops talking and stares at me in anticipation. I then ask people who had different answers to discuss their methods. Again, the students *invariably* direct their explanations at me, the teacher. Occasionally, once an answer is proposed, other students are reluctant to propose or even explain a different answer for fear that they are wrong. It is almost an unspoken rule: A new answer is not offered until the first one is rejected.

The students again stare at me, the instructor, in anticipation. At this point I reply, "You didn't think I was going to give you the answer, did you?" This leads to much anger and rebellion from the students. "But you have to tell us," "How will we know if we are right?" and my favorite, "This will bug me forever if you don't tell me the answer." This is my favorite because it is exactly the response I want from my future teachers. I have to be careful not to give this activity until the end of class; otherwise I will not be able to do anything else the rest of the class period. Students will spend the time whispering back and forth trying to solve the problem. The goal of every math teacher should be to give a problem that intrigues their students so much that they discuss it with friends and family until they are convinced of an answer. This is possible in the early childhood mathematics classroom. Imagine the response you might have from children who are naturally driven to make sense of their world, and exhibit limitless curiosity!

Answers: How long did it take you before you looked at this box? Perhaps you came up with a cursory guess and then looked to check your answer. This process is what most students have been trained to do from our very earliest education. Before you read on, try discussing it with your friends until you are all convinced of the right answer. Try not to look at the answer until you are all convinced of an answer. If you still have a burning desire to know, read on— but reflect on why you have this burning desire if you have already proven your answer to others. Are you looking because you are tired of thinking about it? 1) The 4-cup container can measure exactly 8 cups. We need 1 more cup. The difference between 7 and 8 is 1. If you pour 4 cups into the 7-cup container, refill the 4-cup container, and fill the 7-cup container from the 4-cup container, there will be 1 cup left in the 4-cup container. 2) There are many different answers to this question. Here are a few: beginning, cousins, fountain, elephants, excellent, towers, wizard, writing. Actually, one of those might not be a 100-value word. Can you tell which?

This is the basis of constructivist teaching: a focus on the *process* of thinking and an understanding that wrong answers are just as important or more important than right answers in promoting discussion and thinking. **Constructivism** is a theory that emphasizes the active participation of children in building their own understanding and learning. This book advocates taking a constructivist approach to teaching mathematics. Learning mathematics skills and content is only a part of learning mathematics. NCTM proposes content *and* process standards. The constructivist approach encourages children to actively construct mathematical content knowledge, develop the skills to be fluent in mathematics, while using the process skills to engage with mathematics in a developmentally appropriate and mentally active way. In order to use these techniques in the classroom, there are a number of theoretical tools that we need to focus on.

UNDERSTANDING CHILD DEVELOPMENT

Teachers need to know what research says about children of specific age ranges. What are their abilities? How do they learn math? How do they think about math? What does a child need from a teacher? The reflective process we discussed earlier helps teachers examine their own feelings about students' learning. Many of us come to a classroom with preconceived notions about how children learn and how they should be taught. Sometimes, our ideas are not based on research or what we know about children, but rather on ways we were taught or methods we understand as "common sense." As you read about these theories in the following pages, think about their implications for educational practice and which ones best fit your personal philosophy. Reflective teachers understand that all teaching methodologies have a theoretical basis.

These theories can be thought about in terms of how teacher-directed the mathematics lessons are. In Figure 2.1 you can see that these theories fall on a continuum between very teacher-directed and very child-centered. The designation of where they fall is dictated by what major contributors to the theory assumed about how children learn and develop. Let's start at the teacher-directed end and move toward child-centered.

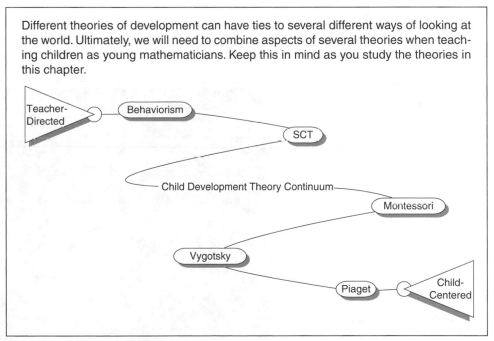

Different theories of development can have ties to several different ways of looking at the world. Ultimately, we will need to combine aspects of several theories when teaching children as young mathematicians. Keep this in mind as you study the theories in this chapter.

Figure 2.1   Continuum of Theories.

The Behaviorist Approach

Mathematics has been a central educational topic for hundreds of years. It is one of the "three Rs" of reading, writing, and arithmetic. In the early days math was known as "learning your sums." Learning was accomplished through repeated practice, drills, and rote memorization. According to this philosophy, math is seen as a set of "facts" to be learned or internalized—as, in a history class, you might memorize a date (e.g., "in 1492 Columbus sailed the ocean blue"). To many it seems intuitively correct that to learn how to add, subtract, multiply, and divide one must practice, practice, and practice some more. This method of teaching mathematics was given scientific validity and turned into a solid methodology by a group of educational theorists we call the *behaviorists*. These include Pavlov, John Watson, and B. F. Skinner.

To the behaviorist, all behavior (including mathematics) is learned from the environment through internalization and reinforcement (Miller, 2002). Therefore, mathematics can be taught by rewarding children for correct answers and withholding reward—or even punishing—for incorrect answers. In this way mathematics learning can be engineered in each child by building more and more complex behaviors. Returning to timed tests in primary school, the student first memorizes the small numbers (adding single-digit numbers, for example) and moves on to more complex problems as the lower-level problems are mastered. Once the basic facts are memorized the student begins memorizing double-column addition and so on. Unfortunately, the behaviorist approach does not ensure or even value problem solving or the learner's thought processes. Behaviorists are only concerned with observable behaviors or outcomes. The goal is to engineer a child that can produce correct answers, somewhat like training a dog to roll over.

An offshoot of behaviorism, Social Cognitive Theory, focuses on modeling and intrinsic or self-reward and has some interesting implications in mathematics

Math games let the child reason about math rather than just memorize facts.

Eugene Geist

(Bandura, 2002). For example, if children see a teacher or parent complaining about doing mathematics, they will model a dislike for mathematics. Mathematics should be presented as an activity that is intrinsically rewarding and meaningful to the student. Teachers and parents should also be modeling positive mathematics behaviors. Unfortunately, we tend to see more of the negative aspects of behaviorism in mathematics teaching.

Behaviorism and Mathematics

Behaviorism is probably the most widely used method for teaching mathematics in the United States. Repetitious problems, homework, graded tests, worksheets, and even stickers for good performance are all based on behaviorist ideas of teaching mathematics. The problem with this mechanistic view is that it never addresses a conceptual understanding of mathematics. Conceptual understanding is not a focus of behavioral approaches to mathematics because it is not directly measurable. Since only external behaviors are measurable, behaviorists such as Skinner chose not to be concerned with *how* the child was thinking, but only on his ability to complete the task (and perhaps receive good grades). This perspective does not acknowledge emergent math concepts, and by itself does not support treating children as young mathematicians.

Teachers of math must make the distinction between behavior and understanding. A purely behaviorist approach does not make this distinction, nor do many children's mathematics textbooks. Today's math textbooks consist of a plethora of activities based on repetition and behavior modification. These activities are designed to train students to say or write the correct answer rather than focusing on understanding. Drilling for speed, for instance, is not focused on thinking or problem solving. This type of assessment is a memorization and reward task. Timed tests are another example that uses classical conditioning through the repetition of behavior and external rewards—in this case, gold stars and class recognition.

Teaching skills are an important part of mathematics education and should eventually be incorporated into the early childhood mathematics curriculum. The ability to use mathematical skills efficiently and quickly is as important as problem solving. A top-down approach, however, begins with a concept and then moves toward skills. These skills, then, are taught in relation to meaningful context. This is the opposite of the "bottom-up" approach associated with behaviorist instruction. Instead of repetitious drills or worksheets, children could play math games where they have to apply their understanding of numbers while getting repeated skills practice. A good example is a commercially available game called Tens. It is a collection of cardboard triangles with numbers 0–10 on each edge so that each triangle has three numbers on it. Children build patterns by matching sides that add up to 10. Kindergartners love to play this game and need little encouragement to continue. Even though they may only match two numbers, they are getting skills practice on sums up to 10. Beyond these skills, Tens also encourages the building of early geometrical concepts and pattern recognition.

*A child-centered approach
links learning to the child's
experience.*

Anne Vega/Merrill

The Montessori Method

Next on our continuum is the Montessori Method. The Montessori Method values the freedom of the child and is designed to support learning through a clean and stimulating environment. Throughout the program children are given choices of what to study and for how long (American Montessori Society & Educational Video Publishing, 2000).

Montessori emphasized practical and domestic skills such as cooking, cleaning, and hygiene. To develop her concept of freedom she developed a curriculum that gave children choice and the freedom to learn at their own pace. Educational objectives and materials were also developed around the five senses, and were designed so that the child could tell if he was right or wrong without a teacher's assistance. On the continuum, this program lies just to the child-centered side of the middle because the curriculum was designed and set by the teachers. The materials were meant to be used in a specific way and children were expected to learn to use them "correctly."

John Dewey and many other contemporaries of Maria Montessori felt that a *child-centered* approach could be a viable alternative to the drill-and-recitation methods of their day. Dewey espoused the notion that learning and education should be grounded in experience (Dewey, 1915). He also argued that education should be based on the child's psychological and physical development, as well as the world outside the schoolroom (Dewey, 1938). This approach put the child at the center of the curriculum and made it important for teachers to know about children's development, their environmental context, and their interests before beginning to teach. These ideas are still true today, and a child-centered approach is instrumental in treating children like young mathematicians.

For Montessori, when learning mathematics is facilitated through sensory experience, children see and touch mathematics and mathematical concepts to learn and internalize them. Montessori's materials were a breakthrough for the teaching of mathematics in this way (American Montessori Society & Educational Video Publishing, 2000). Earlier methods of math instruction were centered on memorization and remained very didactic and teacher-directed. She introduced the concept of the prepared environment in education by giving children child-sized furniture, specially designed materials, and freedom and choice in the classroom. By developing a curriculum focused on the needs and abilities of the children, she helped promote the child-centered approach first proposed by Dewey.

Montessori's Materials and Mathematics

Montessori developed a set of educational materials to use in her schools, many of which focused on mathematics, and for which she is probably best known. They were made according to high standards and included both direct objectives, such as learning numbers, and more subtle objectives. For example, knobs on many of her materials were designed to be the same size as a standard pencil. This was to help children train their sense of touch to prepare for writing with a pencil.

One of the most famous Montessori materials is the "Knobbed Cylinders," wooden blocks with 10 cylinders of various heights and diameters (see Figure 2.2). These materials are considered self-correcting and self-assessing. If a child puts a knobbed cylinder in the wrong hole, he can see his error and correct it without a teacher's intervention. Many Montessori materials allow the child freedom to explore and interact with the object individually. Montessori believed that training the senses would have a positive effect on a child's ability to do mathematics. For example, the more familiar a child is with judging sizes and making visual representations of abstract concepts such as place value, the better he will be at higher-level mathematics such as geometry (Educational Video Publishing, 2003).

Another example of materials designed around a sensory experience is "Number Beads" (see Figure 2.3). Individual beads represent **ones**. To represent **tens**, 10 beads

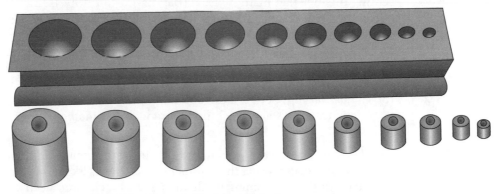

Figure 2.2   A Set of Montessori's Knobbed Cylinders.

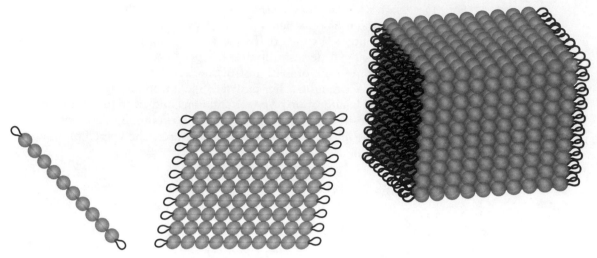

Figure 2.3 Montessori's Number Beads, from Left to Right: A String of 10, a Hundred Square, and a Thousand Block.

are strung together in a row. *Hundreds* are represented by a square with 10 beads across and 10 down, and *thousands* by stacking 10 squares to make a cube. Students then represent numbers using these materials. The idea was for children to "see" the size of the number so they could understand the concept of quantity and place value, and eventually the concept of "squared" or "cubed" numbers. Cuisenaire rods, manipulatives often used in classrooms today, operate on the same principle, using solid cubes instead of beads.

A Visual Approach to Learning Mathematics

We see these methods incorporated in modern math series that discuss "number" as a physical property of a group of items, as if numbers were the same as colors, presenting the idea that math is visual (Baratta-Lorton, 1994). Just as behaviorism has a "common sense" appeal, the idea that we can look at objects and "see" the math just seems to make sense. If a child is shown a group of five and a group of seven objects, he can look at it and can tell which group has more. However, this is a deceptive picture of how the mind is actually working. There is more going on besides just visual sensory activity. The child's brain acts on the objects that are seen with the eyes and forges relationships between the objects.

Many textbooks also teach using a model that mathematics is learned in three stages:

1. The first stage is the "concrete stage," in which young children are expected to do mathematics using three-dimensional objects like blocks or other manipulatives. In these beginning mathematics stages, children need to use a lot of manipulatives to be able to "see" the math that they are learning.

2. After internalizing some of the math, children can move to the "semiconcrete" stage, which includes doing math on two-dimensional surfaces such as chalkboards or paper. These older children have developed enough to not need three-dimensional manipulatives, but not quite far enough to be able to think about math without visual cues.

3. The final, or the "abstract" stage, is where students have internalized mathematics enough to be able to do math in their heads. They can now visualize objects rather than actually having to see them.

Unfortunately, there is little research that supports children actually learning mathematics this way. This assumes that mathematics is a physical property of an object that a child has to see and touch. Research in teaching children mathematics supports the idea that mathematics is not a sensory activity but a mental activity and series of relationships. To teach mathematics, we must stimulate the mind (Ambrose, 2002; Kamii, O'Brien, & Teacher Center, Southern Illinois University at Edwardsville, 1980).

This does not mean that the use of manipulatives and pencil and paper are not vital to learning mathematics—they are! When activities are designed using any materials, we must reflect upon our general assumptions about why we are conducting an activity in a specific way. We should always be asking "What assumptions about learning am I making?" and design activities accordingly.

The Constructivist Approach

The missing element in behavioral and sensory approaches is the role of cognition in the learning of math. Without a strong focus on cognition, learning can only be observed on the surface. Constructivist theory has its roots in research done by cognitive theorists. Cognitive theorists believe that whenever we learn something it causes the mind to change in some way, and that knowledge is structured and builds on previous knowledge (Elkind & Piaget, 1979; Piaget, Yale, & Media, 1977). The next two theories we will discuss lie on the child-centered end of the spectrum: the constructivist theories of Vygotsky and Piaget. Vygotsky's theory relies more on a teacher or more experienced peer to scaffold the learning. For this reason, it lies just to the left of Piaget on our continuum.

Lev Vygotsky is considered a **socio-constructivist** (Sinclair, & Kamii, 1994) and his theory includes many of the same elements as Piaget's theory. Vygotsky's view was that as children learn they need the help of a more experienced peer to develop cognitively. This is known as scaffolding.

Vygotsky felt that interaction within the **social context** (whether with peers, teachers, or parents) was the most important aspect in constructing new knowledge, and brought this belief into cognitive theory. He felt that children who interact with more experienced peers could, through this interaction, improve their performance. He described this in one of the most prominent aspects of his theory—the **Zone of Proximal Development (ZPD)**. We can think of the ZPD as a space in the child's knowledge between what they know and can do individually without any outside help and what they can't do at all, no matter how much help they are given. Between these two extremes is an area where the child can successfully complete a task with a certain amount of help from a more experienced peer or adult (see Figure 2.4). Vygotsky's idea was that the more experienced peer or adult would initially assist the child in accomplishing the task beyond his understanding, gradually offering less and less support until the child could perform the task by himself. This process, of supporting the child's thinking until it is strong enough to stand alone and then slowly removing the support, is called **scaffolding**.

To restate, a child has an independent performance level, an assisted performance level, and a level at which he is unable to complete or understand a task even with assistance. For example, most 4-year-olds will not be able to understand multiplication because the concept is above their zones of proximal development, but they may be able to, individually, count to 10 without help. When the typical 4-year-old is confronted with 20 cubes to count, the child miscounts them when trying alone. Maybe he counts some cubes twice, or skips or repeats numbers. This task falls within the child's ZPD and with the help of a more experienced peer or adult, he should be able to complete it. Holding the child's finger, the teacher says, "Let's count together," and helps him point to the cubes one at a time while saying the number. Next time, perhaps she lets the child count alone while still holding his counting finger. The teacher removes this support when the child begins to complete the task on his own. She must have knowledge of what concepts and activities are developmentally appropriate for the child.

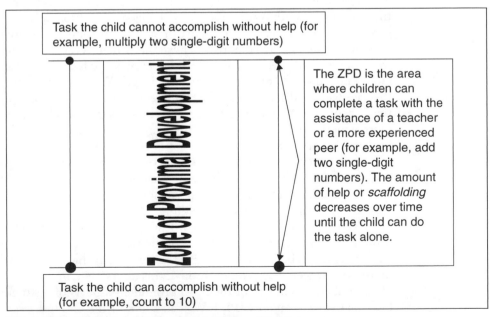

Figure 2.4 Vygotsky's Zone of Proximal Development.

Unlike Vygotsky's idea of the ZPD and scaffolding, Piaget viewed children as "solitary scientists" constructing knowledge without another acting as a "tutor." Teachers and other children were facilitators of knowledge rather than transmitters or trainers. For example, teachers would set up a mentally stimulating experience and the child would grow cognitively because of it. The teacher is not concerned with whether the child completes the activity "correctly," as we saw in Montessori's method, but rather views the simple act of thinking as important.

If we look at the practical implications of Piaget's theory for mathematics, the environment is vitally important, as are social interaction, argument, contextual variables, family input, belief systems, ethnic background, and more. While theoretically Piaget was not as concerned with individual differences as was Vygotsky, the practical implications of both theories are filled with opportunities to apply principles of the contextual paradigm in very diverse settings. For these reasons, I will present both Vygotsky's and Piaget's learning theories as examples of contextual theories.

Piaget placed more emphasis on the cognitive aspect of learning and less on the social aspect described by Vygotsky. While Piaget believed that social interaction was vitally important, he did not feel that it had to be with a more experienced peer or adult. Piaget felt that discussion and even argument would lead children to reexamine what they knew and eventually progress in their construction of knowledge. Piaget's research demonstrated how a child's natural thinking ability leads to increasingly complex ways of thinking. He described how the mind changes **qualitatively.** Instead of understanding learning as gaining *more* knowledge, or **quantitative** change, he showed that the brain goes through stages where the child actually thinks differently in each stage. In other words, the quality of the thinking has changed.

Have you ever wondered why preschoolers are so different from second graders? How they look at the world, play, interact with friends, investigate, and problem solve are all very different. Piaget thought this difference needed to be explained in a better way than through the idea that the child has collected *more* knowledge. He felt that there must be some developmental change in how the child thinks about things. He began to study children in depth, asking them questions and studying their answers. Remarkably, he learned more from their *wrong* answers than from their correct ones. He felt that children got the answers wrong not because they were less intelligent or had less knowledge; rather, they were very intelligent beings applying their own natural thinking ability to solving the problem. The reason different aged children gave different answers was that they thought about the problem in a different way.

As children develop, their thinking tends to become more symbolic and abstract. They also become increasingly better at using logic to help them solve problems and resolve internal conflicts. Piaget felt that children develop through these stages at the same general rate, though some children could be a bit slower or quicker. This development was based on an interaction of biological factors and, more importantly to Piaget, environmental factors. Piaget felt that immersing children in a stimulating and challenging environment that makes them think and use their natural thinking ability causes development through the stages.

Let's take a quick look at these general stages of cognitive development. Each of these stages is qualitatively different from the previous or next stage in the sequence. Most importantly, these stages describe qualitative differences in children's understanding and how they think about their world. A 4-year-old thinks about a math problem differently than an 8-year-old, not because the child has gained a larger quantity of math "facts," but because the way the child thinks, the quality of his thinking, has changed.

Piaget's four stages of cognitive development:

1. Sensorimotor
2. Preoperational
3. Concrete Operational
4. Formal Operational (Inhelder & Piaget, 1958, 1964, 1999)

Each of these stages has its own sub-stages of development, but the important part of the theory is how the child's thinking changes and how children of different ages think and reason. Our study of the nature of mathematics and how it is learned will benefit from examining these stages briefly here and in depth in later chapters.

Sensorimotor Stage. This stage lasts from birth until about age 2. In this stage, infants and toddlers learn about their world through their senses. They like to see, touch, and manipulate objects to learn about them. This stage begins soon after birth, the child having only simple reflexes with which to interact with the environment. Through interaction with a stimulating environment, he begins to modify and control these innate reflexes into actions, or what Piaget called **schemes.** A scheme is just a way of doing something—children learn how to shake things to produce a sound and eventually, how to use things to achieve a goal.

Sensorimotor intelligence has a few characteristics that are important for us to remember when thinking about supporting mathematics with infants and toddlers:

Object Permanence. Children develop the concept that things exist even when they are not seen or observed by the child. This ability begins to develop at about 6 months of age and continues to strengthen over the next year. This is important for mathematics because mathematics in most cases is based on the idea that objects exist outside of perception. It is a bit difficult to do mathematics if you can't assume that an object exists when it is hidden.

Use of Symbols. For most of the duration of the sensorimotor stage children lack the ability to **represent,** or to make a mental or written symbol of an object stand for the real object. For example, they cannot link the word "tree" with a mental representation of a tree because they have not yet developed that mental representation. They lack the ability to make present mentally something that is not in front of them. The symbolic nature of mathematics is important to all future intellectual pursuits even to the youngest mathematician. We see this later manifesting itself as pretend or imaginative play (at 18 months to 2 years). When children pretend to feed a doll or ride a stick horse, their ability to represent is beginning to emerge.

Preoperational Stage. This stage includes the preschool and kindergarten ages (ages 2–6). In this stage children begin to use symbols and signs to stand for other things. For example, words (written and verbal) begin to represent objects in the child's world. Children also begin to use representational symbology such as numbers to stand for specific quantities. They may put up two fingers when asked how many shoes they have. Another example of this representational thought is the copious amount of imaginative and fantasy play in which children engage.

> Qioping and Amit are playing in the housekeeping area of a preschool class-room. Qioping says, "Pretend you are sick, O.K.?" Amit sits in a chair and sticks his tongue out and groans. Qioping then says, "I'll call the doctor!" There is no phone in the play area, so Qioping picks up a block on the shelf and pre-tends to dial a number. "Come quick! He's sick!"

Even though there was no direct mathematical engagement in this example, this type of play, such as pretending to use the phone, strengthens children's representa-tional ability and their ability to think more abstractly—both important abilities for learning mathematics. This type of play should be widely encouraged. Vygotsky pro-posed that children's use of imagination helped them to detach the thought or idea of the object from the actual object. This way, children could use other objects to "represent" the real object, such as a block standing in for the phone.

Some other characteristics of the preoperational stage are:

Intuitive Thinking. Children in this stage tend to think intuitively rather than logically. They are widely curious about their surroundings and will ask "why?" about every-thing. They are not bound by adult logic and their explanations and ideas about how the world works are more based on what "seems right."

Logical thinking strengthens in Piaget's concrete operational stage.

Valerie Schultz/Merrill

Animism. Animism is the idea that inanimate objects have human characteristics. A child may want to put a blanket on the car to keep it warm at night. This shows how hard the child is trying to understand the world as he applies rules about the world in places where they may not work.

Concrete Operations. This stage covers the primary and elementary school ages (approximately age 7 until 11). Here we observe children beginning to think logically, though their logic is limited and not as systematic or abstract as it will become in the formal operational stage. They can now use logical precepts to solve problems and to think about the world. The child can use his logic to overcome visual and perceptual information. Before this, the child's logic can falter when he is presented with conflicting perceptual information. However, his logic is limited to what Piaget referred to as "concrete" circumstances. This does not mean that he can only think about concrete objects or that he needs to touch or see things to think logically, but it does mean that his logic is not as abstract as an adult's.

Some characteristics of concrete operational thought are:

Conservation. Concrete operational children are conservers. In the conservation task the same amount of a substance is changed in shape. Younger children think there is more or less of substance based on its appearance, but conservers know that since only the shape has changed, it must, logically, be the same amount. This demonstrates the dependency on logic to make decisions. Tasks such as this one or the conservation of volume task show the ability of a child's logic to overcome perception. In the conservation of volume task, a child is asked if two identical glasses of water have the same amount of liquid. When the child says "yes" the researcher pours the water from one of the glasses into a taller but skinnier glass. The child is then asked if the quantity of liquid is still the same. Nonconservers *centrate* or focus on one aspect (the height) of the liquid in the skinny glass and say that it has more. So, perception overcomes logic because the child's logic is not able to overcome this perceptual "trap."

> Evan, age 4, and his mommy are having cookies and milk. Both cookies are the same size, and Evan picks the cookie closest to him on the plate. As his mommy puts her cookie on her plate it breaks in two. Evan says, "Mommy! It's not fair! You have more cookie!"

Trial-and-Error Thinking. While children think logically, their logic is not systematic and they often take "the long way around" when solving problems. Since children in this stage cannot take all levels of comparisons and possibilities into account at once, they must attack each idea individually, using a trial-and-error method. It may take them longer, but they get there in the end.

Games with Rules. Children at this stage love games with rules, such as board games or baseball. This links to their newly developed logic. Everything happens for a reason and has an explanation, so the games that children play shift from imaginative (where they exercise representational thought) to rule-based and logical. Games of strategy and logic appeal to these children immensely. While children might start with simple games like tic-tac-toe and checkers, they quickly develop a desire for more complex and challenging games such as Chess, Monopoly, Sorry, or Risk.

Formal Operations. This is adult logic. It begins to develop around age 12 and continues through life. Formal operations consist of a freeform, abstract logic that allows adults to discuss abstract ideas like "freedom," to use deductive and inductive reasoning, and to see all possible outcomes and possibilities.

We will not discuss this stage in depth in this book, but you should be aware of it because it shows how your thinking is vastly different from that of the children you are teaching. Part of this difference goes back to the **nature of number** and where the concept of number originates. For adults, the idea of counting and sorting is so natural we forget that there was a time when we did not have the ability to count, order, and sort things using numbers. Let's look at the development of this idea, as it will be very important to our teaching of math to young children.

The Importance of Piaget to Mathematics. To Piaget, a stimulating environment that allows the child the freedom to make mistakes and be confronted by other conflicting solutions (a similarity with the Montessori Method) causes the child to experience disequilibrium. When confronted with a new idea or piece of information from their environment, children either **assimilate** it into their already existing ideas (what Piaget called schemas), or they have to **accommodate** their thinking to adapt to the new information. The more stimulation in the environment, the more opportunity there is for the child to either assimilate or accommodate.

Disequilibrium is the sense of confusion a child feels when confronted with new information that contradicts his expectations. The child eventually finds a way to adapt and again reach equilibrium. This idea supports the creation of stimulating active learning environments in classrooms. Environments characterized by a focus on the needs and development of the child, and his freedom to develop and construct mathematical knowledge for himself, better fosters the child's development of deep mathematical understanding.

If a child can learn a math concept or skill by playing a math game available in the classroom, there is no need for a teacher-directed activity that may not be as developmentally appropriate or engaging. When the child plays the game of Tens discussed earlier, the child is still "learning," but is constructing instead of internalizing (Kamii & DeClark, 1985; Kamii & National Association for the Education of Young Children, 1982). Any game that uses dice, logical deduction, or score keeping is teaching math skills in a more enjoyable and meaningful way for children.

Instead of the teacher scaffolding information, as seen in Vygotsky's ZPD, she acts as a facilitator and sets up a classroom environment that allows children to think and problem solve either alone or with other students, even if they are on differing levels of understanding. Important to this process for Piaget was the free exchange of multiple answers and solutions between both student and teacher and between the students themselves.

The best way Piaget can be used as a basis for educational practice, however, is his contention that a child or individual constructs knowledge through interaction with his or her environment (Elkind & Piaget, 1979; Kamii, 2003; Piaget, 1970). For Piaget, development is not the result of pure maturation, nor is it the result of pure environment. Rather, it is an interaction between the subject's developmental level and his environment that causes disequilibrium and leads to growth and development (Piaget, 1952).

Constructivism and Mathematics

Piaget's theory is the basis for many of the teaching ideas in this book. However, the other theories mentioned here do have some role to play in all mathematics programs. A child-centered approach often needs to be tempered with some level of teacher direction.

The idea that mathematical ideas are constructed through interaction with our environment and not simply through direct teaching approaches is central to our understanding of how to teach mathematics to young children. As we learn that children learn in different ways at different ages, we come to understand that we must adapt how we teach mathematics for these different ages.

Vygotsky's Zone of Proximal Development gives us a framework for peer teaching and helping children to learn specific mathematical skills with the help of a more experienced peer or adult. It becomes obvious because of this theory that we should not be introducing mathematical concepts to children that are way above their comprehension. Likewise, drilling students on things they can already do without help is a waste of time. We should focus on the area between, where children need support to strengthen and build concepts and ideas about mathematics.

NCTM and Theoretical Basis for Mathematics

The NCTM Principles and Standards for School Mathematics underscore the importance of understanding developmental theory in teaching mathematics. It states:

> Learning the "basics" is important; however, students who memorize facts or procedures without understanding often are not sure when or how to use what they know. In contrast, conceptual understanding enables students to deal with novel problems and settings. They can solve problems that they have not encountered before.
>
> Learning with understanding also helps students become autonomous learners. Students learn more and better when they take control of their own learning. When challenged with appropriately chosen tasks, students can become confident in their ability to tackle difficult problems, eager to figure things out on their own, flexible in exploring mathematical ideas, and willing to persevere when tasks are challenging.

To help children learn with understanding, we must use our knowledge of child development to create new, exciting, and innovative mathematics programs for young children. Encouraging the child as a young mathematician is our goal. We want children to go through the process of solving 20 + 25 in the same manner as a Ph.D. mathematician solves theoretical calculus equations. To do this, we have to use the best aspects of all of these theories.

UNDERSTANDING YOUR STUDENTS

Understanding your students and their needs, strengths, differences, and abilities is a crucial element of a constructivist mathematics program. While we will examine multiple ways to accomplish this, Howard Gardner's Theory of Multiple Intelligences (MI) in particular has radically changed the way we think about children (Gardner, 1999, 2006; Gardner, Gardner, Dinozzi, Harvard Project Zero, & Into the Classroom Media [Firm], 1996). Gardner asks us not to ask "how smart" a child may be, but rather to ask *how* children are smart. This has vast implications for our current processes of testing and assessing children. Children are subjected to many standardized tests each year. Some of these test proficiency, some test achievement, but all are looking at how much a child knows or how "smart" a child is. Gardner outlined eight different intelligences, which are described in Figure 2.5. He developed the idea that each child had a different modal intelligence, or a particular intelligence that is stronger than others.

It is important to remember that these intelligences are not labels that we attach to children so that we can stereotype their learning. Instead, Multiple Intelligences

---

Linguistic—Verbal-linguistic intelligence has to do with words, spoken or written. People with verbal-linguistic intelligence display a facility with words and languages. They are typically good at reading, writing, telling stories, and memorizing words and dates. They tend to learn best by reading, taking notes, and listening to lectures, and via discussion and debate. They are also frequently skilled at explaining, teaching, and oration or persuasive speaking. Those with verbal-linguistic intelligence learn foreign languages very easily as they have high verbal memory and recall and an ability to understand and manipulate syntax and structure.

Logical-mathematical—This area has to do with logic, abstractions, inductive and deductive reasoning, and numbers. While it is often assumed that those with this intelligence naturally excel in mathematics, chess, computer programming, and other logical or numerical activities, a more accurate definition places emphasis less on traditional mathematical ability and more reasoning capabilities, abstract pattern recognition, scientific thinking and investigation, and the ability to perform complex calculations.

Spatial—This area has to do with vision and spatial judgment. People with strong visual-spatial intelligence are typically very good at visualizing and mentally manipulating objects. They have a strong visual memory and are often artistically inclined. Those with visual-spatial intelligence also generally have a very good sense of direction and may also have very good hand-eye coordination, although this is normally seen as a characteristic of the bodily-kinesthetic intelligence.

Figure 2.5   Gardner's Multiple Intelligences.   *(continued)*

Bodily-kinesthetic—This area has to do with movement and doing. In this category, people are generally adept at physical activities such as sports or dance and often prefer activities, which utilize movement. They may enjoy acting or performing, and in general they are good at building and making things. They often learn best by physically doing something, rather than reading or hearing about it. Those with strong bodily-kinesthetic intelligence seem to use what might be termed *muscle memory* (i.e., they remember things through their body, rather than through words (verbal memory) or images (visual memory). It requires the skills and dexterity for fine motor movements such as those required for dancing, athletics, surgery, craft making, etc.

Musical—This area has to do with rhythm, music, and hearing. Those who have a high level of musical-rhythmic intelligence display greater sensitivity to sounds, rhythms, tones, and music. They normally have good pitch and may even have absolute pitch, and are able to sing, play musical instruments, and compose music. Since there is a strong aural component to this intelligence, those who are strongest in it may learn best via lecture. In addition, they will often use songs or rhythms to learn and memorize information, and may work best with music playing.

Naturalistic—This area has to do with nature, nurturing, and classification. This is the newest of the intelligences and is not as widely accepted as the original seven. Those with it are said to have greater sensitivity to nature and their place within it, the ability to nurture and grow things, and greater ease in caring for, taming, and interacting with animals. They are also good at recognizing and classifying different species.

Interpersonal—This area has to do with interaction with others. People in this category are usually extroverts and are characterized by their sensitivity to others' moods, feelings, temperaments, and motivations and their ability to cooperate in order to work as part of a group. They communicate effectively and empathize easily with others, and may be either leaders or followers. They typically learn best by working with others and often enjoy discussion and debate.

Intrapersonal—This area has to do with oneself. Those who are strongest in this intelligence are typically introverts and prefer to work alone. They are usually highly self-aware and capable of understanding their own emotions, goals, and motivations. They often have an affinity for thought-based pursuits such as philosophy. They learn best when allowed to concentrate on the subject alone. There is often a high level of perfectionism associated with this intelligence.

Other Intelligences—Other intelligences have been suggested or explored by Gardner and his colleagues, including spiritual, existential, and moral intelligence. Gardner excluded spiritual intelligence due to its failure to meet a number of his criteria. Existential intelligence (the capacity to raise and reflect on philosophical questions about life, death, and ultimate realities) meets most of the criteria with the exception of identifiable areas of the brain that specialize for this faculty. Moral capacities were excluded because they are normative rather than descriptive.

Figure 2.5 Gardner's Multiple Intelligences (*continued*).

Sources: Gardner, H. (1999). *Intelligence reframed: Multiple intelligences for the 21st century.* New York: Basic Books.

Gardner, H. (2006). *The development and education of the mind: The selected works of Howard Gardner.* London; New York: Routledge.

Gardner, H., Gardner, H., Dinozzi, R., Harvard Project Zero, & Into the Classroom Media (Firm). (1996). MI answers [videorecording]. Los Angeles, CA.: Into the Classroom Media.

Kitchens, A. N. (1995). *Defeating math anxiety.* Chicago: Irwin Career Education Division.

Kornhaber, M. L., Fierros, E. G., & Veenema, S. A. (2004). *Multiple intelligences: Best ideas from research and practice.* Boston: Pearson/Allyn & Bacon.

Theory should be used to better understand children and ensure that their different strengths are valued. Teachers can then provide children with mathematical activities they find meaningful and exciting.

For mathematics teaching, Gardner's Multiple Intelligences Theory is quite revealing. We traditionally define smartness in terms of language and mathematical skills, but Gardner's theory considers children that are musically gifted as being smart in a different way. Children who exhibit exceptional musical intelligence may show great ability at logical and mathematical tasks dealing with patterns, expressed as a musical talent. When we limit our conception of intelligence to reading and math ("book smart" and "number smart"), many children are left behind, labeled "below average," or worse. If we understand **how** the child is smart, we can use that knowledge to inform how we teach them mathematics, even if it is not the intelligence in which they excel. Mathematics can be incorporated into art, music, reading, physical activities, and even into what Gardner called interpersonal, intrapersonal, and environmental topics. For example, music contains a number of mathematical elements such as fractions (whole, half, quarter, eighth notes) and patterns in the rhythm and beat. Books such as *Math Curse* and *One Hundred Hungry Ants* include grouping, patterns, and addition in the prose. Children may set up a pretend store in the classroom or on the playground. If they have access to pretend coins and paper money they could become adept at making change for the pretend purchases, encouraging interpersonal intelligence.

Just like reading, math is everywhere and in everything. First, we need to look and find it (or help the child find it). Family members can help inform you about their children's interests and strengths. Discuss their interests in conferences or through other forms of communication, such as a parent questionnaire at the beginning of school. Careful observation on your part can also help to inform you about the intelligences that each child in your class demonstrates.

Gardner's Multiple Intelligence Theory supplies us with another perspective on our young mathematicians, before we allow their initial frustrations with the content to develop into full-blown math anxiety. Another way to look at the individuality of students is by looking at how they learn. While M.I. Theory focuses on which intelligence is predominant in each child, learning styles focus on how each child learns and takes in information.

Learning Styles

Studies show that children have different learning styles that influence how they might learn best (see Table 2.1). The most common of these are Visual, Aural, Read/Write, and Kinesthetic (Fleming, 2005). Do you know what your learning style is? How do you take notes in class? Do you find that you learn best by attending lectures, reading outside of class, or engaging in an activity or project? While we all might answer these questions differently from time to time, these learning styles can help guide teachers in preparing lessons that engage all their students effectively.

Table 2.1 Learning Styles, Characteristics, and Appropriate Materials

Learning Style	Characteristics	Examples of Appropriate Classroom Materials
Visual learner	• Often swayed by the appearance of an object • Interested in color, layout, and design • Aware of their place in the environment • Likely to draw something to aid their comprehension	• Colorful pictures and aids • Markers and crayons
Auditory Learner	• Like to have things explained verbally • Words heard are more valuable than those read for learning • Like to be told	• Lecture audio books • Class discussion
Read/Write Learner	• Learn by reading a book • Like lists and words to learn by • Meaning is in words	• Books • Texts • Worksheets • Pencil and paper
Kinesthetic Learner	• Experience learning to understand it • Ideas only valuable if they are sound and practical • Learning needs to be real and relevant	• Blocks • Manipulatives • Math games

SUMMARY

Treating children as young mathematicians means encouraging their natural ability to think, problem solve, and make sense of their world. This is best accomplished when teachers continually engage in reflective practice and become decision makers in their classrooms. Throughout this book, we will be examining methods and ideas that will ensure our students never experience "math anxiety" as they instead explore mathematics with natural zeal, curiosity, and a sense of accomplishment.

Behaviorism, however, remains the most prominent theory used in traditional classrooms today. The emphasis on direct instruction and rote memorization to instill a behavior harkens back to Pavlov, Watson, and Skinner's original work with dogs and pigeons. This mechanistic approach to teaching breaks down the task of learning into its smallest components and reinforces learning with rewards for correct answers. This is not conducive to creating a child-centered classroom or a problem-based approach to teaching mathematics.

Maria Montessori developed many very high-quality and useful manipulatives for her child-centered school in Italy. Her materials were very sensory-oriented, but modern Montessori teachers also include many of the cognitive aspects that are the hallmark of a good use of manipulatives.

Piaget and Vygotsky, the constructivists, focused on the active nature of the child. They felt that the child's mind was not a passive vessel, but an active constructor of knowledge. While differing in some aspects, their theories include many of the best aspects of the others, in developing a constructivist-based eclectic approach to teaching mathematics. These theorists assume that mathematics is constructed by the child through interaction with people and objects. Children are viewed as active thinkers rather than just as passive collectors of facts.

An "eclectic" approach to mathematics instruction acknowledges that different classroom philosophies and theoretical traditions all play an instrumental role in treating children as young mathematicians. A teacher's knowledge base is the foundation for her decision making. Her experience, knowledge of developmental theory, and understanding of important instructional methods allows her to easily adapt to different situations and different students.

Individual differences also affect how children learn mathematics. Gardner and Learning Styles Theories show that children have different learning styles that can be used to develop individualized mathematics programs them. The assumption is that, since all children are different, teaching them with one standardized method is not efficient or effective. By presenting math activities with the understanding that different children learn differently, we are better able to support the individual differences in the children we teach.

WEB SITES

PBS Parents - Child Development
http://www.pbs.org/parents/childdevelopment/

Information on the development of children from birth through 6. A specific section is included on mathematics.

Project Construct National Center
http://www.projectconstruct.org/

The Project Construct National Center supports educators' implementation of Project Construct through a comprehensive, ongoing, and participant-centered professional-development program.

NCTM Illuminations
http://illuminations.nctm.org/

Information for parents on the mathematical development of their infant child.

US National Science Foundation - Mathematics Research Overview
http://www.nsf.gov/news/overviews/mathematics/index.jsp

Information for parents on the mathematical development of their preschool-age child.

Eisenhower National Clearinghouse
http://www.goenc.com/
K–12 math and science teacher resources for teaching and professional development.

DISCUSS AND APPLY WHAT YOU HAVE LEARNED

Observe

1. Observe a teacher and try to identify what theories inform the math activities the teacher does with the class. How many are behaviorist? Cognitive? Social-constructivist?
2. Is there any individualization of instruction in classrooms that you have observed? How do teachers you have observed deal with different learning styles? Different intelligences?

Apply

1. Design a mathematical activity for a prekindergarten 5-year-old and for a 7-year-old second grader based on behaviorist theory. Adapt it so that it is based on constructivist theory, and then social-constructivist theory (Hint: encourage student interaction). Finally, adapt it to address one of Gardner's multiple intelligences. What differences do you notice? Was there any overlap?

Reflect

1. Think about how you learned mathematics in your early school years. Which theories do you feel influenced the methods used to teach you mathematics?
2. Why is it important to know about developmental theory when teaching mathematics to young children? What beliefs do you have about how children learn mathematics?

REFERENCES

Altermatt, E. R., & Kim, M. E. (2004). Getting girls de-stereotyped for SAT exams. *Education Digest, 70*(1), 43.

Ambrose, R. C. (2002). Are we overemphasizing manipulatives in the primary grades to the detriment of girls? *Teaching Children Mathematics, 9*(1), 16.

American Montessori Society, & Educational Video Publishing. (2000). An introduction to Montessori philosophy and materials [videorecording]. Yellow Springs, OH: Educational Video Pub.

Bandura, A. (2002). Social cognitive theory in cultural context. *Applied psychology: An International Review, 51*(2), 269.

Baratta-Lorton, M. (1994). *Mathematics their way: Complete revised anniversary edition.* Boston: Center for Innovation in Education.

Burns, M. (1998). *Math facing an American phobia.* Sausalito, CA: Math Solutions Publications.

Dewey, J. (1915). *The school and society* (Rev. ed.). Chicago, IL: The University of Chicago Press.

Dewey, J. (1933). *How we think, a restatement of the relation of reflective thinking to the educative process.* Boston, New York: D.C. Heath and Company.

Dewey, J. (1938). *Experience and education.* New York: The Macmillan Company.

Educational Video Publishing. (2003). Montessori math curriculum demonstrations [videorecording]. Yellow Springs, OH: Educational Video Pub.

Elkind, D., & Piaget, J. (1979). *Child development and education: A Piagetian perspective.* New York: Oxford University Press.

Fleming, N. D. (2005). *Teaching and learning styles: VARK strategies* (Rev. ed.). Christchurch, N.Z.: Neil Fleming.

Fosnot, C. T. (1989). *Enquiring teachers, enquiring learners: A constructivist approach for teaching.* New York: Teachers College Press.

Gardner, H. (1999). *Intelligence reframed: Multiple intelligences for the 21st century.* New York: Basic Books.

Gardner, H. (2006). *The development and education of the mind: The selected works of Howard Gardner.* London, New York: Routledge.

Gardner, H., Gardner, H., Dinozzi, R., Harvard Project Zero, & Into the Classroom Media (Firm). (1996). MI answers [videorecording]. Los Angeles, CA: Into the Classroom Media.

Hatton, N., & Smith, D. (1995). Reflection in teacher education: Towards definition and implementation. Retrieved May 12, 2007, from *http://alex.edfac.usyd.edu.au/LocalResource/originals/hattonart.rtf*

Inhelder, B., & Piaget, J. (1958). *The growth of logical thinking from childhood to adolescence: An essay on the construction of formal operational structures.* London: Routledge & Kegan Paul.

Inhelder, B., & Piaget, J. (1964). *The early growth of logic in the child classification and seriation.* London: Routledge and Kegan Paul.

Inhelder, B., & Piaget, J. (1999). *The growth of logical thinking from childhood to adolescence: An essay on the construction of formal operational structures.* London: Routledge.

Kamii, C. (1990). *Achievement testing in the early grades: The games grown-ups play.* Washington, DC: National Association for the Education of Young Children.

Kamii, C., & DeClark, G. (1985). *Young children reinvent arithmetic: Implications of Piaget's theory.* New York: Teachers College Press.

Kamii, C., Joseph, L. L., & Livingston, S. J. (2003). *Young children continue to reinvent arithmetic—2nd grade: Implications of Piaget's theory.* New York: Teachers College Press.

Kamii, C., & National Association for the Education of Young Children. (1982). *Number in preschool and kindergarten: Educational implications of Piaget's theory.* Washington, DC: National Association for the Education of Young Children.

Kamii, C., O'Brien, T. C., Teacher Center, Southern Illinois University at Edwardsville (1980). *What do children learn when they manipulate objects?* Edwardsville, IL: The Teachers' Center Project, Southern Illinois University at Edwardsville.

Kitchens, A. N. (1995). *Defeating math anxiety.* Chicago: Irwin Career Education Division.

Levine, G. (1995). Closing the gender gap: Focus on mathematics anxiety. *Contemporary Education, 67,* 42.

Miller, P. H. (2002). *Theories of developmental psychology* (4th ed.). New York: Worth Publishers.

Piaget, J. (1952). *The child's conception of number*. London: Routledge & Paul.

Piaget, J. (1970). *Science of education and the psychology of the child*. New York: Orion Press.

Piaget, J., Yale, U., & Media, D. S. (1977). *Piaget on Piaget*. New Haven: The Studio.

Sinclair, H. & Kamii, C. (1994). *Piaget and Vygotsky on collaboration, argumentation, and coherent reasoning*.

Stuart, V. B. (2000). Math curse or math anxiety? *Teaching Children Mathematics, 6*(5), 330.

CHAPTER 3

Diversity, Equity, and Individualized Instruction

CHAPTER OBJECTIVES

After you have read this chapter, you should be able to:

- Explain how effective mathematics experiences can contribute to student achievement
- Identify, analyze, and compare the needs of diverse populations of mathematics learners
- Identify ways to individualize mathematics instruction to overcome disparities in student achievement
- Identify and explain the effect of teacher expectations
- Explain how cultural and environmental factors (such as socioeconomic status and family background) can affect mathematics achievement
- Demonstrate an understanding of working with children with special needs when teaching mathematics
- Explain how language barriers can be overcome in teaching mathematics
- Demonstrate an understanding of gender differences in mathematics achievement

Are you who you are because of your genes or because of your environment? This is the old "nature vs. nurture" debate that has been raging ever since science began to study human nature. Philosophers as far back as Socrates, Plato, and Aristotle have debated this issue. John Locke's concept of "Tabula Rasa"—Latin for "blank slate"—held that children are neither good nor bad by nature but rather products of the environment they were raised in. The child's environment ultimately determines his emotional and moral development. On the other side of this argument were philosophers who believed that certain type of knowledge, traits, and abilities are innate.

New research on the brain has raised new questions in this debate—especially concerning mathematics learning. For example, how can biology and the environment interact to enhance students' ability to learn mathematics? (Butterworth, 1999; D'Arcangelo, 2001; Gurian, Henley, & Trueman, 2002; National Association for Women in Education, 1993; Shaw & Peterson, 2000). Recent research has shown that there are some genetic and biological structures in the brain that aid in the learning of mathematics and help explain differences in inherited intelligence (D'Arcangelo, 2001; Gurian et al., 2002). These structures and differences, however, are affected by a number of variables in the environment, such as the quality of teacher-student interactions, the student's expectations, the student's socioeconomic status, and the educational methods used. Some research on the human brain suggests that we are prewired for mathematics, yet other data seems to show that environment has a large influence on mathematics achievement (Butterworth, 1999; D'Arcangelo, 2001). While you cannot change the genetic "nature" of a child, as a teacher, you *can* affect how a child is "nurtured" mathematically.

Other important questions that need to be considered are how factors such as socioeconomic status, ethnicity and culture, special needs of the child, giftedness, English language learning, and gender affect the child's learning of mathematics. Horace Mann said, "Education, then, beyond all other devices of human origin, is the great equalizer of the conditions of man, the balance-wheel of the social machinery." Education can be the tool to overcome poverty and other social issues, and as a teacher you are one of the tools in the toolbox. Can one teacher make a difference when the problems seem so vast?

When looking at mathematics achievement, certain trends emerge around these issues that lead back to the debate over whether environment or biology makes the most difference in a student's educational achievement. As you continue to grow in your understanding of mathematics learning, try to imagine how nature and nurture might work together to facilitate learning.

NATURE AND NURTURE IN THE MATHEMATICS CLASSROOM

Consider how mathematics is taught in classrooms today, or reflect back to your first years in school. Can you identify elements or assumptions of the nature vs. nurture debate in the educational practices used in modern classrooms?

The National Assessment of Educational Progress (NAEP) reveals some interesting and disturbing trends in mathematics achievement. The data from these tests show that there are disparities between different groups of children. Our schools contain children from many diverse backgrounds and the data suggests that they are not all achieving at the same levels mathematically. One of the overriding aims of teaching mathematics from birth through third grade should be to ensure that all children achieve to the highest level of their ability. This means addressing many of the environmental issues that help us to "nurture" the learning of mathematics. The first step is to make sure that each child is seen as an individual learner with individual needs.

INDIVIDUALIZED INSTRUCTION

Each year on your first day of teaching, you will look out at a class full of unique individuals, all of whom have differing developmental levels, needs, and issues. Your task is to identify these issues and devise innovative ways to address the needs of each individual student. One standardized curriculum will not and cannot meet the needs of all of your students. To begin the process of individualizing the curriculum, you need to understand some of the unique issues of the diverse populations with which you will be working. Understanding these differences will help you support each student to achieve to the best of his/her ability.

Individualized instruction refers to not just a method of teaching, but a general attitude toward how children learn. The first assumption about individualized instruction is that a teacher recognizes that all children in the classroom are at differing levels. Most teachers recognize that all children have different strengths and weaknesses when it comes to learning mathematics. The second assumption is that a teacher must make sure that children receive instruction and assessment based on their level of understanding and learning style. The third assumption is that assessment includes measurement of each child's progress, as well as in relation to standards and other students. The second and third assumptions are what sets teachers, using individualized instruction, apart. Consider the following example.

> Mrs. Garcia is a new teacher and has a first-grade classroom of 16 boys and 12 girls. They all vary in mathematical ability. The other first-grade teacher in the school teaches mathematics through the use of worksheets and chapter and unit tests. This teacher knows the "slow" students and the "smart" students in her class by the grades they get on these worksheets and tests. Mrs. Garcia thought this was an efficient way of teaching mathematics, and considered adopting the method. When she asked the other teacher about individual children, however, the teacher knew little about them except their grades.
>
> Mrs. Garcia chose to use an individualized instruction approach to teaching mathematics. Her first goal was to assess the level of the students' mathematical thinking. She gave open-ended problems and observed how her students went about solving them.

Classroom discussions allow children to explain their solutions and individualize their learning.

Lori Whitley/Merrill

One problem was, "Juan has 45 cents and he wants to buy some candy. The candy he wants costs 5 cents. How many pieces of candy can he buy?" She observed that some children solved the problem using tally marks, while others counted by fives. She also noted that some children used more advanced ways of thinking about the problem that involved more standard multiplication techniques. She observed and documented each child's methods in a notebook.

Mrs. Garcia's next goal was to develop a mathematics program based on each child's unique abilities and understanding. She used her state's standards and developed lesson plans featuring problems and activities that could be solved in many different ways, depending on the level of mathematical understanding and learning style of the child. She incorporated games, brainteasers, and discussion time into her lessons to achieve this goal. By observing the learning styles of her students, she determined what help each child needed in different circumstances. She documented when the child made a step forward in his understanding of mathematics concepts or skills, and developed individual goals based on her assessment and documentation. Mrs. Garcia ensured that all children could succeed in solving the problems she selected. Instead of focusing on the number of incorrect answers on a worksheet or a test, she focused on the child's method of solving problems as her basis of assessment.

Mrs. Garcia noticed that in parent-teacher conferences she had much more to say about each child's mathematical ability. Instead of just scores and grades, she had detailed documentation of the child's mathematical development over a period of weeks. Parents were excited to learn how their child had grown mathematically.

Classrooms not based on individualized instruction often make assumptions similar to those made by the teacher across the hall from Mrs. Garcia's classroom. Some of these assumptions are: 1) that all children learn the same way and teachers should use one method to teach all students in the classroom, 2) assessment should differentiate children by sorting out which ones receive As and which receive lower grades, 3) children who are "slow" or "behind" need to work harder to catch up to the curriculum, and 4) assessment is performed with paper-and-pencil tests.

Problems arise when we teach only one way to only one level. Children with different learning styles are left out. Children who are behind or struggling in their development of mathematical concepts receive the message that they are "slow" or "not good at math," when, in reality, they may just need a bit more time to understand. Not everyone "gets it" at the same time. Development, including the development of mathematics concepts, is not the same for all children. Individualized instruction addresses the needs of all the children in the class.

Schools should be ready for children, not the other way around. In reality, however, students that cannot adjust to the curriculum are at a disadvantage. Meeting diverse needs demands a teacher's reflection and adaptability. We need to ask "why" a student succeeds or fails, and what can be done to ensure the child's success.

Howard Gardner stated that we should ask, not "how smart are kids," but instead, "how are kids smart." Instead of classifying children as "smart" or "slow" based on tests, we should be looking deeper at the strengths and weaknesses of each individual child. All we know about a child that does well on a test is that they are good at taking tests. If we use this as our only assessment of a child's competence, we run the risk of not meeting the needs of all students.

Individualized instruction leads the teacher to assess the needs of each and every student in the classroom and develop a mathematics program that addresses all their needs. Initially, it may seem a monumental task—and it does mean a shift in the way that instruction is normally done—but it is an achievable goal and one that has great benefits for all involved. It can be especially beneficial when working with a diverse student body in the classroom. Instead of developing a mathematics program that expects uniform ability and demands that your students adapt to your curriculum, you will develop teaching strategies that adapt to their various needs and backgrounds. Figure 3.1 provides guidelines for individualized instruction in mathematics.

Mathematics programs require a great deal of individualized instruction because all classrooms have students with varying special needs. Using individualized instruction practices, children with identified special needs, such as learning disabilities and developmental delays, as well as children with advanced abilities, can be better addressed in the everyday classroom. Understanding a student's differences helps teachers to have realistic high standards for all children.

Holding High Expectations for All Students

Expectations teachers have of their students, whether male, female, white, children of color, children of poverty, or children with disabilities, make a big difference in the long-term results that students achieve. Research has shown that, when a teacher expects a child to succeed or fail, the student tends to live up to that expectation. This is called the **Self-Fulfilling Prophecy** or **Pygmalion Effect** (Rosenthal & Jacobson, 1968, 1992; Tauber, 1998).

- *Use authentic assessment* such as observation, work samples, and portfolios to assess students, rather than just paper-and-pencil tests. The rich data that is collected will help you in the planning process and when talking to parents about their child.
- *Develop a math program that is focused on process rather than product.* Ask children "how" they got their answers and watch their problem-solving methods rather than just noting whether the answer is right or wrong. Many times the child's process may be advanced, but includes a slight error that produces a wrong answer. Examining the process involved in how he arrives at an answer provides great insight into the child's thinking.
- *Use open-ended problems in lessons*, and encourage students to use any method they want to reach the solution. Problems with many different correct answers better demonstrate the problem-solving ability of students. For example, "How many ways can we make 50 cents?" More traditional mathematics problems such as 12 + 14 can also be made open-ended by letting the children go about solving the problem in ways that make sense to them.
- *Incorporate mathematics into other content areas* such as science, reading, social studies, music and art. Some children excel at reading and writing, others at mathematics, while others may have strengths in social skills or interpersonal skills or musical performance. Allow children to experience mathematics in the area of their strength.
- *Present mathematics in multiple ways to take advantage of different learning styles.* Have activities that require children to solve problems through bodily movement, or through discussion, sharing, and listening. Other activities can address the visual learner, such as Venn diagrams, charting, and graphing. Traditional paper-and-pencil mathematics helps the read/write learner understand mathematics using their area of strength.
- *Listen to your students and understand what they know.* Their interests can help develop your mathematics program. By incorporating projects into your early childhood mathematics program, you link mathematics with the real world. Children will then not only use mathematics in context, but in a way that they understand and that is linked to their individual experience.

Figure 3.1   Guidelines for Individualized Instruction.

The basis of the self-fulfilling prophecy is that, once a student has been labeled by the teacher as a "troublemaker," "C-student," or as having a low IQ, the teacher's treatment of that student may very well contribute to those negative expectations becoming a reality. Positive effects are also possible. Teachers don't consciously make these decisions and are often not aware that they are treating children differently.

Think back to a teacher you've had that you felt really believed in you. How did this teacher's belief affect your work and performance in the classroom?

Teachers' expectations can influence their interactions with children.

Scott Cunningham/Merrill

All teachers strive to provide opportunities for success in all their students. The NAEYC has acknowledged this in their Code of Ethical Conduct. It states:

> P-1.2—We shall not participate in practices that discriminate against children by denying benefits, giving special advantages, or excluding them from programs or activities on the basis of their race, ethnicity, religion, sex, national origin, language, ability, or the status, behavior, or beliefs of their parents. (This principle does not apply to programs that have a lawful mandate to provide services to a particular population of children.)

However, in practice, self-fulfilling prophecies are subtler than outright discrimination. Even excellent teachers can let their assumptions of a student's ability or intelligence color their interactions with the student. Decisions about what certain children can and cannot do, based on assumptions made about the child's ability, are often based on what is known about the child. If a teacher knows that a child has an IQ of 90 and comes from a low socioeconomic level single-parent household, they might not expect him to achieve as much a child who has an IQ of 125 and comes from an affluent, two-parent family. Is this a valid assumption to make? Just because a child has a higher IQ does not guarantee that the child will achieve at a higher level. Poverty and marital status can have detrimental effects on a child's achievement, but that too is not always true (Borman & Overman, 2004; Myers & Educational Resources Information Center, 1986).

For example, a child may have a very high IQ but lack motivation to do mathematics. He consistently fails to turn in homework assignments and is off task during mathematics lessons. Another child may have an average IQ but be fascinated with mathematics and ask questions constantly. This child needs more time to do the math problems and is not as advanced as some of the others but he loves math and works hard at understanding the concepts. If a teacher takes the time to individualize an approach to each of these children and holds both to the same high standard, both children will succeed at higher levels.

All students, regardless of ethnicity, family background, gender, or ability, should have every opportunity to achieve to the highest level possible. This has been the goal of American education for many years. Governmental initiatives, such as Goals 2000 and No Child Left Behind, have attempted to make this goal a national mandate. To make this ideal a reality, teachers must understand the special needs and characteristics of a diverse group of learners.

There is little that good teachers cannot overcome if they believe that the child can achieve at high levels and offer opportunity and support for the child to advance. Teachers should not lower standards for certain students, but offer extra help and attention. If teachers are attuned to all a student's needs, and individualizes the curriculum appropriately for each student, the students will achieve at a higher level. Even the best teachers make assumptions about students based on many different factors. We must be careful that these assumptions do not affect how we teach each and every child.

SOCIOECONOMIC FACTORS

There are other factors that affect student achievement besides what happens in the classroom. Poverty, parental education level, single-parent households, and school funding also have a very significant effect on outcomes for students in mathematics and other subjects (Borman & Overman, 2004; Byrnes, 2003; Feiler & Webster, 1997; Kamii, 1965; Lubienski, 2003). Socioeconomic status, or SES, is a way of grouping people by their educational, occupational, and economic characteristics. Socioeconomic status implies certain inequities between groups based upon 1) the prestige of their occupations, 2) differing levels of educational attainment, 3) different educational resources, and 4) differing levels of access to the power to influence a community's institutions (such as schools). These inequities produce unequal opportunities for children in life, education, and mathematics (Lubienski, 2003).

While ethnicity has been linked to some differences in home environment, there is more evidence that the cycle of poverty explains certain deficits in mathematics achievement (Bradley, Corwyn, McAdoo, & Garcia Coll, 2001; Payne & Biddle, 1999). The cycle of poverty refers to the fact that it is very difficult to overcome the detrimental effects of poverty. A child living in poverty may have parents who did not receive good educations or even graduate from high school. Subsequently, educational support is lacking in the home (Lewis, 2001; Lubienski, 2003; Waxman & Educational Resources Information Center, 1996). This student may also live in an impoverished area where access to a high-quality education is not available. Add to this the lowered expectations that lead to a self-fulfilling prophecy, and you have a child that is at-risk for failure in school who will experience many challenges in trying to rise out of poverty. As parents, these children then pass on many of the risk factors to their children. The data on poverty and minority achievement overlaps because the poverty rate tends to be much higher in minority populations. In 2005, the poverty rate for non-Hispanic whites under the age of 18 was about 10 percent compared to about 34 percent for African Americans, and about 28 percent for Hispanics (U.S. Census Bureau, 2007).

The impact of poverty is staggering. In fourth grade, the *average* score on the NAEP mathematics assessment for students in the upper 25 percent of family income level was 269, the average for the middle 50 percent was 234, and the average for the lowest 25 percent was 191 (Clements & Bright, 2003; Lindquist, 2001; Thompson & Preston, 2004). This is one of the largest gaps related to any predictor of mathematical achievement. The wealthier the family, the better the student does in mathematics, period—regardless of race, gender, or any other factor (National Center for Educational Statistics, 2007).

Parent's educational attainment is related to and has a major effect on student achievement. While not as dramatic as the poverty statistic, it is nonetheless a potent predictor of success in mathematics. Figure 3.2 shows the scores of fourth graders from 1978 to 1999 grouped by their parents' highest level of educational attainment. As you can see, the better educated the parents the better their children do in mathematics. These effects begin as early as age three. Children see what is important through the social interactions in the home, so many of the child's first experiences will help determine his attitude toward math (New, 1998).

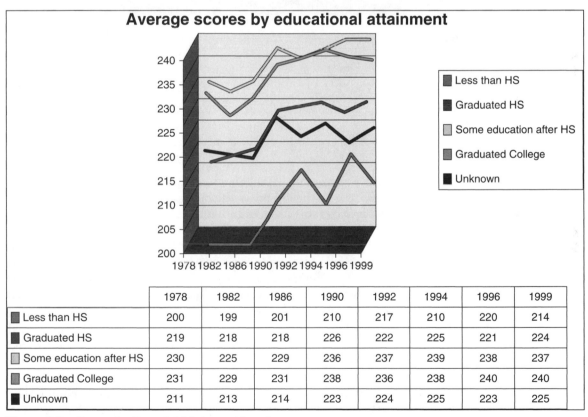

	1978	1982	1986	1990	1992	1994	1996	1999
Less than HS	200	199	201	210	217	210	220	214
Graduated HS	219	218	218	226	222	225	221	224
Some education after HS	230	225	229	236	237	239	238	237
Graduated College	231	229	231	238	236	238	240	240
Unknown	211	213	214	223	224	225	223	225

Figure 3.2   Scores by Parental Attainment Level.

Source: National Center for Educational Statistics, 2007.

(*Note:* X-axis are dates of scores, Y-axis represent average test scores of 12th graders)

Mathematics-rich early experiences can help children from falling behind in mathematics and other subjects.

Scott Cunningham/Merrill

Wanda's daughter, Whitney, comes home from school with math homework. Wanda wants her daughter to succeed, but math scares her and she was never good at it in school. She does not want to let her daughter know that she doesn't understand fractions, but she tries to help. After 10 minutes, both Wanda and her daughter are tired of doing math and take a break to make dinner. By the time they get back to the math homework, it is past Whitney's bedtime. The homework is left undone.

Wanda's situation is not unique. Many times parents want to help, but just don't have the time or skills to help their child as much as the teachers expect. Lower educational attainment and comfort level with mathematics means that these parents may avoid helping their children with mathematics.

One of the most successful programs that helps to deal with this issue is Head Start. Head Start is a national program that promotes school readiness by enhancing the social and cognitive development of children, offering educational, health, nutritional, social, and other services to enrolled children and families. Children are eligible to participate in Head Start if they are from low-income families or if their families are eligible for public assistance. The Head Start Act established income eligibility for participation in Head Start programs based on the poverty guidelines which are updated annually.

Head Start serves preschool-age children and their families by offering a stimulating preschool program designed to help children that are at risk for falling behind when they enter kindergarten and the primary grades (Klein & Chen, 2001). Head Start programs can give children from low-SES a stimulating mathematical environment also (Arnold, Doctoroff, & Fisher, 2002). The program recognizes the importance of addressing other risk factors related to low-SES. It includes home visits by the teachers to

1) *Lack of access to high-quality educational experiences.* Underfunded and over-crowded schools may have classrooms and facilities that are 30 to 50 years out of date, and only one in four students may have textbooks (Kozol, 1991).

2) *Parental adaptive and responsive functioning (Santrock, 2006).* Parents living in poverty often do not have the skills or resources to provide an intellectually stimulating environment for their children in the very early years. As the child grows, they might also lack the ability to adapt and to respond to the child's needs.

3) *Parents' educational level.* Parents that did poorly in school may pass on negative attitudes that can affect their child's orientation toward learning. Parents who cannot read or understand their child's math homework will likely not become involved in mathematics programs, placing their children at a disadvantage.

4) *The self-fulfilling prophecy.* Children in poverty are often not expected to achieve at high levels by parents, teachers, and even schools. Such messages can have devastating effects on their achievement.

5) *Lack of adequate materials.* Textbooks, manipulatives, computers, Internet access, workbooks, and even essentials like paper, pencils, and chalk are often in very short supply in underfunded and overcrowded schools.

Figure 3.3   The Five Characteristics of Children, Families, and Schools Experiencing Poverty.

make sure that activities begun in the classroom spill over into the home. Nutritional support is also addressed to ensure that children are receiving adequate nutrition.

Head Start attempts to address problems related to the two most telling NAEP statistical categories—poverty and parental education attainment—while children are still young. To further develop ways to overcome these detrimental effects, we must understand the characteristics of children who live in poverty. Figure 3.3 revisits five important characteristics these students may share. They have special needs and concerns that need to be addressed on a daily basis to allow mathematics to be successfully taught.

Overcoming SES Obstacles

Parent education is the first step we must take. Head Start, Even Start, and other parental education programs have long-term positive effects in overcoming the cycle of poverty (Lewis, 2001; B. F. Waxman & Educational Resources Information Center, 1996). Actively working with parents to teach them how to interact in a positive way with their child can improve cognitive functioning. The more comfortable parents feel with mathematics the better able they will be to help their child. The earlier this intervention takes place, the better for the child.

Reach out to parents to help them learn how they can interact mathematically with their child. Ensure them that it does not take a college degree in mathematics to help their young child learn how to count or compare objects. Math games and carefully selected brainteasers that the family can do together are good suggestions. In addition, let them know that list making, totaling purchases while

Lack of funding means some schools defer maintenance of their facilities.

Laima Druskis/PH College

grocery shopping, measuring and following directions while cooking, and measuring while doing woodworking or other household projects are also valuable. Direct contact with the parent or primary caregiver and discussions about positive interactions with their child are essential.

For example, send things home that are fun for the whole family. Games that use dice or other mathematics tools to move around a game board are usually not as threatening as a worksheet. Songs, games, and puzzles are also less anxiety-producing for parents.

Whitney brought home a "math suitcase" from school. Inside was a game and a set of instructions. Whitney was excited and wanted to play it right away. Whitney's mother, Wanda, read the instructions for a game called "Fraction War." At first she was scared by the fractions, but felt better when she looked at the cards and instructions. Each card had a pie cut into different numbers of slices (2–8). Each pie also had a different number of missing or "eaten" pieces. The fraction, for example ⅛, was indicated below the pie. Each player turned over one card and the player who had more of their pie uneaten won the round. Wanda thought to herself, "This is easy!"

Since poverty and parents' educational level have such a huge impact on students' ability to achieve, it is vital that there be a teacher–parent relationship. Just as teachers make assumptions about children, we also make assumptions about parents that many times are not positive. Teachers need to understand that what is going on in the child's home is as important as what happens in the classroom. Forging relationships with parents is often not easy. Many parents, especially those who live in poverty or who have little education themselves, find schools to be oppressive and

Math Suitcase with items for Double War.

Barbara Schwartz/Merrill

they often feel intimidated by the surroundings. Their own experiences in school may not have been positive. Find a way to get in touch with parents that may include meeting outside your classroom. Parents want what is best for their children and will appreciate your extra effort.

Making this decision means that you need to make a special effort to make sure your children have access to the materials they need to learn mathematics. Children who come from impoverished backgrounds may not have materials in the home to extend their mathematical learning. Developing materials and activities that can easily be done at home with parents can help overcome some of these problems. Math suitcases that children can check out and take home (just like a library book) are one great way to achieve this goal. A plastic lunchbox works well for this task. Put a mathematics game inside that the child can play with the parents. For example, include easy card games such as War or Double War. Include all the materials needed. This gets even the most resistant parents involved, especially if you can design a game that is fun for both child and adult.

This strategy also involves getting parents involved in the classroom, but in community-building experiences. Ask parents about their child and their activities at home. You can also field suggestions from parents about what is working and what is not working in your classroom. Have high expectations for all students regardless of their ethnicity or socioeconomic background. Expect the school children to exceed the standards for each grade in your state. Find ways to make sure the children, who seem to have a lack of ability or interest in math, succeed. Always ask yourself "why" before coming to any conclusions about a student. For example, "why is that child not playing math games?" or "why is that child not participating in mathematics discussions?" It is doubly important that these children see the usefulness of mathematics in their lives.

Whitney's teacher sent a note home to parents inviting them to attend an "Exhibition of Children's Work" at the school. Wanda always felt uncomfortable going to parent–teacher conferences, thinking the teacher was going to tell her she was doing everything wrong in raising Whitney. Whitney, however, insisted that Wanda come to the exhibition. When Wanda and Whitney arrived, Wanda was greeted warmly and asked to come in and have come cookies and punch. Whitney then acted as a "tour guide" and showed her mom all the great math activities they had done in the 2 months since school started. Wanda and the other parents sat at their children's desks and the children put on a short program about what they had learned. Before leaving, Whitney's teacher spoke with Wanda about Whitney's schoolwork, how well she was doing, and what Wanda could do at home to help. Wanda thought as she was walking out of the school, "That was easy!"

Parental education level can affect the ability of the parent to help and support the child's learning at home. If parents do not feel comfortable with mathematics, they will not want to help their child (Levine, 1995). They may also have negative attitudes toward mathematics and school in general. For many people living in poverty, school was not a positive experience (Bullard & Oborne, 1997; DelCampo & DelCampo, 1995; Ricciuti, 2004). Perhaps education was not seen as important or relevant to their lives. While these parents encourage their children to succeed in school, they may not be capable of providing "critical experiences" that foster early mathematical learning. The negative effects of both poverty and lack of "critical experiences" on achievement have been known for decades (Myers & Educational Resources Information Center, 1986).

In single-parent households, the issue may be as simple as a lack of time. When one parent has to take on the responsibilities of two parents, creating time for helping with schoolwork is often very difficult. Single-parent households often deal with poverty, and many single parents work two or more jobs just to make ends meet.

School funding is also an issue. In the past decade, the courts have decided that the school funding process in some states is unfair to people living in poorer areas. Poverty-stricken areas, both urban and rural, do not have a sufficient tax base to fund quality schools. Schools in affluent neighborhoods with large homes, and, therefore, a large property tax base, have money to maintain very well-supplied schools. While money does not solve all the problems inherent in schools, a school with enough money to buy the best materials and hire the best teachers has a better chance of producing students that succeed.

MINORITY STUDENT ACHIEVEMENT

Many risk factors associated with socioeconomic status are disproportionately found in minority populations (see Figure 3.4 on page 81), and this puts students from minority populations at a disadvantage (Loveless & Coughlan, 2004; Lubienski, 2002). Minorities have less access to higher levels of mathematics and, as a group, experience a less rigorous curriculum (Barlow & Villarejo, 2004; Lubienski, 2002). Sadly, some schools, districts, and teachers might have lower expectations of minority students. Limited resources complicate this lack of support. Some schools in poor districts do not even have the funding to hire teachers qualified to teach the upper levels of mathematics (Holloway, 2004). In addition to placing a huge burden on the student, this is not in keeping with the NAEYC Code of Ethics position stated earlier, as it excludes these students from completing the courses and reaching their full potential.

For decades, the United States Department of Education has been collecting data in the form of the National Assessment of Educational Progress (NAEP). This is often referred to as the "nation's educational report card." The NAEP is a wealth of data that is broken down by gender, ethnic group, and socioeconomic subgroups (Table 3.1). We can compare the performance of many diverse populations of students and come up with some hypotheses as to why there are such differences. By doing this, we can find ways to ensure that every student achieves in mathematics. Factors we've discussed such as poverty, home environment, and study habits (all of which are included in the NAEP data) affect mathemantics outcomes.

In 1978, the NAEP showed a disparity of 31.7 points between white and black students and 21.2 between white and Hispanic students. Twenty-six years later, the disparity had improved but it was still disturbing. In 2004, the difference between white and black was 22.9 and the difference between Hispanic and white was 17.6 (National Center for Education Statistics, 2007). Why, in over 25 years, do we still have such a large gap in achievement?

A report done by the National Center for Education Statistics found that:

> Throughout elementary and secondary school, blacks scored lower, overall, on mathematics and reading tests than whites. Even for children with similar test scores one or two grades earlier, blacks generally scored lower in mathematics and reading than whites.
>
> The black–white mathematics gap differed in size across grades, in a manner consistent with, but not necessarily demonstrating, a narrowing of the gap during elementary school, followed by a widening of the gap during junior high school and little change during senior high school. The black–white reading gap also differed in size across grades, but not in an entirely consistent manner; it grew wider between grades within two elementary school cohorts, but was narrower for cohorts observed in grades 9 and 12 than for a cohort observed in grade 2 (Jacobson, Olsen, Rice, Sweetland, & Ralph, 2001, p. 1).

Studies have also shown that black and Hispanic students begin to fall below grade level as early as second grade, at the same time that white and Asian students begin to advance (Borman & Overman, 2004; Fusarelli & Boyd, 2004; Hoff, 2000; Holloway, 2004). Once these students fall behind, it is not likely that they will be able to catch up. Negative attitudes toward mathematics do not emerge until later.

Table 3.1   Historical Scores of Male, Female, White, Black and Hispanic Students on the NAEP

Gap Between Male and Female

	Male	Female
2004	242.61	239.91
1999	232.88	231.17
1996	232.95	229.04
1994	232.2	230.05
1992	230.84	228.43
1990	229.1	230.16
1986	221.7	221.72
1982	217.11	220.79
1978	217.31	219.87

Gap Between Minority Groups—White/Black

—	White	Black
2004	247.27	224.38
1999	238.77	210.92
1996	236.95	211.65
1994	236.8	212.13
1992	235.11	207.98
1990	235.18	208.37
1986	226.92	201.58
1982	223.95	194.94
1978	224.08	192.37

Gap Between Minority Groups—White/Hispanic

—	White	Hispanic
2004	247.27	229.7
1999	238.77	212.92
1996	236.95	214.66
1994	236.8	209.88
1992	235.11	211.94
1990	235.18	213.75
1986	226.92	205.44
1982	223.95	204
1978	224.08	202.88

Scores from the Math Sections of the National Assessment of Educational Progress

Significant differences in students' enjoyment of mathematics only emerge as students move up in grade level (Hall, Davis, Bolen, & Chia, 1999).

Students who go to schools that lack the necessary resources are sent the message that they are not expected to succeed. Unpainted walls, water-damaged ceilings, or other signs of underfunding and neglect send a message of low

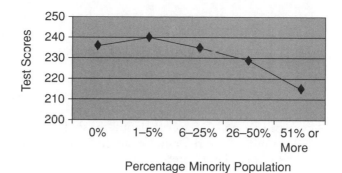

Figure 3.4 Test Scores by Percentage of Minority Enrollment (Y-axis is the mathematics test scores for 12th-grade children and the X-axis is the percentage of minority enrollment).

Source: National Center for Education Statistics, 2007.

Many teachers find dealing with diverse students their biggest challenge and their greatest reward.

expectation and low commitment to these students (Madon, Jussim, & Eccles, 1997; Tauber, 1998; Weinstein, 2002). If higher-level mathematics courses are not taught in more poverty-stricken areas, students may never know that they are capable of achieving at that level.

Above all, these students need to see themselves as successful and competent mathematicians. Their environment may be sending them signals to the contrary, but the teacher must find ways to foster positive feelings about their ability. For example, you can organize an after-school mathematics club where you can offer young mathematicians fun and engaging mathematical activities. You can take field trips to places that use mathematics on a daily basis, such as construction sites or accounting offices.

Many of the active learning methods and mathematical procedures in this book can make a big difference in minority achievement in mathematics. Schoenfeld (2002) and Holloway (2004) cite research that shows that under a traditional curriculum model, fewer than one-third of minority students met or exceeded the skills standard and reference exam in Pennsylvania. With a new reform curriculum in the same schools, 50% of minority students met the standards. Other research also supports the contention that an active reform curriculum benefits minority students immensely.

CHILDREN WITH SPECIAL NEEDS

Years ago, children with special needs were not in the regular classroom with their peers. Many times public schools denied services to these students, and they were instead placed in special education classrooms or other special facilities. Change began when PL 94-142, the Education of All Handicapped Children Act, was passed in 1975. It stated that in order to receive federal funds, states must develop and implement policies that assure a free and appropriate public education (FAPE) to all children with disabilities. Since 1975, the law has gone through many changes and revisions. Today, known as the Individuals with Disabilities Education Act (IDEA), it has expanded its scope and services for preschool children and families of children with disabilities from the time of birth.

When IDEA was originally enacted in 1975, Congress recognized that many children with disabilities were unnecessarily separated from their peers and educated in alternative environments. The goal of IDEA is to allow children with disabilities, to the greatest extent possible, to be educated with their peers in the regular classroom. Under IDEA, states are required to provide a free and appropriate public education to these students in the least restrictive environment (LRE) possible. Children are entitled to special needs evaluation at no cost, and if identified with a special need an individualized education plan (IEP) is developed for that child. While this may seem complicated, IDEA ensures that the expenses associated with special needs education are a public responsibility and that each child is educated in as normal a setting as possible (Rivera, 1998; Schumm, 1999).

There are many ways to meet the general requirements of IDEA. LRE may change from child to child, school to school, and district to district. The **individualized education plan,** or **IEP,** is a document developed by the parent, the child's teachers, and related services personnel that lay out how the child receives a free and appropriate education in the least restrictive environment. In developing the IEP, parents and the local educational agency are empowered to reach appropriate decisions about what constitutes LRE for the individual child, including placements that may be more or

Children with special needs can be integrated easily into classrooms with typically developing children.

Anne Vega/Merrill

less restrictive, in order to maximize the child's benefit from special education and related services (Apling & Jones, 2007). Among other components, the IEP:

- Describes and reports the child's academic achievement and functional levels,
- Describes how the child will be included in the general education curriculum,
- Establishes annual goals for the child and describes how those goals will be measured,
- States what special education and related services are needed by the child,
- Describes how the child will be appropriately assessed including through the use of alternate assessments, and
- Determines what accommodations may be appropriate for the child's instruction and assessments.

For children, birth to age three, there is an Individual Family Service Plan (IFSP). An IFSP is the infant and toddler equivalent of an IEP. Developed through an assessment and evaluation process, the IFSP identifies the child's present levels of development and performance, establishes goals for future development and performance, and outlines how the child will receive early intervention and other services. Unlike an IEP, the IFSP explicitly integrates the needs of the family with those of the child and presents a comprehensive plan that enables the family to meet its goals (Apling & Jones, 2007).

In an early childhood classroom, you may have children with identified special needs and who therefore have an IEP or an IFSP. Special needs that specifically affect mathematical learning and achievement might include:

- Learning disabilities such as Attention Deficit Hyperactive Disorder (ADHD), which affects the child's ability to sit still and attend to mathematical experiences
- Dyslexia, which affects the child's ability to decode text
- Dyscalculia, which affects the child' ability to understand and decode mathematics. Just as some children have trouble reading, some children have mathematical

learning disabilities. These disabilities can range from letter reversals to an in-ability to understand word problems.

More serious disorders include mental retardation, autism, and Asperger's Syn-drome and physical disorders such as Muscular Dystrophy or Cerebral Palsy—in which children often need wheelchairs and special physical attention—and sensory disorders such as hearing or vision deficiencies.

The IEP outlines the services a student with disabilities will receive, where those services will be provided, and educational goals for the student. The members of the IEP team work together to develop the student's IEP. The IEP team is composed of the special education teacher(s), appropriate general education teachers, appropri-ate related services personnel, a local education agency representative, and, if appro-priate, the student.

Performance on standardized tests in mathematics is becoming a reality, for bet-ter or worse. Children with special needs require alternative forms of assessment. The law requires individualization of instruction and assessment for these children. For many students with disabilities, standardized tests fail to measure how they are progressing toward meeting a state's instructional goals and objectives. Instructional

For children birth to age three, special services are provided to the family to help them support their child's initial development. According to IDEA, the IFSP shall be in writing and contain statements of:

- The child's present levels of physical development, cognitive devel-opment, communication development, social or emotional develop-ment, and adaptive development;
- The family's resources, priorities, and concerns related to enhancing the development of the child with a disability;
- The major outcomes to be achieved for the child and the family; the criteria, procedures, and time lines used to determine progress; and whether modifications or revisions of the outcomes or services are necessary;
- Specific early-intervention services necessary to meet the unique needs of the child and the family, including the frequency, intensity, and method of delivery;
- The natural environments in which services will be provided, in-cluding justification of the extent, if any, to which the services will not be provided in a natural environment;
- The projected dates for initiation of services and their anticipated duration;
- The name of the service provider who will be responsible for imple-menting the plan and coordinating with other agencies and persons;
- Steps to support the child's transition to preschool or other appro-priate services. (Bruder, 2000)

planning that combines assessment and instruction can be adapted to link any mathematics education curriculum objectives with the goals and objectives delineated in a student's individual education plan (IEP) (Richards, 2005).

The IEP and IFSP ensure that you are not alone in creating an inclusive and stimulating environment for these children. If you are using the principles of teaching we have been studying, such as individualized instruction, you have already done half the work. See Figure 3.5 for guidelines for working with children with special needs.

- **Think of every child as special and unique.** Each child in your classroom has special characteristics and that should be capitalized upon. Children with identified special needs may need more accommodations than most, but making accommodations should be the rule, not the norm. Avoid "canned" or scripted lectures that assume that all children learn the same way and are on the same level.

- **Be prepared to modify the environment.** Children with special needs also have environmental needs. Some may be in wheelchairs or have trouble seeing; others may need to have distractions such as noise minimized.

- **Focus on strengths, not just the disability.** All children have strengths that can be tapped, even if they have a disability. Make sure that the child is allowed to feel successful in the classroom by giving him the opportunity to shine. Deaf children may be able to help hearing children learn to sign or do math in a nonverbal way. Vision-impaired children may be able to help others talk through problems and solve problems verbally.

- **Create a community of learners.** Children should understand that everyone has different strengths and weaknesses. Talk about differences and encourage children to tutor each other in their strengths. Involve the child with special needs in all aspects of the classroom rather than developing a special isolated curriculum just for that child.

- **Involve the parents and other members of the IEP team in the classroom as much as possible.** Realize that family members or parents have unique insights and can collaborate to help you develop effective methods of teaching math to their child. The other professionals on the team can help you with research on the specific disorder and give you some instructional ideas.

- **Have high expectations.** All children can learn. Even those with a disability are still competent learners. While these children may achieve at a lower level than others in the class, assess them on their individual progress rather than on their achievement compared to others.

- **Use alternative assessment practices.** You would never expect a child with severe visual impairments to take a written test so why expect a child with ADHD to take a 45-minute paper-and-pencil test? Find other ways to assess a student's progress whenever possible.

Figure 3.5 Guidelines for Individualizing the Instruction for Children with Special Needs.

Creating Inclusive Environments

Having children from different backgrounds and at different levels of ability is more beneficial than having children segregated into ability groupings. These "ability groupings" allow teachers to sort and label children quickly and easily, but keeps them from really getting to know "why" a child is doing well or not. As a teacher you must have an affirmative attitude toward diversity of all types. Diversity can mean color, race, personal factors, ability, and parents' sexual preference. Your personal beliefs affect the children in your classroom subtly and often unconsciously. Celebrating diversity is more than just being tolerant or accepting: it is making sure that children and their families feel valued in the classroom.

Get to know the backgrounds and interests of your children and their parents and customize the mathematical experience for them. Children want to see people that look like them and their parents in your books, examples, and problems. This means faces of all different shapes and colors and families that are not "typical." The children may come from a mixed race family, a stepfamily, an extended family, or a family with two mommies or two daddies. This is a reality for many children. No family is inherently more positive or negative than any other. I *once* heard a principal say, "We are accepting of all types of families here at this school, mixed-race parents, single parents, homosexual parents, step families, and families with other problems." These are not "problem families"; they are normal families. Family structures seen less frequently in many communities should be depicted and accepted in the classroom.

Individualized instruction allows a teacher to address diversity in the classroom, whether the student has an identifiable special need or risk factor, or just has a different way of learning or level of understanding. Developing strategies that meet the needs of all children should be your mathematical goal on a daily basis. However, there are a few extra steps to take and more specialized modifications required for these students.

For example, if we use developmentally appropriate instructional practices, we recognize that a young child's ability to pay attention is limited by his developmental level. A 7-year-old can pay attention for about 20–25 minutes before he begins to get restless (Gazzaniga, 2004; Goldstein & Mather, 1998). Educational experiences need to be designed in 15–20 minute chunks with opportunities for children to move around, discuss things with other children, or play math games. A teacher once told me that half of her class must have ADHD. When I observed the mathematics lesson, she had them sit quietly and listen to her lecture for 45 minutes and then do worksheets silently for another 45 minutes, without a break. Any child will have trouble attending in this situation; it could only be that much more difficult for a child diagnosed with ADHD (Birsh, Potts, Potts, & Vineyard Video Productions, 1997; Campbell, Zazkis, & NetLibrary Inc., 2002; Mather & Goldstein, 2001).

As you read the following vignette (see Figure 3.6), identify how the teacher individualizes instruction in an appropriate fashion given each of the student's special needs.

Mr. Baum, a second-grade teacher in an inclusive classroom, is helping his students with a project on construction. Today, they are working on exploring and understanding scale drawings and blueprints. He has several students with identified special needs. Lina, a shy 7-year-old, is nearly deaf and communicates primarily through sign language. Sheena, who has been identified as gifted, seems to love art class and produces very advanced paintings. Tommy is an outgoing child, but has some problems with socialization. A psychologist has diagnosed him with moderate ADHD that is primarily expressed as inattention, however, some impulsivity is also observed. Michaela has muscular dystrophy and gets around the classroom in her wheelchair. She is very friendly and well liked in the classroom.

Mr. Baum walks over to a table where Lina is working with two other students to convert inches to feet on a blueprint. Mr. Baum knows Lina's strength in addition and multiplication, and playing to that strength he asks her, using the little sign language he has learned, how long the front of the building is in the blueprint. Lina grins and signs, "75 feet."

Across the room, Tommy seems to be having trouble staying on task and his group members are getting frustrated with him. Mr. Baum has identified several ways to focus Tommy's attention. He asks a more open-ended question, rather than the specific one he asked Lina.

"Tommy, can you tell me about this blueprint?"

"It's a school."

"What do you like about this school?"

"It has big rooms and a science lab."

"Are the rooms bigger than this room?"

"Yes, much bigger."

"How do you know that?"

Tommy shrugs and his attention begins to drift. Mr. Baum refocuses him by giving him a kinesthetic task.

"Could you and your group measure this room and then compare it to the one in the blueprint?"

"Yes! And I can use the tape measure!" Tommy goes off to measure the room. Mr. Baum has learned that putting Tommy in charge of a task tends to keep him focused.

Sheena is helping Michaela draw a blueprint of the school. Mr. Baum recognizes Sheena's artistic strengths as well as Michaela's ability to work well with others.

"Michaela, how is the blueprint coming along?"

"We drew the outside walls to scale. Now we're trying to figure out the walls inside." Mr. Baum is impressed by the detail of Sheena and Michaela's blueprint. Each classroom is extensively labeled.

"Have you made some measurements?

"We measured our room. All the other classrooms were exactly the same as ours," says Sheena.

"Well, at least on the first floor," says Michaela. "We haven't checked the second floor yet."

"It is all the same! I know it!" says Sheena.

"The office is on the first floor, and that's different from the second floor," replies Michaela.

Mr. Baum interjects, "It sounds like you don't agree about this. How could you solve your disagreement?" Mr. Baum knows that Sheena and Michaela have teamed up to solve similar disagreements in the past.

"We could go to the second floor and measure some classrooms, I guess," says Sheena. "It would only take a few minutes for me to sketch the layout."

"Let's go. You take the stairs and I'll take the elevator and we'll see who gets there first!" says Michaela.

Figure 3.6 The Inclusive Classroom.

- **Create assessments that allow for differences in understanding, creativity, and accomplishment.** Give students a chance to show what they have learned. Ask them to explain their reasoning both orally and in writing.

- **Choose textbooks that provide more enriched opportunities.** Because most early childhood math textbooks repeat topics from year to year and are written for the general population, they are not always appropriate for the gifted. Several series that hold promise for gifted learners have been developed recently under grants from the National Science Foundation; they emphasize constructivist learning and include concepts beyond the basics.

- **Use multiple resources.** No single text will adequately meet the needs of these learners. Integrate technological resources and multimedia such as colorful photos to encourage mathematical connections to the student's experience of the world around them.

- **Be flexible in your expectations about pacing for each student.** While some may be mastering basic skills, others may work on more advanced problems.

- **Use inquiry-based, discovery learning approaches that emphasize open-ended problems** with multiple paths to solutions. Allow students to design their own ways to find the answers to complex questions. Gifted students may discover more than you thought was possible.

- **Use higher-level questions in the justification and discussion of problems.** Ask "why" and "what if" and "explain how you arrived at that answer."

- **Differentiate assignments.** Provide activities, or problems that extend beyond the normal curriculum. Offer challenging mathematical recreations such as puzzles and games. Give students a choice of regular assignments, or activities that are task-tailored to their interests.

- **Expect high-level products** (e.g., writing, proofs, projects, solutions to challenging problems).

- **Provide access to male and female mentors who represent diverse linguistic and cultural groups.** They may be within the school system, volunteers from the community, or experts who agree to respond to questions by e-mail. Bring speakers into the classroom to explain how math has opened doors in their professions and careers.

- **Provide activities that can be done independently or in groups, based on student choice.** If gifted students always work independently, they are gaining no more than they could do at home. They also need appropriate instruction, interaction with other gifted students, and regular feedback from the teacher.

- **Provide useful concrete experiences.** Even though gifted learners may be capable of abstraction and may move from concrete to abstract rapidly, they still benefit from the use of manipulatives and hands-on activities.

Figure 3.7 Guidelines for Working with the Gifted Child in the Mathematics Classroom.
Source: D. T. Johnson, 2000.

Gifted Students

While gifted students are also children with special needs, they do not fall under the auspices of IDEA. These children also need special attention and will require adjustments in your curricular planning. A United States Office of Education document defined **gifted and talented students** as those who have outstanding abilities, are capable of high performance, and who require differentiated educational programs in order to realize their contribution to self and society (Johnson, 2000; Waxman, Robinson, Mukhopadhyay, & Educational Resources Information, 1996; Waxman & Educational Resources Information, 1996). They also may have demonstrated ability in a specific academic aptitude, creative or productive thinking, leadership ability, talent in visual or performing arts, or psychomotor abilities (Brown, 2008).

This is a broad definition and relies heavily on subjective judgment (see Figure 3.7). Gifted students often resist direct instruction, choosing instead to figure things out for themselves. They often "march to a different drummer" and exhibit divergent thinking. While these traits might be seen as behavior difficulties, in reality these students are just trying to get their needs met.

Parents may be concerned that their gifted child is being "held back" by being in a classroom with typically developing children or in a classroom with children with special needs. Some feel that more of the teachers' time is given to the children with special needs than to their child with advanced abilities. Reassure the parent of a gifted child that being in an inclusive classroom has been shown to be beneficial for both the special needs child and the gifted child (Johnson, 2000). The gifted child can act as a mentor and a tutor for less advanced children. Each time he explains a concept, he improves his own knowledge of the concept. Also, the social aspects of being in an inclusive classroom are invaluable. The gifted child learns communication and socialization skills that are often missing in isolated or pull-out gifted programs.

ENGLISH LANGUAGE LEARNERS AND LINGUISTIC DIVERSITY

English Language Learners (ELLs) are students whose native language is not English and who are in the process of learning it. These students usually use their native tongue when communicating with family members and peers at home and in their community. It is possible that by the time they enter preschool they will be quite proficient at their native language but their English language skills may not be up to the task of communicating mathematically. It is not their ability to understand math that is impeded, but their communication with other students and their ability to understand the teacher and the directions. One of the important parts of teaching mathematics in a constructivist, child-centered way is the social interaction between students. Unfortunately, there is no easy answer. These young children are in a continuing process of learning English. ELL students may misunderstand directions or miss the point of word problems.

In the preschool years, children are still very receptive to learning new languages. Teachers can involve students in learning English through their understanding of mathematics. While the child may not be using many of the same words to describe the math, the math itself can be communicated through using symbols such as fingers or hash marks.

Overcoming the Language Barrier

Your school may use one of several instructional approaches proven to work with ELLs, and you may or may not have specialist teachers to assist you with day-to-day needs. However, there are a number of things you can do to help these students in the mathematics classroom. Remember that while mathematics itself is a universal language that crosses language barriers, it can be confusing if not first presented in a child's native language, a fact which places the linguistically diverse child at a disadvantage from the beginning.

Liang is a 5-year-old Vietnamese child who has recently moved to the United States. He understands some English, but speaks very little. While Mrs. Lopez speaks English and Spanish, she does not know Vietnamese. She does know a few general strategies for teaching mathematics to ELL students. First, she assesses what language barriers in mathematics Liang might have. She realizes she must present concepts to Liang in a way he can understand.

Language becomes a barrier when representation, such as writing and saying numbers and problems, is introduced. Mrs. Lopez researches the Vietnamese representational system, such as the names for numbers and how to write them. She then develops a lesson for the whole class in which Liang helps them learn to count to 10 in Vietnamese while he learns to count to 10 in English.

Once Mrs. Lopez overcomes the basic representation barrier by learning the Vietnamese characters and names for numbers, she is able to use both English and some Vietnamese in her lessons. Math problems involve communication whenever possible. She has built common ground where Liang can communicate with his peers about math concepts. She can rely more on symbolic representation of numbers until Liang is able to use English words and Arabic numerals to represent the numbers. She can rely more on gestures and use manipulatives to communicate the math concepts she is trying to encourage.

ELL students can understand mathematics even if they struggle with language. With a little preparation and understanding from the teacher, mathematics becomes a context for learning English. It can also provide the ELL student with a bridge to understanding other students in the classroom. See Figure 3.8 for specific guidelines for working with English language learners.

- **Find ways to use symbols or other representations** of mathematics that the child understands to allow interaction with the mathematics curriculum. Begin by using counters, tally marks, or other counting devices before introducing numerals to these students.
- **Give the ELL students other ways to show their knowledge than speaking English.** ELL students develop a *receptive* vocabulary earlier than a *productive* vocabulary, so they may understand what the teacher wants but will not be able to respond. Allow them to point, show fingers, use manipulatives, or use native language to respond. For example, a teacher may ask the child what 2 + 3 is, and they can respond "Cinco!"
- **Give them instruction in their native language as much as possible.** Many textbooks have modifications for ESL students. Use these as a starting point. Overcoming the representational barrier in mathematics is vital for learning mathematics for ELLs. Simply learning the numbers of the child's representational system from 1 to 20 can help immensely. Most Western languages use the Arabic written numbers system, so using written numbers can help bridge this gap. However, Western Arabic is not the only way to write numbers. There are many different numerical representations, such as those of Vietnamese, Korean, or other Eastern languages. It will be important for the teacher to learn to use this system to build a bridge across the language barrier.
- **Encourage verbal interactions between students.** Teaching the ELLs language and representational system to the class encourages them to interact with the ELL student mathematically. Your native-language students can be a resource for helping ELL students learn the English terms used in mathematics. All the while, the ELL student is teaching their English-speaking peers their language and representational system. We know that verbal interaction strengthens conceptual understanding in mathematics, especially when it takes place in the context of play. A math game between an ELL student and a native English speaker is a good opportunity for both children to learn to understand each other.

  > Liang and Elizabeth are both 5 years old and they choose to play a math game. Mrs. Lopez has been careful to design many of the math games to be intuitive in the instructions and game play so Liang can grasp how to play without too much reading or explanation. The game consists of using two rolling number cubes and moving along a path to the end. The first one there wins. Liang has no problem rolling the cubes and counting the dots and Mrs. Lopez has designed the game to incorporate some Vietnamese characters as well as English ones, with help from Liang's parents. Elizabeth and Liang use their native languages to talk to each other. Perhaps not all of the conversation is understood by the other, but they try and, each time they play, get better and better at understanding each other. Even with partial language understanding, they are both able to play and enjoy the game and grasp the mathematical content of the game.

- **Encourage the use of gestures and manipulatives when doing mathematics.** Language may be a barrier, but there are other forms of representation. For example, knowing the names of shapes is a language activity, but knowing the properties of different shapes and being able to classify or sort them is a mathematical activity. Using manipulatives allows the ELL to use their mathematics thinking ability rather than language to structure the mathematics activity. To get the point across as to what the activity involves, the teacher may need to demonstrate how to sort the shapes or point and gesture along with language. A preschool ELL student could sort large plastic shapes by color and type, while the teacher holds up two similar shapes and encourages the child to identify their relationship in his native language.

Figure 3.8   Suggestions to Help Overcome Language Barriers.

GENDER DIFFERENCES

New evidence reveals that while boys' and girls' brains do develop differently (Gurian et al., 2002; Gurian & Stevens, 2005; Pollack, 1999b), these differences do not seem to greatly affect achievement in mathematics (Bielinski & Davison, 2001; Clements & Bright, 2003; Loveless & Coughlan, 2004; Wenglinsky, 2004).

From the long-term NAEP data, the results between girls and boys are fairly similar over the past 25 years (Clements & Bright, 2003; Johnson, Owen, & National Center for Education Statistics, 1998). (See Table 3.2 for a summary of these results.) Boys' and girls' scores have been within two points of each other during this time. The "back to basics" changes implemented over the past 20 years in mathematics education seems to have benefited boys more than girls, as boys have taken the lead since 1992.

This leads us to examine many of the assumptions about the differences between boys' and girls' achievement in mathematics (Table 3.2) (Perie, Grigg, & Dion, 2005). Many people assume that girls receive unintended or unconscious messages that they are inferior to boys when it comes to higher-level mathematics. While evidence shows that girls are subject to a different set of expectations regarding their mathematical achievement, the consequences may not be what you expect.

Blevins-Knabe (1987) found that parents expect their young sons to develop mathematical skills earlier than parents of young girls expect their daughters to develop these skills (Leedy, LaLonde, & Runk, 2003). Parents of older children believe that their daughters must work harder to attain good grades in mathematics, while parents of boys place more emphasis on the importance of learning mathematics. Parents, quite naturally, expect different things from their children, but their attitudes and expectations have a direct correlation to their children's achievement in mathematics (Leedey et al., 2003).

Research has also shown that girls tend to feel less confident about their answers on tests and often express doubt about their performance. Boys, however, tend to show more confidence, and sometimes overconfidence. This uncertainty on the girls' part and overconfidence on the boys' part often extends beyond individual problems into their general view of mathematics (Ai, 2002; Becker, 2003; Bevan, 2001; Leedy et al., 2003; Li, 1999; Tiedemann, 2002). There is evidence that, as children progress through the grades, girls' enjoyment of mathematics falls off much more drastically than that of boys. The traditional curriculum and pedagogy of schools seem to perpetuate this disparity (Bevan, 2001).

There are important differences between boys and girls and how they learn mathematics in the early childhood years, the time when the seeds of future achievement

Table 3.2 Boys and Girls: NAEP Scores for Fourth Grade

4th	1978	1982	1986	1990	1992	1994	1996	1999	2004
Male	217	217	222	229	231	232	233	233	243
Female	220	221	222	230	228	230	229	231	240

8th	1978	1982	1986	1990	1992	1994	1996	1999	
Male	264	269	270	271	274	276	276	277	283
Female	265	268	268	270	272	273	272	274	279

Source: National Center for Education Statistics, 2007.

Table 3.3   Differences in Learning Styles Between Boys and Girls

Girls	Boys
Girls tend to be linguistic, read/write, or auditory learners. Read/write learners respond to reading to solve the problem. They understand mathematics better if it is written, and might prefer to turn in written homework. Auditory learners like to have things explained to them and enjoy talking through problems. These students respond well to working in groups or having a partner to discuss a problem with.	Boys tend to be visual and kinesthetic learners. They may respond by using drawings to solve math problems or seeing a problem on a chalkboard. Kinesthetic learners learn by doing. They use objects to solve problems or act out a scenario. These children understand mathematics best if they can use it to solve everyday problems. Contextualizing mathematics is vitally important for them.
Girls' fine motor development is more advanced than boys, therefore they find writing and completing worksheets much easier.	At birth, boys are developmentally a few weeks behind girls and remain so until late adolescence (Gilbert, 2001). Boys' fine motor skills develop slower than girls, and they may have difficulty with handwriting tasks (Pollack 1999). Boys in the earlier grades may do better with manipulatives and verbal mathematics, while girls excel at written activities.
Girls respond to open-ended, process-based experiences that encourage independent thinking.	Boys tend to get bored more easily than girls and require more stimulation to keep them attentive and on task.
Girls may work quietly in chairs for long stints.	Repetitive activities are often difficult for boys to attend to positively.
Girls are often less active and use the space provided in the manner specified by the teacher.	Boys are more physically active and like to engage in more exploratory play (Barnett & Rivers, 2004; Boland & Educational Resources Information Center, 1995; Campbell, Storo, & Educational Resources Information Center, 1996).
They tend to use language to reach their goals and deal with problems.	Boys tend to be more "rough and tumble," or, as it is often referred to, "boys being boys."
Girls are better at verbal processing, which enables them to retrieve semantic and phonological information from their long-term memory (Halpern, 2004).	Boys tend to be better at visual-spatial tasks such as mental or spatial perception and spatial visualization (Halpern, 2004).

are sown (see Table 3.3). Below are a few accommodation methods that early childhood teachers can do to ensure that the curriculum is individualized to meet the needs of both boys and girls.

Accommodating Differences in Boys' and Girls' Learning Styles

Avoid Labeling and Gender Stereotyping.   It is very easy to assume that girls are bad at math and boys are bad at language even at a very young age, but this is a dangerous way to think (Barnett & Rivers, 2004). Many teachers believe that girls achieve in mathematics due to hard work while boy's achievement is attributed to talent (Jussim & Eccles, 1990; Jussim & Eccles, 1992; Madon, Jussim, & Eccles, 1997; Smith, Jussim, & Eccles, 1999). These differing expectations by teachers and parents may lead to boys receiving preferential treatment when it comes to mathematics. Children may internalize these attitudes and begin to believe what their teachers and parents do. As a result, girls' enjoyment of mathematics falls much more drastically than boys as they move through the grades (Gurian, 2001; Halpern, 2002). These attitudes may shape the experiences that children have as they are learning mathematics.

Understand Developmental Gender Differences. Because of the differing rates of mylenization (the insulation around the nerve cells that improve signal flow) of the cerebral cortex (the "grey matter" of the brain where all higher level thought occurs), boys may not be able to sit still and pay attention for long periods of time. Girls, however, seem better at self-managing boredom; therefore, they tend to be more attentive in class. This is why boys tend to be more vocal and receive the lion's share of reprimands for poor behavior (Pollack, 1999a).

Allow Children to Solve Problems in Many Different Ways. Because of variance in developmental and learning styles, there are different ways children go about solving problems. A mathematics program needs to be flexible enough to allow children to use their natural thinking ability and strengths to solve problems. Many of the worksheets and problems presented in textbooks, however, do not promote thinking and discussion.

Teachers have direct contact with the students and can better develop engaging mathematical activities that are appropriate for the needs of both boys and girls. The teacher is the decision maker about instructional methods. Using one's knowledge base to inform the curricular process can help teachers design appropriate activities for all students in the class.

Standardized Testing and Gender Differences

It is interesting to note that while there are only slight differences between the sexes in NAEP tests that were given 21 years apart, in 1999 girls were *always* outperformed by boys at all grade levels, whereas in 1978 boys only came out on top at the 12th grade level. We might ask, "What has changed in the past 20 years?" It would seem that the impact of standards, back-to-basics approaches, and high-stakes testing have benefited boys more than girls. This is exactly what we would expect, given the learning differences between boys and girls and the rigidity of traditional mathematics curriculum.

These results strongly suggest that the question is not whether boys are more capable at mathematics than girls, but is one of how our teaching practices in mathematics affect the boys and girls differently and who benefits more. Given the TIMSS results and other achievement scores we have discussed, it may be that neither boys nor girls benefit from a standardized skills-based approach brought about by an emphasis on proficiency testing and "No Child Left Behind." If we truly want children to excel in mathematics, no matter the gender, their natural learning styles and thinking ability must be acknowledged and utilized.

SUMMARY

Traditional approaches to mathematics emphasize memorization, repetition, and skills practice with little interaction between students. These approaches do not meet the needs of students of any gender, ethnicity, family background, or socio-economic status. The most damaging aspect of these approaches is the lack of understanding of individual students' needs as learners. All students are not identical. Even with math curriculum that is based on where "most" children will be at a particular time, teachers must find ways to acknowledge the unique attributes of each of their young learners.

Understand your students' different needs. Acknowledging linguistic, ethnic, cultural, and gender diversity, as well as making appropriate modifications for children with special needs, are all vital parts of your mathematics program. Basing your instructional choices on the principles of individualized instruction will help to meet the needs of these diverse students and ensure that all of your students can succeed.

Environment plays a vital role in a child's cognitive and mathematical development. This is the "nurture" part of the nature-nurture balance. Factors such as socioeconomic status and parental education level affect how children will perform in mathematics. These issues do have an effect on the support that children get at home and the messages sent by parents and teachers. The expectations that parents and teachers have for children also affect mathematical achievement, as children tend to live up to the expectations that adults have of them. If they are constantly sent messages of success, they usually succeed. If expected to fail, they usually do. This is called the self-fulfilling prophesy. Have high expectations and standards for all students, and be aware of what assumptions you might bring into your classroom.

On the "nature" side of the equation, some learning differences are biological. Research has shown that children have different learning styles. Some may learn by doing, others by hearing, and others by reading. Mathematics education programs in early childhood need to be individualized for each child's level of understanding and the learning style to which he is most responsive. In working with gender differences in mathematics, learning styles are especially important. Research suggests that boys' and girls' brains are different and that they have different needs when it comes to learning. While neither gender is better at mathematics, they do tend to think about mathematics and problem solving differently. A method of teaching mathematics that uses a single method for solving problems does not address the needs of either gender when it comes to learning mathematics.

Children with special needs also require an individualized approach to ensure their success. They may have a diagnosed special need that requires the teacher, along with the parent and a team of other professionals, to develop an individualized education plan (IEP). These children can be incorporated into the regular mathematics classroom with little adjustment when all children are treated as individuals and their individual needs addressed regardless of whether they have a diagnosed special need.

The same is true for the growing student population of English Language Learners. While there is an intense debate over the best way to teach these children, you, as teachers, must always ensure that all of your students have an equal opportunity to succeed. While mathematics is a universal language, there are some aspects of doing mathematics that are limited by language. By incorporating an ELL's native language into your mathematics program in a way you are comfortable with, all of your students become familiar with another language.

WEB SITES

Teaching Tolerance
http://www.tolerance.org

Teaching Tolerance provides educators with free educational materials that promote respect for differences and appreciation of diversity in the classroom and beyond.

Girls Go Tech
http://www.girlsgotech.org/

Girl Scout site aimed at making sure that girls feel successful at math and science. The site contains tips for parents as well as games and career resources.

Girlstart
http://www.girlstart.org/

Girlstart is a nonprofit organization created to empower girls to excel in math, science, and technology. Founded in 1997 in Austin, Texas, Girlstart has quickly established itself as a best-case practices leader in empowering, educating, and motivating girls to enjoy and become more proficient in math, science, and technology.

Girls Inc.
http://www.girlsinc.org/gc/

Aims to inspire girls to be strong, smart, and bold. The site contains articles and games that promote girls to study math.

Hispanic Math Initiative at the University of Illinois at Chicago
http://www.uic.edu/educ/outreach/programs/hmsei.htm

Research concerning why there are achievement gaps in mathematics.

Learning Point Associates on Achievement Gaps
http://www.learningpt.org/gaplibrary/text/changesin.php

A library of literature from Learning Point Associates about narrowing achievement gaps in schools.

Council for Exceptional Children
http://www.cec.sped.org

Contains information about children with special needs. Council for Exceptional Children (CEC) is the largest international professional organization dedicated to improving educational outcomes for individuals with exceptionalities, students with disabilities, and/or the gifted. The web site contains resources and professional development opportunities.

DISCUSS AND APPLY WHAT YOU HAVE LEARNED

Observe

1. Observe children in a classroom setting. How much diversity do you see? Do you see evidence of multicultural materials in the classroom? For example, posters, musical instruments, or books?
2. Observe the way that the teacher treats boys and girls when doing mathematics. Is there a difference?
3. How does the teacher deal with different levels of abilities in the classroom? How does the teacher individualize the curriculum and instruction?
4. Is there any linguistic diversity in the classroom? How does the teacher deal with non-native English speakers? What challenges do you see to incorporating the child into mathematics?

Apply

1. Design a mathematics activity that incorporates linguistic diversity, such as a problem-solving activity that needs minimal verbal or written explanation, or a group lesson that involves English and another language in a group activity about mathematics.
2. Design a standard mathematics lesson that meets one or two mathematics standards. How would you modify it to incorporate differences in gender? Socioeconomic differences? A child with ADHD?

Reflect

1. Do you believe there are gender differences when it comes to mathematics?
2. What can schools do to try to overcome the effects of poverty on mathematics achievement?
3. Why do you think the gap in achievement on the NAEP between minority and white students has not narrowed? How might we address this disparity in the classroom?

REFERENCES

Ai, X. (2002). Gender differences in growth in mathematics achievement: Three-level longitudinal and multilevel analyses of individual, home, and school influences. *Mathematical Thinking & Learning, 4*(1), 1-22.

Arnold, D. H., Doctoroff, G. L., & Fisher, P. H. (2002). Accelerating math development in Head Start classrooms. *Journal of Educational Psychology, 94*(4), 762.

Barlow, A. E. L., & Villarejo, M. (2004). Making a difference for minorities: Evaluation of an educational enrichment program. *Journal of Research in Science Teaching, 41*(9), 861.

Barnett, R. C., & Rivers, C. (2004). The persistence of gender myths in math. *Education Week, 24*(7), 39.

Becker, J. R. (2003). Gender and mathematics: An issue for the twenty-first century. *Teaching Children Mathematics, 9*(8), 470.

Bevan, R. (2001). Boys, girls and mathematics: Beginning to learn from the gender debate. *Mathematics in School, 30*(4), 2.

Bielinski, J., & Davison, M. L. (2001). A sex difference by item difficulty interaction in multiple-choice mathematics items administered to national probability samples. *Journal of Educational Measurement, 38*(1), 51.

Birsh, J. R., Potts, M., Potts, R., & Vineyard Video Productions. (1997). LD–LA, learning disabilities, learning abilities. West Tisbury, MA: Vineyard Video Productions.

Blevins-Knabe, B. (1987). Remembering and constructing an order. *Journal of Genetic Psychology, 148*(4), 453.

Boland, P., & Educational Resources Information Center. (1995). *Gender-fair math.* Newton, MA: Education Development Center, Inc.

Borman, G. D., & Overman, L. T. (2004). Academic resilience in mathematics among poor and minority students. *The Elementary School Journal, 104*(3), 177.

Bradley, R. H., Corwyn, R. F., McAdoo, H. P., & Garcia Coll, C. (2001). The home environments of children in the United States part I: Variations by age, ethnicity, and poverty status. *Child Development, 72*(6), 1844.

Brown, V. (2008). BEST PRACTICES IN GIFTED EDUCATION: An evidence-based guide. *Childhood Education, 84*(3), 175.

Bruder, M. B. (2000). The Individual Family Service Plan (IFSP). Retrieved May 19, 2007, from *http://www.cec.sped.org/Content/NavigationMenu/NewsIssues/TeachingLearningCenter/ProfessionalPracticeTopicsInfo/EarlyChildhood/The_Individual_Famil.htm*

Bullard, J., & Oborne, L. (1997). *Yes you can! Help your kid succeed in math, even if you think you can't.* Seattle, WA: Yes You Can! Press.

Butterworth, B. (1999). *What counts: How every brain is hardwired for math.* New York: Free Press.

Byrnes, J. P. (2003). Factors predictive of mathematics achievement in white, black, and hispanic 12th graders. *Journal of Educational Psychology, 95*(2), 316.

Campbell, P. B., Storo, J. N., & Educational Resources Information Center. (1996). *Teacher strategies that work for girls and boys.* Newton, MA: WEEA Resource Center, Educational Development Center, Inc.

Campbell, S. R., Zazkis, R., & NetLibrary Inc. (2002). *Learning and teaching number theory: Research in cognition and instruction.* Westport, CT: Ablex Pub.

Clements, D. H., & Bright, G. W. (2003). *Learning and teaching measurement: 2003 yearbook.* Reston, VA: National Council of Teachers of Mathematics.

D'Arcangelo, M. (2001). Wired for mathematics: A conversation with Brian Butterworth. *Educational Leadership, 59*(3), 14.

DelCampo, R. L., & DelCampo, D. S. (1995). *Taking sides*. Guilford, CT: Dushkin Pub. Group.

Feiler, A., & Webster, A. (1997, September). *Teacher predictions of young children's literacy success or failure in four primary schools*. Paper presented at the annual meeting of the British Research Association, York, England.

Fusarelli, B. C., & Boyd, W. L. (Eds.). (2004). Curriculum politics in multicultural America. *Educational Policy, 18*(1), 5.

Gazzaniga, M. S. (2004). *The cognitive neurosciences* (3rd ed.). Cambridge, MA: MIT Press.

Genshaft, J., Naglieri, J. A., & Educational Resources Information Center. (1987). *A mindset for MATH techniques for identifying and working with math-anxious girls*. Columbus, OH: Ohio State University.

Gilbert, M. C. (2001). Applying the equity principle. *Mathematics Teaching in the Middle School, 7*(1), 18.

Goldstein, S., & Mather, N. (1998). *Overcoming underachieving: An action guide to helping your child succeed in school*. New York: J. Wiley & Sons.

Gurian, M. (2001). *Boys and girls learn differently: A guide for teachers and parents* (1st ed.). San Francisco: Jossey-Bass.

Gurian, M., Henley, P., & Trueman, T. (2002). *Boys and girls learn differently: A guide for teachers and parents*. San Francisco: Jossey-Bass.

Gurian, M., & Stevens, K. (2005). *The minds of boys: saving our sons from falling behind in school and life*. San Francisco, Jossey-Bass.

Hall, C. W., Davis, N. B., Bolen, L. M., & Chia, R. (1999). *Gender and racial differences in mathematical performance*. Heldref Publications; Washington D.C.

Halpern, D. F. (2002). Sex differences in achievement scores: Can we design assessments that are fair, meaningful, and valid for girls and boys? *Issues in Education, 8*(1), 2.

Halpern, D. F. (2004). A cognitive-process taxonomy for sex differences in cognitive abilities. *Current Directions in Psychological Science, 13*(4), 135–139.

Hoff, D. J. (2000). Gap widens between black and white students on NAEP. *Education Week, 20*(1), 6.

Holloway, J. H. (2004). Closing the minority achievement gap in math. *Educational Leadership, 61*(5), 84.

Jacobson, J., Olsen, C., Rice, J. K., Sweetland, S., & Ralph, J. (2001). Educational achievement and black-white inequality. Retrieved May 19, 2007, from *http://nces.ed.gov/pubs2001/2001061.PDF*

Johnson, D. T. (2000). Teaching mathematics to gifted students in a mixed-ability classroom. ERIC Digest E594 (pp. 4): ERIC Clearinghouse on Disabilities and Gifted Education, Council for Exceptional Children, 1920 Association Dr., Reston, VA 20191-1589. Tel: 800-328-0272 (Toll Free); e-mail: ericec@cec.sped.org; Web site: *http://ericec.org*

Johnson, E. G., Owen, E., & National Center for Education Statistics. (1998). *Linking the National Assessment of Educational Progress (NAEP) and the Trends in Mathematics and Science Study (TIMSS) a technical report*. Washington, DC: U.S. Dept. of Education, Office of Educational Research and Improvement, National Center for Education Statistics.

Jussim, L., & Eccles, J. S. (1990). *Expectancies and social issues*. New York: Plenum Pub. Corp. for the Society for the Psychological Study of Social Issues.

Jussim, L., & Eccles, J. S. (1992). *Teacher expectations II: Construction and reflection of student achievement*. American Psychological Association.

Kamii, C. (1965). *Socioeconomic class differences in the preschool socialization practices of Negro mothers*. Unpublished vii, 152 leaves.

Klein, M. D., & Chen, D. (2001). *Working with children from culturally diverse backgrounds*. Albany, NY: Delmar Thomson Learning.

Kozol, J. (1991). In public schooling, social policy has been turned back almost 100 years. (cover story). *Publishers Weekly, 238*(43), 2.

Leedy, M. G., LaLonde, D., & Runk, K. (2003). Gender equity in mathematics: Beliefs of students, parents, and teachers. *School Science & Mathematics, 103*(6), 285-292.

Levine, G. (1995). Closing the gender gap: focus on mathematics anxiety. *Contemporary Education, 67*, 42.

Lewis, A. (2001). *Add it up: Using research to improve education for low-income and minority students*. Washington, DC: Poverty & Race Research Action Council.

Li, Q. (1999). Teachers' beliefs and gender differences in mathematics: A review. *Educational Research, 41*(1), 63.

Lindquist, M. M. (2001). NAEP, TIMSS, and PSSM: Entangled influences. *School Science and Mathematics, 101*(6), 286.

Loveless, T., & Coughlan, J. (2004). The arithmetic gap. *Educational Leadership, 61*(5), 55.

Lubienski, S. T. (2002). A closer look at black-white mathematics gaps: Intersections of race and SES in NAEP achievement and instructional practices data. *The Journal of Negro Education, 71*(4), 269.

Lubienski, S. T. (2003). Is our teaching measuring up? Race-, SES-, and gender-related gaps in measurement achievement. *Yearbook (National Council of Teachers of Mathematics), 2003*, 282.

Madon, S., Jussim, L., & Eccles, J. (1997). In search of the powerful self-fulfilling prophecy (Vol. 72, pp. 791): American Psychological Association.

Mather, N., & Goldstein, S. (2001). *Learning disabilities and challenging behaviors: A guide to intervention and classroom management*. Baltimore, MD: P.H. Brookes Pub. Co.

Myers, D. E., & Educational Resources Information Center. (1986). *The relationship between school poverty concentration and students' reading and math achievement and learning*. Washington, DC: U.S. Dept. of Education, Office of Educational Research and Improvement, Educational Resources Information Center.

National Association for Women in Education. (1993). *Gender equity in math and science*. Washington, DC: National Association for Women in Education.

National Center for Educational Statistics. (2007). NAEP Data Explorer. Retrieved May 16, 2007, from *http://nces.ed.gov/nationsreportcard/nde/*

New, R. S. (1998). Playing fair and square: Issues of equity in preschool math, science, and technology [Electronic Version]. ERIC Document Reproduction Service No. ED423954.

New, R. S., Mallory, B. L., & Mantovani, S. (2000). Cultural images of children, parents and professionals: Italian interpretations of home-school relationships. *Early Education and Development, 11*(5), 597–616.

Payne, K. J., & Biddle, B. J. (1999). Poor school funding, child poverty, and mathematics achievement. *Educational Researcher, 28*(6), 4.

Perie, M., Grigg, W., & Dion, G. (2005). *The nation's report card: Mathematics 2005 (NCES 2006-453)*: U.S. Department of Education, National Center for Education Statistics. Washington DC: U.S. Government Printing Office.

Pollack, W. S. (1999). *Real boys rescuing our sons from the myths of boyhood*. New York: Henry Holt & Company.

Pollack, W. S. (1999a). *Real boys: Rescuing our sons from the myths of boyhood* (1st Owl Books ed.). New York: Henry Holt & Company.

Pollack, W. S. (1999b). *Real boys: Rescuing our sons from the myths of boyhood*. New York: Henry Holt & Company.

Ricciuti, H. N. (2004). Single parenthood, achievement, and problem behavior in white, black, and Hispanic children. *The Journal of Educational Research, 97*(4), 196.

Richards, A. (2005). Retooling the classroom to incorporate alternate assessment. Retrieved May 19, 2007, from *http://www.cec.sped.org/AM/Template.cfm?Section=Home&TEMPLATE=/CM/ContentDisplay.cfm&CONTENTID=5827*

Rivera, D. P. (1998). *Mathematics education for students with learning disabilities: Theory to practice*. Austin, TX: PRO-ED.

Rosenthal, R., & Jacobson, L. (1968). *Pygmalion in the classroom: Teacher expectation and pupils' intellectual development*. New York: Holt.

Rosenthal, R., & Jacobson, L. (1992). *Pygmalion in the classroom: Teacher expectation and pupils' intellectual development* (Newly expanded ed.). New York: Irvington Publishers.

Schumm, J. S. (1999). *Adapting reading and math materials for the inclusive classroom*. Reston, VA: Council for Exceptional Children.

Shaw, G. L., & Peterson, M. (2000). *Keeping Mozart in mind*. San Diego, CA: Academic Press.

Schoenfeld, A. H. (2002). Making mathematics work for all children: Issues of standards, testing, and equity. *Educational Researcher, 31*(1), 13.

Smith, A. E., Jussim, L., & Eccles, J. (1999). *Do self-fulfilling prophecies accumulate, dissipate, or remain stable over time?* Journal of Personality and Social Psychology, 77(3), 548-565.

Tauber, R. T. (1998). Good or bad, what teachers expect from students they generally get! ERIC Digest. ERIC Clearinghouse on Teaching and Teacher Education, Washington, D.C. ERIC Document Reproduction Service No. ED426985.

Thompson, T. D., & Preston, R. V. (2004). Measurement in the middle grades: insights from NAEP and TIMSS. *Mathematics Teaching in the Middle School, 9*(9), 514.

Tiedemann, J. (2002). Teachers' gender stereotypes as determinants of teacher perceptions in elementary school mathematics. *Educational Studies in Mathematics, 50*(1), 49.

U.S. Census Bureau. (2007). Historical Poverty Tables. Retrieved May 18, 2007, from *http://www.census.gov/hhes/www/poverty/histpov/hstpov3.html*

Waxman, B., Robinson, N. M., Mukhopadhyay, S., & Educational Resources Information Center. (1996). *Teachers nurturing math-talented young children*. Storrs, CT: National Research Center on the Gifted and Talented.

Weinstein, R. S. (2002). *Reaching higher: The power of expectations in schooling*. Cambridge, MA: Harvard University Press.

Wenglinsky, H. (2004). Facts or critical thinking skills? What NAEP results say. *Educational Leadership, 62*(1), 32.

CHAPTER 4

Creating a Constructivist Classroom

CHAPTER OBJECTIVES

After you have read this chapter, you should be able to:

- Explain the importance of a child-centered approach to teaching mathematics
- Explain the significance of teachable moments
- Demonstrate methods of overcoming resistance to child-centered curriculum
- Demonstrate optimal ways of arranging classrooms to effectively teach mathematics
- Analyze materials, textbooks, and mathematics curriculum programs based on standards, theoretical, and pedagogical characteristics
- Describe the first steps necessary to prepare an effective mathematics program for young children

By now, you may be thinking, "what activities and lessons can I use in the classroom?" You may also feel that your math skills are not up to par to teach young children mathematics. Math anxiety, as we have discussed previously, is one of the fears that teachers have about teaching mathematics. Rest assured that the mathematics you will be presenting to children of this age is not advanced algebra or calculus. Perhaps this book's title should be "DON'T PANIC!" (Adams,

1979). The best thing you can do to overcome any anxiety you have about teaching math (or any other subject) is to prepare. Preparation and planning are vital to developing mathematical experiences for children that will engage, educate, and interest them. Instead of shying away from math, children will look for mathematics opportunities throughout the day. A first-grade child may make a mathematical observation while eating dinner, stating, "I have 3 carrots and 5 potatoes. That equals 8!"

We can cultivate this interest if we stick to the principles outlined in previous chapters and always treat our students as young mathematicians. When children are engaged in problems that are meaningful to them, they will be interested. The "holy grail" of education is a lesson or experience that children don't know is a learning activity—one they will even continue without direct teacher intervention. Children know more than we often give them credit for, and can learn and construct even more if given the opportunity.

THE CHILD-CENTERED CURRICULUM

A **child-centered curriculum** is one that is built on, led, and informed by children's interests and development (Helm & Katz, 2001; Katz & Chard, 2000). This doesn't mean that the teacher simply does the things children want to do and lets them run around like little hooligans. It means that the teacher knows each child's abilities, developmental level, and interests and builds a curriculum around this knowledge. A child-centered curriculum begins with the child's ideas and questions and then moves on to content. In other words, the curriculum is designed to fit the child, not the other way around.

Teaching does not have to be about standing in front of a class drilling facts into student's brains. A child-centered approach will work just as well if not better and your students will enjoy the learning process (Helm & Beneke, 2003; Helm & Katz, 2001; Katz & Chard, 2000). Yet many teachers have a list of reasons why they cannot implement child-centered curricula in their classrooms. You may even hear some of these arguments in your lab placements, field observations, student teaching, or practicum.

A child-centered approach to mathematics requires teachers to think of the child as an active, thinking being rather than just an empty vessel to be filled up with bits of isolated math knowledge (Helm & Beneke, 2003; Katz & Chard, 2000; New, 1999; New, 2002). The ideas that underlie this approach recall our discussion of how to treat all children as young mathematicians:

1. When children act as facilitators to the learning process, they can construct mathematics in a more beneficial way.
2. The process of problem solving is just as important as knowing how to get the right answer.
3. Giving children a say in the learning process and listening to their ideas about mathematics can guide the mathematics curriculum development process.

4. There is not just one way to solve any particular problem; letting the child solve it in a way he understands, rather than imposing a method for him to use, leads to his gaining a deeper conceptual understanding of mathematics.

These ideas should help broaden your understanding of what teaching can and should be. Applying these ideas about how children learn mathematics to national and state standards opens up opportunities for a child-centered mathematics curriculum that is individualized to meet the need of each student. This is important because not all of your students will be at the same level of competence in mathematics. For example, if two students work on a math problem and arrive at the same answer, we cannot assume that just because the children achieved the same task and got the same answer they were both thinking about the problem the same way or even at the same cognitive level.

A good example of child-centered and constructivist curriculum can be found in the video *First Graders dividing 62 by 5* (Kamii, Clark, Housman, & Teachers College Press, 2000). The teacher, Leslie Baker Housman, gives children the following problem:

> Joe has 62 cents. Erasers at the school store cost 5 cents each. How many erasers can Joe buy?

Leslie then lets the children work on the problem individually at their seats. While this is going on, she is doing four important things that make this activity child-centered and constructivist. First, she has the children explain how they are solving the problem by asking them questions. Second, she refrains from telling the children if they are right or wrong or making any judgmental or leading remarks about their methods. Third, she encourages them to discuss their answers and methods with each other, and even to argue, until they are convinced that one method is best.

The fourth thing she does is to tap into the contextual and cultural background of the children. Children understand erasers and know how to buy them at the school store. This is an act they have had the opportunity to engage in daily. This makes the whole process relevant and more engaging, and helps them to understand the reasons for learning mathematics.

After they have had sufficient time to think and discuss their answers, Leslie brings the class together in a large group in front of the chalkboard and asks each child to give his solution. Again, she does not judge the "rightness" of the answer, but rather asks the children if they agree or disagree with the answer and the method. What quickly becomes clear is that, even though they may be giving the same answer of 12 with 2 cents left over, their methods show a large range of cognitive abilities.

One child drew 62 hash marks, then made circles around groups of 5. She then counted the circles to get 12. Another child counted to 60 by 5s, writing a 5 each time like this:

5 5 5 5 5 5 5 5 5 5 5 5 2

As he wrote each 5 he would say "5," "10," "15," and so on until he reached 60, then wrote the 2 and said he had 2 cents left. Another child said that ten 5s were 50 and two more

Recognizing teachable moments requires teachers to value children's explanations, even when they are incorrect.

Kevin Fitzsimons/Merrill

5s were 10 more and that was 12. Some children in the class seemed to have trouble understanding this method because it was a bit more advanced.

Even though children arrive at the same answer, it does not mean they are all at the same level of understanding. The core of child-centered instruction is to design activities that allow children to use their natural and inborn ability to think and problem solve. Teachers need to allow students to use these processes as frequently as possible (Kamii & Chemeketa, 1982; Kamii et al., 2000).

We will be featuring elements of the child-centered curriculum throughout Chapters 5 to 8. Implementing this approach demands flexibility, spontaneity, and self-belief. All of these traits are evident in a concept central to the child-centered curriculum: the teachable moment.

Teachable Moments

Time spent on preparation is seldom wasted. Many teachers have problems simply because they fail to plan and prepare. Other teachers plan so rigidly that there is little room for spontaneity and flexibility. The trick is to find a balance between planning, preparation, flexibility, and the ability to take advantage of teachable moments.

Teachable moments are those special times when all the stars and planets align just right and something magical happens in your classroom: a child asks a question about what you are teaching because he is truly interested in the lesson. These are opportunities for you to help the student make a connection between a new concept and his own life. While it might seem like a digression from the planned lesson, a teachable moment gets at the core of the child-centered curriculum because your student's interest guides both your instruction and the mathematical content you are covering. There are requirements of teachers when a teachable moment occurs. First, you have to recognize it. Many teachers do not always value what children in their classrooms have to say, and therefore miss the opportunities when a child's comment could lead to a teachable moment. Listening to your students and taking their comments and questions seriously are vital for recognizing teachable moments.

Second, teachers must be willing to devote time to the child's question or comment. Often this means abandoning what you have planned and following a new course. This can be difficult because teachers are under pressure to cover a vast amount of material in a certain amount of time. However, teachable moments offer many opportunities to give depth to the curriculum. Flexibility is important, as is the ability of the teacher to think and act quickly.

Third, some teachers don't feel confident enough about certain subjects and therefore, feel uncomfortable taking the lesson into uncharted waters. Teachers like to have the answers to every question, but with teachable moments this is not always possible. Often, the most difficult thing for a teacher to say is "I don't know." But this can become something else entirely if the teacher says, "I don't know. Do any of you have any ideas how we can find the answer?" Remember Leslie Baker Housman and children dividing 62 by 5? She used questioning to guide the children's thinking rather than as a way to tell them they were right or wrong. This is the skill we need to develop as teachers.

Finally, teachers must value and encourage this intellectual exchange. Many teachers do not see the usefulness of teachable moments in the larger scheme of things. However, in a child-centered classroom, the teacher is a facilitator of knowledge; the children and the teacher together are learners. Using this model, children become more empowered to ask questions and seek out answers for themselves.

Common Objections to the Child-Centered Approach

Many teachers can sense that a child-centered approach is more beneficial. Students are more motivated to learn when we build a curriculum around their natural thinking ability (Byrnes, 2003; Elkind & Piaget, 1979; Kamii, 1984; Kamii et al., 2000; Kamii & DeVries, 1976). Some even say things like "If I had been taught math this way, I would have loved it." Doubts seem to emerge in other teachers. Many times it is easier to explain why something *cannot* be done rather than finding a way to do it. Because of this, teachers and administrators often build "roadblocks" that keeps teachers from embracing a child-centered curriculum. To help you counter these roadblocks, here is a list of the most common reasons why teachers do not adopt a child-centered curriculum, and ways to overcome this resistance.

- I would love to teach this way, but my school district requires that I teach using a prepared mathematics curriculum adopted by the school board.

Make your voice heard. Prepared curricula consisting primarily of direct instruction, with very few components of appropriate practice, are usually selected because a school needs or wants to improve their scores on one of the many standardized tests prevalent in the United States (Schoenfeld, 2002). As teachers and advocates for children, we need to make sure that parents, administrators, school board members, and other interested parties know that these types of programs are detrimental to the future academic health of our children (Parker, 1999).

If we value the types of active learning that promote deep understanding of content and which are supported by NAEYC and other learned societies such as NCTM, NSTA, NCSS, and IRA, then we need to act as advocates to get this message to those making the decisions about assessment in early childhood programs. This includes parents. Parents have an important voice in how their children are educated. They elect the school boards and the state representatives. Through educating the parents, school boards, and politicians, we can promote positive changes in our schools. It's not easy and often feels like our efforts go unrewarded, but if enough people speak up, our voices can and will be heard.

Becoming active in local affiliates of groups such as NAEYC is a great way to be an advocate. Participating in a group that is associated with educators in your state and across the country adds to your firepower when working with people that make decisions about curricula in the schools. In the United States, we value the local control of schools so that they can be responsive to local and regional needs. This system was developed so that local input would have an effect. We need to take advantage of that basic premise of our schooling system and affect change through advocacy.

To be a great mathematics teacher, you need to be empowered to make decisions. This means becoming an advocate for yourself, your children, and your curriculum. If you believe that a child-centered approach is best for your children in mathematics, you need to stand up and say so, during and outside of school hours. Consider creating a "support group" of others that believe in a child-centered approach.

- Child-centered strategies such as project work and classroom discussion seem great, but I don't have the time do all that and still teach all the subjects necessary for children in my class to perform well on proficiency tests. It takes too much time.

If we value project work, we will find time for it in our busy schedules. Projects, while just one aspect of an appropriate curriculum, can be great incubators of ideas and skills that relate directly to information seen on many proficiency tests. They are also child-initiated and provide children many opportunities to pursue their own interests through self-directed activity.

The **Project Approach** lends itself well to the integration of content goals and assessment into classroom activities (Helm & Katz, 2001). Projects offer excellent opportunities for teachers to integrate many curricular areas. An integrated approach

Overcoming resistance to active learning can have a big payoff.

Barbara Schwartz/Merrill

addresses content-related goals by blending several subject areas. This approach allows the curriculum to be child-centered rather than subject-centered, a tenet central to appropriate educational experiences for young children.

The benefits of child-initiated activities, such as projects, are well documented. Preschool children can take a trip to the fire station and learn all there is to know about the fire engine. They may draw pictures of it, look for different shapes on it, and ask questions about the truck. Back in the classroom, they could use this information to extend their study of the fire station. In primary grades, children can use reading, writing, and mathematics to study a topic. They could do a project on rivers and streams, measuring water levels in a nearby stream, or examine, count, and classify the different kinds of wildlife that use the stream as a habitat.

Children who have the opportunity to thoroughly investigate topics of personal interest grow academically and socially/emotionally (Helm & Katz, 2001). Evidence shows that children who are taught using methods of an active curriculum do as well, if not better, on proficiency tests than children taught using a "cookbook" curriculum (Cain, 2002; Heiney, 1998). Projects are compatible with other curricular approaches and should complement, expand, and support other classroom activities.

- There are only so many hours in the day and it seems like a lot of work.

Incorporating appropriate practices into your classroom **is** a lot of work. The teacher must continually assess students, actively develop curricula, and have significant interactions with parents. Teachers who implement appropriate approaches may do more work than teachers using traditional methods, but their work will be more fulfilling, empowering teachers and students to take control of the curricula and the entire educational experience. In a classroom where textbooks or "canned" curricula are used, teachers are reduced to technicians who simply implement preplanned lessons. Teachers should be leaders, developers of curricula, and an empowered part of the child's educational experience rather than a mechanical vessel that presents information.

- I know that children should have many opportunities for choice and exploration, but I am concerned that the lack of structure will lead to behavioral problems in the classroom.

Through careful planning and implementation of a child-centered curriculum, many behavioral problems common to traditional classrooms may be reduced or avoided (Marion, 2007). Children engaged in projects or activities of interest to them will be less likely to demonstrate "bored" or inappropriate behavior. All classrooms need limits and guidelines to ensure both the safety of children and a positive experience for everyone involved. Classrooms can be flexible and spontaneous and still have clearly defined behavioral expectations and consequences (Kostelnik, Soderman, & Whiren, 2007). This will provide a consistent and predictable environment for children, allowing them to make informed decisions, appropriate choices, and to stay on task.

One goal of early childhood education is to foster the development of social competence in children (Brophy-Herb, Lee, Nievar, & Stollak, 2007; Han & Kemple, 2006; McClelland, Acock, & Morrison, 2006). Good teachers view themselves as facilitators of this process, as children develop such traits as self-discipline, self-control, autonomy, and intrinsic motivation. Thus, behavior guidance in a child-centered classroom may look different than in classrooms where teachers regard themselves as authority figures that dispense external rewards and punishments (see Figure 4.1 for a comparison). Instead, many teachers may find that advanced planning and sensitivity to children's learning needs and interests is the best defense against inappropriate behavior (Marion, 2007).

- Adding depth to the math curriculum is great, but I have to get through the entire math book by the end of the year.

A textbook is a tool to aid in the development and implementation of curriculum, not the curriculum itself. It is best utilized as a tool or resource to explain basic knowledge, or as an introduction or reference for further exploration and learning. Textbooks should never be the sole basis for learning any subject at any age. They are developed to have a very broad scope, in order to ensure their potential adoption in as many different states and school districts as possible. Therefore, many contain material that may not be part of an individual school district's plan of study. Textbook companies assume that teachers and administrators will choose not to include the section of the book covering superfluous material. In addition, a textbook assumes that all children are at the same level at the same time. Students that are not at the "level" of the book will fall behind while students who are ahead will become bored or restless (Fosnot, 1996).

Teachers need to be the developers of curriculum in their classroom, as they are most familiar with their students and know their abilities, needs, and interests.

	Child-Centered	Behavioral
Role of Teacher	• Facilitator • Community Leader • Builder of Consensus	• Authority figure • Setter of rules • Keeper of answers, rewards, and punishments
View of the Child	• Active participant in the guidance process • As a developing being	• Passive vessel • Bundle of collected behaviors (some bad) • In need of a powerful figure to tell them right from wrong
Classroom Management	• Rules negotiated and created by the children and teacher together • Focus on feelings and emotional development of the child • Attempt to understand the motivation for misbehavior • Avoidance of direct reward and punishment	• Rewards schedules • Punishments • Token economies • Time-out • Restriction of privileges (no recess) • Possible physical punishments • Promoting positive and extinguishing undesirable behaviors
Determinants of Behavior	• Developmental level • External influences (hunger, fatigue, discomfort) • Emotional regulation	• Modeling • Inadvertent reward of an undesirable behavior • Poor environment

Figure 4.1   Guidance Techniques.

The teacher is in the best position to develop a course of study that meets children's needs and promotes their active learning and development. A textbook cannot do any of those things. The end of a textbook lesson should be the beginning of further in-depth investigation, experimentation, and construction.

• I think a child-centered curriculum is great, but the teacher in the next grade is not going to teach that way and I don't want to confuse the children.

No positive classroom experience can be negative. As teachers, we deal with this concern constantly. We work to provide relevant and meaningful experiences for children, only to see the child placed in a less child-centered classroom the next year.

While this is disappointing, disheartening, and sometimes angering, we cannot use this as an excuse for not doing what we know is best for the child.

The high-quality, positive experience that you give a child in your classroom cannot be erased (Fosnot, 1996; Katz & Chard, 2000). Children will learn from their experiences in the child-centered classroom and use these experiences in their later schooling and throughout life. As the child adapts to other teachers' methods and styles, he will always carry with him that positive, active, and fulfilling educational experience.

There are, however, some important things that we can do. We can try to change the attitudes of our colleagues. By becoming advocates for high-quality instruction, we can attempt to change the less appropriate practices of teachers around us. By being able to address our colleagues' "Yeah, but . . ." responses, we can work to improve the future educational settings of the students in our care. We should envision our role in children's education to include not only what happens in our own classroom, but what happens throughout children's entire early childhood experience.

We can also think creatively about our concepts of schooling and grade levels. Many schools incorporate a multiage or **looping** program in primary and elementary grades so that teachers have children in their classes for two consecutive years. Multiage programs have been shown to be beneficial to a positive educational experience for children (George & Lounsbury, 2000; Miletta, 1996). Not only does a teacher have the child for multiple years, but groups of children are stable for longer periods of time. The students' broad range of abilities allows for peer-to-peer teaching, and older or more advanced children have opportunities to help younger or less advanced children.

Teachers can also implement collaborative projects between pre-K–3 classrooms. For example, if the topic for a project is "insects," children could work collaboratively between the grades, in addition to focusing on grade-specific mathematics activities

Projects allow teachers to easily integrate math and other subjects.

Patrick White/Merrill

within the topic. Kindergarteners might compare sizes of different insects and count the body sections, while third graders might compare weights of spiders or study the geometric patterns in webs to learn about angles. The interaction across age groups is a valuable addition to the curriculum and definitely qualifies as best practice for young children (Bacharach, Hasslen, & Anderson, 1995; Chase & Doan, 1996; Kuntz, 2005).

- These "new" approaches sound good, but I am afraid my students' parents will be concerned that I am not doing my job to "teach" their child.

The best way to address parents' concerns is through communication. The more the teacher communicates with parents about what is going on in the classroom, the more likely the parents will recognize the value of a child-centered approach. Our work with parents is just as important as our work with children. Most parents want what is best for their child and the majority of their questions and concerns can be addressed through information, involvement, and empowerment.

Providing parents with information is the first step in gaining their acceptance and support for appropriate practices. Many times, they will become great allies in your efforts to incorporate best practices into your classroom. You can inform them by explaining how you are not only meeting state and local standards, but going beyond the minimum requirements by teaching their child to engage in independent thinking and academic and social problem solving. You can also provide helpful articles to help them understand child development and best practice for young children. Figure 4.2 includes a suggested list of materials that can help parents understand how important best practices are in primary classrooms.

Parents need to know that implementing child-centered practices does not mean decreasing the amount of academic rigor in your classroom. The better you are at communicating that this approach to curriculum development is based on research and knowledge of child development, the more likely they are to support your efforts.

Empower parents to take a hand in their child's education. Work with them to continue investigative work begun at school at home. Inform them about your math

---

NAEYC Position Statements on developmentally appropriate, child-centered schools are available online to distribute to parents. These can help parents see the research and commitment behind what teachers are doing in the classroom. *http://www.naeyc.org/about/positions.asp*

NAEYC also offers a number of brochures that can be ordered through their web site on many different topics including curriculum issues and guidance. Issues of NAEYC's journal *Young Children* also has articles that can be copied and distributed to parents.

Order NAEYC Resource Catalog
http://sales.naeyc.org/Frm_Order_Catalog.aspx

Figure 4.2 Suggested List of Materials That Can Help Parents Begin to Understand How Important Best Practices Are in Primary Classrooms.

activities at school. Encourage them to help their children count money, read the clock, and participate in measuring ingredients while cooking. Assigning homework is a good way to involve families, so make sure that parents know what is happening in the classroom and how to extend that learning at home. Newsletters, e-mails, and even class web pages are great ways to keep parents involved in their child's mathematics learning.

- How can I be sure that children are learning?

Assessment is an integral part of an appropriate curriculum. Assessment helps the teacher to gauge children's learning, and determine how the curriculum needs to be modified for each child. This type of assessment requires more than formal testing. Assessment is too often thought of as a test, usually at the end of a chapter, to see how much information a child has retained. However, tests are not the only form of assessment, and often are not the most effective. Assessment is an ongoing process and needs to occur every day.

Authentic assessment consists of children's work samples; portfolios of their work; and anecdotal, running records that the teacher collects throughout the day. In other words, authentic assessment can be everything that the child makes, says, or does. Teachers and parents can take pictures, collect writings and drawings, and write down mathematical interactions that they have with the child and keep them in a folder. Methods such as these can help parents understand their child's development. Traditional report cards with letter grades or the equivalent are not very descriptive. However, if a teacher has been collecting samples of a child's work for many months in a portfolio, it can be very informative for the parents when they are invited to sit down with the teacher and the child to review the child's learning and development.

This does not mean that formal assessments should be completely eliminated. There may be times when that type of assessment is appropriate. The challenge for the teacher is to decide when formal assessment is really necessary and when it might be more beneficial to use authentic assessment. In most classrooms, assessments come in one form—paper-and-pencil tests that focus on a child's ability to come to a correct answer. Tests have their place, but most assessments in the child-centered classroom should be based on a child's mathematics work, personal development, and achievement; on process rather than product.

A child-centered approach to teaching requires teachers, children, and parents to work together to create an atmosphere of lively engagement in mathematics and the other subjects. Children have a great deal of choice in the process and their individual needs are addressed in the curriculum planning process. However, there is another element of the child-centered classroom that is often overlooked and is vitally important—the physical environment in which these interactions will take place every day. A child-centered approach requires that the teacher pays special attention to the physical environment in the classroom, in order to ensure that the children can interact with materials and others in a constructive manner.

An interactive environment supports an interactive curriculum.

Getty Images, Inc, - PhotoDisc

PREPARATION OF THE CHILD-CENTERED ENVIRONMENT

Preparing the environment for mathematics includes planning, flexibility, and observation skills to follow children's interests and include them in the learning process. Even before the children arrive in the classroom, the teacher needs to decide how it is to be arranged. The way a classroom is prepared tells a lot about how a teacher believes that children learn. Think about a classroom you were in recently. How was it set up, and what does it say about how mathematics is being taught?

Preparing the Environment

Everything that we do in our lives happens in space. Whether outdoors or indoors, space influences how we behave. When walking through a church, temple, or mosque, we whisper and show reverence, but at a water park, we yell, scream, and have fun. We respond very differently to different environments.

When we think about the mathematics classroom environment and the school environment as a whole, what is the message they are sending? From the paint on the walls to the lighting and windows, schools should exalt and project the message that learning is valued. Yet many times this is not the case, especially with school buildings that are older or located in impoverished areas. Teachers may not have control over the school's neighborhood, but they do have control over their own classrooms and how they are set up.

It is your first day at your new school and you are shown to your new classroom. As you look around the room for the first time, you should see it as a blank slate. It

Addition of blocks to primary grade classrooms is rare, but beneficial.

Krista Greco/Merrill

might be bare or already decorated. Either way, it is not ready for you because it is not YOUR classroom. Your goal is to create a vibrant, intellectually stimulating classroom that allows and encourages children's learning and inquiry and also reflects your personal teaching style.

Placement of Teacher's Desk. This is an important and telling decision because it reflects your role in the classroom. Some teachers put the desk front and center, facing the students. What this arrangement lacks in space utilization, it makes up for in a projection of power and authority. In this arrangement, the teacher says, "I am in charge and I am watching you." This teacher is most likely using a direct instruction model of teaching in which she is transmitting knowledge to the students.

Other teachers may choose to put their desks in a corner of the room. This frees up space in front of the chalkboard while retaining the "overseer" status of the teacher. In both of these arrangements, the teacher plans on sitting at the desk as children are engaged in learning. If she plans on moving around the classroom, the desk does not need to face the children.

Other teachers choose to place their desks at the back of the class to free up even more space at the front near the chalkboard for group discussions. The teacher is relinquishing the desk as a symbol of power and instead relegates it to a work space to grade papers and store items that she may need in the course of teaching. Other teachers may choose to arrange their desks among the children's desks to send the message that "we are all in this learning process together." This works best if the children's desks are not arranged in rows. You might want to do away with the teacher's desk all together. If so, you will need to find places to store all the things you need for teaching.

Arrangement of Children's Desks or Tables. Effective mathematics instruction allows children to discuss problems and solutions with their classmates. They should have ample opportunity to look at each other's faces. In traditional settings, the desks are in rows and the only face they get to see is the teacher's. This sends the subtle signal that the only information that matters is that which comes from the teacher.

What other arrangements might work better? One example is a double horseshoe arrangement, as shown in Figure 4.3. This is effective because it leaves a lot of open space in front of the chalkboard or whiteboard for children to work on problems or play math games on the floor. It also gives the teacher room to interact with them in a more natural way.

Another suggestion is the pod approach, as illustrated in Figure 4.4. This is where four desks are placed in a "pod" arrangement, or tables with space for four chairs are used. Both arrangements allow children to face one another. These arrangements work well for mathematics instruction because they facilitate group work, and allow the teacher to assist students individually or in small groups. Presenting problems that involve discussion and group problem solving is very easy to manage in this type of arrangement.

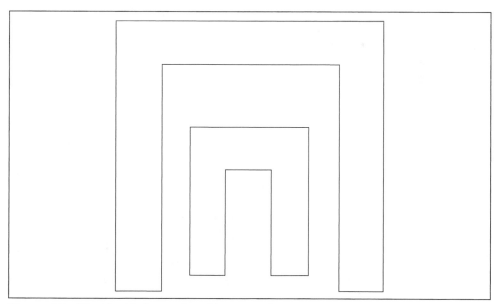

Figure 4.3   The Double Horseshoe Classroom Arrangement.

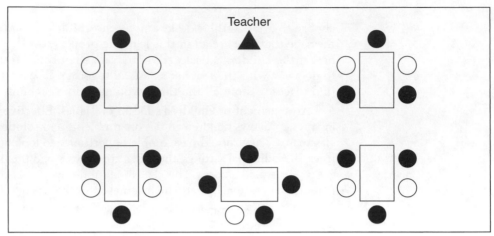

Figure 4.4   Pod.

Tips for Ownership
1) Allow children to make their own rules
2) Allow children to decorate their desks using their own style
3) Use pictures of children whenever possible
4) Give students a say in decisions about the classroom or major events
5) Use voting as a strategy for making decisions
6) If using bulletin boards, allow children to plan, design, and construct the content of the board
7) Avoid an overreliance on "store bought" or "premade" decorations. Let the children plan and design the classroom materials
8) Develop a homelike environment rather than an institutional one. Include cozy spaces as well as work spaces; quiet spaces as well as noisy areas
9) Allow for social interaction among students at appropriate times
10) Bring your students' cultural diversity and home life into the classroom as much as possible

---

MATERIALS

After setting up your physical space, the next thing you will need is materials. Choosing the materials you need in your classroom is as important as setting up your environment and knowing your students. Just as the environmental setup reflects a teacher's method of teaching mathematics, the materials he or she chooses reflects his or her philosophy of mathematics education as well. If the teacher only has math textbooks and piles of worksheets, that teacher is probably going to have children sitting at their desks quietly doing worksheets, which is considered a direct instruction approach.

Interaction between students is vital for construction of mathematics.

Scott Cunningham/Merrill

Integrating Music, Art, and Physical Education

Music
   1) Use beat to help young children count in steady time
   2) Use rhythm to help children see the patterns in the world around them
   3) Use melodies to help children with memory tasks (such as multiplication tables)

Art
   1) Use children's drawings to emphasize the use and names of different shapes
   2) Use creative art activities to encourage and strengthen representational abilities
   3) Use sculpture to help children work with three-dimensional shapes

Physical Education
   1) Use physical games to help children use mathematics in their everyday activity
   2) Physical play offers opportunities for children to use problem-solving skills in a social situation
   3) Large motor activity such as building with large hollow blocks offers many opportunities for numerical and shape comparisons

---

In order to foster interaction, discussion, and problem solving in the classroom, you will have to choose your materials more carefully. This does not mean avoiding textbooks and worksheets, but does mean including materials that allow more flexibility and variety in how you implement your mathematics teaching strategy. In the following discussions we will first address various types of manipulatives, which are appropriate for all ages. Then we will discuss math series textbooks used in kindergarten and the primary grades.

Manipulatives

Manipulatives are a buzzword for teaching mathematics. Supply houses and sales representatives will extol the virtues of "hands-on" and "3D" objects. While manipulatives can be great to have in your classroom, it is the mathematical thinking fostered by the manipulative that is important (Kamii, Joseph, & Livingston, 2003; Kamii & National Association for the Education of Young Children, 1982; Kamii, O'Brien, Southern Illinois University, 1980). In other words, the math is not "in" the manipulative, it is in the child's mind (Kamii & National Association for the Education of Young Children, 1982).

When selecting any manipulative, you should remember that teaching math is not about "seeing" or "touching," nor is it about cute objects. It is all about how you are going to get children to THINK about mathematics. You should be asking yourself how you and the children are going to use the objects. In subsequent chapters, we will discuss at length how these items can be used, but for now here is a list of the basics.

- **Counters**—A counter is any object that children can count. Supply houses make these in many different shapes and colors to entice you, the teacher, to buy different sets for different classroom "themes." Shapes like teddy bears, dinosaurs, monkeys, trucks, dogs, and pumpkins are all available, but you only really need one set (maybe two if you have a large class). There is no need to buy a different set for each season.

- **Chips**—Chips can be seen as a kind of counter, but they can be used in different ways. They can be stacked and moved around easily, and can be used in math games where counters might not work as well. Plastic poker chips of various sizes and colors are great to have around the classroom. Chips can be used for demonstrations, in problem solving, and even in creating problems.

- **Decks of Cards**—Card games are a great way to promote mathematical thinking. One of my favorite activities is a game called "double war" where each child pulls two cards from his pile and whoever has the greater sum gets to take the pile. This activity focuses on repetition and fluency. While a teacher could teach these skills with worksheets, students often self-select to play this game. Since cards have numerals and the corresponding amount of suit markers (hearts, diamonds, clubs, and spades), they are valuable for all sorts of mathematics. One caveat you need to be aware of: a standard card has an extra suit marker under the numeral. Children counting ALL the markers will end up with two more than they should. You can try using white out to cover up these extra markers however, some stores do offer special cards without them.

- **Blocks**—A basic set of wooden building blocks is appropriate for preschool, kindergarten, and grades one to three. Block play is an excellent mathematical and spatial activity that is child-selected and directed. Concepts such as measurement, spatial ability, counting, and planning, as well as gross and fine motor ability and social-emotional development are all rolled up into block play. Block play is also very open-ended. It draws on children's creativity and imagination and allows them to incorporate their knowledge into a play situation (Adams & Nesmith, 1996; Hewitt, 2001; Moore, 1997; Phelps & Hanline, 1999; Pickett, 1998; Reifel, 1995;

*Curriculum development is a
group effort.*

Stephens, 1995; Stritzel, 1995; Weiss, 1997; Wolfgang, Jones, & Stannard, 2001). Soft blocks and shapes can be introduced into infant and toddler classrooms. Babies use their senses and motor activity to explore their world, so giving them items they can look at, touch, stack, squeeze, and throw will emphasize the development of early mathematical abilities (Wittmer & Petersen, 2006).

- **Board Games**—Games like Sorry, Parcheesi, Chutes and Ladders, Monopoly Junior, and Monopoly are great ways to foster mathematics. With a bit of modification, these games can take the place of individual seatwork using worksheets. For example, replace the cards in Sorry with number cubes or cards that require a mathematical function. One benefit is that other children playing the game act as assessors, not letting another child get away with moving too many spaces in the game. While these games are readily available at stores, you can create your own materials. All you need are a few counters, a piece of poster board, and some number cubes. Draw a path from "Start" to "Finish" in any winding shape you like (such as a pumpkin for Halloween).

- **Number Cubes**—Number cubes come not only as standard 6-sided cubes, but in all shapes, sizes, and number combinations, including 4-sided, 8-sided, 10-sided, 12-sided, 20-sided, and even 24-sided. Using various number cubes can help children learn about three-dimensional solids. You can also change the character and complexity of a game by replacing the number cube set. Blank number cubes are available that you can put anything on, such as multiples of three, pips (the dots on the number cubes) in nonstandard patterns that encourage children to count or even function symbols like $+$, $-$, $\times$, and %. For example, children throwing two numerical number cubes and one function number cube do whatever functions come up. A 10-sided number cube labeled with multiples of 10 can help children learn place value.

- **Puzzles**—If you look at any intelligence test, many of the "mental flexibility" questions deal with mentally rotating shapes. Two- and three-dimensional puzzles and tangrams offer children the experience of interacting with these types of activities in a play situation. Children must mentally rotate different shapes in many different planes to solve a puzzle. Mental imagery helps the child with mental mathematics and geometry activities. Much of mathematics can be represented in graphs and charts and many calculus problems represent very complex visualizations.

- **Recycled Materials**—There are many useful items that you, your students, and their parents throw out every day. Pill bottles and caps, liter-sized plastic bottle tops, egg cartons, milk jugs, and so on can all be used to create mathematical experiences. Other things that are thrown away also have math in or on them. For example, most packaged food items have nutritional information on the packaging. Before the child throws it out, why not look at it mathematically?

This should give you a start on collecting math materials and manipulatives for your classroom. Paper, pencils, calculators, and computers are also good to have. While paper and pencils are often impossible to live without in a classroom, calculators and computers, despite popular opinion, are not necessary to develop a good math program.

Textbooks and Math Series

Almost every school and school district uses math series or textbooks to guide and implement a mathematics program in kindergarten through grade 3. Many popular series are distributed by Scott Foresman, Saxon Math, SRA, Sadlier-Oxford, McGraw-Hill, and other major publishers. These series divide the learning objectives for each grade level into small, related chunks. They include a teacher's manual and suggestions for teaching. The teacher's manual always includes a "Scope and Sequence" chart that tells what topics the book or series covers, and in what order.

As a teacher, it is your job to not just use a textbook that is plopped down in front of you by a school board or state selection committee. The teacher's manual is an important resource for more than just teaching procedures. It should also give you hints as to the teaching philosophy of that series. Some series are more process-based and others use more direct instruction. Some series are even laid out in a "script" format. In these cases, the teacher basically reads from a script and assigns related things. She has no flexibility or choice, and is just a technician reading and implementing someone else's words. Judging by the five principles of a good environment, this is not a good thing.

There are a number of things that you need to consider when presented with a math textbook.

- **What is the philosophy of the book?** Each book is constructed accordingly to a specific idea of how mathematics is learned. Sometimes these philosophies are based on developmental theory, as we discussed in previous chapters. Other times the philosophy is more pragmatic and practical in nature. Either way, you should critically examine the series and decide how it fits with your personal philosophy of mathematics education.

- **How does the textbook relate to your state's mathematics standards?** Every state has its own set of standards that lay out what children should learn in each grade. Since most textbooks are marketed in all 50 states, they often include more material than your state requires.

- **How can you expand on the book's lessons?** Textbooks are the beginning of developing mathematics lessons, not the end. Teaching math is more than just following the book and handing out worksheets or following a premade script. Many books require strict adherence to scope and sequence, while others allow for more creativity and innovation on the teacher's part. Some school districts and schools may be more stringent regarding the freedom teachers have to develop additional lessons or skip around in the textbook. Either way, these textbooks should be used as resources and guides rather than as a complete curriculum.

- **Could you teach mathematics without a book?** This may seem like a strange question, but it helps you think about exactly why you need a book in the first place. If your answer is "Yes," then you can try to move ahead with less direction from the text. However, you will most likely say "No," in which case you need to ask, "Why do I need the book?" This will help you to select and use the most useful aspects of your text.

- **How does this textbook foster a good home–school relationship?** A good mathematics program will involve parents as much as possible in their child's learning of mathematics. Too many parents pass on their negative feelings toward mathematics if a textbook is too confusing. We want to avoid this if at all possible. Instead we want parents saying, "If I had been taught math this way, I would have really enjoyed it!"

- **How does the textbook provide lessons and activities for the individual differences and levels of your children?** Teachers of mathematics must ensure that their curriculum is relevant to all students and meets each student at his developmental level. Many textbooks primarily measure student success through tests. These books' lessons tend to be focused at the level of children who achieve at the middle of the class. Therefore, children who are significantly ahead are bored, and those who are significantly behind are lost and usually do poorly on tests. Children are individuals with unique needs and strengths. As a teacher, you need to be ready to teach them no matter what their level of mathematical understanding.

WHAT TO DO BEFORE THE FIRST DAY

If this is your first day teaching, understand that you will feel overwhelmed. You will be nervous, anxious, frightened, uninformed, underprepared, and experience a multitude of other feelings. Even after a few years, the first day of school will still give you butterflies. You need to be sure that you are ready well before that first day. Here is a checklist of things you should do before the first day of class.

Prepare a Letter Home to Parents About How You Intend to Teach Mathematics. This is especially important if you plan on doing some of the more child-centered and constructivist things that we propose in this book. This is appropriate no matter what age children you will be teaching. If you are teaching K–3, include the title of the textbook series you will be using and discuss how you plan to use it. Also include your contact information, including a phone number and perhaps an e-mail address where the parents can reach you for questions. Let parents know what you expect from their children in class and at home, and what you expect the parents' role to be in the mathematics education of their child. You can also ask for any items such as manipulatives the families might be able to supply.

Review Your Textbook. Review your textbook, the textbook's scope and sequence chart, and your state's standards for instruction, usually found on your state's Department of Education web site. Determine which lessons are vitally important for your state and which you can spend less time on or omit altogether. Reviewing the textbook should become a vital tool in your lesson planning. Also, judge the quality of the lessons presented and ask yourself if you could come up with a lesson that achieves the same outcome in a more child-centered, engaging, and motivational way. Determine whether the book's activity or your own activity has a better chance of achieving the standard.

> Mrs. Reyes had used the same third-grade textbook series for three years and wanted to find a more interactive way to do some of the activities. This book provided daily worksheets for the students to practice fluency. The children did not look forward to the time they had to spend doing the worksheets, but Mrs. Reyes felt that the practice was important. Because she wanted more student engagement, activity, and discussion she made the worksheets a group activity. Children worked in groups of three and discussed different ways to solve each problem on the sheet. Everyone in the group had to understand how they got the answer before moving on to the next problem. She found that children were coming up with very innovative ways to solve the problems and to explain their methods so others in the group could understand. She was a bit concerned about how loud her classroom had become during math time and worried about what other teachers or even her principal might think, so she made sure to document what was happening in the groups through pictures, collections of their work, and narrative observations.

Talk to Your Principal or Administrator. Get to know the administration at your school and its educational philosophy and personality. If the school administrators such as the principal, the assistant principal, or the curriculum director are strict and dogmatic, you may be required to follow the book and conform to a "party line" teaching strategy. However, most principals are willing to look for innovative ways to teach and make their school exemplary. When you meet with your principal to discuss your ideas for your mathematics program, be prepared to support your ideas with research and efficacy studies. Talk to him or her about the textbook and what you learned while reviewing it, and discuss state standards and the priorities of the school district. You may also ask about opportunities for additional materials, continuing education, or further training.

Talk to Other Teachers in the School. You will find a wide range of personalities and philosophies. Some may even try to "tempt you to the dark side of the Force." Don't underestimate the power of the "Dark Side." It is alluring in its simplicity and ease. The "Dark Side" is populated by teachers who have given up on research or exploring what works best for them. They have been seduced by the ease of ready-made worksheets, the ability to teach with little planning or understanding of students' needs, and the power of asserting domination over a classroom. Most insidious is their ability to turn new teachers to the dark side through the simple words, "forget what you learned in college, this is the real world." Avoid their negative energy and find teachers who are still excited about teaching children and trying new things. Create study groups or group planning sessions one night a week, perhaps at a local restaurant to be a little festive. In your first few years, it will be difficult to do everything you want to do in your mathematics program to make it constructivist and child-centered. Having a support group of others who think similarly can help you achieve your goals.

When Planning Lessons for Mathematics, Begin with the Mathematics Standards. Planning for instruction is the most important thing teachers do. Time spent planning is never wasted. Planning, however, does not just mean making a lesson plan. It includes researching a topic; gauging interest from students; assessing the ability levels of students in the class; and linking the idea to national, state and local standards. A good lesson plan begins with a good objective. The objective of the lesson is the most important part of the teaching and planning process. Why are you doing this lesson? What do you want children to learn from this lesson? What standards are you trying to meet with this lesson? These are all questions that a teacher must ask when thinking of the objective. You can use your state's standard of instruction manual to help with this. However, there may be others that are not in the manual.

Perhaps select one standard to be your primary objective, such as "sort, classify, and order objects by size, number, and other properties." Develop an activity or lesson around that objective. After you have made a first draft, go back to the mathematics standards for your state. Are there any other standards that you can include in your lesson? While you might need to adjust your initial idea, this usually improves the lesson. Next, go to the standards documents for Language Arts, Social Studies, Science, and even Art and Music to see if there are any related standards you can include in your mathematics lesson. This type of planning will lead to a multidimensional lesson that engages children on many levels.

Example: A lesson whose primary objective is to promote understanding of all the different combinations that make the number six can be combined with other objectives such as art and science. Have kindergarten children work in pairs. First, the teacher takes the children on a nature walk, looking at leaves and insects. Back in the classroom, the children draw and color pictures of one of the leaves they saw on their walk. Each child then draws pictures of three insects he saw on small, one-inch circles, one insect per circle. The children then put their three insects on their leaf. The teacher then says "Can you and your partner put the ladybugs on the leaves another way? How many different arrangements can you find?" (Note: $1 + 5$ and $5 + 1$ are different arrangements.) The students' findings are recorded on the chalkboard, and they are encouraged to find the patterns that emerge by the teacher asking "How do you know if you found all possible arrangements of six?" (Example: The first number gets smaller by 1, the second number gets larger by 1, and the answer is always 6.)

Other Standard Items to Include in Lesson Plans. In addition to the objective, there are some other standard things that need to be included in the lesson plan. There are many different formats, and while your school may require you to format lesson plans differently, they will generally include the items listed and described here (which is the format we use in Chapters 5–8 for children of different ages).

- Name of the Lesson
- Grade Level—What grade or age group is this lesson for?
- NCTM Standards met—This may seem redundant, but better to say it twice. Remember these are the most important parts of this document.
- Materials—List all the materials you will need for this activity. You will want to make sure you have access to all of these materials well in advance.
- Initiating the Lesson—This is how you, as a teacher, will tap into children's prior knowledge. This has two purposes. First, it helps to build interest and excitement in the children because they will see how this activity is relevant to their own lives. Second, it allows you to gauge the level of understanding the children have about your proposed topic. You may need to adapt or revise your initial plans based on what you learn. Remember, flexibility leads to taking advantage of teachable moments. For example, a teacher might start a lesson on coins by bringing in some coins and asking the children to talk about what they know about them. "How much are they worth?" "What are they called?" "Who is on the front?" "What is on the back?" "Where do the coins come from?" and "Have you ever seen coins that look different?" Perhaps, even coins from other countries could be introduced.
- Procedure—This is where you describe the activity and how it is to be implemented. Pretend you are writing it for a substitute teacher who will have to carry out the lesson. Write it in the first person such as "Have the children find a partner or two. Each group of children should select two nonstandard units to measure how tall they are. That way you will be sure to be detailed. Be sure to include any preparations you will need to make before the day of the lesson."

- Assessment—This is the second most important aspect of a lesson plan. How are you going to know if your students actually met the objectives you set out at the beginning of the document? Assessment can be anything from a paper-and-pencil test to direct observation of the child or small group of children. Assessment is more than just testing. You can keep detailed notes about your student's problem-solving methods, take photos of the learning process, and develop a portfolio of the children's work. In assessing mathematics, it is important to know whether a child can produce a correct answer, but also to assess his mathematical thinking process. There are many different paths to get to the same endpoint. By examining those paths we get a better picture of the child's ability and progress (assessment will be discussed for various ages and grades in Chapters 5–8).

- Extensions—How can this activity be extended into future lessons or other subject areas? I suggest that you make sure that the lesson itself is linked with everyday usage, as well as adding a piece about how to extend the lesson into everyday activities.

- Adaptations—How can the lesson be adapted for children with special needs (those who are gifted or with attention deficit disorder or with physical disabilities)? How can the lesson be adapted to accommodate students who do not speak English as their first language, as they struggle with terminology or comprehension of instructions or steps?

Acknowledge Your Limitations and Learn from Experience. Many teachers go into a classroom with grand plans and dreams, not seeing the obstacles that lay between their plans and reality. To teach effectively in a child-centered and constructivist way, you need to see the obstacles in order to avoid them. There is one last limitation to be aware of—yourself. Teachers go through changes as they develop professionally. At each stage a teacher must realize what his or her professional needs are, in order to continue to grow and develop in the profession (Helm & Katz, 2001; Katz & Chard, 2000).

- **Survival Stage**—Teachers in the survival stage feel overwhelmed by the job of teaching. They ask questions like "Can I make it until the end of the week?" or "Can I really do this work day after day?" It is difficult for survivors to be reflective or concerned about children's needs in the classroom because they are focused on their own needs and survival. Survivors tend to place blame rather than look for solutions themselves. These feelings are normal for a teacher's first few years. Gauge how ambitious you can be in your lesson development and planning. You may find that you use worksheets and rely on direct textbook instruction more than you would prefer. Realize that you will move on from being a survivor to the next stage, when you will be able to do more.

- **Consolidation Stage**—After one or two years in the survival stage, you should feel more comfortable as a teacher. As you continue to develop, you begin to consolidate what you have learned. Teachers in the consolidation stage begin to focus on instruction and curriculum. They may ask questions like, "How can I help a child who does not seem to be learning?" or "How can I deal with a child with a specific discipline problem?" Teachers in this stage effectively implement class rules and routines, and have lessons that meet the differing needs of their students. Gather support and develop relationships with other teachers in order to discuss your teaching and begin growing.

- **Renewal Stage**—Teachers in the consolidation stage will often reach a point referred to as "burn out." Many choose to quit teaching after a few years and change professions. Without renewal, teaching can become monotonous and unfulfilling. Teachers in the renewal stage ask questions such as, "What new materials, techniques, approaches, and ideas can I try in my classroom?" or "What is the teacher with my specialization doing in the next building?" or "What ideas have emerged since I was last in class?" Renewal teachers often pursue professional development opportunities, attend conferences, or become members of professional associations. At this stage, consider examining your teaching through videotaping or action research projects. Visit other classes and welcome visitors to your classroom to get new ideas from your peers and to share your own.

- **Maturity Stage**—Mature teachers are leaders in their field. Respected by other teachers and administrators, they begin to ask questions of themselves and their teaching that focus on insights, perspectives, and beliefs about teaching children. Teachers in the maturity stage are still interested in new ideas and resources; however, they begin to ask deeper questions about their philosophy of teaching and the impact they make in and out of the school setting. These questions might include, "How will schools change society?" or "What is my role to assist in change?"

SUMMARY

Now that you know how to prepare for teaching mathematics, all that is left to learn is what should be taught to each student in each grade level. You should now be able to pull together all your resources in preparation for your first day in the classroom.

Don't panic when you think about your first day in the classroom. It is natural to feel overwhelmed, but you will make it. Your planning and preparation process will have started long before that moment. Incorporate a child-centered approach to teaching mathematics in your classroom. This involves finding ways to make sure that the individuality of each of your students is reflected in the curriculum. While there are many difficulties in implementing child-centered mathematics programs, with work and conviction you will overcome any doubts and become better able to support children working and acting as young mathematicians.

Preparing your environment effectively will make the planning and teaching process much easier. The way you position your desk and arrange the students' workspace will have an impact on how you teach mathematics. Develop a sense of ownership in your classroom and make your spaces defensible, relevant, responsive, and significant.

The materials that you select for your classroom also will help you to develop a child-centered classroom. Textbooks are a useful tool, but relying on them as your sole resource will lead to a very limited mathematics experience for your students. Learn how to analyze your textbook and use it most effectively. Supplement it with materials such as counters, chips, decks of cards, blocks, board games, number cubes, puzzles, nonstandard forms of measurement (such as string, rope, toothpicks), math games, items from nature, and other materials.

Preparing before your first day by sending letters to parents and talking to your principal and other teachers will help you to feel a part of the school and give you an idea of what is expected of you. You should also begin the planning process and think about curriculum, relevance, standards, lesson planning, and how to engage and maintain interest. Finally, you need to recognize that you are empowered to make a change. As a teacher you need to take charge. Your students' education depends on the choices you make. Be prepared and ready to make the right ones.

WEB SITES

NCTM e_Resources—Teaching Children Mathematics Home
http://my.nctm.org/eresources/journal_home.asp?journal_id=4

Resources for teaching math from NCTM.

National Mathematics Advisory Panel
http://www.ed.gov/about/bdscomm/list/mathpanel/index.html

This is the web site for the National Mathematics Advisory Board. It is important for teachers to know what is going on with this group. The panel advises the president and secretary of education on the best use of scientifically based research on the teaching and learning of mathematics.

Math Forum: Teacher2Teacher (T2T)
http://www.mathforum.org/t2t/

Teacher2Teacher is a resource for teachers and parents who have questions about teaching mathematics.

Teach-nology
http://www.teach-nology.com/

A collection of worksheets, Teaching Tips, Teacher Resources, Lesson Plans, and Rubrics from Teach-nology.com to help teachers develop interactive mathematics programs.

Teacher Resources by Annenberg Media
http://www.learner.org/index.html

A searchable database of information from Annenberg Media. Search by discipline and by grade.

FREE—Federal Resources for Educational Excellence
http://www.free.ed.gov/

A goldmine of educational resources, many of them free.

U.S. Department of Education—Mathematics and Science Partnerships Program
http://www.ed-msp.net/protected/index.jsp?.lat=null

The goal of the MSP program is to improve academic achievements of elementary and secondary students in mathematics and science by increasing instructional quality.

DISCUSS AND APPLY WHAT YOU HAVE LEARNED

Reflect

1. Why might teachers resist a child-centered approach? List three possible objections to this approach and responses to each.
2. Do you feel prepared to implement a child-centered mathematics curriculum?

Discuss

1. What fears do you have about your first year of teaching?
2. What aspects of mathematics teaching do you feel most prepared to do? Least prepared?
3. List and describe some ways to engage interest and make lessons relevant to young children's interest.

Apply

1. On a piece of graph paper, design a preschool classroom layout. Why did you choose that particular layout? How does it facilitate the teaching of math? Point out the five different categories of space discussed in this chapter.
2. Identify one of your state's mathematics standards for a particular age group or grade and develop a practice mathematics lesson around it. Develop the lesson plan as described in this chapter.
3. Write a "first-day" letter to students' parents based on how you plan to teach mathematics. Share it in groups or with the whole class. What kinds of things do you think parents need to know? What would you not tell them?
4. How would you explain your philosophy of mathematics education to your principal? What if he or she is resistant? How could you go about convincing him?
5. How might you ensure that you don't get "stuck" in one of the stages of teacher development? In other words, what is your plan to develop to the *maturity stage*?

Observe

1. Observe a new teacher and a seasoned teacher in action. What differences do you see between the two?

2. Observe any early childhood classroom. What elements of the mathematical teaching you observe are child-centered? What do you see that is not child-centered and what changes would you make?

REFERENCES

Adams, P. K., & Nesmith, J. (1996). Blockbusters: Ideas for the block center. *Early Childhood Education Journal, 24,* 87–92.

Bacharach, N., Hasslen, R. C., & Anderson, J. (1995). *Learning together: A manual for multiage grouping.* Thousand Oaks, CA: Corwin Press.

Brophy-Herb, H. E., Lee, R. E., Nievar, M. A., & Stollak, G. (2007). Preschoolers' social competence: Relations to family characteristics, teacher behaviors and classroom climate. *Journal of Applied Developmental Psychology, 28*(2), 134–148.

Byrnes, J. P. (2003). Factors predictive of mathematics achievement in white, black, and Hispanic 12th graders. *Journal of Educational Psychology, 95*(2), 316.

Cain, J. S. (2002). An evaluation of the connected mathematics project. *Journal of Educational Research, 95*(4), 224.

Chase, P., & Doan, J. (1996). *Choosing to learn: Ownership and responsibility in a primary multiage classroom.* Portsmouth, NH: Heinemann.

Derman-Sparks, L. (1993). Empowering children to create a caring culture in a world of differences. *Childhood Education, 70*(2), 66.

Elkind, D., & Piaget, J. (1979). *Child development and education: A Piagetian perspective.* New York: Oxford University Press.

Fosnot, C. T. (1996). *Constructivism theory, perspectives, and practice.* New York: Teachers College Press.

George, P. S., & Lounsbury, J. H. (2000). *Making big schools feel small: Multiage grouping, looping, and schools-within-a-school.* Westerville, OH: National Middle School Assn.

Han, H., & Kemple, K. (2006). Components of social competence and strategies of support: Considering what to teach and how. *Early Childhood Education Journal, 34*(3), 241–246.

Heiney, C. J. (1998). *Effect of problem of the day on Ohio ninth grade proficiency test mathematics scores.* Unpublished Masters, Salem-Teikyo University, Salem, West Virginia.

Helm, J. H., & Beneke, S. (2003). *The power of projects: Meeting contemporary challenges in early childhood classrooms—Strategies and solutions.* New York: Teachers College Press.

Helm, J. H., & Katz, L. (2001). *Young investigators: The project approach in the early years.* New York: Teachers College Press.

Hewitt, K. (2001). Blocks as a tool for learning: Historical and contemporary perspectives. *Young Children, 56*(1), 6–13.

Kamii, C. (1984). *Autonomy as the aim of childhood education: A Piagetian approach.* Galesburg, IL: Knox AV.

Kamii, C., & Chemeketa Community College. (1982). *Piagetian research on how children construct number concepts.* Salem, OR: Chemeketa Community College.

Kamii, C., Clark, F. B., Housman, L. B., & Teachers College Press. (2000). First graders dividing 62 by 5: A teacher uses Piaget's theory. New York: Distributed by Teachers College Press.

Kamii, C., & DeVries, R. (1976). *Piaget, children, and number: Applying Piaget's theory to the teaching of elementary number*. Washington, DC: National Association for the Education of Young Children.

Kamii, C., Joseph, L. L., & Livingston, S. J. (2003). *Young children continue to reinvent arithmetic—2nd grade implications of Piaget's theory*. New York: Teachers College Press.

Kamii, C., & National Association for the Education of Young Children. (1982). *Number in preschool and kindergarten: Educational implications of Piaget's theory*. Washington, DC: National Association for the Education of Young Children.

Kamii, C., O'Brien, T. C., Teacher Center, Southern Illinois University at Edwardsville. (1980). *What do children learn when they manipulate objects?* Edwardsville, IL: The Teachers' Center Project, Southern Illinois University at Edwardsville.

Katz, L., & Chard, S. C. (2000). *Engaging children's minds: The project approach* (2nd ed.). Stamford, CT.: Ablex Pub. Corp.

Kitchens, A. N. (1995). *Defeating math anxiety*. Chicago: Irwin Career Education Division.

Kostelnik, M., Soderman, A., & Whiren, A. (2007). *Developmentally appropriate curriculum: Best practices in early childhood education* (4th ed.). Upper Saddle River, NJ: Merrill/Prentice Hall.

Kuntz, S. (2005). *The story of Alpha: A multiage, student-centered team, 33 years and counting*. Westerville, OH: National Middle School Association.

Marion, M. (2007). *Guidance of young children* (7th ed.). Upper Saddle River, NJ: Merrill/Prentice Hall.

McClelland, M. M., Acock, A. C., & Morrison, F. J. (2006). The impact of kindergarten learning-related skills on academic trajectories at the end of elementary school. *Early Childhood Research Quarterly, 21*(4), 471–490.

Miletta, M. M. (1996). *A multiage classroom: choice and possibility*. Portsmouth, NH: Heinemann.

Moore, G. T. (1997). A place for block play. *Child Care Information Exchange*, (115), 73–77.

New, R. S. (1999). What should children learn? making choices and taking chances. *Early Childhood Research & Practice, 1*(2), 15.

New, R. S. (2003). Reggio emilia: New ways to think about schooling. *Educational Leadership, 60*(7).

Parker, K. (1999). The impact of the textbook on girls' perception of mathematics. *Mathematics in School, 28*(4), 2.

Phelps, P., & Hanline, M. F. (1999). Let's play blocks!: Creating effective learning experiences for young children. *Teaching Exceptional Children, 32*(2), 62–67.

Pickett, L. (1998). Literacy learning during block play. *Journal of Research in Childhood Education, 12*(2), 225–230.

Reifel, S. (1995). Enriching the possibilities of block play. *Child Care Information Exchange*, (103), 48–50.

Schoenfeld, A. H. (2002). Making mathematics work for all children: Issues of standards, testing, and equity. *Educational Researcher, 31*(1), 13.

Stephens, K. (1995). Resources on block play: On the floor with kids! Teachers as block play partners. *Child Care Information Exchange* (103), 54.

Stritzel, K. (1995). Block play is for all children. *Child Care Information Exchange,* (103) 42.

Stuart, V. B. (2000). Math curse or math anxiety? *Teaching Children Mathematics,* 6(5), 330.

Weiss, K. (1997). Let's build! *Scholastic Early Childhood Today, 12,* 30–32.

Wittmer, D. S., & Petersen, S. H. (2006). *Infant and toddler development and responsive program planning.* Upper Saddle River, NJ: Merrill/Prentice Hall.

Wolfgang, C. H., Jones, I., & Stannard, L. L. (2001). Block play performance among preschoolers as a predictor of later school achievement in mathematics. *Journal of Research in Childhood Education, 15*(2), 173–180.

CHAPTER 5

Infants and Toddlers

CHAPTER OBJECTIVES

After you have read this chapter, you should be able to:

- Describe what infants and toddlers are like physically, cognitively, emotionally, and socially
- Identify what mathematical concepts infants and toddlers are learning
- Explain the importance of the NAEYC–NCTM Joint Statement on Early Childhood Mathematics
- Demonstrate optimal ways of arranging environments to effectively support mathematics for infants and toddlers
- Develop developmentally appropriate mathematics activities for infants and toddlers
- Explain the role of the teacher and the parent in the learning of mathematics in infancy and toddlerhood

Now that we have laid the foundation of teaching mathematics in the early childhood years, it is time to move on to some of the practical aspects. Chapters 5 through 8 will cover material related to teaching mathematics to children from birth through third grade. We will begin by examining mathematics with infants and toddlers.

NAEYC and NCTM produced a joint statement on teaching mathematics in early childhood entitled *Early Childhood Mathematics: Promoting Good Beginnings* (NAEYC, 2004). In this document, the basic philosophy governing the standards for prekindergarten mathematics is presented in light of NCTM's *Principles for School Mathematics.* To help achieve the goal of developmentally appropriate and engaging mathematics for the early years, the position statement sets forth 10 research-based essential recommendations to guide classroom practice. It also recommends four goals for policies, system-wide changes, and other actions needed to support standards-based, developmentally appropriate mathematics teaching.

This statement's focus is on children over age three, primarily because there is more research on mathematical learning for this age group. However, research indicates that infants and toddlers, age birth to 36 months (3 years), enjoy and benefit from various kinds of mathematical explorations and experiences as well (Brannon, Lutz, & Cordes, 2006; Spelke & Kinzler, 2007; Wynn, 2000; Xu, Spelke, & Goddard, 2005). Additionally, the basic principles of the position statement can be applied to infant and toddler mathematical learning because they deal with the active, environmental, and experiential learning of mathematics. Infants and toddlers construct mathematics through interaction with their environment and with objects in that environment. These mathematical constructions, while vitally important, often go unnoticed by the adults around the child.

WHAT ARE INFANTS AND TODDLERS LIKE?

Infants and toddlers are interesting to observe. They need a lot of care and nurturing from a responsive adult and, for the most part, their whole world revolves around adult caregivers (Lally et al., 2001; Lally & California Dept. of Education, 1990; Lally, Mangione, & Young-Holt, 1992; Lally & Zero to Three, 2003).

Socially, infants and toddlers are mainly attached to their parent or primary caregiver. However, by 5 months, they do begin to reach out socially to others, vocalizing to each other and even smiling and laughing in social situations. At 8 months, they begin to show objects to each other and play together. At 18–24 months, children begin to develop friendships and will offer toys and food to another child. They begin to take turns playing with objects. By 24–36 months of age, children are exchanging information about objects and experiences. They readily invent new ways of doing things and can work with peers to achieve common goals.

Physically, children in the first two years of life grow faster than at any other period of development (Santrock, 2005). They consume vast amounts of calories and gain weight at phenomenal rates (Lamb, Bornstein, Teti, & NetLibrary Inc., 2002). During this time their gross motor skills, which use large muscle groups that allow the child to crawl, sit, stand, and lift things, develop to the point where many children are proficient at walking within the first year of life. Their fine motor skills, responsible for more delicate maneuvers like stacking blocks and stringing beads, develop more slowly, but by age 4 most children are able to zip zippers and button buttons (Wittmer & Petersen, 2006).

Many of these physical abilities stem from the brain's development during this time. **Neurons** become more efficient at sending signals to other neurons through mylenization—the development of a coating on the brain cells. Neurons also begin to group together into neighborhoods to allow for more complex actions (Puckett, Black, & Black, 2002). Therefore the child's thinking and body control becomes more sophisticated. Because of mylenization, the brain will grow from 25% of its final adult weight at birth to 75% of its final adult weight at age two (Santrock, 2005).

New research on the brain has shown that there are sensitive periods in its growth and development when it is more attuned to learning certain things (Bremner & Slater, 2004; DelCampo & DelCampo, 2006; Otto, 2006). For example, we know that language seems to be a priority for the young brain and many children seem to learn to speak effortlessly (Chomsky, 2006). Children are also attuned to mathematics during this time, although its development seems to be independent of language (Brannon & Jordan, 2006).

As children grow and learn, they develop the ability to categorize. This process begins at about 3 to 5 months. Recent research on infants and mathematics suggests that by 5 months infants are using organizational systems such as spatial reasoning and mathematics (Feigenson, Carey, & Spelke, 2002; Lourenco & Huttenlocher, 2006; Sodian & Thoermer, 2004; Spelke & Kinzler, 2007). At about one year of age, they can group these newfound categories, such as "things that are round" or "things that are soft," into concepts, such as "things with no corners are round" and "things that don't make loud noises when banged together are soft." This includes properties of objects that can be "known" but not "seen" such as an object's purpose. For example, soft objects can be used to cuddle (Wittmer & Petersen, 2006). As their brains become more and more complex, children are able to do more and more complex actions physically, mentally, and emotionally. They can stack blocks to build a high tower, their ability to pay attention increases, and they are better able to control their emotions.

Cognitively, as we will see in more detail later in this chapter, children are learning about the world by experiencing it through the senses: sight, smell, touch, taste, and sound. But they are also learning by thinking about things, forming hypotheses and testing them, and problem solving (Bower, 1992; Brannon, 2002; Dehaene, Spelke, Pinel, Stanescu, & Tsivkin, 1999; Jordan & Brannon, 2006). This is known as sensorimotor thought (Piaget, 1952, 1953). Children use their senses to explore their environment. As they progress through Piaget's sensorimotor stage of development, they begin to develop an understanding of object permanence, causality, and spatial awareness. **Object permanence** is vital to mathematics because it is the understanding that an object continues to exist even if it is not seen. It would be difficult to count objects if their existence was in question. The concept of object permanence is also the first step toward representation. When a child knows something exists even when he can't see it, it means he has a mental concept of the object in the absence of its presence. This is one of the bases upon which more advanced mathematics will be built. Numbers are representative of objects and quantities even if we do not see them.

Causality is the understanding that one action can cause another action to occur and that a child has the power to make these things happen. This understanding, which occurs between 6–9 months, changes the way an infant interacts with the world. Now they can actually make things happen in their environment, such as pushing a ball to cause it to roll, picking up objects, and moving them. Since the environment is vital to learning mathematics for infants and toddlers, an understanding of causality is vital. **Spatial awareness** refers to the understanding that we live in a three-dimensional world, and more importantly, that things have fronts and backs (Ginsburg, 1988).

Babies' minds are developing many of the basic structures that will be needed for later "formal" mathematics and there is a lot that adults can do to support this learning (Brannon & Jordan, 2006; Brannon, Lutz, & Cordes, in press; Geist, 2003; Lipton & Spelke, 2005). Refer to Table 5.1 for a list of the mathematical developmental milestones you will observe in an infant and toddler classroom.

Language development in the first 3 years of life is nothing short of astounding. Children's receptive vocabulary, the ability to understand what is heard, develops as early as 5–6 months of age. They may be able to understand words but are as yet unable to produce them due to limitations of the mouth, tongue, and vocal chords. Vocal communication does not occur until about one year of age. By the second year children have about 200 words in their productive vocabulary.

Object permanence is an important development for children in the first year of life.

Doug Goodman/Photo Researchers, Inc.

Table 5.1 Infant and Toddler Developmental Milestones

Concepts	0–6 Months	6–12 Months	12–18 Months	18–24 Months	24–30 Months	30–36 Months
Numbers		• Begin to develop understanding of "more"	• Start to recognize patterns and understand shapes as they play with objects. • Begin to sort familiar objects by one characteristic, such as "hard" or "soft." • May enjoy filling and emptying containers. • Notice that night is followed by day, and that socks go on feet before shoes. • Know that when an object is hidden, it is still there. • Many can complete simple insert puzzles when the puzzle pieces show whole objects.	• Begin to use a few number words without understanding quantity (e.g., imitating a simple counting rhyme). • Some begin to understand the words "one" and "two" (e.g., can distinguish "one" or "two" from many; identify pairs of items as "two", identify three or more items as "many" rather than as "one" or "two"; ask for "one" or "two" of something; know their age; respond appropriately to the request, "Take just one," or "Give me two").	• Learn important math skills from their play and daily routines. • Show symbolic thinking with pretend play, and recognize patterns with daily activities. • Understand what "tomorrow" and "yesterday" mean. • Begin to use logical reasoning to solve everyday problems. • Can sort shapes, complete puzzles with eight pieces or less, and stack sets of rings on a peg by size. • Understand addition and subtraction with the numbers "one" and "two." • Around 24 months, the average child uses a few number words without understanding quantity (e.g., imitates a simple counting rhyme). Some may not do so until later this year.	• Some children will be able to determine the number of items in a collection of up to five items by using one-to-one counting, or "enumeration" (i.e., labeling each item in a collection with one and only one number word from the counting sequence to determine the total number of items in the collection). • Understand the words "one" and "two." • Some 2-year-olds begin to understand the word "three." • Very few may grasp the concept of "four."

(continued)

Table 5.1 Infant and Toddler Developmental Milestones *(continued)*

Concepts	0–6 Months	6–12 Months	12–18 Months	18–24 Months	24–30 Months	30–36 Months
					• Some children can correctly use the size terms *many* and *same* when making comparisons. • Some children begin to appropriately use the size word, "more," to identify the larger of two obviously different-sized collections. • Some children will be able to verbally count by ones up to "three," and sometimes beyond, but not necessarily in the correct order. The average child will be able to do this later this year. • A few 2-year-olds may even be able to count in the correct order up to "five."	
Operations		• Begin to develop an understanding of causality. Discovering that one thing can cause another thing to happen feeds yearning to explore their environment.		• A few children begin to nonverbally and mentally determine that one item added to another makes "two," and that one item taken away or subtracted from "two" makes "one." The average child will be	• Some 2-year-olds intuitively recognize that if you change the size of a part of a collection, then you also change the size of the whole collection.	• A few children may use informal knowledge gained from everyday experiences to nonverbally estimate sums up to "five" (e.g., for "3 + 2," puts out four to six items to estimate the answer) and their subtraction

140

(continued)

					complements (e.g., for "5–2," puts out around three items to estimate the answer).
			able to do this during their second year.		
Measurement	• As infants become mobile, they begin to understand concepts such as "here" and "there," and "near" and "far."	• Adjusts reach based on the distance and size of an object (e.g., accurately reaches and closes hand around an item instead of missing the object or closing hand before contact). • Adjusts grasp of an object based on its weight (i.e., no longer grasps all items tightly or allows arm to drop when given heavy items).	• Children will explore objects by filling and emptying containers (e.g., with sand or water). • May believe that a cracker broken into many pieces is more food than a whole cracker of the same type. • Begin to develop a sense of time through participation in routine daily activities (e.g., know about when it is time to eat, nap, etc.). • A sense of time develops gradually over the next several years.	• Explore objects by filling and emptying containers (e.g., with sand or water). Some children continue such explorations throughout the year. • Some children can fill a shape with solids or liquids (e.g., ice cubes or water), and know that different-sized containers will hold more or less. • A few 2-year-olds recognize, informally discuss, and develop language to describe attributes such as big v. small (height/area/volume), long or tall v. short (length/height), heavy v. light (weight), and fast v. slow (speed).	• Some children understand the concepts of "same" and "different," and describe items in these terms. • Continue to develop a sense of time through their participation in daily activities (e.g., know about when it is time to eat, go home, nap, etc.).
Patterns, Reasoning, and Algebra	• Object permanence begins to develop in some children.	• Object permanence is firmly established by the end of the first year.	• Some children recognize that there is an order to the day (e.g., Mommy comes to get me after story time).	• Some children notice patterns in the environment (e.g., day follows night, patterns in carpeting or clothing, etc.).	• Some children notice patterns in the environment (e.g., day follows night, patterns in carpeting or clothing, etc.). • Between 30–36 months, a small number of 2-year-olds will be able to use deductive reasoning (using what we know to logically reason out a conclusion about what we

Table 5.1 Infant and Toddler Developmental Milestones *(continued)*

Concepts	0–6 Months	6–12 Months	12–18 Months	18–24 Months	24–30 Months	30–36 Months
				• Some children use the terms *tomorrow* and *yesterday*. • Some children show a greater understanding of daily time sequence and patterns (e.g., time to eat, time to nap, etc.). • Some children show interest in patterns or sequence (e.g., attempts to follow patterns with stringing beads, magnetic shapes, peg boards). • Some children can classify, label, and sort familiar objects by a known group (e.g., hard v. soft, large v. small, heavy v. light). • Some children can pick up blocks in the order of size.	• Use the terms *tomorrow* and *yesterday*. • Some children show interest in patterns or sequence (e.g., attempts to follow patterns with stringing beads, magnetic shapes, peg boards). The average child develops this interest during the second half of the year.	do not know) to solve everyday problems (e.g., figures out which child is missing by looking at children who are present). • Classifies, labels, and sorts familiar objects by a known group (e.g., hard v. soft, large v. small, heavy v. light).
Geometry and Spatial Sense	• Begins to construct the concept of three-dimensionality. • Some children begin to construct the understanding		• Understand that when an object is completely hidden, it is still there ("object permanence"), and can be recovered. (Some children may	• Some children informally identify and play with solid objects (e.g., picking out a familiar object by touch when that object is placed in a bag with two other objects).	• Some 2-year-olds will match shapes, first with the same size and orientation, then with different sizes and orientations (e.g., matches simple shapes in form	• Between 24–36 months, children are typically able to work simple "insert" puzzles (e.g., complete a three-piece simple puzzle where pieces are whole objects). • Remove parts from a toy (e.g., a

that things have fronts and backs.

understand this between 18–24 months.)

- Recover objects that have been hidden in one place, and then visibly moved to a second position and rehidden. (The average child will establish such "object permanence" during the second half of this year.)
- Recover objects that have been covered with one item, and then covered with something else while remaining in the same position.
- Work simple "insert" puzzles (e.g., complete a three-piece simple puzzle where pieces are whole objects).
- Remove parts from a toy (e.g., a wheel) and replace them.
- Build three-dimensional structures using one type of item (e.g., a cube).

- Some children create pictures using one shape, but don't use shapes in combination.

boards and puzzles, sorts simple shapes in a sorter box, etc.).

- Some children will still be learning how to recover an object that has been hidden in one place, and then visibly moved to a second position and rehidden.
- Some children may still be learning how to recover an object that has been covered with one item, and then covered with something else while remaining in the same position.
- Informally identifies and plays with solid objects (e.g., picks out a familiar object by touch when that object is placed in a bag with two other objects). Some children will learn to informally identify objects in this way during the second half of this year.
- Some 2-year-olds will be able to sort, order and build

wheel) and replace them.

- Complete increasingly complex puzzles (e.g., 4-piece to 8- or 10-piece interlocking puzzles)
- Progress in ability to put together and take apart shapes (e.g., understand that a whole object such as a pizza can be separated into parts).
- Build three-dimensional structures using one type of item (e.g., a cube).
- A small number of 2-year-olds understand and use words representing physical relations or positions (e.g., "over," "under," "above," "on," "beside," "next to," "in front," "behind," "in," "inside," "outside," "between," "up," "down," "top," "bottom," "front," "back," "near," "far," "left," "right").
- A few 2-year-olds will be able to informally create two-dimensional shapes and three-dimensional buildings that have symmetry.

(continued)

Table 5.1 Infant and Toddler Developmental Milestones (continued)

Concepts	0–6 Months	6–12 Months	12–18 Months	18–24 Months	24–30 Months	30–36 Months
					with solids (e.g., when playing with a ring-stacking toy, ignores any forms that have no hole and stacks only rings or other objects with holes; can stack rings on a peg in order of size). The average child can do this during the second half of this year.	

Source: Chart adapted from PBS Parents website at *http://www.pbs.org/parents/childdevelopment/©* 2002–2007 Public Broadcasting Service. Reprinted from *www.pbsparents.org* with permission of The Public Broadcasting Service.

144

WHAT MATHEMATICAL CONCEPTS DO INFANTS AND TODDLERS LEARN?

Some of children's first thinking happens when they begin to distinguish between things that they have seen before and new stimuli (Wiebe et al., 2006). A child becomes **habituated** to objects in their environment. When this happens, they tend to pay attention to it less and less. To recognize something as familiar means that the child knows that they have previously experienced it. When a new or **novel** stimulus is introduced, the child will spend more time examining it than the familiar object (Brannon, Abbott, & Lutz, 2004; Brannon et al., 2006). The implication of this is that infant's minds are actively engaged in observing new objects and stimuli in their environment. Every aspect of a new object fascinates them. Once it becomes familiar they spend less time looking at it because their brains are more accustomed to it. Infants are acting on objects not only with their hands, mouths, and eyes, but with their brains.

Research shows us that even very young babies have an abstract understanding of quantity and a more concrete, object-related sense of number. Infants as young as 6 months can tell the difference between large sets of objects based only on number, provided the ratio of difference is great enough (they can discriminate 8 vs. 16 but not 8 vs. 10) (Barth, Mont, Lipton, & Spelke, 2005; Feigenson et al., 2002; Jordan & Brannon, 2006; Xu et al., 2005).

Research has also shown that children as young as 7 months of age are developing an understanding of mathematics (Brannon, 2002, 2003; Feigenson et al., 2002; McCrink & Wynn, 2004; Wynn, 2000). Consider the following observation in an infant-toddler program.

Infants interact with objects and other people to construct an understanding of their world.

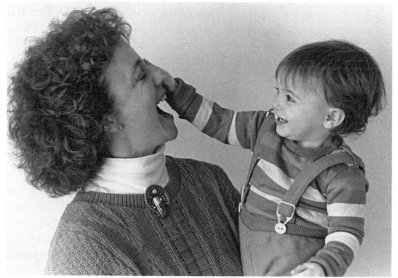

Susan Woog Wagner/PH College

The teacher shakes a rattle in front of a child and says, "See the rattle?" The infant, sitting in a high chair, reaches for the rattle and grabs hold. She then drops the rattle. When the teacher picks up the rattle and gives it back to the child, she drops it again on the right side of the chair with eyes steadfastly fixed to the floor. The teacher picks up the rattle, saying "Oops! The rattle fell on the floor!" as she returns it to the child. The child then takes the rattle and drops it on the left side of the chair, again watching it fall and staring at it on the floor.

The infant originally drops the rattle to test the precepts of gravity. When the teacher picks up the object and gives it back to the child and she drops it again, the child is testing the constant nature of gravity. When the teacher gives the child the object again and the child drops it again, but this time on the other side of the chair, the child is testing whether gravity works on both sides of the chair. The child is testing theories about her environment. She is learning, and the teacher responds, "Did the rattle fall? Can you do it again? Can you make it fall over here?" Children are actively and systematically constructing the world around them. They are acting as scientists to construct **physical knowledge of object**. This is the knowledge of an object that can be observed. Physical properties like shape, texture, and color are examples of physical knowledge. **Social knowledge** is knowledge acquired through interactions with others. Mathematics incorporates many types of social knowledge, such as "saying the numbers to 10" or the "names of the shapes," but should not be the primary focus for infants and toddlers.

Most mathematical learning at this age is what Piaget called **logico-mathematical knowledge.** This is the knowledge of relationships between objects. Piaget felt this knowledge was the basis for logical and mathematical thinking. These mathematical ideas are not a tangible physical property of an object or group of objects or something that needs to be taught by someone else. They are constructed by making relationships between the objects (Piaget, 1952; Kamii & DeClark, 1985). For example, a rattle and a teddy bear can be put into many different kinds of relationships. One relationship might be that they are "different" because the rattle makes noise and the teddy bear does not. Another relationship might be that they are the "same" because both are toys. "Difference" or "sameness" is not a physical property of either item and one does not have to be taught this. Instead, the objects are put into a comparative relationship in the mind.

Another logico-mathematical relationship is "two." The "twoness" is not a physical property of either the rattle or the teddy bear, but exists in the mind in the form of a relationship. Mathematics is based on our ability to put things into mathematical relationships (Kamii & Chemeketa, 1982).

Children as young as age one try to find answers systematically, as can be seen in the previous example. While, this may seem like a haphazard process, they are mentally organizing their thoughts and their worlds mentally with an often remarkable ingenuity. Children will repeat actions or introduce other methods in order to test the regularity of the observed phenomena. Answers raise new problems and questions in the children's mind, which they immediately set about resolving.

Bobby, a 2-year-old, stacks a set of blocks on the floor. He builds a tower four blocks high and then pushes it over with his hand. He seems pleased by his actions. He then builds the tower again and knocks it over by throwing a ball at it. Again he seems pleased. Bobby then builds the tower five blocks high and pushes it over with his hand, then rebuilds the five-block tower and throws the ball at it.

This example shows how a child acts like a scientist by testing many different variables, including the height and number of blocks, as well as experimenting with the method of knocking over the tower. Infants use logic and scientific processes to reconstruct, mentally, the world around them. (Forman, 1982; Sinclair & Kamii, 1995). Progressive organizing behaviors, such as the following, exist at a very young age:

- making comparisons between and among objects based on similarity
- putting one object in one hole (one-to-one correspondence)
- putting objects into a series from smallest to biggest as preparation for more complex number concepts

As teachers of children of this age, we have to be mindful of the complex constructions going on in their minds. Every time they touch, see, smell, taste, or move something they put it into their minds in a certain way (Sinclair & Kamii, 1995). The brain instinctively wants to make sense of this new information and puts it into a framework that Piaget called a **schema**. For infants and toddlers, these schema are very concrete and are directly linked to their senses and motor activity. From 24–36 months, children are developing some **representational thought**, that is, they begin representing their knowledge using language, drawings, and objects. As the child grows, representational thought is going to be very important in the construction of mathematics. A large part of mathematics is based on representational thought. Representation is the process of making one thing stand for another.

For example, we use the numeral "4" to stand for ||||. We use all sorts of symbols and signs to represent more abstract ideas in mathematics such as addition (+), subtraction (−), and multiplication (×). In the infant and toddler years, the simple act of supporting a child's burgeoning representational thought process is supporting his future mathematical ability.

Teachers of children from 2–3 years are on the cutting edge of fostering this vital intelligence. Children this age will begin to incorporate what they know into their imaginative play and this becomes a fertile area for mathematics. When a child pretends to use a block as a telephone, he is using representational thought. He has made a block stand for the phone just like "4" stands for ||||. Many times, children develop a better understanding of these concepts if they are presented in a play context.

For example, children playing in the housekeeping area could be asked questions like "how many apples or spoons?" or "how much soup will you need?" They could be asked to put toy cans in their places in the pantry, which supports one-to-one correspondence. The children are also developing rudimentary counting and number skills and can be asked to count, even if they are not always accurate. "Let's see how many spoons are here. Let's count together: 1, 2, 3, 4. . . ." Even before infants can count, however, they begin to discern similarities and differences in their environment that form the basis for forming mathematical relationships (Brannon et al., 2004; Kuhlmeier, Bloom, & Wynn, 2004; McCrink & Wynn, 2004), as in the following observation:

> Twelve-and-a-half-month-old Xu is given a set of cups that fit inside one another and a group of sticks of different lengths. He takes the second-to-longest stick, looks at it, and keeps it in his left hand. With the other hand, he takes the second biggest cup. With the stick he firmly touches the cup. Then using the rod he firmly touches the largest cup, then the next smallest cup, and then the cup he is holding.

As children try to apply order to their environment, through mentally and physically acting on objects in their environment, they are thinking logically and even mathematically. When they do very simple actions such as using a stick to touch three cups in sequence they are systematically applying order to their environment using number, and logic (Forman, 1982). This is the child making sense of the world. As teachers in programs for young children, we need to recognize the rich mathematical learning that is occurring, and that the environment is vital to the infant's construction of mathematics. Setting up a stimulating environment is the most important thing a teacher can do for infants and toddlers. Make objects available that

Children are thinking logically and even mathematically as they mentally and physically act on objects in their environment.

Getty Images - Stockbyte

children can observe, sort, and act on mentally, as we saw in the vignette with Xu. Interactions with objects will aid the child in developing the basic concepts needed for higher-level mathematics, such as one of the first basic concepts they will learn: the concept of "more."

The Concept of "More"

As infants interact with their environment, they begin to develop one of the first basic concepts—the concept of "more." Children begin to order their environment using quantity. They have not yet developed to the stage where they can use "one" or "number," but they can make judgments of "more" (Brannon, 2003; Brannon et al., 2004). They will make piles of objects and can then choose piles that have more things in them. The infant does not distinguish the objects in these piles as things that can be individually counted. They are instead viewed as masses of "stuff" in which some piles have more. Notice that I have not said "more and less." Research has suggested that children will use words like "more" almost exclusively when making these comparisons. It seems as if "less" is a more complex understanding (Kamii & National Association for the Education of Young Children, 1982).

The Concept of "One"

The concept of "one" is the next concept that a child needs to construct before any advanced mathematics is possible. As we've explored, children understand "more" very early on. They ask for "more milk," "more food," or more of other objects that please them as early as 8 months, but what about "one"? It takes a while before a child can ask for "one" of something.

Infants begin to understand that "one" means that there are single objects—not just masses of "more" stuff. They recognize there are distinct objects that can be counted, or at least put into a numerical relationship. This is a refinement of the earlier concept of "more" (Lipton & Spelke, 2005, 2006; Spelke & Kinzler, 2007). This understanding of distinct objects is the basis of all numerical concepts. Understanding that cookies, for example, are separate entities means that they can now be counted rather than just lumped together in a mass.

Infants begin to construct this by actively observing their environment and organizing all the information acquired. When do they learn the concept of one? They can understand "one" when asked to "take one cookie" as early as 20–24 months, but may not be able to explain how they know that one cookie is "one" (PBS, 2006).

Making Relationships

Very young children begin to **make relationships** between and among objects. They are looking at and touching objects; hearing sounds, rhythms, or beats; or even smelling and tasting things and comparing them to one another. Every interaction infants and toddlers have with their surroundings creates relationships such as "same" or "different" and "near" or "far." Some of these relationships have to do with mathematics and quantity. Early concepts such as "bigger" or "smaller" or "more" eventually

*Comparison of objects happens
as early as infancy.*

Eugene Geist

develop into the concept of "one," as previously mentioned. Since **number** is just one of the many types of relationships that a child can make, encouraging them to make as many relationships as possible promotes their mathematical thinking. Number is the understanding that objects can be put into a numerical relationship like "two" or "three." For example, "twoness" is not a physical property of the objects themselves, but a relationship that the child places the objects in, like "bigger" or "smaller." Relationships are, fundamentally, one way of **classifying** something.

Promoting mathematical concepts such as "more," "one," and "number" in infants and toddlers is not a question of teaching but of facilitating a stimulating environment. Ensure that children use their natural thinking ability wherever they go in the classroom. This is the child's innate capacity to think and problem solve. It is the human defense system. Even if they can't yet walk or crawl, children's minds are still active and are making all sorts of relationships and constructions (Gardner, 1999, 2006; Gardner, Gardner, Dinozzi, Harvard Project Zero & Into the Classroom Media (Firm), 1996; Davidson Films & Piaget, 1968; Piaget & Inhelder, 1974). By touching and moving objects, they mentally construct how the world works.

Refer to Table 5.2 for a complete list of mathematical concepts infants and toddlers are beginning to develop.

Table 5.2 Infant and Toddler Mathematical Concepts

Concept	Age	Description	Example
Numbers			
One-to-One	24–36 mo.	The understanding that one thing can be matched up with another.	Children playing musical chairs understand that there is one chair for everyone. When one chair is removed the one-to-one correspondence is disturbed (which is what makes the game fun).

Object Permanence	6–12 mo.	The understanding that an item still exists when it is not seen. The child understands that it is just hiding.	A baby plays with a ball, and then an adult covers it up with a handkerchief. The infant will cry as if the ball no longer exists. A 1-year-old; will remove the handkerchief and retrieve the ball.
More	12–18 mo.	The understanding that groups of objects or items have a quantity.	Children can tell an adult that there is "more" in a group of five than in a group of two however, they cannot explain how they know this (in other words they cannot use "one" or number)
One	24–36 mo.	The understanding that items have a distinct quantity and can be counted.	Children understand when asked to "take one cookie" or "take two cookies." They can point to a group of objects and begin to count them; however, many times they get the numbers incorrect or count the same object twice.
Counting	24–36 mo.	Children can recite some number words.	Children can recite the number words but often not in the correct order. Also, quantity is usually not attached to their recitation of the numbers at this age. It is more similar to saying the "ABCs" than to counting for quantity.

Geometry and Shapes

Matching	12–18 mo.	Children can match shapes and colors to other objects of the same shape and color.	Children can begin to use "peg and hole" toys. They can match a shaped peg to the same-shaped hole.
Stacking	24–36 mo.	Children can stack towers from different-sized objects.	Children may use nesting cubes to stack a tower of cubes with the largest on the bottom and the smallest on top.

Measurement

Judging Distance	6–12 mo.	Infants begin to be able to judge "near" and "far."	Infants are able to judge how close or far away objects are. They know if things are within their reach or too far away for them to reach.
Quantity Measurements	12–24 mo.	Using concepts of "more," children are comparing quantities.	At sand and water tables children will pour sand or water into bigger or smaller containers and observe the result.
Size Comparisons	24–36 mo.	Children use words to make relative comparisons such as "bigger" and "smaller."	Children might say, "I am bigger and my little brother is smaller."

Patterns, Reasoning, and Algebra

Sorting	12–24 mo.	Grouping items that are exactly alike.	A child makes a pile of all small yellow circles, large yellow circles, small blue circles, large blue circles, small yellow squares, large yellow squares, etc.

Table 5.2   Infant and Toddler Mathematical Concepts *(continued)*

Concept	Age	Description	Example
Multiple Classification	18–24 mo.	Grouping items by only one or more (but not all) characteristic.	A child makes a pile of all yellow shapes, all blue shapes, etc.
Sequence	24–30 mo.	A child puts items in an order based on either arbitrary or nonarbitrary characteristics.	A child puts letter blocks in alphabetical order, beginning with A and going as far as they are able.
Seriation	30–36 mo.	A child puts objects in a numerical sequence from smallest to largest.	A child sorts a group of different-sized items in order from smallest to largest. Older children may be able to put groups of objects into a series using "fewest" to "most."
Patterns	18–24 mo.	Children can recognize, replicate, and produce patterns.	18-month-olds can replicate patterns they have heard on a drum. Older children may be able to replicate numerical patterns that are shown to them, like one red bead, two green beads, one red, two green, etc.

Source: Adapted from information from PBS Parents (PBS, 2006).

MEETING STANDARDS WITH INFANTS AND TODDLERS

Some states have adopted Infant and Toddler Early Learning Guidelines (check your state's Department of Education web site for more information). Since these are usually based on NCTM's *Principles for School Mathematics* for children 3 to 6, let us reexamine these principles and think about how they apply to younger children. While not intended for formal assessment purposes, they will help us further understand what concepts infants and toddlers are constructing during this important developmental stage.

1. *Enhance children's natural interest in mathematics and their disposition to use it to make sense of their physical and social worlds.* Infants and toddlers are using their natural thinking ability to structure their world. Everything is new to them, such as the idea that things have tops, bottoms, fronts, and backs. Infants primarily learn through their senses and their relationships (Inhelder & Piaget, 1964; Rochat, 2001), so creating a contingent, responsive, tactile, visual, auditory, and kinesthetic environment is vital. For example, mobiles with different shapes and patterns can be hung in cribs. A room filled with interesting objects of varying size, shape, color, and function will offer new information for the child to process. There should be plenty of materials to manipulate and opportunities for children to interact with each other

during play, even though most of this exploration may be solitary (Parten, 1932). Remember that infants and toddlers act mentally on every object as they classify it, and each interaction they share with an object changes the way they view the world.

Nothing is as important to the infant or toddler learner as the adults who help the child to experience the world. Much of what the child experiences during this time is mediated by the adult. The adult prepares the environment, introduces novel stimuli, and interacts with the child in rich ways. When we think about the "3 Es," these children rely on learning mathematics through a stimulating environment created by the parent, teacher, or caregiver.

Use children's dispositions to support and expand on their natural ability to make sense of their world. What do infants and toddlers like to do? How do they explore their world? How will the child respond to particular environmental stimuli? All of these questions are important for a teacher to consider so that they can prepare an environment that allows children to construct the basic ideas of mathematics.

2. *Build on children's experience and knowledge, including their family, linguistic, cultural, and community backgrounds; their individual approaches to learning; and their informal knowledge.* The child's learning happens in the classroom as well as at home. Infants and toddlers are strongly attached to a parent or caregiver and receive most of their social input from that person. Most of the knowledge infants have, therefore, can be considered "informal"—that is, not formally taught by a teacher. An active and engaging environment, individualized to encourage family input and cultural differences, supports mathematical development in every child.

Formal teaching might involve a teacher developing a worksheet with specific activities and then teaching a lesson on what "one" means. Infants learn by exploring and interacting with their environment rather than by listening, reading, or writing. We should use more informal ways of supporting their internal construction of "one," such as singing songs from the child's cultural background or using musical rhythms from different cultures.

Talk to families about your goals and help them understand that the basic concepts of mathematics are growing in their child. Show them what you are doing in the classroom and explain how basic toys like blocks promote mathematics. Explain the importance of play and informal interactions with the child.

3. *Base mathematics curriculum and teaching practices on knowledge of young children's cognitive, linguistic, physical, and social-emotional development.* It is important to understand how children develop physically, emotionally, and cognitively in order to build developmentally appropriate curriculum.

This is especially important when working with infants because they are growing and changing so rapidly.

Most infants' and toddlers' mathematical learning is directly related to interactions with adults. Very little is rooted in direct teaching. It is important to make sure that experiences designed and developed for infants and toddlers are developmentally appropriate and build on the child's way of thinking about the world (sensorimotor and, later, preoperational thought).

4. *Use curriculum and teaching practices that strengthen children's problem solving and reasoning processes as well as representing, communicating, and connecting mathematical ideas.* A responsive teacher can focus on problem-solving abilities using a play-based model. Older infants and toddlers can be encouraged to make choices about everyday things such as what snack to eat and which toys they wish to play with. There are many other easy things that teachers can do to promote the emerging mathematician in every child. An active, stimulating environment coupled with a teacher who sees the child's ability to construct mathematical concepts can be an invaluable asset. Wittmer and Petersen (2006) discuss many ways to promote math, space, and shape in a responsive infant and toddler program.

For example, adults around the child can model counting behavior in play situations. Counting toys, books, and even the children themselves supports this concept. For toddlers, try counting "one" while letting the

An infant's and toddler's cultural, linguistic family and community context has an effect on their mathematical development.

Scott Cunningham/Merrill

child count the next number, "two." Any opportunity to count should be taken advantage of whether it is counting toes and fingers or places at the snack table (Wittmer & Petersen, 2006).

Toys that support the concept of one-to-one correspondence, such as toy cars and garages can be made available in the imaginative play area of the home or classroom. Each car should have one garage to park in. Preparation for eating can have many one-to-one opportunities. Those for toddlers include putting one plate at each seat at the snack table. An adult can model this by saying, "One plate for Daddy, one for Mommy, and one plate for you" as they are setting the dinner table (Wittmer & Petersen, 2006, p. 300).

5. *Ensure that the curriculum is coherent and compatible with known relationships and sequences of important mathematical ideas.* While there is no consensus regarding the sequence in which infants and toddlers acquire mathematical ideas, we know that very basic concepts of quantity are being formed in the child's mind.

   Developmentally appropriate practice for infants and toddlers is age appropriate, individually appropriate, and culturally appropriate. If an 18-month-old holds up any amount of fingers in response to a counting question, that is an **age-appropriate** response. The child knew that the question called for a numerical response. This may be advanced for an 18-month-old child, so being **individually appropriate** means that we tailor our response to what we know specifically about that child. Being **culturally appropriate** includes valuing the child's home environment and incorporating it into the classroom as a learning tool.

6. *Provide for children's deep and sustained interaction with key mathematical ideas.* Through a play-based approach, children constantly interact with two of the key points of mathematics: quantity and representation. As a teacher, you can use the methods discussed earlier to promote both of these concepts. Signing is one way to promote representational thinking and imaginative play is another. Teachers should appreciate the importance of imaginative play in a child's development. Play is a key way that young children practice and strengthen their representational ability.

   When a child pretends to cook dinner, or pretends that a stick is a horse, they are substituting one item for another. He pretends that the toy stove and plastic eggs are real. The stick stands in for a horse. The child knows they are not the "real thing" but uses those items to represent the real thing. In mathematics, we use numerals to represent or "stand in" for the actual quantity. When talking about four sticks lying on the sidewalk, we write the numeral 4 instead of showing the actual four sticks. Younger children might even draw the four sticks, which is also representation—the drawn pictures are representing the actual objects.

Supporting children's use of imagination and representation as we discussed in the section on children's play is, ultimately, supporting their mathematical thinking ability. All math is representational. The more advanced math becomes, the more abstract the representation involved.

7. *Integrate mathematics with other activities and other activities with mathematics.* All mathematics is integrated with other content areas during the infant and toddler period. They do not distinguish between math, reading, or science. There will be very few times when you encourage mathematical thinking out of the context of the child's routine or play setting. However it is important that you, as the teacher, are aware of where this learning is happening in your classroom and that you capitalize on the opportunities you observe.

8. *Provide ample time, materials, and teacher support for children to engage in play, a context in which they explore and manipulate mathematical ideas with keen interest.* Spending enough time supporting children's learning and interacting with them is vital to achieving curricular goals. Limiting playtime to a few minutes does not allow for the free flow of discovery and construction of concepts that we want to see in infant and toddler classrooms.

Allow children time to interact with objects. Teachers, parents, and caregivers can use questioning strategies to help support children's interaction and learning when interacting with objects.

> Kamile sees 25-month-old Dylan playing with some beads and a piece of string but not stringing them. She sits next to Dylan and asks him if he can put the beads on the string. Dylan puts two blue ones on the string. Kamile says, "You put two blue ones on the string!" Dylan smiles and says "more blue." Kamile says, "Do you want all the blue beads?" Dylan nods yes and Kamile finds three more blue beads and Dylan puts them on the string. Kamile then counts each bead and says "You have five blue beads on a string." Dylan grins broadly.

Here, time with play materials and teacher questioning made a play situation more robust. Kamile helped Dylan expand his play to include one-to-one correspondences, number, patterning, and counting.

9. *Actively introduce mathematical concepts, methods, and language through a range of appropriate experiences and teaching strategies.* Play is the medium by which infants and toddlers learn the most about mathematics. Whether it is imaginative play, block play, music, or sand and water play, children will be interacting with objects and their minds will be making many connections. Research is still not clear on how very young children learn with such amazing speed and agility. Don't underestimate the child just because

he can't yet communicate with language. There are many other ways that the children can communicate. If you listen and observe carefully, they will tell you a lot.

10. *Support children's learning by thoughtfully and continually assessing all children's mathematical knowledge, skills, and strategies.* With infants and toddlers we are going to bypass most formal math assessments, but as a teacher you should constantly be aware of what the children can do and what they are capable of doing. Identifying children with special needs is important. Observational strategies help to identify behaviors that may be indicative of special needs such as autism, or developmental delays.

Diagnosis of learning disabilities in mathematics, literacy or other areas is difficult in children under the age of three. However, sensory disorders (hearing, vision), or other disorders such as autism, could be interfering with the natural learning process. The earlier these conditions are diagnosed, the earlier an intervention can be developed for the child.

Observing and recording a child's progress and documenting his abilities will help you plan future interactions with the child. Since mathematics during this stage is closely linked to cognitive and physical development, monitoring his developmental milestones is useful in marking the growth of his mathematical ability. Documenting progress using portfolios containing photos or video are an excellent idea.

WHAT DOES AN INFANT AND TODDLER LEARNING ENVIRONMENT LOOK LIKE?

The director of a preschool related an experience to me about infant and toddler environments. A new building was being renovated for their preschool. Architects and facility planners worked up a set of drawings for her to review. When she saw the plans, she noticed that the infant classrooms were very tiny and contained no windows. When she pointed this out, she was told that the sizes of the rooms met state minimum guidelines, and furthermore, what do infants need windows and sunlight for when all they do is sleep and crawl around and can't see out of them anyway?

Fortunately, the director was knowledgeable enough to make her case and the infants got more room and some windows. This example, however, shows how some people misperceive how infants learn from their environment. Natural light and windows are a must, even if infants can't see out of them. The sense of comfort and well-being that comes from a well-designed environment is especially critical to infants and toddlers. The mathematics environment for infants and toddlers should support the child physically, emotionally, mentally, and cognitively.

Scott Cunningham/Merrill

Good environments for infants include the following characteristics:

- Spaces that are responsive to children's sensory needs and their need to explore.
- Spaces that encourage play, such as sand or water tables, or a dress-up area.
- Aspects that support children's development of trust and security, such as caring teachers and soft spaces and items for children to go to when they are upset—perhaps even some stuffed toys for comfort.
- Support for children making their own choices and developing a sense of mastery (Curtis & Carter, 2003; Fitzgerald, Karraker, & Luster, 2002).

> Nell watched as 23-month-old Nicholas tried to stack some graduated blocks. He chose to put the smallest block on the bottom and work up to the biggest. After three blocks his tower repeatedly fell over. Nicholas was beginning to get frustrated and upset. Instead of telling Nicholas he should start with the biggest block, Nell sat with Nicholas and asked what the problem was. Nicholas said "Fall down." Nell asked if they could play together and Nicholas nodded. Nell took the biggest block and set it in front of Nicholas. Nicholas then put a smaller block on top of it and then Nell put another smaller one on top. They took turns until no more blocks would stack.

Nell let Nicholas make his own choices. She structured the activity to help Nicholas feel a sense of mastery of the task.

Learning should take place in all areas of the room. Environments should have cozy spaces; creative spaces; spaces that are safe for physical play; and places to sleep, nap, and relax. Other spaces are needed for more practical aspects of being an infant and toddler such as changing tables, rockers for soothing adult-child interactions, and feeding areas.

Mathematics takes place in all of these areas. During time in a rocker, the adult may sing to the child a song with a repeated pattern; during feeding time the adult may count how many bites the child has eaten. Children can make relationships between objects in the sensory area, or can use musical instruments to bang out a beat or rhythm. In block areas, children can play with games that support the discovery of sorting. Classification and seriating takes place in the manipulatives area of the classroom.

An infant classroom should have carpeted areas for children to crawl and move comfortably and tile surfaces that are easily cleaned for messier activities such as sand and water table activities. These activities help infants and toddlers explore causality. Children may pour water into the top of a waterwheel and watch as it makes the wheel move. This type of activity also supports quantity constructions such as "more" and "one" as for instance, children put sand into containers of different sizes and make numerical and quantity comparisons between them. Children also make sensory and tactile relationships between and among objects, such as how the water and the sand feel different, and act differently in containers.

The environment should contain climbing and mobility toys such as mats and objects for helping children to pull themselves up to a standing position. Infants before the age of one year interact with things closer to the ground because they are usually crawling, and their gaze is usually fixed downward. After age one, they become more mobile as they begin to walk. Opportunities in the environment for infants to move are important. Padded mats of different shapes allow children a safe environment to experiment with movements such as jumping, climbing, and running.

Materials in the classroom need to be large, easy to clean, "low density," and have rounded edges. Large objects allow the child ease of use considering their lack of fine motor skills. They also prevent children from putting whole objects in their mouths; because of this tendency, easily cleaned objects are vital. Low-density objects are light and, more importantly, less dangerous when thrown or dropped. There should be objects that have some weight to build the children's muscles, but avoid small, heavy, sharp, or edged objects.

Materials should be of various shapes and sizes to promote classification. Series of different-sized objects can support seriation. Musical instruments such as drums, tambourines, rattles, sticks, and even keyboards of various sizes and construction can be available in the classroom. Rhythm, beat, and music incorporate elements that help a child construct the concepts of "one" and use patterning to promote higher-level mathematical thinking.

Finally, infants and toddlers need ample room. Small spaces do not give the infants or toddlers room to crawl around and experience their movement through space, or allow a toddler to march around the room beating a drum.

DEVELOPMENTALLY APPROPRIATE STRATEGIES AND ACTIVITIES FOR INFANTS AND TODDLERS

Because of what we know about how infants and toddlers learn, direct teaching of basic mathematics concepts is not developmentally appropriate. We need to devise other ways to introduce mathematics. This can be achieved by integrating logical thinking, decision making comparison, and the making of relationships throughout the child's day into everything they do. This method of teaching can be thought of as **emergent mathematics.** The goal of emergent mathematics should be to immerse children in mathematics, number, and number concepts through special attention to the environment and activities that children participate in during the day.

Mathematics should be taught through experiences that allow the infant or toddler to grow mathematically. Many of these experiences, as we will also see through preschool and even into kindergarten, will be based on play. An understanding of the play-based nature of children's learning is especially important in these early years since it is the exclusive way children construct knowledge (Clements & Sarama, 2000a; Clements & Sarama, 2000b; Clements & Sarama, 2006; Sarama & Clements, 2004).

Play does not guarantee mathematical development, but it offers rich possibilities, according to the NAEYC and NCTM position statement on mathematics (Clements, 2003). As a teacher, it is up to you to observe and develop a vital classroom where children have many opportunities to discover mathematical concepts through play. Here are a few suggestions for developing an engaging play-based setting for infants and toddlers.

Rhythm and Music. Rhythm and musical activities and materials are excellent for promoting emergent mathematics. Any activity that encourages making relationships is beneficial to mathematical learning. When children use beat, rhythm, and melody, they can begin to recognize mathematical patterns. Beat and rhythm with young children also supports the construction of "one." Different rhythms are made up of different patterns. Some of the beats may be long and some short. Children can hear the differences between these rhythms and begin to discern patterns.

> Three-month-old Julie sits in her mother's lap as her mother sings her "Twinkle, Twinkle Little Star." Julie stares at her mother's face as she sings. Her mother finishes the song and Julie smiles broadly.
>
> Thirteen-month-old Patel sits in the middle of an infant and toddler classroom. He hears a Raffi song on the stereo and picks up a nearby tambourine. He begins to bang the tambourine and march around a table keeping a regular rhythm that roughly matches the song. Occasionally he vocalizes using recognizable and unrecognizable utterances.

Music is often one of the first communicative expressions for children. Julie's mother sang her a song with a very distinctive rhythm. Replacing the words to "Twinkle, Twinkle Little Star" with the words "one" and "two" shows the beat. Try singing these numbers to the tune of "Twinkle, Twinkle Little Star:"

1,2,1,2,1,2,1 (rest)
1,2,1,2,1,2,1 (rest)

1,2,1,2,1,2,1 (rest)
1,2,1,2,1,2,1 (rest)
1,2,1,2,1,2,1 (rest)
1,2,1,2,1,2,1 (rest)

Can you recognize the regular and predictable pattern of the rhythm? Children in the sensorimotor stage of development can recognize the pattern. By the time they are Patel's age, they can link what they hear with the action to be performed.

The teacher or parent can also use drums or a makeshift alternative with infants and toddlers. For instance, the teacher and child can take turns repeating each other's beat. The teacher beats the drum twice, then the child beats the drum twice. If the child takes the lead, the teacher can echo his rhythm. This helps support a one-to-one correspondence relationship in the child's mind. Movement activities can also be supplemented by tapping cymbals, shaking bells, and marching to recorded music.

You do not need special training to do musical activities with children. Many teachers don't feel they can sing, so they don't include music in their classrooms. However, children are not judgmental when it comes to a teacher's musical ability. They just love to sing, dance, and play instruments, and they love it when their teacher joins in and encourages them.

Blocks and Shapes. Children who are surrounded with interesting objects, such as different-sized and -shaped blocks, are naturally promoted to make relationships between them. "Same and different" relationships require the child to focus on a certain quality of an object in order to make a comparison. Children go through distinct developmental stages of sorting objects by their characteristics (Piaget & Inhelder, 1974). Very young children tend to make exact groupings such as placing matching objects into piles. A 32-month-old might separate plastic shapes by grouping all the yellow triangles together, all the yellow squares together, and follow suit with the

Music is the first mathematical patterning activity that many children experience.

Todd Yarrington/Merrill

yellow circles, the blue triangles, the blue squares, and so on. *All* characteristics must be shared exactly to be included in the child's grouping.

As the child gets older, he is better able to do more of what Piaget called "class inclusion." **Class inclusion** means that children can sort things that share some characteristics, but not others. Therefore, the groupings don't have to be exact. Consider the sorting abilities of the two children below.

> Thirty-one-month-old Darryl is playing with a set of red, blue, and green blocks of many different shapes. Darryl begins to make piles of the blocks that he thinks are the same. He puts all of the red circles in a pile, all of the blue circles in another pile, and all of the green circles in yet another pile. He does the same for the squares and triangles.
>
> Four-year-old Tamika plays with the same blocks. When asked by her mother to sort them, she makes a pile of circles, a pile of triangles, and a pile of squares, ignoring the color differences. When her mother asks her if there is another way to make piles out of the objects, she puts the red ones in one pile, the blues ones in another pile, and the green ones in another.

Darryl is unable to group blocks with differences in his method of classifying. However, Tamika is able to say that "these are all triangles, and these are all squares" even though the grouped objects are different colors, and therefore could be placed in groups in which blocks are red, blue, and green. This is an example of **multiple classifications**, and exemplifies the growing mobility of children's thinking. The relationships children are capable of making are becoming more and more complex.

Infant classrooms should have colorful blocks and shapes in soft, plush forms. Other common fixtures include mobiles hung above the infant's crib that can be manipulated by the child (kicked with feet or batted with fists). These offer the very young child an opportunity to interact with and be stimulated by different shapes and colors, and help develop the concept of causality during the sensorimotor stage. Children see that their actions make things happen, and by the age of 5 months, are beginning to find ways to affect change in their environment.

> Four-month-old Roji lies on his back looking up at a hanging mobile. He grins when it moves and stops grinning when it stops. Roji moves his arms randomly until he hits it and it begins to move. Roji has learned that when he flails his arms the mobile begins to move again and he is happy.

It is useful to remember that while colorful objects are very nice and are appealing to adults as well, infants are more interested in contrasts than colors. Human faces also fascinate them. Be sure the mobiles have lots of black and white contrasts, such as bull's-eyes and pictures of faces.

> Eleven-month-old Ahmad crawls over to a pile of large plastic blocks and a plastic bucket. He picks up one block, walks over to the bucket, and drops

it in. He then toddles back to the blocks, selects another, and puts it in the bucket. When he has filled the bucket, he turns it over, then smiles and giggles.

Infants should have fairly large blocks with soft edges that the child can carry and manipulate with his hands. An infant's fine motor skills are not developed enough to grasp smaller blocks with one hand. Large cardboard blocks and stuffed pillows are best for this age. Babies love to manipulate objects, and a more solid block can be introduced at about 10–12 months. These blocks come in many different shapes so children can make comparisons, as we see with Ahmad. After age one, plastic and eventually wooden blocks can be introduced. Wooden blocks make a nice sound when clicked together and have a substantial weight and a feel that is pleasing to a toddler. As they develop to ages two and three children's hands are better able to grasp these, and their grasping and stacking ability makes them especially interesting (Lally & Zero to Three, 2003; Rochat, 2001).

Everyday Activities. Even children under the age of two can be exposed to math during everyday tasks and activities. Just as reading to children helps them develop literacy skills, using numbers and counting helps them develop number concepts. Children this age can understand the concept of "more," and asking them to compare groups of objects or quantities encourages the development of this idea. The concept of "more" is the concept of quantification which will later be built upon.

A group of five toddlers are sitting around a table in the classroom waiting for a snack. The teacher is circulating with a plate of graham crackers. To each child she says, "Please take one cracker." When she comes up one cracker short, she asks, "How many more do I need?" When no one responds she says, "I need one more cracker," and gets one and gives it to the last child.

There are many ways the teacher can handle similar situations. She can count how many people are at the table and ask, "How many crackers do I need?" or walk around the table and tell each child, "Take two crackers." Teachers should use math whenever possible and ask children questions such as "who has more?," "who needs more?," or "how many more do we need?" This type of interaction helps children recognize the importance of numbers and promotes the construction of emergent mathematics. Children as young as 5 months of age can begin to enumerate items such as crackers in their everyday or play environments. The importance of this type of interaction cannot be overstated (Wynn, Bloom, & Chiang, 2002).

As children begin to move out of the sensorimotor thinking stage and into the preoperational stage, they begin to think representationally and to acquire a certain degree of abstract thinking. They can think about objects that are not right in front of them and begin to make connections to previous experiences. Children of this age can make more complex relationships between objects. This is important for emerging number concepts because it is during this time that the mental structures which allow a child to understand quantity are constructed. Children begin to make mental

Toddler indoor and outdoor environments should offer opportunities for mobile explorations and mathematical experimentation.

Eugene Geist

numerical relationships that build on and refine the idea of "more" into "one more" or "two more." This refinement will eventually lead to the understanding that "three" is one more than "two" and two is more than "one." This is the core idea behind quantification.

Manipulatives. We have discussed blocks and shapes in great detail, but there are other manipulatives that should be included in the infant and toddler classroom as well. Objects such as large stringing beads, multicolored balls, musical instruments, and especially items that encourage imaginative play will support mathematics. Large beads that can be strung help children develop their fine motor skills while also supporting mathematical development. Interactions with objects such as different-sized balls help children to make relationships. The habituation/novelty comparison is one that children make very early in life. Babies also begin to recognize and compare balls of different sizes.

Musical instruments, toys for use at sand and water tables, and dress-up materials for the fantasy play area are also considered types of manipulatives. In essence, any object in the room that a child can act on physically or mentally can be considered a manipulative. For example, a child sits in his high chair playing with a "sippy-cup," rolling it back and forth around the tray. The sippy-cup has become a manipulative as the child explores its properties.

Everyday Routines and Common Activities. The everyday activity of infants and toddlers can be used to support the construction of mathematics.

Martina is changing 9-month-old Gregory's diaper. As she tapes up the fasteners she counts "One side, now two," and makes eye contact with Greg.

As Martina is feeding Gregory she asks him questions such as "Would you like more?" and "How much more can you eat?" She lines up and counts five cheerios on his tray and also counts them as he eats them. "There's one, that's two . . ."

We use mathematics everyday and it is not difficult to simply point out and talk about its usage even to children as young as Gregory. Older children can help distribute snacks at snack time or put out plates and napkins for each child at their table. Giving them the responsibility to help with some of these tasks allows teachers to incorporate mathematical thinking and problem solving into these chores.

Math Games. Games in which children are encouraged to make mathematical relationships are good for supporting emergent mathematics. For infant and toddlers, this could be as simple as "pat-a-cake" or as complex as cover-up games in which a child rolls a dice or other counter and covers up the same number of items.

> Twenty-two-month-old Frank draws a card with three bears on it from a pile. He looks at the card and takes one teddy bear counter from a basket and puts it on one of the bears. He does the same with the other two bear pictures on the card. Thirty-five-month-old Francie is playing a game using an oversized six-sided die, teddy bear counters, and an old dozen-egg carton. The dice faces have one, two, or three pips (dots) on them. She rolls a two. She touches one pip, takes one teddy bear counter out of the basket, and puts it in the egg carton. She then touches the other pip and puts another teddy bear counter in the carton. She repeats this action, rolling one, two, or three, until the entire carton is filled.

Like Francie, children may count one pip and pick up one teddy bear, count another pip and grab another teddy bear, and so on until they have counted all the pips. Others might count all the pips and then count out that many counters. Either method is an acceptable way of achieving the task. Because the children invented the method for themselves, it was based on their understanding of numbers and rooted in their own developmental level.

These "cover-up" games are good for one-to-one correspondence. With 30–36 month-old children, you can use egg cartons or other materials to create the game. The game can be played alone or with a partner (however, this does not usually happen until preschool).

Infants and toddlers are rarely interested in competitive games. They are very egocentric and do not understand the idea of someone winning or losing. They are much more task-directed. They understand completing a task and get joy simply from filling up all the holes in a counter game.

Supporting Emergent Mathematics

Emergent math begins to construct mathematical understanding from the day a child is born. This understanding occurs through interactions with his environment and through his mentally and physically acting on objects. It is not something that can be taught to a child. He must construct it for himself. The role of the teacher is to facilitate this process by offering different opportunities and materials to promote the child's construction of number.

Early mathematical concepts develop over the first three years of life, emerging from children's development and through their interactions with the environment. Table 5.3 gives a time line of some of the more important concepts that develop during this time. As a teacher, you should be aware of them so you are able to design curricular experiences for infants and toddlers that support their construction.

Let's look at a few sample activities for infants and toddlers. The objectives and focal points in these lessons are either taken directly from NCTM's Standards or Focal Points documents. As you look at these, think about what would make them developmentally appropriate for infants and toddlers and what mathematical concepts are being learned in each example. After you review them, think about how you might adapt the activity to meet other mathematical objectives. Try developing a mathematical experience for infants and toddlers on your own using these ideas as a guide.

Table 5.3 Supporting Infant and Toddler Mathematics

What You Might Observe Children Doing	How It Relates to Mathematics	What Teachers and Parents Can Do
Dumping out a bucket of blocks and putting all of the blue ones in a pile.	Infants and toddlers look for exact matches when classifying objects. They cannot understand that something can be the same and different at the same time (e.g., round and blue vs. square and blue). Classification will one day be used for the mathematical content areas of measurement, patterning/algebra, and geometry/spatial sense.	• Provide plenty of blocks and tiles of different shapes, colors, and sizes. • Play with children; notice what they do and record observations. • Use words that describe attributes such as size, shape, and color. "You made a big pile of blue blocks."
Beating on a drum, shaking a tambourine, or playing another musical instrument.	Infants and toddlers are slowly constructing number sense, concepts of quantity, and other concepts through their interaction with the environment. These concepts will one day lead to the ability to use numbers in a conventional sense, for example, in one-to-one correspondence and quantification.	• Provide plenty of sound-makers (e.g., wrist bells, pots and pans, wooden spoons) and rhythm instruments so children can experiment with and experience rhythm and beat. • Encourage children to play and move along with recorded music. • Talk with children and describe what they are doing. "Shake, shake—shake, shake, shake. You made your own music."
Pretending to drink from a cylindrical block, filling and zipping	To a child, a cylindrical block looks like a cup so he pretends to drink from it. In pretend play children make	• Set up a simple dramatic play area with many props that encourage children to compare,

up a backpack, or pushing buttons on a phone.

decisions, solve problems, and notice how objects are related to each other. Encouraging children to compare, contrast, and relate is vital to the construction of future mathematics. Making relationships will eventually lead to children being able to use numbers to compare and relate groups of objects. This will begin with relationships of "more" and "less" and develop into addition and other mathematical functions.

sort, manipulate, and explore properties.

Stacking rings on a post, matching blocks to the appropriate openings in a shape-sorting box, patting a piece of corduroy in a homemade texture book.

There are many toys that can promote making relationships. Infants learn through their senses and by using their motor skills. Toys that capitalize on the way infants interact with the world can encourage children to make relationships.
Order and sequence are important concepts that will eventually lead to quantification and numerical comparisons.

- Provide a variety of toys that invite children to explore with their senses and motor skills and allow them to make relationships and compare objects by size, color, texture, and sounds.

Holding a piece of apple in each hand, returning books and toys to the shelf, or touching a furry caterpillar crawling up a leaf.

We use mathematics every day to help make sense of our world, solve small problems, and order our universe. Infants and toddlers do the same thing as they engage in everyday activities such as eating snacks, cleaning up, and taking walks.
It is important for all children as they grow to understand the importance of mathematics in their daily life. Children who relate to math in this way will be more comfortable with mathematics as adults.

- Point out mathematical and relational comparisons during daily activities. For example, serve two kinds of fruit and say, "These apples are hard and crunchy. The bananas are soft and mushy."
- Offer several sizes of balls on the playground, or point out the colors, sizes, shapes, and sounds that children experience on a walk.

Filling and emptying containers at sand and water tables.

Infants and toddlers do not understand the concept that simply changing the shape or arrangement of an object or group of objects does not change their quantity. This ability is known as conservation and will not begin to emerge until about age four. As with other mathematical concepts, these ideas are constructed slowly over time as children play with objects, containers, and substances such as sand and water.

- Offer materials such as sand and water (or other safe materials) and containers of different sizes, shapes, and capacities.
- Allow children to interact by filling and emptying the containers and noticing what happens. Focus a child's thought by asking questions such as, "What might happen if you pour that into this jug?" or "Do you think all of the sand will fit in this bucket?"

Continued

Table 5.3   Supporting Infant and Toddler Mathematics *(continued)*

What You Might Observe Children Doing	How It Relates to Mathematics	What Teachers and Parents Can Do
Making patterns using blocks or beads and string.	Patterning activities require children to make and repeat relationships and even use rudimentary number concepts. To create patterns with blocks or beads a child must make specific relationships between the objects. For example, a child might alternate colors (red, blue, red, blue), sizes (large, small, small, large), or numerical patterns (1 block, 2 blocks, 1 block, 2 blocks). Patterning will lead to the ability to seriate (put objects in an order based on number or size).	• Observe and comment on the patterns children make. • Engage in patterning with the children. • Make or provide a pattern (e.g., on cardboard) and invite children to make a pattern that looks the same as the model.

Source: Geist, 2003.

SAMPLE INFANT AND TODDLER LESSON PLANS

Developing mathematical experiences for infants and toddlers is mainly about preparing the environment. The developmental variability is very broad with children this age. Because of this, the lesson plans presented here are formatted differently than in later chapters. Beginning the Lesson, Standards, Focal Points Extensions, Adaptations, and Assessment sections are not included because they are not relevant to these types of activities. However, a section on Preparing the Environment is included here.

LESSON PLAN

▼ ▲▼ ▲▼ ▲▼ ▲▼ ▲▼ ▲▼ ▲

Lesson Title: Singing and Rocking

Age: 0–6 Months

Subject Area: Mathematics

▼ ▲▼ ▲▼ ▲▼ ▲▼ ▲▼ ▲▼ ▲

Objective: Introduce a steady pulse or beat to the very young infant.

Lesson Summary: As the parent or caregiver comforts the baby, she sings, rocks, or gently pats the baby on the back, leg, or arm using slow, comforting beats matching her own heartbeat.

Preparing the Environment: This activity is mainly based upon the nurturing that a mother gives. The environment should be set up to be relaxing and supportive of a bonding experience between the parent and the child. Soft, soothing background music can be playing to enhance the experience.

Procedures: As the caregiver holds and comforts the baby, she uses regular rhythms to soothe the baby. This can be in the form of singing a simple song with a regular beat to the infant while rocking him in time.

Materials: Rocking chair.

LESSON PLAN

▼ ▲▼ ▲▼ ▲▼ ▲▼ ▲▼ ▲▼ ▲

Lesson Title: Manipulatives

Age: 6–12 Months

Subject Area: Mathematics

▼ ▲▼ ▲▼ ▲▼ ▲▼ ▲▼ ▲▼ ▲

Objective: Introduce objects into the environment that allow infants to make comparisons and relationships.

Lesson Summary: Preparing the environment for infants to interact and compare interesting objects.

Preparing the Environment: Infants in this age range are exploring their environment. Some may be crawling and others may be walking with support of furniture. The environment should be as safe as possible, with soft surfaces and no sharp corners or edges, and should contain objects with which the child can interact using his senses, such as mobiles; objects of differing colors, shapes and textures; and things that make different sounds when used or struck.

Procedures: Teachers should choose materials that infants can easily interact with, for example, graduated objects such as nesting blocks or cylinders, and graduated plastic rings for stacking. Behavior such as clapping and beating drums is rarely seen in children less than 6 months, but after this age they will clap their hands or bang objects together. Drums, tambourines, and other percussion instruments support their early patterning by using repeated rhythmic beats. Teachers can imitate beats made by children on drums, or can encourage them to imitate different beats or replicate an action. Imitation is developing during this time and is an important part of beginning representation.

Teachers should introduce manipulatives to the infant or toddler in a one-on-one situation, for example, a set of stacking rings. The teacher can get the infant's attention and say "Would you like to play with the rings?" while retrieving them and bringing them to where the infant is sitting. The teacher should demonstrate how the manipulative can be used by stacking the rings from largest to the smallest. She should then let the child interact and play with the manipulative as he likes. This can be done occasionally during the next few weeks as the child becomes familiar with the manipulative. Eventually he should be encouraged to retrieve and use the toy himself and even to interact with other infants and toddlers.

Teachers should observe the child's interaction with the manipulative and take notes on the various ways the child uses it. This will offer data for the introduction of new manipulatives into the environment.

Materials: Various. Any manipulative that supports the child making comparisons.

LESSON PLAN

▼ ▲▼ ▲▼ ▲▼ ▲▼ ▲▼ ▲▼ ▲

Lesson Title: The Gallop Game

Age: 12–36 Months

Subject Area: Mathematics

▼ ▲▼ ▲▼ ▲▼ ▲▼ ▲▼ ▲▼ ▲

Objective: Strengthen understanding of one-to-one correspondence and help children recognize different rhythmic patterns.

Lesson Summary: Drums or other percussion instruments can be placed in the play area for children to choose. The teacher interacts with one or a small group of children while playing the drum, offering stimuli such as a steady beat or a rhythmic pattern and observing the child's reaction.

Preparing the Environment: Children are going to be active and moving during this experience, and will need a lot of room to move around. Children this age are very mobile, but still a bit wobbly on their feet. Sharp edges should be protected and soft surfaces provided for safe interactions. Music is central to this activity so teachers should have some music ready to play for children before, during, and after this experience. Physical movement, interaction with objects, and musical interactions help them develop mathematical understandings and spatial awareness. This should be taken into account when preparing the environment.

Procedures: Percussion instruments such as drums or tambourines can be placed in the music area of the classroom for children to interact with. Teachers can model the use of the instruments during interactions or songs by keeping a steady beat with the instrument while singing. She can then interact with the child when she notices him playing with an instrument. She can try to initiate a call and response with the child, such as tapping the drum three times and seeing if the child does the same. Movement can be added, such as marching while playing the drum.

Materials: Drums or tambourines for the children. Note cards for observational assessment purposes.

LESSON PLAN

▼ ▲▼ ▲▼ ▲▼ ▲▼ ▲▼ ▲▼ ▲

Lesson Title: Finger Plays

Age: 24–36 Months

Subject Area: Mathematics

▼ ▲▼ ▲▼ ▲▼ ▲▼ ▲▼ ▲▼ ▲

Objective: Strengthen understanding of one-to-one correspondence and develop the concepts of equal, more, and fewer.

Lesson Summary: The teacher sings a song such as "Five Fat Peas" with children individually or in small groups. Children can just listen, sing along, or just do the movements.

Preparing the Environment: This activity can be conducted individually or in small groups. The environment needs to be conducive to holding the child's or children's attention. Find a quiet corner of the classroom and minimize distractions from other children running or throwing objects. Maintain eye contact with the children while singing, encouraging them to use their fingers and hands as you sing. It is also helpful to have this song recorded so children can listen to and revisit it during the day. This can be through a tape recorder and headphones or a computer.

Procedures: Teacher sings "Five Fat Peas" while doing the finger play for the children. This can be done in a one-on-one situation or in small groups.

> Five fat peas in a pea pod pressed
> (Children hold hand in a fist)
> One grew, two grew, and so did all the rest.
> (Put thumb and fingers up one by one)
> They grew and grew
> (Raise hand in the air very slowly)
> And did not stop,
> Until one day
> The pod went POP!
> (Children clap hands together)

Extension: More advanced finger plays that involve using numbers, addition, and counting can be introduced such as:

> Five little monkeys jumping on the bed
> One fell off and bumped his head
> Mama called the doctor and the doctor said,
> "No more monkeys jumping on the bed!"
>
> (The teacher could ask, "How many monkeys now?")
>
> Four little monkeys jumping
> On the bed, three little monkeys jumping on the bed, (and so on).

Materials: Tape player and headphones (optional).

LESSON PLAN
▼ ▲▼ ▲▼ ▲▼ ▲▼ ▲▼ ▲▼ ▲

Lesson Title: Washing Up

Age: 12–36 Months

Subject Area: Mathematics

▼ ▲▼ ▲▼ ▲▼ ▲▼ ▲▼ ▲▼ ▲

Objective: Strengthen understanding of one-to-one correspondence and help children counting fingers.

Lesson Summary: During hand washing time the teacher can count the children's fingers as they are being washed, using the "Ten Little Indians" song.

Preparing the Environment: Bathroom and washup time is a part of everyday life for toddlers and their teachers. Teachers can take advantage of the environment by introducing a counting song while washing the child's fingers. This will take place in a bathroom or near water, so teachers should take precautions to avoid slippage or drowning risk.

Procedures: As the parent or teacher helps the child wash their hands she can sing to this song, to the tune of "Ten Little Indians":

> One clean, two clean, three clean fingers
> Four clean, five clean, six clean fingers
> Seven clean, eight clean, nine clean fingers
> Ten clean fingers washed.

As children become more familiar with the song, they can sing along while washing their hands. As they become more independent they can sing and wash with less help from a teacher or parent.

Materials: Soap, water, and drying towels.

ASSESSMENT

When most parents and teachers think of assessment, they think of either oral or written tests. However, assessment is much more, especially with infants and toddlers. It is a major part of any educational program and, used efficiently, can inform and guide the teacher in designing mathematics curricula for his or her students.

Standardized vs. Authentic Assessment

The first distinction we need to make in assessment is between standardized testing and authentic assessment. Standardized tests are used to compare children to each other. Generally we use this term for tests that measure IQ achievement, or proficiency. You may think that these types of tests are not used for infants and toddlers, however, there are many tests that are routinely administered to children this age, such as the *Denver Developmental Screening Test, The Bailey Scale of Infant Development II*, or the *Wechsler Intelligence Scale for Children III*. Young children may be given the *Test of Early Mathematical Ability—Third Edition* (Ginsburg & Baroody, 2005). Generally, these scores are used to diagnose developmental delays in infants and toddlers rather than achievement in mathematics.

Authentic assessment in mathematics is based on the individual child and is designed to illustrate what that child knows and can do mathematically. Authentic assessment does not create artificial situations in which children demonstrate their competence and knowledge, but rather real situations in which children use mathematics in their everyday life. With infants and toddlers, most if not all assessment is authentic. It includes observation, collection and documentation of children's work, and teacher-child interactions just to name a few.

Formal vs. Informal Assessment

Teachers should understand that assessment can either be a formal procedure such as a paper-and-pencil test or an informal one such as observation. With infants and toddlers, formal mathematics assessments are not only developmentally inappropriate, but also very difficult to administer. The standardized assessments listed above often use parents to help structure the assessment activity in a "one-on-one" process. In a classroom, this is not always possible.

Informal assessments with infants and toddlers are usually more effective at collecting information about the children's mathematical development and abilities. Where formal assessments can test a child's performance in an isolated, carefully controlled setting, an informal assessment, such as observing a child playing at a water table, can give information about how the child uses mathematics concepts in an authentic setting.

Informal assessment occurs throughout the day, requiring no set time or special arrangements. Informal assessment of infants and toddlers attempts to take snapshots of children as they work. A written observation of a child interacting with blocks is a slice of that child's day that shows how he or she is thinking mathematically.

Formative vs. Summative Assessment

Teachers also need to consider, when planning an assessment program, what the assessment is going to be used for and why it is being done. These questions are central to designing an assessment program that meets the needs of everyone involved.

Formative assessment helps teachers decide how to move forward. It can guide the direction the lesson or curriculum takes. Teachers observe students and their interactions with people and objects to help guide this process. For example, if a 1-year-old playing with stacking rings can complete the task quickly, the teacher knows that it is time to introduce a more difficult task to that child. If the teacher observes that the other children are interested in stacking all sorts of objects, she might design an experience for the class that incorporates blocks in a mathematical way.

Summative assessment is used to determine how much the child has learned from an experience or lesson. Most of us are familiar with this type of assessment, in the form of a "unit test" or a "midterm exam." It can also take the form of a standardized achievement test, in which schools assess how much a child has learned.

Summative assessment need not include only these more formal assessments; informal assessments can also be summative. Teachers can create a mathematics portfolio for an infant or toddler that documents the child's development mathematically. She can take pictures of the child engaging in mathematics, collect drawings or other artifacts that demonstrate mathematical development, include a written observation of a situation in which the child was interacting mathematically with a person or object, or all of these. This portfolio can then be used in meetings with parents to show their child's progress in the classroom.

Using Assessment with Infants and Toddlers

With infants and toddlers, we almost exclusively use informal assessment for both formative and summative purposes. However, the summative goal in this case consists of documenting the child's development, rather than "testing" goals and outcomes which would be inappropriate for a child this age. Our goal in assessing infants and toddlers is simply to see what types of things they are doing, so that we can better support their learning through challenging and interactive curricula, and document their progress as they develop. Occasionally, the documentation process can also help to identify special needs in children.

The main instrument in the infant and toddler teacher's assessment "toolbox" is the **anecdotal record**. An anecdotal record is a short one- or two-paragraph description of something the child did during the day that was significant, interesting, or new. You can also record problems that may arise that need to be dealt with, such as biting and the antecedents of this behavior.

To use anecdotal records, the teacher needs a place in which to keep them. A three-ring binder with a section for each child works well for this purpose. Some teachers choose to use 3×5 cards and a card box with a divider for each child (see Figure 5.1). The teacher should try to observe each child and take notes during each day. At the end of the day, using these notes, she should write a paragraph about each child or two in

Name: Gregory
Age: 18 months
Date: November 9
Time: Approx 10:35 am

I watched as Gregory walked about 10 yards over to the shelf with the tambourines on it. He is still a little uncertain on his feet and he stumbled once. He grasped the tambourine in his left hand and threw it on the ground. I walked over to him and sat on the floor next to him. I asked him what he could do with the tambourine and he picked it up and threw it down again. I picked up the other one and tapped it with a steady beat at about a 1-second interval. While doing so I chanted, "What can Gregory do with the musical instrument?" Gregory picked up the tambourine and shook it while I chanted. He did not keep the same beat, but he did not throw the tambourine down and he began to shake it occasionally to produce sounds.

Figure 5.1   Anecdotal records are good for describing general developmental patterns over time. Three-by-five cards are useful for this type of assessment.

the notebook or on a card. These written observations can be as simple as describing a child's interaction with a certain toy, even if it seems nothing new is happening.

At the end of the week, the teacher should have a few pages or a number of note cards with rich, narrative descriptions on them. At this time, she can read and compile them into a weekly assessment of the child's development. Things that do not seem significant when noticed on a daily basis become more significant when compiled into a weeklong review.

The teacher should record where and with whom the child chooses to play. How does the child talk? What causes him difficulty? What does he enjoy the most? What mathematics do you see in the child's activities? Is he making or recognizing patterns? Does he seem to comprehend the concept of "more"? These are just some sample questions the teacher can think about when observing the child (Dobbs, 2005; Klein, Starkey, & Wakeley, 1998).

Another technique is the **running record**. This is similar to the anecdotal record but is a bit more detailed and focused on one activity or one specific period of time. When a specific period of time is selected we call it a **Time Sample**. With a running record the teacher observes the child doing a specific task until he is finished with that particular task, no matter how long it might take. With a time sample, a teacher observes a child for a set period of time, such as 5 or 10 minutes, and writes down everything he does during that time, marking the beginning and end times, trying to be as detailed as possible (see Figure 5.2). These methods are more time intensive than anecdotal records, but can yield more detailed information about the child. Teachers should try to avoid making judgments while recording the data. Only write down what you can directly observe. Don't try to guess what the child is thinking or analyze his motivations while recording. You will have time to do that later.

For example, if the teacher notices in her weekly anecdotal records that Janet seems to be creating interesting patterns when playing the drums, she may choose to

Name: Gregory
Age: 18 months
Date: November 9
Time: 10:35–10:40 am

[10:35—Observation Begun] He is sitting on the floor in the northeast corner of the room. He glances at two children playing on the mats. He makes a noise to try to get their attention. I do not recognize the utterance as a word. The children do not respond. He pushes himself to a crawling position and then by pushing with his hands to a standing position. He begins to walk toward the musical instruments that are on a shelf in the southeast corner of the room. He walks 5 yards and stumbles. He regains his feel and reaches the shelf after walking another 5 yards. He takes a tambourine from the shelf. He examines it. He throws it to the floor. Ms. Katie goes over to him and sits with him. She asks him, "What can you do with the tambourine?" Gregory bends down and grasps the tambourine, stands up and throws it down again. Ms. Katie takes the other tambourine from the shelf and begins a steady beat of about 1 second and chants "What can Gregory do with the musical instrument?" Gregory looks at Ms. Katie while she chants this. He then watches the tambourine for about 10 seconds. He then shakes the tambourine he is holding but does not follow Ms. Katie's beat or pattern. He opens his mouth while shaking and laughs. He continues to shake the tambourine—[Observation ended 10:40]

Figure 5.2 Running records provide more detailed information about children's behaviors. A spiral-bound notebook is useful for this type of assessment.

spend time observing and recording Janet when she is playing in the music area. It may seem like useless data, but you can never be sure. After several minutes, the teacher can stop the running record. Later, she can review what was written and produce a few paragraphs describing what she observed. She should do this soon after the observation, while the experience is still fresh (sometimes notes taken in haste are terse and difficult to understand if too much time has elapsed).

Photos also help tell the story. These can be used with running records or anecdotal records. With narrative assessments such as these, it is always good to have multiple forms of data. Pictures and videos also make it easier to show parents the progress their child is making. With new computer editing software, it is easy and inexpensive to make short DVDs of a child's progress and activities in the classroom, and allows parents to have actual video evidence of their child's development.

SUMMARY

Newborns', infants', and toddlers' brains are undergoing phenomenal development. The neurons developed during the prenatal period are building into more complex neighborhoods by linking. They are also developing a fatty coating called myelin, which makes them more efficient at handling information.

Infants are in the sensorimotor stage of development and learn mathematics using their senses and motor skills. They learn by looking, hearing, touching, and tasting things and by acting on objects with their bodies and, as toddlers, mentally. Socially, infants and toddlers are bound to their parents or primary caregivers. Toddlers, however, begin to play together in groups. Their language development makes this social play easier. They begin to speak single words at age one and, by the age of three are beginning to use rudimentary sentences. This rapid growth of language also indirectly supports mathematics development.

Basic math concepts like "more" begin to develop by the child's first birthday, which soon develop into the concept of "one." By the age of three, many children can count to five or higher. The environment in which the child explores and plays is a fertile venue to support mathematics in the infant and toddler. The environment should include aspects of rhythm and music, blocks and shapes, numbers and counting, manipulatives, and math games to support mathematics learning. Math is all around the child and just needs a teacher or parent to point it out. Sitting at the lunch or dinner table and saying, "There are six people at this table—one, two, three, four, five, six," is a good example. Even if children cannot count, you are focusing their attention on critical prenumber concepts throughout their day.

WEB SITES

The NAEYC's Position Statement on Preschool Mathematics
http://www.naeyc.org/about/positions/psmath.asp

National Association for the Education of Young Children's position statement on how mathematics should be introduced to children before the age of six.

NAEYC—Early Years and Learning Years
http://www.naeyc.org/ece/eyly/

Articles and information on teaching children in infant and toddler years.

PBS Parents—Math for Infants
http://www.pbs.org/parents/earlymath/infant_flash.html

Contains developmental information about infants' and toddlers' mathematical development and suggestions for teachers and parents.

Math Mom
http://www.math-mom.com/list/top-picks-for-infants

Picks of materials for stimulating infants mathematically.

Baby Einstein
http://www.babyeinstein.com/

Line of Disney products that claim to stimulate the brain in ways that can promote mathematics.

DISCUSS AND APPLY WHAT YOU HAVE LEARNED

Reflect

1. Why is it important to encourage mathematical learning this early? How much mathematics would you consider developmentally appropriate?

2. Name four important environmental considerations that support mathematics learning in infants and toddlers.

3. Why is music such a good activity for infants and toddlers mathematics programs?

Discuss

1. Role-play the part of a teacher describing to the parents of an 8-month-old infant the importance of teaching mathematics. What do you tell the parents about their child's abilities? As the parent, what questions and concerns might you have?

2. As a group, discuss and compile a list of 10 objectives you would have for infants and toddlers in your classroom.

Apply

1. Develop an activity that supports the concept of number and numeracy in the infant and toddler classroom. Include objectives from NCTM or your state, a procedure, and a way to expand and assess your activity.

2. Place the following developmental milestones in order from least to most sophisticated based on the Developmental Milestones table in this chapter (Table 5.1). Justify your answers to a partner.

    • Understands what "tomorrow" and "yesterday" mean.
    • May enjoy filling and emptying containers.
    • Understands addition and subtraction with the numbers "one" and "two."
    • Begins to sort familiar objects by one characteristic, such as whether they are "hard" or "soft."
    • Begins to develop understanding of "more."

3. Develop a set of guidelines for teachers on how to incorporate mathematics into everyday activities. Mention specific chores, materials, and interactions.

Observe

1. Observe an infant and toddler classroom. What are the teachers doing to support mathematics? What opportunities are they missing?

2. Observe an infant or toddler in a classroom or home setting. What do they do that is mathematically based or involves problem solving using sensorimotor thought? Is there any evidence of toddlers using early representational thought?

REFERENCES

Barth, H., Mont, K. L., Lipton, J., & Spelke, E. S. (2005). Abstract number and arithmetic in preschool children. *Proceedings of the National Academy of Sciences of the United States of America, 102*(39), 14116–14121.

Bower, B. (1992). Infants signal the birth of knowledge. *Science News, 142*(20), 325.

Brannon, E. M., & Jordan, K. E. (2006). The multisensory representation of number in infancy. *Proceedings of the National Academy of Sciences, 103*(9), 3486–3489.

Brannon, E. M., Lutz, D., & Cordes, S. (in press). The development of area discrimination and its implications for numerical abilities in infancy. *Developmental Science*.

Brannon, E. M. (2002). The development of ordinal numerical knowledge in infancy. *Cognition, 83*(3), 223.

Brannon, E. M. (2003). Number knows no bounds. *Trends in Cognitive Sciences, 7*(7), 279.

Brannon, E. M., Abbott, S., & Lutz, D. J. (2004). Number bias for the discrimination of large visual sets in infancy. *Cognition, 93*(2), B59–B68.

Brannon, E. M., Lutz, D., & Cordes, S. (2006). The development of area discrimination and its implications for number representation in infancy. *Developmental Science, 9*(6), F59–F64.

Bremner, J. G., & Slater, A. (2004). *Theories of infant development*. Malden, MA: Blackwell Pub.

Chomsky, N. (2006). *Language and mind* (3rd ed.). Cambridge: Cambridge University Press.

Clements, D. H. (2003). MATH: A civil right. *Early Childhood Today, 17*(4), 4.

Clements, D. H., & Sarama, J. (2000a). The earliest geometry. *Teaching Children Mathematics, 7*(2), 82–86.

Clements, D., & Sarama, J. (2000b). Standards for preschoolers. *Teaching Children Mathematics, 7*(1), 38–41.

Clements, D. H., & Sarama, J. (2006). Early math: Young children and geometry. *Early Childhood Today, 20*(7), 12–13.

Curtis, D., & Carter, M. (2003). *Designs for living and learning: Transforming early childhood environments*. St. Paul MN: Redleaf Press.

Davidson Films (Producer), & Piaget, J. (Director). (1968). *Growth of intelligence in the preschool years: Conservation*. [Video/DVD]

Dehaene, S., Spelke, E., Pinel, P., Stanescu, R., & Tsivkin, S. (1999). Sources of mathematical thinking: Behavioral and brain-imaging evidence. *Science, 284*(5416), 970.

DelCampo, R. L., & DelCampo, D. S. (2006). *Taking sides. Clashing views in childhood and society* (6th ed.). Dubuque, IA: McGraw-Hill Contemporary Learning Series.

Dobbs, D. (2005). Big answers from little people. *Scientific American Mind, 16*(3), 38–43.

Feigenson, L., Carey, S., & Spelke, E. (2002). Infants' discrimination of number vs. continuous extent. *Cognitive Psychology, 44*(1), 33.

Fitzgerald, H. E., Karraker, K. H., & Luster, T. (2002). *Infant development: Ecological perspectives*. New York: Routledge Falmer.

Forman, G. E. (1982). *Action and thought: From sensorimotor schemes to symbolic operations*. New York: Academic Press.

Gardner, H. (1999). *Intelligence reframed: Multiple intelligences for the 21st century*. New York: Basic Books.

Gardner, H. (2006). *The development and education of the mind: The selected works of Howard Gardner*. London, New York: Routledge.

Gardner, H., Gardner, H., Dinozzi, R., Harvard Project Zero & Into the Classroom Media (Firm). (1996). Los Angeles, CA: Into the Classroom Media,.

Geist, E. (2003). Teaching and learning about math—Infants and toddlers exploring mathematics. *Young Children, 58*(1), 4.

Ginsburg, H. (1988). *Piaget's theory of intellectual development / Herbert P. Ginsburg, Sylvia Opper* (3rd ed.). Englewood Cliffs, NJ: Prentice-Hall.

Ginsburg, H., & Baroody, A. (2005). *Test of early mathematics ability* (3rd ed.). Austin, TX: PRO-ED.

Inhelder, B., & Piaget, J. (1964). *The early growth of logic in the child: Classification and seriation.* London: Routledge and Kegan Paul.

Jordan, K. E., & Brannon, E. M. (2006). The multisensory representation of number in infancy. *Proceedings of the National Academy of Sciences of the United States of America, 103*(9), 3486–3489.

Kamii, C., & Chemeketa, C. (1982). *Piagetian research on how children construct number concepts.* Salem, OR: Chemeketa Community College.

Kamii, C., & DeClark, G. (1985). *Young children reinvent arithmetic implications of Piaget's theory.* New York: Teachers College Press.

Kamii, C., & National Association for the Education of Young Children. (1982). *Number in preschool and kindergarten: Educational implications of Piaget's theory.* Washington, DC: National Association for the Education of Young Children.

Klein, A., Starkey, P., & Wakeley, A. (1998). *Supporting pre-kindergarten children's readiness for school mathematics.*

Kuhlmeier, V. A., Bloom, P., & Wynn, K. (2004). Do 5-month-old infants see humans as material objects? *Cognition, 94*(1), 95–103.

Lally, J. R., Butterfield, G., Mangione, P. L., Signer, S. M., et al. (2001). *The next step: Including the infant in the curriculum* (videorecording). Sacramento, CA: California Dept. of Education.

Lally, J. R., & California Dept. of Education. (1990). *Infant/toddler caregiving: A guide to social/emotional growth and socialization.* Sacramento, CA: California Dept. of Education.

Lally, J. R., Mangione, P. L., & Young-Holt, C. L. (1992). *Infant/toddler caregiving: A guide to language development and communication.* Sacramento, CA: California Dept. of Education.

Lally, J. R., & Zero to Three. (2003). *Caring for infants and toddlers in groups: Developmentally appropriate practice* (2003 ed.). Washington, DC: Zero to Three.

Lamb, M. E., Bornstein, M. H., Teti, D. M., & NetLibrary Inc. (2002). *Development in infancy: an introduction* (4th ed.). From *http://www.netLibrary.com/Details.aspx* An electronic book accessible through the Internet; click for information.

Lipton, J. S., & Spelke, E. S. (2003). Origins of number sense. *Psychological Science, 14*(5), 396.

Lipton, J. S., & Spelke, E. S. (2005). Preschool children's mapping of number: Words to non-symbolic numerosities. *Child Development, 76*(5), 978–988.

Lipton, J. S., & Spelke, E. S. (2006). Preschool children master the logic of number word meanings. *Cognition, 98*(3), B57–B66.

Lourenco, S. F., & Huttenlocher, J. (2006). How do young children determine location? Evidence from disorientation tasks. *Cognition, 100*(3), 511–529.

McCrink, K., & Wynn, K. (2004). Large-number addition and subtraction by 9-month-old infants. *Psychological Science, 15*(11), 776–781.

National Association for the Education of Young Children. (2004). *Early childhood mathematics: Promoting good beginnings.* A joint position statement of the National Association for the Education of Young Children and the National Council of Teachers of Mathematics. [Electronic version]. Retrieved May 29, 2007, from *http://www.naeyc.org/about/positions/pdf/psmath.pdf*

Otto, B. (2006). *Language development in early childhood* (2nd ed.). Upper Saddle River, NJ: Merrill/Prentice Hall.

Parten, M. (1932). Social participation among preschool children. *Journal of Abnormal and Social Psychology, 27*, 242–269.

Public Broadcasting Service. (2006). PBS Parents—Early Math. Retrieved June 17, 2007, from *http://www.pbs.org/parents/earlymath*

Piaget, J. (1952). *The child's conception of number*. London: Routledge & Paul.

Piaget, J. (1953). *The origin of intelligence in the child*. London: Routledge & Paul.

Piaget, J., & Inhelder, B. (1974). *The child's construction of quantities conservation and atomism*. London: Routledge and Kegan Paul.

Piaget, J., Inhelder, B., & Davidson, F. (1971). *Piaget's developmental theory: Classification*. Davis, CA: Davidson Films.

Puckett, M. B., Black, J. K. (2002). *Infant development*. Upper Saddle River, NJ: Merrill/ Prentice Hall.

Rochat, P. (2001). *The infant's world*. Cambridge, MA: Harvard University Press.

Santrock, J. W. (2005). *Children* (8th ed.). Boston: McGraw-Hill.

Sarama, J., & Clements, D. H. (2004). "Building blocks" for early childhood mathematics. *Early Childhood Research Quarterly, 19*(1), 181–189.

Sinclair, H., & Kamii, C. (Directors). (1995). *Representation a piagetian view*. [Video/DVD] Birmingham, AL: University of Alabama at Birmingham.

Sodian, B., & Thoermer, C. (2004). Infants' understanding of looking, pointing, and reaching as cues to goal-directed action. *Journal of Cognition & Development, 5*(3), 289–316.

Spelke, E. S., & Kinzler, K. D. (2007). Core knowledge. *Developmental Science, 10*(1), 89–96.

Wiebe, S. A., Cheatham, C. L., Lukowski, A. F., Haight, J. C., Muehleck, A. J., & Bauer, P. J. (2006). Infants' ERP responses to novel and familiar stimuli change over time: Implications for novelty detection and memory. *Infancy, 9*(1), 21–44.

Wittmer, D. S., & Petersen, S. H. (2006). *Infant and toddler development and responsive program planning*. Upper Saddle River, NJ: Merrill/Prentice Hall.

Wynn, K. (2000). Findings of addition and subtraction in infants are robust and consistent: Reply to Wakeley, Rivera, and Langer. *Child Development, 71*(6), 1535.

Wynn, K., Bloom, P., & Chiang, W.-C. (2002). Enumeration of collective entities by 5-month-old infants. *Cognition, 83*(3), B55.

Xu, F., Spelke, E. S., & Goddard, S. (2005). Number sense in human infants. *Developmental Science, 8*(1), 88–101.

CHAPTER 6

Preschool Age

CHAPTER OBJECTIVES

After you have read this chapter, you should be able to:

- Describe what preschoolers are like physically, cognitively, emotionally, and socially
- Explain the importance of social interaction for problem-solving and mathematics learning in preschool
- Demonstrate optimal ways of arranging environments and providing meaningful experiences that effectively support mathematics for preschoolers
- Develop appropriate mathematics activities for preschoolers that are based upon NCTM principles and standards and the NCTM Curriculum Focal Points and their interconnected relationship
- Discuss how *both* the environment and experiences support mathematics learning for preschoolers

Preschool years bring new developments and abilities for the child, allowing the child to interact with mathematics in a whole new way. This is the age when NCTM and NAEYC begin to outline things that children should be able to accomplish during these essential years. Both the *NCTM Principles and Standards for School Mathematics*

(National Council of Teachers of Mathematics, 2000) and the *NCTM Curriculum Focal Points for Prekindergarten through Grade 8 Mathematics* (National Council of Teachers of Mathematics, 2006) that were discussed in Chapter 1, begin in pre-K.

A joint statement on preschool and kindergarten mathematics by NCTM and NAEYC focuses on children over the age of 3 (NAEYC, 2004). Connecting curriculum and teaching for children age 3–6 with that for students over 6 is essential to achieve the seamless mathematics education that children need (NAEYC, 2004).

Recognition of the importance of good beginnings underlies the joint position statement. It describes what constitutes high-quality mathematics education for children 3–6 and what is necessary to achieve that quality.

WHAT ARE PRESCHOOL CHILDREN LIKE?

Any mathematics program must take into account that physically, preschool children are extremely active. Emotionally, they are explorative and inquisitive. They identify closely with their parents and are affected by the parent's judgments of their activities. Early in the preschool years, it is difficult for the child to see things from another person's perspective. Cognitively, these children have developed symbolic and representational thought which allows them to let one object stand in for another and eventually use sophisticated symbols and signs such as numbers. They think and solve problems intuitively rather than logically.

Physical Development

Physical development in preschool age children is dominated by mylenization of the brain and the building and organization of connections between neurons. The brain grows at a very rapid rate, building more and more connections and becoming more efficient at processing information (DelCampo & DelCampo, 1995; Gazzaniga, 2004; Santrock, 2005). As the attention centers of the brain mylenate and mature, the child's ability to attend for longer periods of time increases. Gross and fine motor skills become more refined and memory structures develop larger capacities because of brain growth.

For example, a three-year-old might only be able to maintain attention in a group activity for about 5 minutes. I was recently in a classroom where the teachers attempted to conduct a 15-minute activity with three-year-olds. After 5 minutes, the children began to squirm, fidget, and look for something else to do. This often included pinching other children or other antisocial behavior. A three-year-old's attention is just not up to the challenge of a 15-minute activity and this can lead to what is often deemed "misbehavior." A preschooler may be able to handle a 10–15 minute activity of this sort because the attention structures in the brain have mylenated and developed sufficiently to allow them to attend for longer periods of time (Campbell, Zazkis, & NetLibrary Inc., 2002; Gazzaniga, 2004; Mather & Goldstein, 2001).

Cognitive Development

Preschool students are in the preoperational stage of development. Between the ages of three and four, they are developing some very impressive cognitive abilities that they are eager to use with other children or with a adults. One thing to remember is that these children are **egocentric;** they have difficulty seeing another person's perspective and are often inflexible in their beliefs. Teachers need to understand this and plan accordingly, especially when using games. Preschool children's egocentrism makes it difficult for them to understand the concepts of winning and losing as do adults. Games need to allow for interaction and can even have some competition, but should avoid having winners and losers. The focus should be on cooperation.

Symbolic and Intuitive Thought

During this preoperational stage, children are making the transition from primitive symbols to more sophisticated symbols and signs. The first half of the preoperational stage is called the **symbolic function substage**. This stage lasts from about age two to four. During this stage, children develop the ability to represent objects using other objects or symbols. **Representation** is making one thing stand in for another. Children often do this through pretend play. The child can pretend that a stick is a horse as he gallops around the room pretending to be a cowboy. This imaginative play should be supported as much as possible. This representation will lead to the use of more sophisticated symbols in the **intuitive thought substage** that we will see in kindergarten (Inhelder & Piaget, 1958; Piaget, 1959).

    The second substage of the preoperational stage is that of "intuitive thought." While children about ages 4–7 have developed a sense of rational thought, it is mostly intuitive in nature, rather than based on logic. In other words, the child is not concerned whether his answer is logical, but that it is an explanation he can understand. Children want explanations, but they tend to think intuitively rather than logically. Many times this manifests itself as a belief in the magical.

> Four-year-old Saffron's uncle came to visit for the weekend. He took one look at her and said, "Hey, what's that in your ear?" and put his hand to her ear and then showed her a quarter. "Your ear is full of money!" he said. Saffron was very excited by this and went into the bathroom to examine her ear to see where the money was hidden.

Older children recognize this as a simple trick and sleight of hand, but young Saffron believed that money really could be hidden in her ear. This is not logically possible, but logic is not a concern for Saffron. This does not mean that preschool children like Saffron cannot think mathematically. Children are still inventing, observing, and constructing new knowledge, and all of these interactions help them develop mathematically and cognitively (Inhelder & Piaget, 1958; Piaget, 1959). They have developed to a level where they can understand and answer questions fairly well. They are also very curious and ask a lot of questions beginning with "Why?" or "How?"

> After her time in the bathroom, Saffron asked her uncle "How did you find the money in my ear?"
>
> "Well it's all right there. Look . . ." and he proceeded to pull another quarter from her ear.
>
> "Why can't I find it?"
>
> "Well, maybe it is magic!" This seemed to satisfy Saffron, but after a while she went back to her uncle with another question.
>
> "Will you show me how to do the magic to get the money out of my ear?" Saffron's uncle was finally at a loss for words.

Conservation

For children to truly understand the constancy of number and quantities, they need to develop the ability to conserve. **Conservation** is basically the battle between intuitive thought and logical thought in the child. To observe this process, the child is presented with a situation in which logic and intuition are at odds. One of the first conservation tasks that a child is able to correctly complete is the conservation of number task. This construction usually occurs during the preschool years and is important to the child's use of numbers in complex mathematics. Children may be able to count before constructing conservation, but it is required in order for them to actually use mathematics processes such as addition.

Kamii (Kamii & National Association for the Education of Young Children, 1982) states that the importance of this concept lies not in the fact that the children "learn" how to complete the task, but rather in making us ask, "How do children learn number?" While our brains might be prewired to learn math, actual math concepts are constructed through interactions with a stimulating environment.

Centration

Centration is the tendency of the child to focus on one aspect of an object or situation to the exclusion of all others. Here is a description of another experiment Piaget conducted with children 4 and 5 years old.

> The teacher presents a child with two small glasses, A and B, of identical size and shape. Each glass is filled with an equal amount of water. The teacher asks the child to confirm the equality by asking "Is the amount of water in each glass the same?" If the child says no, then the teacher adjusts the levels until the child agrees that the amount is the same. Next, B is emptied into a differently shaped glass C, while A is left as is. Children 4–5 years usually conclude that the quantity of water has changed, even though they are sure none has been removed or added. If the glass C is tall and thin, they will say that there is "more water than before" because "it is higher," or that there is

As children develop cognitively and socially the types of play that they engage in changes also.

less water because "it is thinner." They "centrate" on one of these aspects of the glass, rather than realizing that one is "taller and skinnier" and the other is "shorter and fatter."

This is often called the "conservation of volume" experiment and demonstrates centration in children. In this demonstration the child is focusing on either the height or the width of the glass but not both and is, therefore, unable to conserve the equality of the liquids in each glass. In other words, when the same amount of liquid is poured into a tall, skinny glass, the child focuses on the fact that the water level is higher and looks like more without looking at the fact that the glass is skinnier (Inhelder & Piaget, 1958; Piaget, 1959).

Reversibility of Thought

Reversibility is the ability of a child to think in two directions at once. In preschool-age children, reversibility is still developing. Their thoughts are very linear and move in one direction. A good example of this is the "part to whole" task. Children are shown a group of flowers, separated into five dandelions and two daisies.

Teacher: "How many flowers are there?"

Child: "Seven."

Teacher: "How do you know?"

Child: "I can count them. See? One, two, three, four, five, six, seven."

Teacher: "How many daisies are there?"

Child: "One, two."

Teacher: "And how many dandelions?"

Child: "One, two, three, four, five."

Teacher: "OK. Listen carefully to my question. Are there more dandelions or more flowers?"

Child: "There are more dandelions."

Teacher: "Than what?"

Child: "Daisies!"

Why did the child change the question? Did she not hear the question correctly? Actually, her lack of reversibility of thought made her unable to understand the question, "Are there more dandelions or more flowers?" so she changed the question to one she could understand: "Are there more dandelions or more daisies?" The ability to reverse operations is a step toward logical thinking and concrete operational thought.

Emotional Development

Children in these years are in Erikson's stage of **initiative versus guilt**. Children dealing with initiative versus guilt have a drive to initiate activity. If this activity is supported and encouraged, they will begin to develop a healthy initiative and will enjoy exploring their world. If, on the other hand, they are overly criticized for their failures, they will develop guilty feelings for taking the initiative, and will stop trying new activities for fear of failure or criticism. It is important that in a preschool math program, children have many opportunities to feel successful. Activities should be designed to minimize failure and emphasize problem solving, cooperation, and the fun of mathematics.

Play

Play is the vehicle through which children learn. This is especially true in the preschool years. Math games, fantasy play, manipulatives, puzzles, and other preschool activities rely on play as a basis for learning. The Association for Childhood Education International in the position paper *Play: Essential for All Children* states:

> ACEI believes that play—a dynamic, active, and constructive behavior—is an essential and integral part of all children's healthy growth, development, and learning across all ages, domains, and cultures.

Play is a dynamic process that develops and changes as it becomes increasingly more varied and complex. It is considered a key facilitator for learning and development across domains, and reflects the social and cultural contexts in which children live.

Theorists, regardless of their orientation, concur that play occupies a central role in children's lives. They also suggest that the absence of play is an obstacle to the development of healthy and creative individuals. Psychoanalysts believe that play is necessary for mastering emotional traumas or disturbances; psychosocialists believe it is necessary for ego mastery and learning to live with everyday experiences; constructivists believe it is necessary for cognitive growth; maturationists believe it is necessary for competence building and for socializing functions in all cultures of the world; and neuroscientists believe it is necessary for emotional and physical health, motivation, and love of learning (Packer, Quisenberry, & ACEI, 2006).

Parten (1932) defined six types of play in which children engage. These classifications are based on the social nature of the child and how he enters play situations and interacts with others during play.

1. *Unoccupied*—Not engaged in play.
2. *Solitary (Independent)*—Playing separately from others, with no reference to what others are doing.
3. *Onlooker*—Watching others play. May engage in conversation but not engaged in doing. True focus on the children at play.
4. *Parallel*—Playing with similar objects, clearly beside others but not with them. (Near but not with others.)
5. *Associative Play*—Playing with others without organization of play activity. Initiating or responding to interaction with peers.
6. *Cooperative Play*—Coordinating one's behavior with that of a peer. Everyone has a role, with the emergence of a sense of belonging to a group. Beginning of "team work." (Adapted from parenthood.com—*http://topics-az.parenthood.com/articles.html?article_id=2797*)

These classifications are not stages, but we do see that the older the child, the more time he spends on more sophisticated play behaviors. If a 4-year-old is engaging only in solitary or onlooker play, some intervention may be necessary. Teachers need to be aware of these play classifications when implementing math games in preschool classrooms. Social interaction in math games is an essential part of the reason math games work so well in teaching math concepts to preschool-age children.

Piaget also classified play behaviors, based more on cognitive development than social interaction. By observing Piaget's types of play, we can assess some aspects of the child's cognitive development.

Sensorimotor and Practice Play. This is play that exercises a sensory motor scheme. An infant shaking a rattle or clacking blocks together is a good example of this type of play. During sensorimotor play, infants are practicing schemes as a way to refine and eventually combine them into more complex ways of making things happen in their environment.

Pretence/Symbolic Play. Children begin to include their representational ability into their sensorimotor and practice play. They may build towers out of blocks or pretend to comb a doll's hair. They also begin to bring other people into their play and take on different roles in the play situation.

Constructive Play. Children combine imaginative play with the ability and need to build and represent things. They will use blocks to build houses and then populate them with mini cars and people. It is vital to have building blocks in the classroom for these older preschoolers.

Games with Rules. As children begin to develop logic, they like to have rules to guide their play. Often the rules become more important than actually playing the game. Math games and other board games, where taking turns and adhering to the rules is important, become popular during this stage (DeVries & Kamii, 1975; Kamii & DeVries, 1980; Kamii, O'Brien, & Teacher Center, Southern Illinois University, 1980; Piaget et al., 1972).

Developmental Milestones for Preschool Mathematics

Children's ability to understand mathematics takes a big leap forward in the preschool years. Their strengthening ability to represent using manipulatives, symbols, and signs opens up many new possibilities. As early as age three, children can hold up fingers to indicate a quantity. The child is sometimes incorrect, but it is a mathematics behavior. By age four, children are learning to count. They can usually count to 5 or 10, and can tell you what number comes next in a series. For example,

Play can be a rich experience for integrating mathematics.

David Mager/Pearson Learning Photo Studio

if you counted 1, 2, 3, 4, 5 and asked what comes next, the child could say, "6!" However, at this stage, saying the words and understanding the quantity linked to them is not a certainty (D. Clements & Sarama, 2004; Sarama & Clements, 2004).

In geometric thinking, children can recognize and name shapes that have different sizes and orientations. They are also learning and using directional words such as "up," "down," "over," "under," and many others. By age four or five, they can use these words in a sentence to describe the orientation of an object.

Measurement also takes a leap forward as children begin to compare objects by length. Three-year-olds can put two pencils next to each other and tell you which one is longer. Four-year-olds can begin to use nonstandard units to measure things; for example, they can tell you how many shoes wide the teacher's desk is. They will need a lot of shoes to do this, because they cannot yet use one shoe repeatedly (Clements & Stephan, 2004; Clements, 2001; Clements & Bright, 2003).

Children also make strides in algebra and patterning. As mentioned earlier, they can sequence events in time by age three. By age four, they can re-create patterns or make their own repeating pattern.

During the preschool years, the child's ability to problem solve takes on a new zeal. Children's ability to classify objects is more developed; they can sort and organize objects into different categories and tell which pile has more.

WHAT MATHEMATICAL CONCEPTS DO PRESCHOOL CHILDREN LEARN?

Based on their general developmental patterns, children in the preschool years construct a number of mathematical concepts that will become the basis for more complex mathematics in kindergarten and first grade. These concepts include:

- Construction of numerical concepts such as
  - Writing and saying numbers
  - Use of rote and meaningful counting skills
  - More complex patterning, matching, and classification than infants and toddlers
  - Understanding mathematical functions
  - Understanding of order and seriation
- The construction of shape, measurement, and geometric concepts such as
  - Understanding comparing (bigger or smaller), positional (nearer or farther), and sequence words (first or second).
  - Comprehension and use of shape words (circle, square) and matching attributes of two-dimensional and three-dimensional shapes through play or drawing
  - Use of the language of time (tomorrow, tonight)
  - Understanding of measurement concepts such as unit iteration and using nonstandard units to measure an object (Clements & Sarama, 2004)

Table 6.1   Developmental Milestones in Preschool Mathematics

	3–4 Years	**4–4½–Years**	**4½–5 Years**
Numbers and Operations	Child can count a collection of 1–4 items. He understands that the last word tells "how many" even if his counting lacks numerical understanding. Counting is more like saying "ABCs". There is sequence but not quantity.	Can add by "counting all." For example, children roll two dice that come up three and four. To determine how many spaces to move, the child counts "One, two, three" on one die and "Four, five, six, seven" on the second die.	Can "count on" when using dice to play a math game or in other addition situations. The child rolls two dice. One displays three dots and the other displays four dots. He looks at the first die and says "Three" then counts on with the second die "Four, five, six, seven."
Geometry and Spatial Sense	Child begins to associate names of two-dimensional and three-dimensional shapes with the same size and orientation.	Can identify two-dimensional and three-dimensional shapes regardless of size differences and orientations. A triangle is still a triangle even if it is upside-down.	Can use tangrams to combine shapes into new shapes.
Measurement	Recognizes and labels measurable attributes of objects such as length and weight. For example, they may ask "is this long enough?" Children can use a stick that is longer than the object to be measured to reproduce a length, but is unable to use something shorter.	Begins to use nonstandard suits for measurement. They can use an item that is shorter then the item to be measured, but they need a number of them. For example, the child can measure the teacher's desk with five shoes.	Children begin to use standard units such as rulers to measure objects. They can use a 1-foot ruler to measure a 3-foot desk using "unit iteration."
Displaying and Analyzing Data	Sorts objects and is able to count and compare the categories formed.	Creates categories based on complex characteristics of objects such as "things that cut," which could include knives, scissors, and saws.	Child organizes and displays data through simple numerical representations such as bar graphs. Children can count the number in each group.

Mathematical Concepts in Preschool

Between the ages of 3–5, the concepts children learn can be divided into two types: numerical activities, which deal with discrete quantities—things about which we can ask, "How many?"—can be arranged, sorted, or grouped in a set; and measurements, shapes, and geometric activities dealing with continuous quantities *or things we can ask "how many."* The latter concept usually deals with one object which can be observed for its properties (angles, sides etc. . . .), transformed, and measured using nonstandard (hands or shoes) or standard units (inches) (see Table 6.1). Measurement is dependent on the units used. You can ask a child how many pencils there are and the child just has to say "five" but if you ask how long the pencil is, "five" is no longer a complete answer. The big difference is how the child's mind develops an understanding of these two concepts.

Number concepts require the development of numbers and an understanding of one-to-one correspondence, which begins in infancy and continues into preschool. This understanding enables children to sort and seriate objects and to compare two or more objects. Measurement, shape, and geometry involve the construction of a two-dimensional and three-dimensional coordinate system and the understanding that single items can be mentally segmented into smaller pieces to describe one or more of its properties, such as length or weight.

Numerical Concepts

Numerical concepts determine "how many" in a collection. We call this discrete quantity or things that can be counted "one, two, three. . . ." As children learn to count discrete quantities, it is important to understand the difference between rote counting and meaningful counting. Rote counting is usually emphasized with younger children. Parents and teachers focus on children's ability to say their "A, B, Cs and 1, 2, 3s." **Rote counting** is the ability to say the numbers or to count to a certain number, such as 10. Rote counting focuses on the behavior of being able to say the words in the correct order. **Meaningful counting** focuses on the numerical concepts behind the counting as well as being able to say the numbers. When children count meaningfully, they actually understand *what* and *why* they are counting. They are using their concept of numbers. Comparisons and using counting for meaningful items in play situations are good ways to promote meaningful counting. A child's ability to count meaningfully lags behind his ability to rote count so, while he may be able to count to 20, in mathematical situations, he can only use numbers up to 5.

> When Lily heard her daughter, Lydia, count to 20, she was so proud. She would often have Lydia count for others and Lydia seldom made a mistake. One day, Lily set out 20 small blocks on a table and asked Lydia to count them. She was very confident in Lydia's ability because, after all, she could count to 20; counting the blocks should be easy. To Lily's surprise, Lydia counted some blocks twice and didn't count others. Lily could not understand. Had Lydia forgotten how to count? She asked Lydia to count without the blocks and she counted to 20 flawlessly.

Writing and Saying Words. The representational rules of mathematics are mostly arbitrary. They are based on conventions or societal agreements. For example, most languages and numerical representational systems use a base-10 system because that is what our society decided upon, probably because we have 10 fingers. The decision was also made to put the larger place value to the left of the number—two hundred and thirty four is written 234. Children need to learn these rules of writing and counting and to link them to what they already know in their developing understanding of mathematics.

In preschool, children begin to use language and writing for many activities, and math is no exception. As they grow and develop, they learn to use number words to describe quantity. Teachers can promote the use of this numerical language. As with all teaching, using a constructivist method of questioning and listening is the most valuable tool in the teacher's repertoire.

Writing numbers is more difficult for children. Fine motor skills in their hands must develop to a sufficient stage in order to handle writing instruments. Older preschoolers may be able to write letters and numbers; however, actually using them in a practical situation may still be beyond their ability. Recognizing written number symbols is within their developmental level and writing numbers 1–6 or more can readily be used in activities. This is one reason number cube activities are so useful with preschool children. Six-sided number cubes can have either dots or numbers. They can be used in combination or the child can be allowed to choose one.

> Kendra sits at the math-path game with Josie. The game consists of a curving path with squares to move along it and a cup full of number cubes and playing pieces. Some of the number cubes have dots in a standard arrangement and some have dots arranged in other patterns. Still other number cubes have numerals 1–6 on each face.
>
> "I want to be red!" says Kendra.
>
> "OK. I want to be green!" says Josie, as she selects the numbers cube.
>
> "I don't want to use this cube; I can't count the dots!" says Kendra.
>
> "When it is your turn, you can use one of the other cubes and I will use that one," says Josie.
>
> "What if they are different? You could win!" says Kendra.
>
> "They are the same." Josie counts the dots on Kendra's cube.
>
> "1, 2, 3, 4, 5, 6."
>
> "Oh, okay. I get to go first!" says Kendra.

Written numbers can be used on calendars, charts, shelving and storage units, and in the imaginative play area, just to name a few. The more the children see numbers used in their environment, the better able they are to construct the rules, such as place value, that we all use in writing numbers.

Counting Skills. A child's ability to write and say numbers does not guarantee their application (Seo & Ginsburg, 2004). Just because a child can recognize, say, and even write numbers in the preschool years does not mean he understands that quantity is linked to the numbers. For example, while a child might be able to count to five at age four, it may not be what NCTM considers meaningful counting. Meaningful counting links the concept of quantity to the counting procedure; the child understands that, as they count higher, the quantity increases. To a child without this understanding, saying the numbers "1, 2, 3," is no different than saying "A, B, C." However, there is a big difference; the alphabet is an arbitrary series. "A" comes before "B" simply because our society decided to use this alphabet. One comes before two because the sequence has a numerical basis. Two is always more than one.

Drawings and paintings are a good way to introduce geometrical concepts such as symmetry.

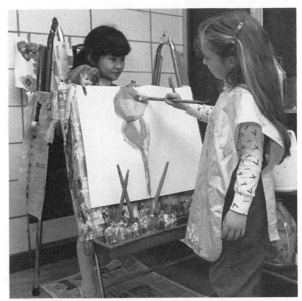

Ken Karp/PH College

Children must link this numerical relationship with the representational system. In the toddler years, children develop an understanding of the concept of "one." In the preschool years, they are constructing a **system of ones.** They begin to put the concept of one into a more complex organization that allows them to count meaningfully; "counting up" means adding "one more." As we count higher, each previous number quantity is contained in the next highest one. For example, the concept of "5" includes everything we know about 4, 3, 2, and 1. This is called **hierarchical inclusion** (Kamii & National Association for the Education of Young Children, 1982). This is true not just for a series of ones, but as we construct a more complex number system, also for 10s and 100s and all other values.

This counting and hierarchical inclusion is the beginning of the child's understanding of **cardinal number**, which answers the question "how many?" Cardinal numbers are the basic or **natural** numbers like one, two, three, and so on, as distinguished from the **ordinal** numbers (first, second, third, etc.) which describe rank or order (Clements & Sarama, 2004).

Order and Seriation. Vital to children's ability to count meaningfully are the concepts of **order** and **seriation**. Order is the ability to count a number of objects once and only once. This requires the child to mentally organize the objects in a way that he can remember which items have been counted and which have not. Once an item has been counted, the child must mentally move that item from the "to be counted" group to the "has been counted" group. **Seriation** is the process of putting objects in a series. For example, a child may seriate four rocks from smallest to largest. For a child to understand that counting is meaningful, he must understand that, with each number counted, the series gets larger.

Classification. Children's ability to group objects by their characteristics becomes more developed during the preschool years. They begin to create sets using properties of objects or even number properties as a classificatory scheme. Preschoolers are able to come up with many different ways to put objects into sets. For example, they can use numbers to classify objects, putting cards with one, two, and three dots into separate piles. They are able to do complex classifications using two or more variables, such as color and shape. Children can use a Venn diagram to demonstrate how they classify objects as "square or not square" and "yellow not blue."

It is not the visual representation of the Venn diagram that helps children learn mathematics, but the process of classifying objects as one or the other or both (see Figure 6.1). For example, children can use hula-hoops to do a Venn diagram activity.

> Mrs. Cho asked all the children that were wearing something blue to stand. She then asked all the children that were wearing something yellow to stand. She saw that Hans and Rosa had on yellow and blue. She laid out two hula hoops and said, "Can we sort the people wearing blue from the people wearing yellow using these rings?"
>
> Bobby said, "Put the blue people here and the yellow people there!"
>
> Mrs. Cho said, "All right, but what should we do with Hans and Rosa? They are wearing both colors."
>
> "I know," Rosa said. "Hans and I can each put one foot in each circle!"

Patterning. In preschool, children explore patterns on four levels. They can **recognize, describe, extend,** and **create** patterns. They make patterns that are more complex and more numerical. They develop the ability to use three types of patterning. **Repeating patterns** are virtually the same as those the children did as toddlers, repeating sequences such as red, blue, red, blue. However, in preschool, children are more intentional about patterning and their repeating patterns become more complex. They may use three or more colors in their sequence and add mathematical elements to the pattern (Seo & Ginsburg, 2004; Singer, Golinkoff, & Hirsch-Pasek, 2006).

The second type of patterning is a **growing pattern** such as "1, 2, 3, 4" or "2, 4, 6, 8." In these patterns, number is the central element. These can be demonstrated either with numerals or with groups of objects. In these patterns, there are numerical or mathematical rules that govern the relationship of the groups. A rule might be "add one more" for "1, 2, 3, 4" or "count by twos" for "2, 4, 6, 8." The third type of pattern is called a **relationship pattern**, in which two numbers are linked using some sort of function. For example, using a box of crayons containing eight crayons, the pattern could be "1, 8, 2, 16, 3, 24." Generally, this type of patterning is not seen until second or third grade due to its multiplicative properties (Clements & Sarama, 2004).

Functions. Functions are a basic building block of mathematics and are repeatedly mentioned in NCTM and other standards and principles. A function is something done to one number or piece of data to make it into a new number or a new piece of data. For example, "add one" is a function that creates the typical way of counting by ones (1, 2, 3, 4, and so on). Because in the preschool years children begin

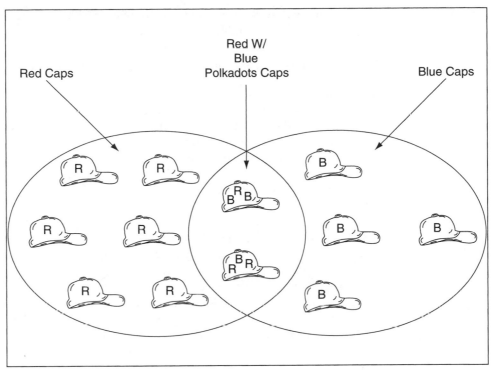

Figure 6.1 Venn Diagram.

to understand functions by using patterning activities, these two concepts are usually mentioned together as Patterns and Functions (Ginsburg & Baroody, 2005; Ginsburg, 1988; Rivera, 1998; Rousso & Wehmeyer, 2001; Singer et al., 2006).

Problem Solving. Problem solving is just as important with preschool children as it is with older children. Encouraging children to use their own natural thinking ability to solve problems is vital to their mathematical development, even if the problem-solving situations are not always mathematical in nature. Children can solve problems in social interactions such as a dispute over a toy. As teachers, we tend to step in and try to solve a dispute for a child, rather than saying, "What do you two think you should do to solve this problem?"

Mathematically, children can be given problems that need mathematics to solve. One example is measurement.

Jason suggested to Mr. Zamarano that they move the couch over by the window. Mr. Zamarano, who knew that the space was too small, said to him, "Before we move it, how can we be sure that it will fit under the window? It looks a little small to me. Maybe we can ask the entire class to help with some ideas?" Later, during group time, Mr. Zamarano said to the class, "Jason has suggested that we move the couch, but before we do, we need to make sure that it will fit. Can we help him come up with a way to solve this problem? Jason, would you like to share your idea first?"

Shape, Measurement, and Geometric Concepts

Understanding the properties of shapes, measurement, and geometry are different types of concepts than the numerical concepts. These concepts have to do with understanding and measuring the properties of continuous quantities, such as shapes or solids, and also with the construction of a positional coordinate system that helps the child figure out his relative position in space and the relationship of other things around him. An example of the development of the coordinate system would be children drawing and understanding maps.

Comparing, Positional, and Sequence Words. Children in the preschool years begin to use **comparing words** such as "bigger" and "smaller" or "longer" and "shorter." These words show their developing ability to make comparisons using quantity or mathematical concepts.

Between the ages of three and four, they also begin to use **positional words** such as "above," "below," "over," "under," "on," "beside," "next to," and "between" accurately. Between four and five, children use these positional words to begin constructing a **coordinate system** that allows them to draw maps of their environment.

During the preschool ages, children begin to use landmarks in conjunction with positional words to create descriptions of a route. For example, if a child is asked to draw a map illustrating how to walk from his home to a friend's house, his description will not correspond with reality but will show how he uses his understanding of relative position to describe a route. The child's map is not based on landmarks such as "the big trees" or "Tommy's house" but on his actions in getting to the friend's house. Preschool age children occasionally put two landmarks into a relationship, such as "Tommy's house" and "the big trees," but these pairs are not indicative of a coordinate system nor necessarily spatial in nature.

Children will also begin to use and understand **sequence words** such as "first," "second," "next," and "last." These words show a beginning understanding of **ordinal numbers**. When objects are placed in an order, we use ordinal numbers to tell their position. For example, in a race between four children, there is a first, second, third, and fourth place. We can also call fourth place "last."

Shape Words and Attributes of Two-Dimensional and Three-Dimensional Shapes Through Play or Drawing. Preschool children build an intuitive and explicit knowledge of geometric figures such as shapes (Clements & Sarama, 2000, 2006). Knowledge of shapes and objects are a big part of their mathematics learning and development during these years. On a language level, they begin to attach names to certain shapes, such as "triangle," "square," or "circle." While this is often an objective for mathematics in preschool, it is actually more of a language arts activity as it does not really involve mathematical thinking or problem solving as we have discussed them. The act of recognizing and classifying attributes of shapes, however, is a mathematical activity.

They also learn to draw geometric shapes, combine them to make designs, and play with three-dimensional blocks and pattern blocks. By the age of four, children can recognize and name basic two-dimensional shapes. They begin to use their developing ability to do more complex classification and to notice different attributes of shapes. They can classify triangles, circles, and squares even if they are different sizes or orientations or both.

Children between ages four and five begin to recognize angles as critical parts of geometric figures and to understand the idea of **transformations and symmetry.** An example of transformation is shapes that are turned or rotated. For example, a square can be turned to make a diamond. Older preschool children are constructing the ability to match corresponding angles and to understand that a diamond is the same shape as a square (Clements & Sarama, 2000, 2006). Children also begin to use different shapes to *compose and decompose* designs and representative pictures. Later in their development, they will be able to combine two or more shapes to make a new shape, for example, to combine two right triangles to make a square.

Symmetry involves a visual balance. **Line symmetry** means that when a line is drawn through the middle of a picture or design, each side will be a mirror image of the other. **Rotational symmetry** means that x and y axis lines drawn through a picture or design will show a mirror image on both axes. Preschool-age children can create drawings and designs that have both line and rotational symmetry, but it is difficult for them to create the other half of a symmetric geometric figure until kindergarten (Clements, 2004).

Time. Concepts of time begin to develop in children as they start to talk about "yesterday, today, and tomorrow" or "earlier, now, and later." Telling time will not develop until after kindergarten; however, preschoolers can use their developing understanding of the passage of time to structure their activities and days. They can understand that events took place before what is happening at the present time.

Asking how many shoes long something is is a fun way for children to measure items and also use unit iteration in their measurement.

Silver Burdett Ginn

Susie: "Do you want to play blocks, Kendra?"

Kendra: "Not right now, I am doing a puzzle."

Susie: "When you are done, do you want to play later?"

Kendra: "OK. Later."

Teacher (announcement to the whole class): "We will be gathering for group time in 5 minutes so start putting your things away."

Kendra: "We can play blocks after group time."

Susie: "But we always have snack after group time!"

Kendra: "That's right. After snack we will play blocks."

Susie: "OK."

Sometimes a child's concept of past, present, and future is also very concrete. For example, I was speaking with a child who had just had a lesson about the past, present, and future. He said, "Yesterday I had a hamburger for lunch. That was in the past." I said, "Well, a few minutes ago you had a grilled cheese sandwich for lunch; that also was in the past." He responded, "No, it is not. The past is yesterday; today is the present!"

Measurement Concepts. Measurement is the process of dividing a continuous quantity into a unit of measurement in order to communicate, describe, or reproduce its length or quantity. Measurement has aspects of both numerical and geometric concepts because we can use numbers to describe a physical property of the continuous quantity. We will use length as an example for this discussion, but the concepts are generally the same for all measurements.

Children's first foray into measurement is through using words such as "equal" or "longer." Next, they learn how to measure connecting number to length, for example (Clements & Sarama, 2000, 2006). Eventually, in the preschool years, they begin to construct the concept of a **unit**. A unit is a measuring standard that is of equal size. This understanding does not happen instantaneously.

The understanding of measurement requires the construction of a number of concepts. The concepts below concern length, but many of them are also needed for the measurement of weight and area.

- Partitioning—This is the mental activity of slicing up a length into smaller but same size units.
- Unit Iteration—This is the ability to think of the length of a small block as a part of the length of the object being measured, and to be able to place the smaller blocks repeatedly along the length of the larger object.
- Transitivity—This is the understanding that if the length of an object is the same as that of a second object and the length of the second is equal to that of a third, then the first object must be the same length as the third object.
- Conservation—This is the understanding that the length of an object is the same no matter how it is moved or aligned.

- Accumulation of Distance—This is the understanding that as you iterate a unit along a length of an object and count the number of interations, the number words signify the space covered by all units counted up to that point.
- Relation to Number—This is the understanding that number is being applied to measurement of a continuous object rather than to discrete objects. (Clements & Stephan, 2004)

Below is an example of preschool children constructing and using these measurement concepts.

> Sasha, who is 3½ years old, has been asked to make a block road exactly as long as the one the teacher made. She has been given a bucket of 1-inch squares, a 12-inch ruler, a 3-foot-long stick, and a 2-foot-long stick. Sasha first picks up the 2-foot-long stick and lays it next to the teacher's road.
>
> "It is too short," she says.
>
> "Can you think of a way to use it to make your road the same as mine?"
>
> "No. It's too short."
>
> Sasha then picks up the three-foot stick. It is about 4 inches longer than the road. She lays it next to the road and aligns one end with the beginning of the road. She then puts her finger on the stick where the road ends. She carefully picks up the stick without moving her finger and moves it to where she will build her road. With her left hand, she picks up the blocks she will need, while keeping the finger of her right hand on the stick so as not to lose her place.

Sasha is a child whose understanding of repeating units is not completely developed. She knows she can reproduce the road using the longer stick, but does not see how using the other objects will help. Let's look at how Petula, who is a little older, handles the same problem.

> The teacher asks Petula, who is a little over 4½, if she can figure out a way to use the 1-inch squares to make a road as long as his. She picks up the bucket of 1-inch squares and lays them out one at a time next to the teacher's road until she has a line of squares as long as the teacher's road. She takes the squares to where she is going to build her road and reconstructs the line. She then lays out her blocks to match the length of the 1-inch squares.

Petula can use units to measure the length of the road. She has constructed a basic understanding of **unit iteration,** which is the concept that a number of units of equal size can be used to measure an object. However, there are still limitations. If Petula were asked if she could measure the road using just one of the cubes, she would likely respond, "no." This true unit iteration does not occur until later, in kindergarten.

Children in most classrooms come from diverse backgrounds and ethnicities and the toys in the classroom should reflect this fact.

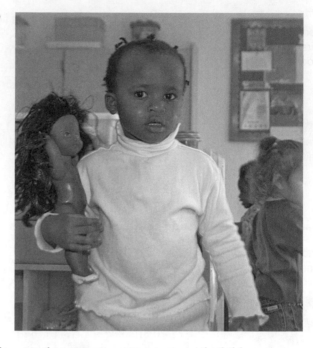

Krista Greco/Merrill

The traditional approach to teaching measurement is to teach children about nonstandard units and put off the use of standard unit measuring devices, such as rulers, until later ages. Recent research (Lehrer, Jenkins, & Osana, 1998) has found that children can use, and often prefer to use, rulers—even in the preschool ages, when measurement using unit iteration is still in its developmental stages. Children seem to enjoy measuring things using a variety of materials such as their own shoes and standard rulers.

Table 6.2   Math Concepts in Preschool.

Topic	2–3 Years	3–4 Years	4–5 Years
Shapes	Match shapes of same size and orientation	Match shapes of different sizes and orientations	Recognize and name variations on the circle, square, triangle, and rectangle
	Informal play with solids such as blocks or tiles	Cover an outline or existing picture with moveable shapes	Build and describe two-dimensional shapes in play settings using their own words
	Use shapes to make a design. Usually in isolation rather than in combination	Break down simple shapes on a tangram puzzle with clues or help	Make representational pictures by combining shapes
			Locate shapes in an arrangement of overlapping shapes or figures

Locations, Directions, and Coordinates	Understand and use ideas such as over, under, above, on, beside, next to, and between	Place toy objects in correct relative position to make a map of the classroom Orient objects vertically or horizontally	Can draw maps of familiar areas or environments that include landmarks, even if landmarks are not in correct relative positions
Transformation and Symmetry	Create two-dimensional shapes and three-dimensional buildings that have line and rotational symmetry in play situations	Can identify slides, flips, and turns of two-dimensional shapes informally	When asked, can identify and create shapes that have line and rotational symmetry
Visualization and Spatial Reasoning	Copy a shape while directly observing it	Copy a shape from memory after seeing the model for a few seconds	Copy a small collection of shapes from memory after seeing the model for a few seconds
Measurement Concepts Measurement Skills and Tools	Use comparing language in play situations, such as bigger, smaller, longer, taller	Compare lengths directly Recognize attributes of volume, weight, area, and time Explore measurement using objects in a play environment, such as building blocks or shoes	Begin understanding transitivity; can use a stick or string to represent and re-create a length. Use nonstandard units to compare objects Comparison of area by placing one object over another Exploratory use of a standard ruler
Number and Systems and Counting	Recognize numerals up to 5 Can recognize small groups of objects (3 and under) as being more or less	Recognize numerals up to 10 Can determine "how many" in groups of 5 or fewer objects Demonstrate one-to-one correspondence	Recognize numerals up to and over 20 Can group and regroup sets of objects (5 blocks can be 2 groups of 2 and 3)
Patterns and Functions	Recognize that a pattern is present in a play situation (music, art, blocks)	Can identify a pattern such as long—long—short or white—white—blue.	Can create new patterns or re-create patterns seen before

MEETING STANDARDS WITH PRESCHOOL CHILDREN

Standards tell us what children need to know in each grade level. As you read the preschool standards and focal points that follow, keep the NCTM's *Principles for School Mathematics* (National Council of Teachers of Mathematics, 2000) in mind.

Mathematical programs for preschool age children should:

- Enhance children's natural interest in mathematics and their disposition to use it to make sense of their physical and social worlds
- Build on children's experience and knowledge, including their family, linguistic, cultural, and community backgrounds; their individual approaches to learning; and their informal knowledge
- Base mathematics curriculum and teaching practices on knowledge of young children's cognitive, linguistic, physical, and social-emotional development
- Use curriculum and teaching practices that strengthen children's problem-solving and reasoning processes as well as representing, communicating, and connecting mathematical ideas
- Ensure that the curriculum is coherent and compatible with known relationships and sequences of important mathematical ideas
- Provide for children's deep and sustained interaction with key mathematical ideas
- Integrate mathematics with other activities and other activities with mathematics
- Provide ample time, materials, and teacher support for children to engage in play, a context in which they explore and manipulate mathematical ideas with keen interest
- Actively introduce mathematical concepts, methods, and language through a range of appropriate experiences and teaching strategies
- Support children's learning by thoughtfully and continually assessing all children's mathematical knowledge, skills, and strategies

General Mathematics Standards and Benchmarks for Preschool Mathematics

Since the publication of the joint NCTM and NAEYC Statement on Preschool Mathematics, many states have begun to develop specific mathematics standards for preschool (see Table 6.2 on page 202). These should be used to guide the activities that occur in the preschool classroom. Below is an example of one state's preschool mathematics standards. Each state may have differences, but they are all based on the principles of NCTM Standards and Practices. Appendix A contains an example of one state's early learning standards.

These standards do not dictate how to teach these concepts. They only set guidelines that teachers of preschool children should try to achieve. By the time the children complete preschool, they should be able to do the things on this list. Standards are simply an aid to help teachers design curricula that are appropriate. They can choose how to teach these standards in class by integrating them into the environment and play experiences of the children. You will notice many of the standards listed above state things such as "in the context of everyday experience or play." The different standards are designed to be met through an integrated approach, rather than by direct instruction.

Sue Bredecamp, one of the authors of the original NAEYC publication on developmentally appropriate practice, wrote:

Any standards document must acknowledge at the outset that there is a wide range of individual variation, and there is a wide range of expectations that are well within the range of typical, that is, developmentally appropriate. Such statements commonly appear on most standards documents, but unfortunately, they are essentially ignored when standards are implemented in assessments or decisions about children. Therefore the most useful strategy is to articulate goals/standards for young children as a developmental or learning continuum. (Bredecamp, 2004, pp. 79–80)

She also states, in the same document, that we need to distinguish between what children *can* learn and what they *should* learn.

The NCTM focal points (Figure 6.2) help us decide which of these standards teachers should focus on in the preschool years. While all of the standards are important, NCTM has discerned a few concepts that should be paid special attention. In the Number and Operations Standard, the focus is on developing an understanding of whole numbers, including concepts of correspondence, counting, cardinality, and comparison. In geometry, the focus is on identifying shapes and describing spatial relationships. In measurement, the focus is on identifying measurable attributes and comparing objects by using these attributes.

WHAT DOES A PRESCHOOL MATHEMATICS LEARNING ENVIRONMENT LOOK LIKE?

Preschool environments are vitally important to all learning, and this is especially true for mathematics. Using the 3E approach to learning mathematics, preschool children are in a transitional period between environment and experience. Therefore, while environment is important, it is also important that the classroom space encourages and supports rich mathematical experiences.

These environments need to have:

- Connections and a sense of belonging for the students—Preschool classrooms should be comfortable and homelike rather than "institutional." By institutional we mean something that looks like a hospital or other public facility. These facilities lack the sense of ownership, relevance and significance that makes a space more homelike. Children are going to do a lot of mathematical learning

Curriculum Focal Points and Connections for Prekindergarten

The set of three curriculum focal points and related connections for mathematics in prekindergarten follow. These topics are the recommended content emphases for this grade level. It is essential that these focal points be addressed in contexts that promote problem solving, reasoning, communication, making connections, and designing and analyzing representations.

Prekindergarten Curriculum Focal Points	Connections to the Focal Points
Number and Operations: **Developing an understanding of whole numbers, including concepts of correspondence, counting, cardinality, and comparison** Children develop an understanding of the meanings of whole numbers and recognize the number of objects in small groups without counting and by counting—the first and most basic mathematical algorithm. They understand that number words refer to quantity. They use one-to-one correspondence to solve problems by matching sets and comparing number amounts, and to counting objects to 10 and beyond. They understand that the last number they state while counting tells "how many." They count to determine number amounts and compare quantities (using language such as "more than" and "less than"), and they order sets by number of objects.	*Data Analysis:* Children learn the foundations of data analysis by using objects' attributes that they have identified in relation to geometry and measurement (e.g.,size, quantity, orientation, number of sides or vertices, color) for various purposes, such as describing, sorting, or comparing. For example, children sort geometric figures by shape, compare objects by weight ("heavier," "lighter"), and describe sets of objects by the number of objects in each set.
Geometry: Identifying shapes and describing spatial relationships. Children develop spatial reasoning by working from two perspectives as they examine the shapes of objects and inspect their relative positions. They find shapes in their environments and describe them in their own words. They build pictures and designs by combining two- and three-dimensional shapes, and solve such problems as deciding which piece will fit into a space in a puzzle. They discuss the relative positions of objects using vocabulary such as "above," "below," and "next to."	*Number and Operations:* Children use meanings of numbers to create strategies for solving problems and responding to practical situations, such as getting just enough napkins for a group, or mathematical situations, such as determining that any shape is a triangle if it has exactly three straight sides and is closed. *Algebra:* Children recognize and duplicate simple sequential patterns (e.g., square, circle, square, circle, square, circle. . .).
Measurement: **Identifying measurable attributes and comparing objects by using these attributes** Children identify objects as "the same" or "different," and then "more" or "less," on the basis of attributes that they can measure. They identify measurable attributes such as length and weight and solve problems by making direct comparisons of objects on the basis of those attributes.	

Figure 6.2   Preschool Focal Points.

Source: Reprinted with permission from *Curriculum Focal Points for Prekindergarten through Grade 8 Mathematics: A Quest for Coherence*, copyright 2006 by the National Council of Teachers of Mathematics. All rights reserved. The Curriculum Focal Points identify key mathematical ideas for these grades. They are not discrete topics or a checklist to be mastered; rather, they provide a framework for the majority of instruction at a particular grade level and the foundation for future mathematics study. The complete document may be viewed at *www.nctm.org/focalpoints.*

through play and they will need to feel comfortable in the environment for this to take place.

- Flexible space and open-ended materials—While children need consistency and predictability in their environments, they also need flexibility. Rooms need not be static, but rather changeable depending on the activity. The guiding principle should be that there are many ways for children and adults to use space and materials.

- Natural materials that engage the senses—Preschoolers rely a lot on their senses to actively explore their environment. The classroom can support mathematics by bringing in interesting objects, textures, and even tastes and aromas. Curtis and Carter (2003) suggest herbs, flowers, leaves, scented candles or soaps, shells, rocks, feathers, branches, pieces of bark, and wood as manipulatives rather than just plastic or polished wood objects.

- Wonder, curiosity, and intellectual engagement—Things that provoke a sense of mystery and wonder encourage children to become curious about how mathematics works. The preschool years are filled with a sense of magic and wonder and a well-prepared environment can support a child's sense of mathematical inquiry.

- Symbolic representations and visual arts—Children need an environment rich in representation, whether printed literary or mathematical in nature. The arts can support mathematics in the preschool years through music, dance, and theatrical expression, as well as through visual arts such as painting and drawing (Curtis & Carter, 2003).

- Diverse materials—Each classroom will be composed of children of different cognitive levels and cultural and ethnic backgrounds. Materials in the classroom should reflect this diversity. Pictures and dolls should include examples of many different ethnic backgrounds, and materials should allow for many different levels of use.

Preschool environments are active places that support exploration. Most importantly, they should be comfortable and as homelike as possible. Creating a homelike environment means that the teacher thinks about how a child interacts with people and objects in their home and tries to re-create that in the classroom. For example, there are places in a home suited to messy types of activities, such as a kitchen, garage, or basement. These spaces may have hard floors and easy-to-clean surfaces. Other spaces, such as a living room, need to be comfortable and quiet for activities such as reading. Some spaces are social spaces where children can discuss mathematical ideas or problems, such as a den. These spaces may include multiple chairs and maybe a table. There are also spaces for work, such as an office, which might include hard surfaces for writing, storage spaces for paper and pencils, a computer, and other items needed to do mathematics work (Curtis & Carter, 2003).

DEVELOPMENTALLY APPROPRIATE STRATEGIES AND ACTIVITIES FOR PRESCHOOL-AGE CHILDREN

During the preschool years, children's ability to use representation and symbolic and intuitive thought enables them to begin to learn through classroom experiences. Using the 3 Es of mathematics learning for children introduced previously, they are still learning through interaction with the environment; however, their new physical, cognitive, and social-emotional abilities make it possible for them to interact with objects and people in more complex ways. Preschool children can manipulate objects with more skill due to improved fine motor skills; can understand, think, and reason about situations and problems; and can interact with the teacher and other students in meaningful ways.

While the environment is still an important factor in the child's learning of mathematics, teachers can also design experiences that meet mathematics goals. With infants and toddlers, teacher-directed mathematics lessons were not a viable option. In preschool, teachers can introduce mathematical activities in the context of everyday activity and group time activities.

It is always prudent to keep to ideas of developmentally appropriate practice when designing a standards-based mathematical curriculum for young children. As mentioned earlier, standards are a tool that, when used carefully, can greatly benefit the learning process. However, if used improperly, they can lead to higher levels of stress in children, poor attitudes to school and mathematics, and math anxiety. Carol Copple, who has written extensively on Developmentally Appropriate Practice,

Manipulatives are a mainstay of preschool classroom mathematics materials.

Katelyn Metzger/Merrill

suggests some basic practices to develop effective mathematics curriculum in the preschool years and avoid some of the negative outcomes.

- Give children opportunities to manipulate a wide variety of things and provide time for children to "mess about"
- Let children pursue their own interests and investigations
- Interact frequently with children and ask open-ended questions
- Integrate the curriculum
- Encourage children to interact mathematically with one another
- Have close contact with families (Copple, 2004)

We should keep these basic practices in mind as we discuss how to create rich and interactive mathematical experiences for young children. There are many ways that mathematics can be integrated into the preschool classroom. The activities and experiences listed here are not exclusive and can be modified and extended into many other areas of the child's life and play situations. Here are 10 suggestions to help you get started developing experiences in your preschool classroom.

Group Time. As with infants and toddlers, everyday activities such as snack and circle time can be used to promote the usage of math. Dividing up snacks, counting plates, and other activities can be assigned to children. They then have to use their own mathematical problem-solving ability to figure out the best way to achieve their tasks. For example, a child assigned to put out the plates for his table of five may do it by going to the stack of plates, getting one plate and placing it in front of one child, going back to get another plate for the next child, and so on until everyone has a plate. Eventually, he will realize that he can count the children, then go to the plates, count out five, and distribute them accordingly. Allowing the child to use his own methods of solving a problem allows his emergent understanding of math to develop.

Assigning two children to figure out how to solve an everyday problem, as described previously, promotes problem solving even more. The children can discuss, plan, and even argue about the best way to solve the problem. This argument will encourage both children to construct new ways of seeing the problem (Kamii & DeVries, 1980; Kamii & National Association for the Education of Young Children, 1982; Kamii et al., 1980). In an argument, the child must clearly communicate his ideas to another person and at the same time evaluate the other person's ideas. In the process, he examines and perhaps modifies his or her own ideas.

Whenever a decision needs to be made and the children can have an input, voting allows the teacher to use math in an integrated way. Not only does it offer an opportunity to count, but to compare numbers as well. Children can be asked to vote on which book the teacher should read to them first. As the teacher counts hands, she encourages the children to count with her. If the vote is six to five, the teacher asks the children which book won.

Manipulatives. An easy way to promote math at this age is simply to ask a child to use mathematical concepts in his activities. If a child is using blocks, a teacher can say, "I see you have some blocks. Can you tell me more about them?" Children are willing and even excited to count objects and make mathematical relationships if encouraged. A 4-year-old child was working alone to make a chain out of different colored plastic links. When I asked him how long he was trying to make the chain he did not respond, so I tried a more direct question. "How many do you have so far?" I asked. He continued to put on the next link and then proceeded to count each link. There were eight. After he put on another link, I asked again, "How many do you have now?" Going back to the beginning, he counted each link again and said, "nine." This time I asked him a more leading question. "You had nine and you added one more. How many do you have now?" Again he counted all the links and said, "10." Each time he put on a new link, he would count all of them, eventually making a chain with 27 links. However, after about 15, his counting became erratic. Sometimes he counted carefully and got the correct answer; other times he missed some of the links in his counting.

After correctly counting to 26 and adding one more, he counted again and missed a few. After completing the counting, he triumphantly announced "15!" Even though he made mistakes and showed an incomplete understanding of number concepts, he was getting closer and closer to using mathematics in a conventional manner. This is similar to the process that children go through when they move from drawing squiggles to learning to write conventionally.

Tangrams. These are geometric puzzles (Figure 6.3) that can help children with rotation and transformation of shapes as well as with other attributes of two-dimensional shapes. If the names of the shapes are marked on the pieces, this can also help with word recognition. Picture puzzles are also valuable tools in teaching rotations and spatial

Children's maps may not be accurate enough to follow, but they reflect the child's spatial reasoning skills. This is a valuable activity in the preschool classroom.

Anne Vega/Merrill

Figure 6.3   Tangram.

awareness. Other manipulatives such as Pattern Blocks and Magna Tiles (Figure 6.4) can help children with two-dimensional (flat) shapes recognition and attributes. Three-dimensional building materials like Legos and building blocks can help with three-dimensional shape recognition and attributes. Patterning beads and string are also very interactive mathematical tools to have in your manipulatives area of the classroom.

Whatever manipulatives you choose, you should make sure that you have a variety of shapes, colors, textures, material (wood, plastic, glass, etc.), and sizes for children to sort, classify, and use for building patterns. Children learn through sensory activities, but math is learned through mental activity. The benefit of manipulatives is that they stimulate the child to think mathematically while sorting, classifying, patterning, and counting the objects.

Blocks. In the classroom, blocks are usually in a separate area, as playing with them often requires a good deal of space. However, there is a benefit to having the manipulative area close by, in that this allows children to bring blocks to the manipulative area and vice versa. This can allow for a cross-pollination of ideas and thought. Blocks

Figure 6.4 Magna Tiles.

have many of the same benefits and uses as manipulatives but they incorporate representational thought much more than other math manipulatives.

Preschool children, especially older ones, use constructive play to learn about the world and mathematics (Burns & Cuisenaire Company of America, 1987; National Association for the Education of Young Children & South Carolina Educational Television Network, 1987; Reifel, 1995). Mathematics is a representational activity and by playing with blocks, children strengthen these abilities. Additionally, block play allows for the meeting of many of the three-dimensional shapes standards. Naming three-dimensional shapes and understanding rotations, symmetry, and making new shapes are accomplished when a child plays with blocks. Often, this understanding happens without the teacher's assistance.

Math Games. Preschool children's social skills have developed to the point that they can communicate and interact with their peers. Math games for infants and toddlers were generally individual games, but group games become a reality with the new cognitive and social abilities of preschool children. Their developing counting skills also make it possible for teachers to introduce games that involve counting and number concepts (DeVries & Kamii, 1975; Kamii & DeVries, 1973,1980; Weikart, 1964).

Math games allow for a large degree of social interaction. If children disagree on a rule or on a move made by another child, they should be encouraged to express their points of view and try to resolve the conflict through discussion. Discussion leads to mathematical thinking and explanation of thought processes and should be encouraged as long as it is not causing emotional distress to one or the other student. Teachers should avoid solving the problem for the children by telling them who is right, but should let them work it out for themselves (Kaye, 1987; Zaslavsky, 1979).

Math games also allow for social problem solving. For example, two children are playing a card game and both put down the same card. What happens? The teacher can explain the rule, but if left open for the children to decide, it encourages them to figure out what to do on their own. They may choose to take the cards back out or to put down another card to create a larger pile. This may not seem mathematical, but the problem solving that occurs is related to mathematical thinking.

Math games are varied and can range from simple, homemade path games to card games and commercially available games such as "Hi, Ho!, Cherry-O." Using math games in preschool requires the teacher to:

1. examine the game and how it is played
2. determine if there is enough mathematical content to justify its use or creation
3. think about what standards are met with the game
4. if it is a commercially available game, determine how it can be modified to include more mathematics
5. determine how the game can be extended to make it easier or harder depending on the developmental level of the students
6. determine if the game will be fun for the students

This last point is often overlooked when creating math games. Remember, these are games that indirectly teach mathematical concepts. Playing with other students makes the games fun, as does the exercising of cognitive thinking ability. The mathematics should be kept open-ended, with many possible ways of getting an answer. These games should require little or no teacher or adult interaction or explanation. The children should, with minimal instructions, be able to figure out what is required. There should also be a goal or "end point" to the game. In a path game, this is the "finishline." Games in preschool should not emphasize winning and losing but should focus instead on process.

Many math games tend to become teacher-directed activities such as using flash cards dressed up to look like a math game. These take too much explanation and interaction from the teacher. Children can easily recognize these weaknesses and the games tend to just sit on a shelf.

The Project Approach. Using the 3E approach to teaching mathematics, preschool-age children begin to learn through experience. Projects in preschool are the best way of integrating experience into the mathematics program. They engage the children physically and mentally. Selecting a topic should be conducted in cooperation with the children and should be based on their interests. Good topics are ones that children see and interact with every day and are narrow enough to allow for a thorough and focused investigation, and integration of many different subject areas.

The project approach to early childhood education allows children to explore the world and construct knowledge through genuine interaction with the environment. Lilian Katz (Helm & Katz, 2001; Hillen et al., 1986; Katz & Chard, 2000) suggests that young children should have activities that engage their minds fully in the quest for knowledge, understanding, and the skills to help them develop and learn.

When engaged in a project children are not just gathering knowledge from a worksheet, structured activity, or teacher, but are actively making decisions not only about what to learn, but also how and where. Through this engagement, children construct problem-solving techniques, research methods, and questioning strategies.

When children work on projects, a number of opportunities arise for them to use math. In the lesson plan on apples presented later, you will see the rich mathematical explorations that can be made available to students through this type of investigative activity (Figure 6.5). They can measure the apples and the trees as well as use measurement in pretend cooking activities. Their measurements may not always be accurate, because their use of standard measurement is still developing, but just as a child who writes squiggles on a piece of paper is learning to write, so these children are learning about measurement.

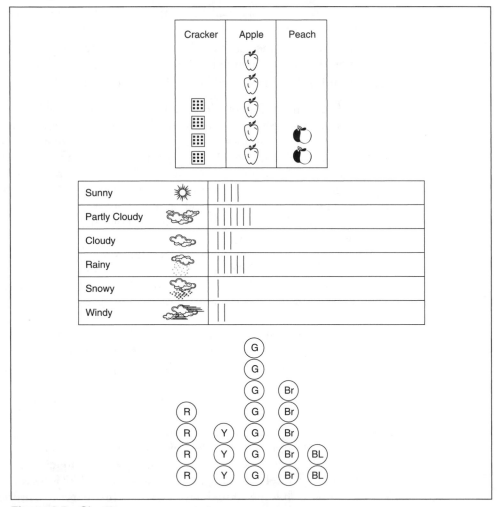

Figure 6.5   Charts.

The children can also learn the science of growing things, allowing for an integration of number concepts with science activities. They can plant apple seeds and mark off days on a calendar until they see a sprout. They can take measurements each day to examine the growth and make a graph of the data they collect. They can look for shapes in the leaves and apples they collect. They can make apple prints and discuss how cutting the apple differently can create different shapes on paper.

Representational aspects of the project can also allow for rich mathematical experiences. If children are painting a picture of a large tree, they can discuss how large the paper needs to be and on what scale they should draw their tree. They can examine where the picture should be hung and discuss how to make it large or small enough to fit the space.

Mapmaking. Children are developing spatial reasoning skills and are constructing a coordinate system that will allow them to represent large areas, such as their neighborhood. When children are asked to make maps of their classroom, school grounds, neighborhood, or routes to favorite places, they have to reconstruct what they know about getting from one place to another and organize it in a systematic way. As adults, we use a scaled coordinate system which shows where things are in relationship to others. When adults make maps, there are aspects of direction, distance, and the coordination of landmarks (where is the grocery store in relation to your home).

Preschool children do not have the concept of a two-dimensional grid coordinate system. However, just because their maps are not accurate does not mean this is not a useful activity in which to engage. As children think about the space and environments they live in and repeatedly represent them, they begin to think about and notice irregularities in their representations (Dehaene, Pica, & Spelke, 2006; Eisenhower National Clearinghouse for Mathematics and Science, 1919; Piaget, Inhelder, & Szeminska, 1960).

> Paula is conducting a mapmaking activity. She has asked her class of four-year-olds to draw maps showing how to get from their preschool classroom to the nearby art museum. She tells them that they will be walking to the museum the next day and she wants everyone to have a map of the route. The maps the children make show lots of landmarks that they remember, such as the "big tree," the "candy store," and the "old bridge." However, their maps do not reflect physical and spatial reality. The children put the candy store closest to the school and the tree and the bridge next to each other.
>
> After the children have completed their maps, they present them to the class. The next day, as they walk to the museum, Paula points out landmarks and mention how far it is from the school to the candy shop. She also points out that when standing on the bridge, she can't see the "big tree" because it is around the corner. She encourages the children to count steps. After the field trip, she talks about all the landmarks they saw. She then has the children work in groups to make a larger map on chart paper. The children discuss with each other and look at their previous maps, saying things such as "The big tree can't be near the old bridge because you can't see it from the bridge. It's around the corner, and the candy store is much farther from the school." The interaction between the children and their recent experience produces group maps that show more of a link to physical reality.

Charting and Graphing. Preschool children use their experiences to organize their environment and mathematics can be used to help them organize and understand these experiences. Just about anything children do in the classroom, at home, or during play can be made into a chart or graph. A simple pictograph is understandable to young preschoolers, as they can recognize that one line of the graph is longer than the other. Older preschoolers can chart the daily weather or other aspects of their school life.

For younger preschoolers, preference graphs can be used. Each child selects a slice of apple or peach, or a piece of a cracker, and tapes or velcros it to a chart. If each child places his selection above the last person's, the selection with the most pieces will be taller and children can easily discern which selection contains the "most."

Older preschoolers can do the same thing using a chart of sunny days, cloudy and partly cloudy days, rainy days, snowy days, and windy days. Each day, they put a mark in the box that best describes the day. Children can also be given a bag of small colored candies and asked to make a chart out of the different colors, putting each color in a line to see which color has the most candy. This activity allows children to relate numbers to the graph; they can count as well as make a graph.

Art and Drawing. Drawing and using art materials such as scissors and paint brushes creates many opportunities for children to interact with shapes and geometry through their artwork. Activities can be directive, giving children many different cardboard shapes (such as squares, circles, triangles) and asking them to cover an existing picture with the shapes, or compose their own picture. Three-year-olds might use the shapes to make a design, while 4-year-olds may construct a picture of a house.

Open-ended and nondirective art activities incorporating, drawing and painting can be used to promote children's understanding of geometry, shape, and symmetry. Free drawing and painting activities offer opportunities for teachers to ask about the child's drawing or painting and perhaps focus his attention on geometric constructs. Teachers should always avoid using judgmental language when talking to children about their art, instead asking questions about the method of production, such as "How did you decide to use a circle here?" or "Why did you put three squares here?" Teachers can also make nonjudgmental statements such as, "You used more blue than green." These types of observations not only keep the teacher's comments genuine, but help focus the child's attention on mathematical concepts such as circles, squares, and more.

Imaginative Play. A great deal of a preschooler's time is spent in imaginary play activity. Wherever the imaginative play takes place, it is a perfect opportunity to promote mathematics. Not only is the representational thinking supported by the simple act of engaging in fantasy play, but the topics of the fantasy play can also be filled with mathematical opportunities.

One of the most popular things children like to do in the imaginative play area is to play "store." They set up a cash register and offer things for sale, take in money, and make change. This is often done without any teacher intervention. With careful observation, a teacher can determine what mathematical props would make the play situations more mathematically rich. For example, play paper money and coins. The teacher could also role-play as a customer in the imaginary store.

Casey (who is almost 5 years old): "Would you like to shop at my store?"

Teacher: "Yes, how much do things in your store cost?"

Casey: "A dollar."

Teacher: "Well, I don't have any dollars . . ."

Casey: "That's OK. Here are some for you (he gives the teacher four play dollars)"

Teacher: "Thank you. What does your store sell, Casey?"

Casey: "We sell hamburgers and french fries and fried eggs and soup (these were all prop items that Casey had collected from the imaginative play area)."

Teacher: "Well, I will take soup and one fried egg please."

Casey: "OK. That will be—um . . ."

Teacher: "If it is one of these dollars for each of these things, how many dollars should I give you?"

Casey: "Um. . . let me see (he takes the money and lays one dollar on each item and then counts it). One, two. Two dollars, please!"

Teacher: "OK, two dollars. Thank you, Casey."

Vygotsky theorized that children perform on a higher level within the context of a play situation than in an academic setting. Using imaginative play situations allows children to use their natural thinking and problem-solving abilities and their intuitive understanding of mathematics.

SAMPLE PRESCHOOL LESSONS PLANS

On the following pages, you will find some Lesson Plans that provide developmentally appropriate ways to promote the development of mathematical concepts in preschool-age children. These suggestions incorporate the concepts you've read about in this chapter. If you have a field experience or observation opportunity in your course, these activities can be introduced to young children. In keeping with developmentally and culturally appropriate practices, keep in mind the individual children you are working with and adapt the lessons accordingly. If you are building a teaching portfolio, place a copy of the lessons, along with your adaptations, comments and reflections in your electronic or hard copy folder.

LESSON PLAN

▼◄ ▲▼◄ ▲▼◄ ▲▼◄ ▲▼◄ ▲▼◄ ▲▼◄ ▲

Lesson Title: Field Trip to Apple Orchard

Age: Preschool

Subject Area: Mathematics

▼◄ ▲▼◄ ▲▼◄ ▲▼◄ ▲▼◄ ▲▼◄ ▲▼◄ ▲

Objective: To use a familiar topic to integrate the use of mathematics into preschool children's day using the project approach. Children will use mathematics to investigate apples and apple orchards through this project.

Standards: Sort and classify similar two- and three-dimensional objects in the environment and play situations (e.g., paper shapes, two balls of different size). Identify, name, create, and describe common two-dimensional shapes in the environment and play situations (e.g., circles, triangles, rectangles, and squares). Identify, name, and describe three-dimensional objects using the child's own vocabulary (e.g., sphere—"ball," cube—"box," cylinder—"can" or "tube," and cone—"ice cream cone").

Focal Points: 1) Developing an understanding of whole numbers, including concepts of correspondence, counting, cardinality, and comparison; 2) identifying shapes and describing spatial relationships; and 3) identifying measurable attributes and comparing objects by using these attributes (use of comparison words).

Lesson Summary: Students will study apples over a period of a few weeks, including a field trip to an orchard. The teacher will help children define questions about apples that they would like to answer, focusing on mathematical concepts. The teacher will direct children to examine the shape of apples ("What shape are the apples?"), the relative size of apples ("Which apples are bigger?" "What are apples smaller than or bigger than?"), the quantities of apples in containers (barrels, bushels, and bags), and ways to count and measure the apples. Children can also learn about apples through science, reading, social studies, music, art, and movement.

Beginning the Lesson: Preschool children have probably had experiences with apples at home and at snack time. Perhaps they have been grocery shopping with a family member and have been overwhelmed with the amount and variety of apples for sale. Because apples contain a rich diversity of color, shape, taste, and other attributes, an apple orchard is an ideal environment for a field trip. You might start the conversation about apples and the upcoming trip by asking, "How many of you like apples? What kind of apples do you like?" This question even provides an opportunity for counting hands.

Procedures: Before the trip, the children should be encouraged to discuss apples in group time and told about the field trip. This will be where much of the initial KWL charting is done. The children are asked to come up with individual questions to ask the people at the apple orchard, using mathematical language such as "how many" and "how much," and sequence words in some of their questions. The teacher has the children tell her their questions in group time and writes them on a piece of chart paper. Before the field trip, she transfers the questions to a regular sheet of paper and makes copies for the children. The copies, as well as two sheets of blank paper, are clipped to clipboards. Each child will carry his own clipboard on the field trip.

Next you can start to develop a KWL chart in which children tell you what they **K**now about apples, what they **W**ant to know about apples, and later, what they **L**earned about apples. Begin by asking them to tell you everything they know about apples. This can be recorded on chart paper with the heading, *What we know*. After they have exhausted what they know about apples, you can move on to recording, *What we want to know* on another piece of chart paper. Many times the questions children have about apples are more revealing than answers to questions put to them by a teacher. Some examples of responses to this might be:

What we know about apples	What we want to know about apples
Apples are red	How do they pick all the apples?
Some apples are green	How many seeds are in an apple?
Apples grow on trees	Why are there different colored apples?
Apples have a skin	Why are some apples bigger?

If children need some guidance coming up with questions to investigate, the teacher could help them along by making statements or asking questions such as:

- I wonder how many kinds of apples there are.
- I wonder if there are blue apples.
- How many different colors of apples you have seen?
- I wonder where apples come from.

The day of the trip, children will take their clipboard and a marker with them to the apple orchard. The host will take the children on a tour of the orchard and show them the buildings and equipment used to run it and how products such as apple cider are made. After the tour, they can sit with the host and ask questions. Afterward, they can break into small groups and choose something that they would like to gather more information on (for example, the cider press, or an apple picker machine). They should be encouraged to draw pictures of what they saw and did during their adventure.

Once back in the classroom, the teacher revisits the KWL chart, asking children what they learned about apples. She will begin to examine the artifacts the children brought back from the orchard to determine what mathematics content can be focused on over the next couple of days (see Figures 6.6 and 6.7). Perhaps she can discuss the different shapes that children saw at the orchard, or help sort what they saw into categories of "big" and "small" or "a lot" and "a little."

Extension: The questions the children asked in the KWL experience and during the field trip can guide activities and investigations over the following weeks. While teachers should follow the children's interests and questions, they can facilitate the learning and

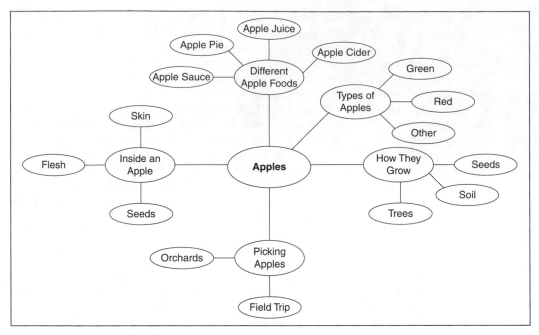

Figure 6.6   Topic Web for Apples.

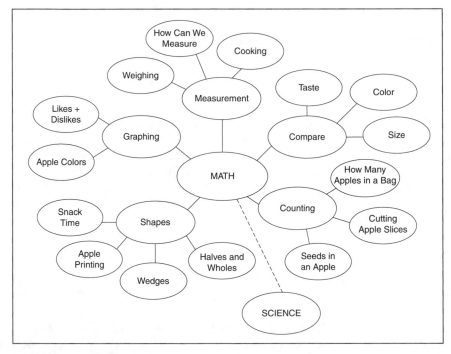

Figure 6.7   Math Web Apples.

investigation process by saying things like, "I wonder how many seeds there are in that apple?" or "I wonder if a bigger apple has more seeds." As children's questions become more and more complex, smaller groups can be assigned to investigate specific questions that arise, such as, "What is the difference between a fruit and a vegetable?"

Adaptations: Help the class learn how to say "apple" in many different languages, such as *manzana* in Spanish or *pomme* in French. Children can examine different fruits grown in the countries of children who are from different cultures. For example, a mango might be more popular in some areas of the world and can be brought in, studied, and compared to the apple. Make comparisons between the fruits such as the shape or number of seeds or the size of the fruit. Hands-on activities lend themselves to children with special needs. If needed, the teacher or another student can help these students with recording information.

Materials: Paper, clipboard, chart paper, markers, a nearby apple orchard, and transportation (parents should be encouraged to come along as additional guides).

Assessment: Assessment should be done through observation and recording the children's responses to the experience. A collection of the children's drawings should be put in their portfolios.

LESSON PLAN

▼◄ ▲▼◄ ▲▼◄ ▲▼◄ ▲▼◄ ▲▼◄ ▲▼◄ ▲

Lesson Title: What Do I Need?

Age: Preschool

Subject Area: Mathematics

▼◄ ▲▼◄ ▲▼◄ ▲▼◄ ▲▼◄ ▲▼◄ ▲▼◄ ▲

Objective: To promote counting as a means of solving problems and to strengthen one-to-one correspondence.

Standards: 1) Explain the rules of counting, such as how each object should be counted only once and that order does not change the number. 2) Determine "how many" in sets (groups) of 10 or fewer objects. 3) Construct multiple sets of objects each containing the same number of objects.

Focal Points: Representing, comparing, and ordering whole numbers and joining and separating sets.

Lesson Summary: Children will make patterns using attributes of the clothes that the children are wearing.

Beginning the Lesson: The teacher says to the class "I was eating my dinner last night. I had my favorite food—SOUP! And you know what! I didn't have a clean spoon! It is really hard to eat soup without a spoon, don't you think? I had to wash a spoon so I could eat my dinner. We need different eating utensils for different foods." Have the children discuss what utensils should be used when eating different types of food.

Procedures: The teacher has four children stand in front of the group. A fifth child is told, "These four are going to eat soup. Can you give each one the utensil he will need?" Then have five children come up and do the same thing, saying, "These children are going to eat carrots. Give them each the utensil they will need." On the third round, have three children stand up and say, "These children are going to eat steak. I think they might need more that just one utensil, what do you all think?"

Observe how the child distributing the utensils completes the one-to-one correspondence task. Does he make four or five trips to the table with the utensils or does he count four utensils and distribute them accordingly?

Extension: Children can make patterns based on height or other measurable attributes. More complex patterns can be developed with children that have two colors on their shirts. The teacher can also create a Venn diagram based on what colors children are wearing. For example, some children might be wearing blue, others white, and some might be wearing both blue and white. Children can discuss in which group the children wearing both colors should be placed.

Adaptations: Musical experiences help to structure activities for children with special needs, such as autism. With careful attention and by varying beat, rhythm, and melody the music can be adapted to involve these children in an activity in which they would not otherwise be able to participate. Teachers may need to help the child clap or keep a rhythm during the song. Drums and other instruments can be incorporated as needed. The following song can be used for this activity.

To the tune of "Head, Shoulders, Knees, and Toes"

We've got some forks, knives, and spoons,
Knives and spoons.
We've got some forks, knives, and spoons,
Knives and spoons.

What do you need to eat _____ (fill in with food)

Some soup?
Green beans?
Some steak?
Some chicken?
Some carrots?

Choose from forks, knives, or spoons? Tap tap tap
Keep a beat by tapping on your own legs and encourage the students to keep the beat with you by tapping their own legs.

Materials: A number of plastic forks, knives, and spoons; drums to help keep the beat.

Assessment: Assessment should be done through observation and recording the children's responses to informal questioning techniques. Individual work can be collected and put in the child's portfolio.

LESSON PLAN
▼◄ ▲▼◄ ▲▼◄ ▲▼◄ ▲▼◄ ▲▼◄ ▲▼◄ ▲

Lesson Title: Distribution of Snack

Age: Preschool

Subject Area: Mathematics

▼◄ ▲▼◄ ▲▼◄ ▲▼◄ ▲▼◄ ▲▼◄ ▲▼◄ ▲

Objective: Strengthen understanding of one-to-one correspondence and help children recognize different numerical patterns.

Standards: 1) Count to 10 in the context of daily activities and play (e.g., number songs). 2) Touch objects and say the number names when counting in the context of daily activities and play (e.g., cookies on a plate, steps on a set of stairs). 3) Demonstrate one-to-one correspondence when counting objects (e.g., give one cookie to each child in group). 4) Determine "how many" in sets of five or fewer objects.

Focal Points: Developing an understanding of whole numbers, including concepts of correspondence, counting, cardinality, and comparison.

Lesson Summary: Children help distribute the snack during snack time. Each day, the teacher has a snack item to distribute that requires a mathematical process. She puts a package of 10 crackers on a table where five children are sitting. One child each day is designated as snack leader and is in charge of equally dividing the crackers amongst the children. Teachers should encourage social interaction among the students and should use mathematical questioning techniques.

Beginning the Lesson: Math can be found in many everyday activities. Snack time is especially rich with mathematical experiences. It is an activity that children enjoy and it is part of their daily routine. It also shows the concrete and practical application of mathematics in the classroom.

Procedures: The teacher introduces the snack for the day and assigns tasks. A few children are assigned as "daily snack helpers." This can be done at the beginning of the day during circle time or at snack time, by assigning one child at a table to be in charge of a specific task. For example, Gaby can be in charge of napkins, Peter can be in charge of spoons, and Ruth can be in charge of plates. Often teachers don't think to emphasize the one-to-one correspondence of putting one spoon or one napkin at every plate. Simply saying to the child, "Can you give one napkin to each person at your table?" or "How many spoons do you need for your table?" emphasizes the rich mathematical substance in this everyday activity.

Teachers can also promote geometry by choosing snacks that have interesting and different shapes, and asking questions such as "How is the shape of today's snack different from yesterday's?"

Students will develop one-to-one correspondence concepts by distributing needed items to the children at the table. The method of achieving these simple tasks will change and develop as the child grows. For example, at the beginning of the school year, the child may make a number of trips to the napkin holder to get napkins for each person at his table; later in the year, he may be able to count five people and five napkins and know that he has enough for everyone.

Students can also examine the shapes that they see at snack time. What shape are the plates or the snack? For example, crackers can be square, rectangular, round, oval, or, in some cases, polygonal.

Extension: Having the children help prepare the daily snack can extend this activity. Instead of just distributing the snack, children can help to prepare it by helping to open boxes or by cutting fruit (use sturdy plastic knives and softer fruit at first). They can also be involved in making cookies or other foods that involve measurement and mixing. As they become more competent in this task, the teacher can introduce uneven quantities. For example, she may give 12 crackers to a table of five children and observe how they handle the problem.

Adaptations: Children can learn words for different foods in other languages and use different languages to say things such as "Please" and "Thank You." Foods from other cultures can be introduced during snack time and ELL students can use their language as well as English to talk about the food. Children with developmental delays may need some assistance with the tasks. Pairing students can be beneficial; they can help each other with the tasks.

LESSON PLAN
▼◄ ▲▼◄ ▲▼◄ ▲▼◄ ▲▼◄ ▲▼◄ ▲▼◄ ▲

Lesson Title: Shape Patterns with Felt Board

Age: Preschool

Subject Area: Mathematics

▼◄ ▲▼◄ ▲▼◄ ▲▼◄ ▲▼◄ ▲▼◄ ▲▼◄ ▲

Objective: Help children to recognize and extend patterns.

Standards: Identify, copy, extend, and create simple patterns or sequences of sounds, shapes, and motions in the context of daily activities and play (e.g., creates red, blue, red, blue pattern with blocks).

Focal Points: Identifying shapes and describing spatial relationships.

Lesson Summary: Children will use the felt board to create, repeat, and extend patterns.

Beginning the Lesson: The teacher will talk to the children about the different shapes to make sure that they know what each shape is called. The teacher might say, for example, "What shape is this?" as she puts a triangle on the felt board.

Procedures: The teacher begins by placing a circle and a square on the felt board. She says, "What shape is this?" pointing to the circle, and then, "And this one?" pointing to the square. She then asks, "If we were making a pattern, what would come next?" Children should be allowed to build the pattern until there is no room left on the felt board.

Extension: Adding different colored shapes, so that children can pattern by two attributes, can extend this activity. Longer patterns can be introduced for children to repeat and extend.

Adaptations: Musical experiences help to structure activities for children with special needs, such as autism. With careful attention and by varying beat, rhythm, and melody the music can be adapted to involve these children in an activity in which they would not otherwise be able to participate. Teachers may need to help the child clap or keep a rhythm during the song. Drums and other instruments can be incorporated as needed. The teacher puts a pattern up on the board, singing the song and keeping a steady beat going. He then asks a child to come up to extend the pattern.

Sing the song as children put shapes up. Change the tempo of the song to fit what the child is doing.

Teachers can replace the word "I" with the name of the child when he makes his own pattern.

> Sung to the melody of "Blue Bird."
> Words to the Song:
> (Example of three-shape pattern song)

Circle Triangle Square, clap clap
Circle Triangle Square, clap clap
Circle Triangle Square, clap clap
(I) _____ just made a pattern.

(Example of two-shape pattern song)

Circle Square, clap clap clap clap
Circle Square, clap clap clap clap
Circle Square, clap clap clap clap
(I) _____ just made a pattern.

(Example of a four-shape pattern song)

Triangle Square Circle Circle
Triangle Square Circle Circle
Triangle Square Circle Circle
(I) _____ just made a pattern.

Materials: Felt board, nine each of a red circle, yellow triangle, and green square.

Assessment: Assessment is achieved through direct observation of the interaction of the child with the materials and experiences. Anecdotal and running records can be employed.

LESSON PLAN

▼◄ ▲▼◄ ▲▼◄ ▲▼◄ ▲▼◄ ▲▼◄ ▲▼◄ ▲

Lesson Title: How Many Ducks?

Age: Preschool

Subject Area: Mathematics

▼◄ ▲▼◄ ▲▼◄ ▲▼◄ ▲▼◄ ▲▼◄ ▲▼◄ ▲

Objective: Aid children in counting and one-to-one correspondence.

Standards: 1) Touch objects and say the number names when counting in the context of daily activities and play (e.g., cookies on a plate, steps on a set of stairs). 2) Demonstrate one-to-one correspondence when counting objects (e.g., give one cookie to each child in group). 3) Determine "how many" in sets of five or fewer objects.

Focal Points: Developing an understanding of whole numbers, including concepts of correspondence, counting, cardinality, and comparison.

Lesson Summary: Children will count ducks during a story and singing activity using a felt board.

Beginning the Lesson: The teacher tells a story such as, "A little while ago, I went to a park where there were lots of ducks swimming in a pond. I saw a momma duck with all her little ducklings swimming behind her. Usually, they all swam in a straight line, but sometimes one or two of the ducklings would get out of line. When this happened, the momma duck would turn around, count her ducklings, and then give a big 'Quack quack' to get them to line up again. Do you think we can count ducklings just like the momma duck?"

Procedures: The teacher should put the white momma duck on the felt board. "OK, so here is the momma duck and she is going to count her ducklings. When we count, do we count the momma duck? What do you think?" Children should decide as a group and the teacher should follow what they decide. The discussion of the question as a group could lead to a "teachable moment"; be careful not to cut it short if children are still discussing.

The teacher should then introduce the Duck Counting song to help them in their counting.

Duck Counting Song:

(Place the mother duck and the little ducks out of line on the felt board. The number doesn't matter. Whatever you want to start with will be fine.)
Start with a steady beat and keep it going throughout.

Sing to the tune of the "Addams Family"

How many ducks? clap clap clap
How many ducks? clap clap clap
How many ducks, how many ducks, how many ducks, clap clap

[Spoken] Let's count
1 2 3 4 5 6 7

How many ducks? SEVEN
How many ducks? SEVEN
How many ducks, how many ducks, how many ducks, SEVEN

[chanted] What does mother duck say to get them back in line?

Quack Quack Quack Quack Quack (repeat until the ducks are put back in line)

(Sing a little slower to allow time for the kids fill in the blanks)
How many ducks? SEVEN
How many ducks? SEVEN
How many ducks, how many ducks, how many ducks? SEVEN

(If all children don't say the number, go back to the "Let's count" line)

Repeat song, placing a different number of ducks out of line.

In the beginning, the teacher should pick about four or five ducklings and line them up behind the mother duck. The teacher then asks, "How many ducklings are there?" Encourage children to count as a group while you point to the ducks.

The next time, the teacher chooses five or six ducklings and puts two of these ducklings out of place behind the momma duck. This will make the counting harder because children have to focus on the *order* of the counting. Have a child come up and point to the ducks while the children count as a group. Afterward the teacher can say, "Do you remember what the momma duck said to get the ducklings back in line? Let's all say it now." Have the children say "quack, quack" as you put the ducks back in a row. Then ask, "Now that the ducklings are back in a straight line, are there the same number of ducklings?"

The felt board can be left up during the day for children to play with during free play time (if possible).

Extension: Children may ask questions such as, "Where is the Daddy duck," in which case you can make another adult duck to put on the felt board. This will also allow you to make size comparisons and estimations.

Adaptations: Translating the song or parts of the song into other languages will help to include children who are still learning English. Songs make this process less difficult. Some children may have trouble with sequencing while counting and may count some ducks twice (especially when they are not in a line). Teachers can help them by holding their hand as they count, in order to scaffold the experience.

Materials: Felt board, felt cutouts of a Momma Duck, Daddy Duck, and at least eight ducklings.

Assessment: Assessment is achieved through direct observation of the interaction of the child with the materials and experiences. Anecdotal and running records can be employed. As the children play with the felt board independently or in groups later in the week, teachers can do more in-depth observations of the mathematical thinking.

ASSESSMENT

As we discussed in the chapter on infants and toddlers, assessment has two purposes: formative and summative. It can also be formal or informal. As with infants, in the preschool years, appropriate assessment will mostly be formative and informal. Changes in the types and uses of assessment from infants and toddlers to preschoolers come from the development of the child himself. As children move into the preschool years, they are much more active, use language to communicate, draw pictures, build with blocks, work puzzles, and use imaginative and symbolic play. In short, they are doing and producing more and this fact can be used to assess a child's progress and development.

As with infants, anecdotal and running records can produce rich data about a child's mathematical development. One of the things that can be recorded is a child's use of materials (Cohen, Stern, & Balaban, 1997). Preschool children are not symbolic in their interactions with objects and in play situations. Teachers should record not only symbolic verbal behavior such as speaking and writing, but also nonverbal behavior. This becomes especially important when assessing mathematics. Nonverbal symbolic activities, including interactions with materials and symbolic play, are the basis for the later use of more abstract forms of symbolization, such as mathematics and numbers (Cohen, Stern, & Balaban, 1997).

Cohen, Stern, & Balaban, (1997) suggest the following sample format and questions for recording a child's use of materials such as blocks.

The Setting
- Include nearby significant people and activities, as in routines, and such things as abundance or scarcity of materials, availability of supplies, amount and kind of adult supervision, and so on.

The Stimulus
- How does the child come to the material? Was it teacher suggested? Self-selected?

Response to Blocks
- What blocks does the child select?
- What forms does she construct?

- How does he use space?
- How flexible is the child in solving problems? Does he or she try different solutions? Repeat the same ineffectual ones? Repeat a successful approach again and again?
- Does the child verbalize while working?
- Is the structure named? Is it used in imaginative or dramatic play? Is the child primarily interested in the process of building?
- Is there a repeated theme or pattern? Are the themes or patterns changeable and varied?
- Does any type of mathematical thought develop during the play? After the play?

Length of Time Spent with Material
- Length of time can reflect concentration span, distractibility, interest, and so on.

According to the authors, the final thing a teacher must do once all this data is collected is to interpret it. He should think about these five questions when interpreting the questions listed above.

1. How did the child use the various materials? What did you notice about the child's physical coordination and the techniques he used in his interaction with the materials? Think about the mathematical content that could have been present in the activity such as patterning, sorting, categorizing, or seriating (small to large for example). Think about how the child used language and nonverbal activities. Record the products of the activity and whether the child reached a satisfactory end to the activity (for example, did he leave frustrated for some reason?). Finally, record what the adult's role was and the child's response to the adult.

2. How did the child seem to feel about the materials? What materials does the child seem to gravitate to and what is the frequency of his use of these materials? What activities are avoided and does the teacher know why? Think about the general attitude of the child. Was the child eager, confident, cautious, tentative, or fearful of the material or activity? How does the child react to failure and success?

3. How does the child use line, color, shape, and form in his drawing and building? Is there symmetry to the work? How does it relate to what the rest of the class seems to be doing? Does this child seem to be advanced or lagging behind? Is there something you can do for this child in this regard?

4. What child-adult relationships are revealed via the materials? Is the child more independent or dependent on the adult?

5. Look for special problems or delays. Does the child get overly distressed over breakage? Does he avoid messiness or concentrate on only one material or idea for an inordinate amount of time? Does he have an inability to concentrate or enjoy? These could be indicators of larger needs in the child that may need to be addressed, such as autism or Asperger syndrome.

Another assessment tool is the checklist, used to assess skills that children are able to complete. They are often used to assess "readiness" skills such as counting to five or sorting based on shape or size; however, they can be expanded to document the growth of a child and his development of skills over time (Helm, Beneke, & Steinheimer, 1998).

Teachers, parents, and the child can cooperate to develop goals, which can then be assessed through observations of the child's interactions in the classroom. Helm, et al. (1998) suggest using the following assessment scale:

- Not Yet—The skill, knowledge, behavior, or accomplishment described by the checklist has not yet been demonstrated.
- In Progress—The skill, knowledge, behavior, or accomplishment described by the checklist is present; however it is intermittent or emergent and is not demonstrated consistently.
- Proficient—The child can reliably demonstrate the skill, knowledge, behavior, or accomplishment described by the checklist.

A portfolio assessment is basically a collection of children's work over time that is collected in one place. The work collected is the authentic work of the children; in other words, it is work that children do in class as part of the ongoing learning process (Helm, et al., 1998).

One way to create portfolios is to collect samples of a child's work. The purpose of this is:

- Capturing the quality of the child's thinking and work
- Showing the child's progress over time
- Involving the child in the process of assessing his or her own work
- Reflecting on the types of classroom experiences available to the child
- Giving teachers an opportunity to reflect on their expectations of students' work
- Giving students, teachers, families, administrators, and other decision makers essential information about student progress and activity in the classroom

This approach, according to Helm, et al. (1998), is based around two types of items. **Core items** reflect a child's work across the whole curriculum as well as his growth over time. Teachers can determine the types of items they want to collect by identifying particular areas of learning within each domain, such as mathematics. Then they collect the same type of documentation five or six times throughout the year.

For example, if the core item for mathematics is an observation of a child playing a math game, then the teacher would observe the child playing the game five or six times throughout the year. At the end of the year, she will have a number of observations about the same game, documenting the child's progress. For mathematics an example of some core items might be:

- Record of a child's interest in counting
- Record of a child's sorting by more than one attribute
- Record of a child's patterning
- Example of a child using numbers to solve a problem

In addition to core items, the teacher will collect **individualized items**, which represent a significant event or learning experience in an area of special interest to the child. Meisels (1996) described individualized items as items that allow the child to display unique characteristics, learning styles, and strengths, as well as integration of skills and knowledge from several domains. These items can be examples of children's "firsts," such as their first time counting to five.

At the end of the year or during midyear assessment or parent-teacher conferences, teachers, using the portfolio and the core and individualized items, can craft a short report reflecting on the development of the child. These documentation items are like snapshots in an album. By themselves, they only tell half the story. A narrative tying the pieces together is needed for the parent or other decision maker to see the true meaning of the portfolio.

Anecdotal and running records, checklists, and portfolios are appropriate ways to assess children in the preschool ages, using observation and assessment of a child's authentic work in the classroom to make both formative and summative decisions about the mathematics learning of each individual child.

SUMMARY

During the preschool years, children are undergoing phenomenal physical, cognitive, and social-emotional growth. Continued mylenization of their brains has improved memory, fine motor skills, and the ability to attend. These developments mean that the way in which preschool children learn and interact with mathematics is different than that of an infant or toddler. Preschool children are in the preoperational stage of development. While still not thinking logically, they can use symbolic thought and intuitive thinking to solve problems.

Socially and emotionally, these children are able to interact with one another in play situations. This is a vital development in preschool, since most of what they learn will be taught through play experiences. For mathematics, this means that important concepts such as number, which is the understanding of the relationship between distinct objects, shape, and measurement and geometric concepts dealing with continuous quantities, are best taught and learned through play.

Using standards during the preschool years should be handled in a developmentally appropriate way. Teachers need to understand the developmental levels of their students and design activities that meet the standards in ways that are physically, cognitively, socially, and emotionally appropriate for preschool-age children. The NCTM focal points for preschool emphasize 1) developing an understanding of whole numbers, including concepts of correspondence, counting, cardinality, and comparison; 2) identifying shapes and describing spatial relationships; and 3) identifying measurable attributes and comparing objects by using these attributes.

To address these standards and focal points in a developmentally appropriate way for preschool-age children, teachers should use a combination of group activities, manipulatives, blocks, projects, math games, mapmaking, charting and graphing, art and drawing, and imaginative play to promote the learning of mathematical concepts.

WEB SITES

PBS Parents—Math for Preschool and Kindergarten
http://www.pbs.org/parents/earlymath/prek_flash.html

Contains developmental information about preschoolers' and kindergarteners' mathematical development and suggestions for teachers and parents.

PBS KIDS
http://pbskids.org/

This site contains activities based on popular PBS shows like *Curious George, Clifford the Big Red Dog*, and many others. The activities have various skill levels which make them appropriate for infants to children through third grade and higher. The activities include patterning, counting, shapes recognition, problem solving, and other mathematical content.

National Library of Virtual Manipulatives
http://nlvm.usu.edu/en/nav/vlibrary.html

An online science museum with explorations that include mathematics, problem solving, and applications of mathematics to other subject areas.

Funbrain.com's MathCar Racing Game
http://www.funbrain.com/osa/index.html

Math game based on NASCAR auto racing. Children choose a skill level and then make their car go around the track by answering math questions.

ICT Games
http://www.ictgames.com/resources.html

Math games for preschool and kindergarten.

Yahooligans
http://kids.yahoo.com/games/index

Yahoo! site for kids. It contains games with a mathematical basis for kids from preschool on up.

Coolmath—An Amusement Park of Math
http://www.coolmath.com/

Contains math games and puzzles for children of all ages. For the youngest, there are jigsaw puzzles and number recognition games.

Nick Jr.
http://www.nickjr.com/

This site contains activities based on popular Nickelodeon shows like *Blues Clues, Dora the Explorer,* and many others. The activities have various skill levels which make it appropriate for preschool through third grade and higher. The activities include patterning, counting, shapes recognition, problem solving, and other mathematical content.

DISCUSS AND APPLY WHAT YOU HAVE LEARNED

Reflect

1. How is the mathematical development of preschool-age children different from that of infants and toddlers?
2. Why is the child's social-emotional development so important to the development of mathematical learning in preschool?
3. Why are the arts a good place for mathematics experiences in preschool?

Discuss

1. Role-play the part of a teacher describing the importance of imaginative play to a child's parent. What do you tell the parent about why it is important to do mathematics? As the parent, what questions and concerns might you have?
2. As a group, discuss and compile a list of 10 possible consequences of teaching preschool standards in a rigid academic way to preschoolers.

Apply

1. Develop a topic for a project that could be done in a preschool classroom. Brainstorm ideas for the activity and mathematics concepts. Include objectives from NCTM or *your state's standards, a procedure*, and a way to expand and assess your project.
2. Develop a set of guidelines for teachers on how to incorporate mathematics into imaginative play. What are some questions teachers could ask?

Observe

1. Observe in a preschool classroom. What are the teachers doing to support mathematics? What opportunities are they missing?
2. Observe a preschooler in a classroom or home setting. What do they do that is mathematically based or involves problem solving using preoperational thought? Representational thought?

REFERENCES

Bredecamp, S. (2004). Standards for preschool and kindergarten mathematics education. In D. Clements & J. Sarama (Eds.), *Engaging young children in mathematics*. Mahwah, NJ: Lawrence Erlbaum Associates.

Burns, M., & Cuisenaire Company of America. (1987). Mathematics with manipulatives. New Rochelle, NY: Cuisenaire Co. of America.

Campbell, S. R., Zazkis, R., & NetLibrary Inc. (2002). *Learning and teaching number theory: Research in cognition and instruction*. Westport, CT: Ablex Pub.

Clements, D. (2004). Geometric and spatial thinking in early childhood education. In D. Clements & J. Sarama (Eds.), *Engaging young children in mathematics*. Mahwah, NJ: Lawrence Erlbaum Associates.

Clements, D., & Sarama, J. (Eds.). (2004). *Engaging young children in mathematics: Standards for early childhood mathematics education*. Mahwah, NJ: Lawrence Erlbaum Associates.

Clements, D., & Stephan, M. (2004). Measurement in pre-k to grade 2 mathematics. In D. Clements & J. Sarama (Eds.), *Engaging young children in mathematics*. Mahwah, NJ: Lawrence Erlbaum Associates.

Clements, D. H. (2001). Mathematics in the preschool. *Teaching Children Mathematics, 7*(4), 270–275.

Clements, D. H., & Bright, G. W. (2003). *Learning and teaching measurement: 2003 yearbook*. Reston, VA: National Council of Teachers of Mathematics.

Clements, D. H., & Sarama, J. (2000). The earliest geometry. *Teaching Children Mathematics, 7*(2), 82–86.

Clements, D. H., & Sarama, J. (2006). Early math: Young children and geometry. *Early Childhood Today (3), 20*(7), 12–13.

Cohen, D., Stern, V., & Balaban, N. (1997). *Observing and recording the behavior of young children* (4th ed.). New York: Teachers College Press.

Copple, C. (2004). Mathematics curriculum in the early childhood context. In D. Clements & J. Sarama (Eds.), *Engaging young children in mathematics*. Mahwah, NJ: Lawrence Erlbaum Associates.

Curtis, D., & Carter, M. (2003). *Designs for living and learning: Transforming early childhood environments*. St. Paul, MN: Redleaf Press.

Dehaene, S., Pica, P., & Spelke, E. (2006). Core knowledge of geometry in an Amazonian indigene group. *Science, 311*(5759), 381–384.

DelCampo, R. L., & DelCampo, D. S. (1995). *Taking sides*. Guilford, CT: Dushkin Pub. Group.

DeVries, R., & Kamii, C. (1975). *Why group games? A Piagetian perspective*. Urbana, IL: Available from Publications Office/IREC, College of Education, University of Illinois.

Eisenhower National Clearinghouse for Mathematics and Science Education. (1919). *Eisenhower National Clearinghouse for Math/Science Education Attachments B-E*.

Gazzaniga, M. S. (2004). *The cognitive neurosciences* (3rd ed.). Cambridge, MA: MIT Press.

Ginsburg, H. (1988). *Piaget's theory of intellectual development / Herbert P. Ginsburg, Sylvia Opper* (3rd ed.). Englewood Cliffs, NJ: Prentice Hall.

Ginsburg, H., & Baroody, A. (2005). *Test of early mathematics ability* (3rd ed.). Austin, TX: PRO-ED.

Helm, J. H., Beneke, S., & Steinheimer, K. (1998). *Windows on learning*. New York: Teachers College Press.

Helm, J. H., & Katz, L. (2001). *Young investigators: The project approach in the early years*. New York: Teachers College Press.

Hillen, J., Mercier, S., Wiebe, A. J., & Ecklund, L. (1986). *Pieces and patterns: A patchwork in math and science*. Fresno, CA: AIMS Education Foundation.

Inhelder, B., & Piaget, J. (1958). *The growth of logical thinking from childhood to adolescence: An essay on the construction of formal operational structures*. London: Routledge & Kegan Paul.

Kamii, C., & DeVries, R. (1973). *Piaget-based curriculum for early childhood education: Three different approaches*. Paper presented at the *Society for Research in Child Development*, Philadelphia.

Kamii, C., & DeVries, R. (1980). *Group games in early education: Implications of Piaget's theory*. Washington, DC: National Association for the Education of Young Children.

Kamii, C., & National Association for the Education of Young Children. (1982). *Number in preschool and kindergarten: Educational implications of Piaget's theory*. Washington, DC: National Association for the Education of Young Children.

Kamii, C., O'Brien, T. C., Teacher Center, Southern Illinois University at Edwardsville. (1980). *What do children learn when they manipulate objects?* Edwardsville, IL: The Teachers' Center Project, Southern Illinois University at Edwardsville.

Katz, L., & Chard, S. C. (2000). *Engaging children's minds: The project approach* (2nd ed.). Stamford, CT: Ablex Pub. Corp.

Kaye, P. (1987). *Games for math: Playful ways to help your child learn math from kindergarten to third grade.* New York: Pantheon Books.

Mather, N., & Goldstein, S. (2001). *Learning disabilities and challenging behaviors: A guide to intervention and classroom management.* Baltimore, MD: P.H. Brookes Pub. Co.

Meisels, S. J. (1996). Using work sampling in authentic assessments. *Educational Leadership, 54*(4), 60.

National Association for the Education of Young Children. (2004). Early childhood mathematics: Promoting good beginnings: A joint position statement of the National Association for the Education of Young Children (NAEYC) and the National Council of Teachers of Mathematics (NCTM) [Electronic Version]. Retrieved May 29, 2007, from *http://www.naeyc.org/about/positions/pdf/psmath.pdf*

National Association for the Education of Young Children, & South Carolina Educational Television Network. (1987). *A classroom with blocks* [videorecording]. South Carolina Educational Television Network,.

National Council of Teachers of Mathematics. (2000). *Principles and standards for school mathematics.* E-Standards ver. 1.0.

Packer, J., Quisenberry, N., & ACEI. (2006). Play: Essential for all children. A position paper of the Association for Childhood Education International. Retrieved June 13, 2007, from *http://www.acei.org/playpaper.htm*

Parten, M. (1932). Social participation among preschool children. *Journal of Abnormal and Social Psychology, 27,* 242–269.

Piaget, J. (1959). *The psychology of intelligence.* London: Routledge & Paul.

Piaget, J., Inhelder, B., & Szeminska, A. (1960). *The child's conception of geometry.* London: Routledge & K. Paul.

Piaget, J., Piers, M. W., et al. (1972). *Play and development: A symposium with contributions.* New York: Norton.

Reifel, S. (1995). Enriching the possibilities of block play. *Child Care Information Exchange* (103), 48–50.

Rivera, D. P. (1998). *Mathematics education for students with learning disabilities: Theory to practice.* Austin, TX: PRO-ED.

Rousso, H., & Wehmeyer, M. L. (2001). *Double jeopardy: Addressing gender equity in special education.* Albany, NY: State University of New York Press.

Santrock, J. W. (2005). *Children* (8th ed.). Boston: McGraw-Hill.

Seo, K.-H., & Ginsburg, H. (2004). What is developmentally appropriate in early childhood mathematics education? Lessons from new research. In D. Clements & J. Sarama (Eds.), *Engaging young children in mathematics.* Mahwah, NJ: Lawrence Erlbaum Associates.

Singer, D., Golinkoff, R., & Hirsch-Pasek, K. (2006). *Play = learning: How play motivates and enhances children's cognitive and social-emotional growth.* Oxford: Oxford University Press.

Weikart, D. P. (1964). *Perry Preschool project progress report, June, 1964.* Ypsilanti, MI: Ypsilanti Public Schools.

Zaslavsky, C. (1979). *Preparing young children for math: A book of games.* New York: Schocken Books.

CHAPTER 7

Kindergarten and First Grade

CHAPTER OBJECTIVES

After you have read this chapter, you should be able to:

- Explain the transitional nature of this age group and the importance of a carefully designed mathematics program
- Describe what five-, six-, and seven-year-olds are like physically, cognitively, emotionally, and socially
- Explain the importance of social interaction for problem solving and mathematics learning in K–1
- Demonstrate optimal ways of arranging environments to effectively support mathematics for K–1 to support experiential learning and educational experiences
- Identify what mathematical concepts kindergarteners and first graders are learning
- Develop developmentally appropriate mathematics activities for K–1 that include emphasis on NCTM standards
- Discuss how experiences and education both support mathematics learning for K–1

The kindergarten and first-grade years are transitional times for children both developmentally and mathematically. They are transitioning from what is traditionally thought of as "a time of play" in the preschool years to "a time of work" in the school-age years. While kindergarten is often thought of as a fun and supportive play-based introduction to school, it is also viewed as an important introduction to school and a transition into first grade and all subsequent grades. Children in kindergarten today are expected to be "ready for school" by the end of their experience (Jeynes, 2006).

In the past 20 years, kindergarten experiences have changed significantly (Kamii, 1990; Klein, Starkey, & Wakeley, 1998). Kindergartens have progressed from optional play-based half-day experiences run by private providers or churches, to a required public school experience with strict curriculum and standards and, in many cases, full-day experiences. In essence, kindergarten has become the "new first grade" (Tyre et al., 2006). Recent research has shown that 5-year-olds are capable of cognitive tasks such as beginning reading and mathematics. The catalyst for this research is the recent emphasis on proficiency tests and the push to begin formal schooling earlier and earlier (Kamii, 1990).

Another important transition that children in the K–1 years are experiencing is the transition to formal schooling. Kindergarten today is seen as the first "real" schooling experience and there are a lot of curricular objectives meant to prepare them for first grade and beyond (Riley, 2000). In kindergarten, it is still common to see play areas, blocks, and other play-based materials. By first grade, there is more of an emphasis on traditional educational experiences (National Association for the Education of Young Children, & South Carolina Educational Television Network, 1987; Phelps & Hanline, 1999).

Kindergarten and first-grade children are transitioning from experiential learning to a more teacher-focused model or, using the 3E model, from "Experience" to "Education." This does not mean that children in the elementary grades do not benefit from experiential learning or that all teaching should be teacher-directed. Children in the elementary grades are, however, more capable of handling traditional teaching and learning. The classroom mathematics environment reflects the growing emphasis on the acquisition of specific content in mathematics. The most effective K–1 mathematics program blends experience with content-based education that meets mathematics standards and the NCTM Focal Points.

This time of transition should be seen as an opportunity of growth for the child. The mathematics activities and experiences that a teacher designs during this crucial transition can have a great impact and produce great rewards for both child and teacher.

WHAT ARE K–1 CHILDREN LIKE?

Many significant changes in the physical, cognitive, and social-emotional domains take place during this time. K–1 children are becoming more capable of achieving physically demanding tasks, are beginning to overcome some of the limitations of preoperational thought, and are beginning to make close friends that will become their support system. As they enter this transitional time, they will begin to identify more with these friends than with their own parents. All of these changes have an impact on how these children learn mathematics and how, as a teacher, you can best facilitate their learning.

Physical Development

Brain Development and Attention. Some areas of the brain are still not completely mylenated; for instance, the areas of the brain associated with attention will not complete this process until adolescence. Between the beginning of kindergarten and the completion of first grade, however, the child's ability to attend will have greatly increased. This increase in the ability to sit and attend is what makes it possible for some formal math education to occur by the time children get to first grade (Helm, Katz, & Scranton, 2000).

Children in kindergarten are still less able to sit and attend long enough to make a formal, teacher-directed approach to education developmentally appropriate or effective. Their functional attention spans are about 10 minutes. The teacher-directed and seatwork portions of mathematics instruction need to be kept to a minimum. Teaching mathematics through experience is still the primary means of teaching math to kindergarteners.

By first grade, children's sustained attention can reach 15–20 minutes. More importantly, they are developing **selective attention**. Selective attention is the ability to decide which things need to be attended to and which things can be ignored. First graders are better at this than kindergarteners. A first grader can focus on a math assignment while other things are going on in the classroom. This skill will still be "under construction" but it does allow for some formal instruction in addition and other first-grade math concepts.

These developments in attention offer the teacher more options in the classroom. Teaching and learning of mathematics should still be linked strongly to the child's experience, but done in a developmentally appropriate way; teacher-directed mathematics instruction, seatwork, and even homework can be useful additions to the mathematics program.

Motor Skills. At this age, gross and fine motor skills are also reaching a point where they enable the child to complete more traditional educational tasks. In the gross motor area, most kindergarteners are quite adept at jumping and climbing. Running becomes more efficient as they begin to coordinate their arms and upper body. Halfway through the first grade, most children will be able to skip.

These developments may not seem like they have much to do with mathematics, but there is research showing that the physical, cognitive, and social-emotional domains do not develop in isolation. The physical development of the child is important to cognitive development and vice versa. These gross motor milestones occur because of cognitive advancements in cooperation with muscle development. Conversely, the development of coordination through physical play such as running, jumping, and skipping helps to strengthen cognitive and mathematical development (Thelen & Smith, 1994, 1996).

Manipulatives are an important part of any K–1 classroom.

Fine motor skills in K–1 develop to a point where writing numbers and letters and using a pencil are possible. Kindergarten children's fine motor skills require thick pencils or markers and their letters and numbers are written large. By first grade, children are becoming much more adept at controlling their hand and fingers. They are now able to write smaller and their writing becomes more precise. This development makes using writing in mathematics possible.

Other developing fine motor skills include better control of finger and hand muscles. Children can use their hands as "tools," allowing them to use more and smaller mathematics manipulatives, such as puzzles. They can tie their shoes, cut and paste, sculpt with clay, and use a knife to spread butter. These abilities open up a new realm of mathematical activity possibilities such as cooking, building, and other activities that require fine motor precision.

Cognitive Development

K–1 children's cognitive abilities are in transition. By the end of first grade, most children have progressed past Piaget's preoperational stage into the concrete operational stage, where logical thinking is more prevalent. During the K–1 years, we see the development of this logical thinking, as children begin to better understand conservation, reversibility, and classification (Santrock, 2005).

Conservation, Classification, and Patterning. Completing the conservation of number task shows that they are able to think about mathematics and numbers in a fairly logical and rational way; however, they are not yet fully logical thinkers, and this fact needs to be taken into account (Dolk, 2004; Inhelder & Piaget, 1964).

Children also become more flexible in categorizing objects. They can now sort things into a number of self-defined categories, such as small, medium, and large, whereas before the categories had to be directly observable (circle, square, triangle).

The categories can include comparisons of length, weight, or other more abstract characteristics of classroom and playground objects.

Graphing data collected from classification tasks becomes more mathematically based than in preschool (Clements & Sarama, 2004). Children will now use counting as a tool to build graphs and compare groups of objects, rather than just the height of the bar on a graph. Even if the answer is easily observable, they will attempt to use counting to confirm it:

> *Teacher:* (referring to three stacks of same-sized blocks, one with five blocks, one with seven, and one with eight). Dylan, which of these stacks has the most blocks?
>
> *Dylan:* (observes the stacks of blocks) Um . . . okay, let's see. I think I will have to count them.
>
> *Teacher:* Can't you tell by looking?
>
> *Dylan:* Well . . . yes, but counting is better.
>
> *Teacher:* Why is counting better?
>
> *Dylan:* I don't know. Maybe, it's because I can add them?
>
> *Teacher:* Are you going to add up all the blocks?
>
> *Dylan:* Yeah! First, I need to see which stack has the most! (He proceeds to count the stacks and pick the one with eight as the most.)

Children in K–1 begin to notice more complex patterns in their environment and everyday life. Musical patterns, even of the most complex nature, are often discernable and describable by these students. They are able to recognize and extend simple number patterns such as 2, 4, 6, 8, or, in first grade, more complex ones such as 2, 4, 8, 16. Sometimes, the errors that children make while looking for patterns show us how active their minds are. In November, I had the following interaction with a first-grade child:

> *Researcher:* "Hi Roger! I have a pattern for you. See if you can find what the next number should be. (The researcher writes down the numbers as he says them.) 1, 2, 3, 5, 8, 13. So, what do you think comes next?"
>
> *Roger:* "Okay, let's see. (He takes the paper and begins to write down a math problem, after 5 minutes he puts down the pencil.) Finished!"
>
> *Researcher:* "So what did you get?"
>
> *Roger:* "32!"
>
> *Researcher:* "What pattern did you see in the numbers?"
>
> *Roger:* "Well, 1 plus 2 is 3 and 3 plus 2 is 5, 5 plus 3 is 8, and 8 plus 5 is 13."
>
> *Researcher:* "So how did you get 32?"
>
> *Roger:* (Showing what he has written on his paper) "I added $1 + 2 + 3 + 5 + 8 + 13$ and that equaled 32!"
>
> *Researcher:* "Wow, that was a lot of adding!"
>
> *Roger:* "Yeah, I'm good at adding."

Many teachers might focus on the fact that Roger came up with the wrong answer. But when we examine the process the child went through to get this answer, it shows a systematic mathematical understanding of many things. First, he was able to recognize a very complex pattern in his work up to the number 13 (known as the Fibonacci series). Second, he was able to write the numbers into a mathematical equation and add them correctly. Finally, his answer is surprisingly close to the third number in the series $(8 + 13 = 21)$. Roger did not quite understand how to get to the next number, probably because he thought of this as a traditional mathematics problem, similar to one of his homework problems, rather than as a pattern extension activity. Overall, even though the answer was wrong, the process shows very advanced thinking about mathematics and patterns.

Memory and Automation. While a child's strengthening memory aids his learning mathematics, many mathematics programs overrely on memory as a teaching tool. From the age of four, a child's memory improves significantly. As children begin to learn more formal mathematics in first grade, their memory allows for the retention and recall of mathematical calculations. Fluency begins to become a factor in the child's mathematical development. The focus of mathematical education, in early childhood and primary grades, remains on conceptual development. However, some research suggests that the ability to automatically retrieve certain mathematical computations from memory greatly improves the chances for mathematical success in the elementary grades.

Linguistic Development

As children encounter writing and print in more contexts, they begin to more firmly make the link between words and concepts. Literacy and reading development builds on the foundation of spoken word development and adds the use of visual symbols to represent objects. The development of reading and writing means that word problems can be used for teaching mathematics and that children can read instructions on homework assignments. In kindergarten, the words should be short and simple and an adult should help with the reading. As a group, reading problems from the board is a good developmentally appropriate strategy for this age. By first grade, children can read and understand longer sentences and follow written instructions. They can use writing as a tool to document their work and their problem-solving process. Math concepts can also be promoted through the use of songs, poems, finger plays, and literature.

Social-Emotional Development

Mathematics instruction should be socially based and interactive during these years. Children need to learn to work together, discuss, and even argue in a civil manner about their mathematical thought process. For this instructional strategy to succeed, teachers need to understand the social climate of the classroom and the social-emotional development of the K–1 child. This may sometimes be a challenge because children are still egocentric in kindergarten and to some degree, in first grade.

In the mathematics classroom for K–1 and subsequent grades, social interaction is important to the learning process. The teacher has an obligation to ensure that some children are not excluded by their peers and that all children have the opportunities and skills to interact with others in a positive way in the classroom. Since the goal of the mathematics program is that children interact and discuss, the children must work to maintain working relationships with the others. This provides the children and the teacher with opportunities to help less social children to interact with their peers. The climate of interaction and civil discussion and argument is an important factor in a constructivist classroom. The teacher needs to be aware of the social development of each child.

The physical, cognitive, social, and emotional development of kindergarten and first-grade children allow them to master many new concepts. Review Table 6.1's developmental milestones as we explore what concepts these children will be learning.

WHAT MATHEMATICAL CONCEPTS DO K–1 CHILDREN LEARN?

Kindergarten and first-grade children are developmentally more similar than they are different. Also, in contemporary schools, kindergarten is usually the entry point to schooling. It is usually a child's first experience with public school and the standards and testing that go with it. Children entering kindergarten are subject to academic standards that are much more intense than those in preschool. In the past 15 years, kindergarten has become the "new first grade" and it is where many textbooks for mathematics begin their scope and sequences. For these reasons, K–1 is grouped together in this chapter (Rathbone, 1993).

One developmental similarity we see in kindergarteners and first graders is the influence that direct teaching has on them. Since kindergarten is where students are usually first exposed to the public school model, it is also where they begin to learn what it means to be a student in schools. If in these first two grades children sit quietly and wait to be told "how" to solve a math problem, it sets the mold for how they will expect to learn in the second grade and beyond. If they get used to passive learning, it will be hard to break that "way of learning" later (Kamii & DeClark, 1985). Kamii and DeClark (1985) found that students who had traditional mathematics instruction in earlier grades had difficulty transitioning into a constructivist, active learning model of mathematics instruction, while children who were taught using a constructivist model in the early grades had no problem adapting to a passive model later in their schooling. They also retained the emphasis on thinking even when confronted with teaching that did not encourage it. Therefore, encouraging intellectual autonomy in K–1 classrooms is vital for the development of active learning and problem solving later in their schooling.

Encouraging Intellectual Autonomy

In *Number in Preschool and Kindergarten* (1986) and other works, Kamii proposes the idea that the major goal of education in the early years should be developing

When children explain and defend their answers, they are building intellectual autonomy.

intellectual autonomy. Intellectual autonomy means knowing something is right or wrong independent of an adult saying so or rewarding (or even punishing) an answer. A continued exchange of points of view with other children, and the discussion of answers and the processes used to get those answers (both correct and incorrect) leads to intellectual autonomy (Kamii, 1984).

The opposite of intellectual autonomy is **intellectual heteronomy,** which means a reliance on others' ideas to assess whether one's work is right or wrong. Classroom routines built around reward and punishment lead to intellectual heteronomy. Children learn to give the answer they think the teacher wants in order to get a reward or avoid punishment, regardless of their own thought processes. Have you ever had the experience of having the right answer marked wrong because either the teacher or the answer key was incorrect? This is not uncommon, and in most instances, children do not challenge the teacher.

As children enter the school ages, they begin to encounter formal schooling. Because formal schooling tends to be directive, teacher-led, and content-based, they run the risk of thinking that answers come from the teacher, rather than from a problem-solving process.

Unfortunately, children are not encouraged to think autonomously. Teachers use sanctions in the intellectual realm to get children to give the "right" answers. An example of this practice is the use of worksheets. In first-grade arithmetic, for example, if a child writes "$4 + 2 = 5$," most teachers will mark it as wrong. The result of this is that children become convinced that truth can only come from the teacher. When I walk around a first-grade classroom as children are working on arithmetic worksheets, I might stop and ask a student how he arrived at a particular answer. The child typically reacts by grabbing his eraser and erasing like mad, even when his answer is correct! Already, many children have learned to distrust their own thinking. Thus discouraged from thinking autonomously, they will construct less knowledge than those who are mentally active and confident. (Kamii & National Association for the Education of Young Children, 1982)

Teachers need to be aware of the danger of creating intellectually "dependent" children. For children to construct mathematics in a meaningful way, their thinking must be valued and supported by the teacher. It is easy to fall into the traditional teacher role of providing methods and answers and then rewarding correct answers with stickers or smiley faces. It seems intuitively like the right thing to do to make children feel good about their progress. However, this method does not promote children's independent thinking and problem solving and should be kept to a minimum. It is important to recognize children's background knowledge and to build from their innate abilities.

K–1 children are making a difficult transition developmentally and mathematically. They are entering a type of schooling which is a new experience for them. They are learning new ways to interact with others and with mathematics. Our goal, as children develop, learn, and construct mathematical concepts, should be to ensure that they also develop intellectual autonomy.

Mathematical Concepts in Kindergarten

Numbers. Most kindergarten children understand one-to-one correspondence concepts and are beginning to develop an understanding of additive relationships and cardinality. Because of the development of a system of ones and hierarchical inclusion, most children of this age can not only count, but also understand that with each number they say, the quantity increases by one. When a kindergarten child counts "five, six," he understands that in essence he is adding "one" to "five."

Because of this additive thinking, children can begin to **compose** and **decompose** sets of numbers. For example, they understand that three red chips and two blue chips make five chips (compose). They also understand that a group of five chips can be broken down into smaller groups of four and one or three and two (decompose). While this is not the formal addition that we will see in first grade, this additive thinking makes it possible to introduce some simple addition games and activities to the curriculum. Kindergarten children may not be able to handle addition with numerical notation such as "3 + 5," but they can count the dots on dominos or other items.

Children in kindergarten may **count all** or, if they are a bit more advanced, they may **count on**. For example, if playing a path game that requires two number cubes to be thrown and the game piece to be moved based upon the resulting number, a child might count all of the dots on both cubes. This is composition of a new number set because the child is combining two smaller sets of numbers to make a larger number, then moving his game piece according to that new number. Another strategy is for the child to count on from the higher number—he might throw a five and a three and say "five . . ." and then count the dots on the other cube, "six, seven, eight." This is called counting on. It is still composition of a new set; it is simply a more advanced strategy than counting all (Smith, 1997).

Kindergarten teachers can encourage these composition strategies through the use of games. To encourage children to use counting on, teachers can replace one of the cubes that has dots with one that has numerals. Since there are no dots to count, it encourages the child to count on. It is possible that the child will still count to the numeral on his fingers and then count the remaining dots. If this is the case, the child is not ready to advance to counting on.

Kindergarten children have sufficient control of their fingers and hand muscles to permit the use of a pencil. In fact, they begin to prefer writing with a pencil rather than a crayon or marker. Their memory level allows them to remember the shapes of numbers and recall them when writing. Number and letter reversals are common in kindergarten children due to factors such as memory or perception. Given their development, this is normal. Children may have no problem aligning numbers on the top-to-bottom axis so they don't write them upside-down, but coordinating both the top-to-bottom axis and the left-to-right axis may be challenging for children this age.

Measurement. During this time, many of the cognitive structures of measurement are still developing. Two of the most important of these are transitivity and conservation of length. An understanding of transitivity allows children to compare two lengths even if they are not right next to each other. For example, if shown two towers that are not next to each other and asked if he can use a dowel rod to compare their heights, a child with transitive thought can compare the first tower to the rod and then use the rod to assess the height of tower two, to determine if they are the same. Conservation of length is the understanding that length remains constant regardless of appearance. These two concepts should be the focus of the kindergarten measurement program. In this way, kindergarten children can begin to develop an understanding of **iterated units of measurement**, such as a ruler broken down into inches (Clements & Stephan, 2004). Iterated units of measurement can be either **standard**, such as inches or meters or **nonstandard,** like shoes or paperclips. Both

Standard and nonstandard units can be used in teaching measurements.

Anthony Magnacca/Merrill

can be used the same way in unit iteration, but a standard unit makes it more efficient for a society to communicate measurements.

Some research has shown that the coordination of these two cognitive developments can take until fourth grade to develop to a point where children can use measurement techniques efficiently and flexibly. However, activities and interactions using nonstandard units to find the length of classroom objects support the early development and coordination of these concepts. For example, kindergarteners can use paperclips to measure the length of their books or desks. Children also begin to understand the measurement of area and can cover a picture with a number of squares and then count the squares. They can compare the number of squares it takes to cover different shapes, objects, and pictures.

Units of Time. Kindergarten children begin to understand that time can be divided into units such as hours, minutes, and seconds. However, it is often hard for them to mentally gauge the passage of time using these units. For example, a child may be told that the class will be going to the playground in 15 minutes. Five minutes later the child may ask, "Has it been 15 minutes yet?" With kindergarteners, it is often a good idea to use clocks to help them gauge time. The teacher can then say, "It will be 15 minutes when the big hand is on the 12."

Time is most relevant to the kindergarten child when it is linked to his daily schedule and everyday activity. It is difficult for him to link the understanding that time can be segmented into units with how long those units are, because the passage of time is based on perception. The old adage "time flies when you are having fun" is true. Fifteen minutes sitting outside the doctor's office waiting to get a shot feels a lot longer than 15 minutes playing on the playground.

Patterns and Algebra. Children's classification schemes are more complex than they were in preschool. Kindergarteners can now sort objects by one or more attributes. They also use mathematical attributes to sort and seriate objects or groups of objects such as, "This pile has eight this one has four, and this one has two." They can also sort objects into three distinct classes, such as small, medium, and large.

Kindergarten children are also becoming better at using their representational abilities to make mathematical models (Dolk, 2004). Katherine Fosnot describes mathematical modeling as part of "mathematizing," or the process of using mathematics to structure the world rather than just "learning" it. In her book *Young Mathematicians at Work* (Fosnot & Dolk, 2001), she shows how children use mathematical models. In one example, a teacher showed children a picture *biscuits on a worksheet* and asked them if there were enough for everyone in the class to have one. Three students decided to use small cubes to model the problem letting the cubes stand in for biscuits. When asked what they were going to do with the cubes, one child began to put red cubes on each of the biscuits while another gave a brown cube to each child in the class. Once each biscuit had a red cube on it, she counted them and got 22. The other child finished handing out the brown cubes and after ensuring that everyone received one, began collecting the cubes and counted 15. The students then said there were enough, because "22 is more than 15."

Geometry and Spatial Sense. Kindergarten children can use positional words in sentences and can give directions to other students. Preschool children learn how to use words like "behind" or "next to" and can understand them, but have difficulty using them correctly. They have no problem saying, "The scissors are on the shelf next to the sink under the paper towels." They can also locate things in three-dimensional spaces using a two-dimensional representation such as a map. For example, children can follow a treasure map around the classroom to find a bag of candy hidden under the sink. If "X" marks the spot under the sink on the map, they can translate that into the three-dimensional world of the actual classroom. They can also use toys to make a fairly accurate map of their classroom.

Data Analysis, Probability, and Statistics. Kindergarteners can use graphs in more dynamic ways than preschool children, using them to collect, analyze, and represent data. They can then use them to make decisions, such as "What snack are we going to have today?" or "What book are we going to read next?" Kindergarteners are good at making graphs out of things in their environment such as shoes, blocks, or even people. They can also use pictures to create graphs to represent data. While preschoolers can construct similar simple graphs, kindergarteners can use the information in the graph to answer questions such as: "Which group has less? Which group has more? Which group is the smallest? Which group is the biggest?" They can also compare individual factors. For example, if a graph is about a favorite color, each student can put a colored square on the board to make a stacked bar graph. They can then answer questions such as, "Do more people like red or yellow?"

Kindergarteners are able to extract useful mathematical information from pictures or other visual media. These can become early versions of "word problems." For example, children can look at pictures of houses and figure out which one has the most windows. They are able to problem solve and should be involved in what Fosnot called mathematizing, or making sense of the world using mathematics. Kindergarten is the beginning of the formal mathematics that children in the first grade and up will be involved with, such as addition, subtraction, multiplication, fractions, and decimals (Burns & Silbey, 2000).

Mathematical Concepts in First Grade

Number. For most children, formal instruction in mathematics begins in first grade. They begin to have homework and work on traditional problems such as addition and subtraction. Traditionally, these concepts are taught as "facts" to be memorized. However, there is another approach to learning and teaching these concepts. If we understand and value how first graders construct mathematics, we can use their natural thinking skills to promote their developing understanding of mathematics (Fosnot & Dolk, 2001; Kamii & National Association for the Education of Young Children, 1982; Kamii, Piaget, & Federation of North Texas Area, 1984).

Addition. Addition is the most noticeable advancement in the mathematical thinking of the first-grade child. Early first graders can add single-digit numbers up to 10.

These problems do not involve place value or carrying, but putting two groups together and getting a sum. They understand the mathematical notations for addition, such as $4 + 5 = 9$.

Understanding principles of addition and memorizing math facts are the two factors necessary to learning early addition. There is a national debate on which of these is most useful (Fosnot & Dolk, 2001). Rote memorization is not sufficient by itself because first graders who learn addition facts by rote and do not understand the relationships between numbers often think there are "hundreds" of facts to learn. Children who focus solely on understanding, however, may struggle to develop the skills needed to use mathematics efficiently. Both memorization and understanding are important to ensure that children are fluent in addition and other mathematical computations.

Katherine Fosnot suggests that we think about automaticity rather than memorization when it comes to fluency (Fosnot & Dolk, 2001). She notes that memorization usually means committing unrelated operations to memory, making thinking unnecessary. With rote learning, the emphasis is on recalling answers, not on mathematical thinking. Research has shown that a focus on the interconnected relationships in addition (such as $2 + 3 = 2 + 1 + 1 + 1$) along with activities that promote automaticity such as math games, actually helped children to remember and recall the math "facts" better (Kamii, Joseph, & Livingston, 2003).

Children in first grade find it easier to remember doubles ($1 + 1, 2 + 2, 3 + 3 \ldots$) than other mathematical combinations. Math games and other mathematical interactions help them to use their developing memory strategies to remember simple addition sums. They remember these sums and retrieve them with an automaticity that

Manipulatives can help children construct the principles of addition.

Patrick White/Merrill

improves fluency. For example, you can ask them what 2 + 2 equals and they will say "four" without having to do the computation. If you ask what 3 + 5 equals, they may have to think about it or count on their fingers. In this case, 3 + 5 is not yet automated.

Children will use the sums they recall automatically to get to more complex sums:

Teacher: "Who can tell me what 4 + 6 equals?"

Benjamin: "I know! It's 10!"

Teacher: "How did you get that answer, Benjamin?"

Benjamin: "I know that 4 + 4 is 8 and then I added 2 more to get 10."

Through first grade, the recall of single-digit sums becomes more automatic. Next, children tend to remember the addends that make 10. It is more useful for teachers to focus on the sums of the problems rather than the addends. Instead of designing a lesson that helps the child become fluent in the "4+" facts such as 4 + 1 = 5, 4 + 2 = 6, 4 + 3 = 7, and so on, it is more efficient for him to remember numbers that make a sum. For example, the lesson should focus on all the different ways to make 10 such as 9 + 1, 8 + 2, 7 + 3, and so on. This strategy also allows the children to experiment with commutivity, as they realize that 7 + 3 is the same as 3 + 7.

Another addition issue that appears in first grade is the use of algorithms. Algorithms are methods that have been developed by mathematicians over the centuries to make certain mathematical operations more efficient. However, in first grade these algorithms are taught as rules to be followed in addition, especially with the introduction of double-column addition that involves carrying. As with the memorization of math facts, teaching an algorithm before children understand the relationship between number, addition, and place value leads to children who follow the rules and get answers without understanding exactly what they are doing mathematically. It also leads to children who have trouble understanding place value, but more on that later (Kamii et al., 1984).

A better approach is to present problems and let children invent ways to solve them. Algorithms are just one acceptable way of finding an answer. They may be more efficient, but are useless if children don't understand what they are doing. Instead of teaching children to do 8 + 13 using the algorithm as in Figure 7.1, encourage them to get the answer any way they can. Then as a group, the class can share all the possible ways to get to the answer. Some examples can be seen in Figure 7.2.

Place Value. Understanding of place value begins to develop in first grade. This is the understanding that where the numeral appears in a number affects its value. For

Figure 7.1   Example of the Traditional Algorithm.

$$\begin{array}{r} 1\,3 \\ +8 \\ \hline \end{array}\quad \text{is changed}\quad 3 + 8 = 11 + 10 = 21$$
to

$$\begin{array}{r} 1\,3 \\ +8 \\ \hline \end{array}\quad \text{is changed}\quad \begin{array}{l} 13 - 2 = 11 \\ 8 + 2 = 10 \\ 10 + 11 = 21 \end{array}\quad$$
to

The child knows $8 + 2 = 10$ so she takes 2 from the 13 to make it 11. Then she adds the 11 to 10 to get 21.

Figure 7.2 Examples of ways children solve the same problem when asked to use their thinking.

example, the 3 in 357 is not a 3, but rather 300. Second- and third-grade teachers usually lament the fact that their students have so much trouble with place value. The problem is not that children in first grade cannot learn or understand the concept of place value; it is a natural outgrowth of learning how to add numbers whose sums are larger than 10. The problem occurs when teachers unwittingly "unteach" place value (Kamii et al., 2003).

If we revisit our discussion of the algorithm, we can see that in trying to make math simple for children, teachers actually make it more difficult. Think about the following problem. Explain to someone else exactly how you would solve it using the standard algorithm for carrying, including all your steps.

$$\begin{array}{r} 34 \\ +29 \\ \hline \end{array}$$

Many people solve this by saying, "4 plus 9 is 13. Carry the one and $1 + 3 + 2$ is 6. So the answer is 63." But was it really a 1 that was carried?

Algorithms are a perfectly reasonable way to do a math problem. The difficulty of using algorithms with K–1 children is that the process takes all place value concepts out of the addition process. Children never have to add any two addends higher than nine.

If, on the other hand, children are not given an algorithm rule to follow and are allowed to use their own inventions, they might do the problem by starting from the left, rather than from the right as the algorithm requires. This is very natural to them because they have learned to read from left to right. Left-to-right problem solving also requires them to think about place value. So, the child might say "30 + 20 is 50 and 4 + 9 is 13 and 13 + 50 is 63." This method may be less efficient than using an algorithm, but for the child who is just beginning to learn addition relationships and place-value concepts, it is much more valuable because it naturally makes them consider place value. Research has shown that children taught using this method understand place value much better when they get to higher grades (Kamii et al., 2003).

Subtraction. Subtraction is the reverse operation of addition. In the child's mind, however, it is not just a simple task of reversing addition. Many first- and even second-grade teachers have noted that their children seem to struggle with subtraction concepts. While addition is a linear process that involves taking two groups of objects and combining them into a new whole quantity, subtraction requires the child to think of the whole quantity and then a part of that whole quantity before arriving at the answer. For example, $3 + 2 = 5$ is the same as $| | | + | | = | | | | |$. All of the items to the left of the $=$ were simply moved to the right and then combined. We cannot as easily represent $3 - 2 = 1$ because $| |$ (2) is part of $| | |$ (3) and it in essence deletes them as they move to the right of the $=$.

Children in first grade have not completely constructed the understanding of part-to-whole relationship. It is difficult for them to think about the whole group and part of a group at the same time. This is exactly what subtraction requires them to do.

Does this mean that children cannot perform subtraction? No, but teachers should understand that addition is going to be much easier and understandable to children than subtraction. If children are allowed to solve subtraction problems using their own thinking processes, they will usually use a "counting up" process, rather than true subtraction. Kamii et al. (2003) suggest that the best way to strengthen subtraction ability is to teach children to be strong at addition. When teaching subtraction in first grade, it should be through word problems that involve concepts such as these.

- Take Away—Susie had five cupcakes and gave two to her friend Maria. How many does each child have?
- Comparison—Nine children wanted to play on the playground at recess and three wanted to stay inside. How many more wanted to play on the playground?
- Completion—Patel had four cards and he picked up some more from a pile. Now he has nine. How many did he pick up?
- Missing Addend—Dora made 12 cupcakes. Four were chocolate, the rest were yellow. How many were yellow? (Smith, 1997)

Using these strategies, children can begin to use the concepts of subtraction in ways that are understandable to them. Many times, they may use addition to solve these problems.

Rules of Operations. As children learn to add, they also begin to construct an understanding of the Rules of Operations. These are basic rules that are important for understanding the relationships between numbers. These rules are often taught to children, but if they interact with numbers daily, the rules should become self-evident through experimentation.

Commutative Property
- The understanding that $2 + 3$ is the same as $3 + 2$.

Associative Property
- The understanding that it doesn't matter in what order you add numbers, the answer is always the same. For example $2 + 4 + 6 = (2 + 4) + 6 = 2 + (4 + 6)$.

Transitivity of Equality

- The understanding that different numbers can be broken down in many different ways. For example $5 = 5 + 0 = 4 + 1 = 3 + 2$. To promote this rule, it is often better for children to learn automaticity by learning all the ways to make each number. Math games are a good way to do this.

Identity

- Addition to 0 is the identity property. In other words, anything added to 0 is still that number—$0 + 5 = 5$. (Smith, 1997)

Multiplication and division are not objectives for K–1; however, by allowing children to use their own problem-solving techniques, they can use addition to solve problems involving multiplication and division concepts by the end of first grade. In this way, they begin to see the uses of multiplication and division. In the video, *First Grade Children dividing 62 by 5*, the teacher presents a problem such as this: "Peter has 62 cents and erasers cost 5 cents at the school store. How many erasers can he buy?"

The children use many techniques, such as drawing 62 tally marks on a sheet of paper and then circling them in groups of 5 until no more can be circled. The children then count the circles to figure out how many erasers Peter can buy. Some children instead counted by 5s, writing 5s on the paper until they reached 60, and then counting the number of 5s they wrote. One child multiplied 10 by 5 and then added 2 more 5s to get 60. She then added $10 + 2$ to get the number of erasers. Many of the children did not understand her answer; one child even said it was "like cheating" (Kamii, Clark, Housman, & Teachers College Press, 2000).

First graders can understand multiplication through counting up numbers. My first-grade son came in and wanted to help me write this book. He and I decided he could make up a math problem and explain how he got his answer. He even helped with the typing. Here is what we wrote:

G: "Can you make up a math problem?"

Dylan: "Yes. $(3 \times 3) + 1 =$"

G: "What does that equal?"

Dylan: "10!"

G: "How do you know that?"

Dylan: "Because 3×3 is 9 and one more is 10."

G: "How did you know that 3×3 equals 9?"

Dylan: "Because when you count by 3s you go 3, 6, 9."

G: "And then one more onto that equals 10!"

Dylan: "Yes!"

[When writing this, he made me put "do me first" symbols around the 3×3 so there was no confusion.]

Number Systems. Construction of number systems occurs in layers. Each layer is built on the one before, increasing the complexity. In kindergarten, we see the construction of the system of ones, which is the first layer. The next layer is being able to mentally

Math games can help children develop fluency with addition.

Karen Mancinelli/Pearson Learning Photo Studio

segment those ones into a base-10 system. Yet another layer is multiplicative thinking, or being able to think of groups of items in terms of both group and individual values. In first grade, most children are not yet thinking multiplicatively; this will not occur until second or third grade or even later. However, they can still work multiplication and division problems using their own invented methods, which usually consist of additive thinking and repeated addition. In fact, this process strengthens their conceptual understanding of numbers and hastens the construction of the more complex layers of numerical understanding, such as multiplicative thinking.

Measurement. Children in first grade can understand the concept of a standard unit. A **standard unit** is a unit of measurement that is widely accepted by a group of people. Children in first grade begin to understand the usefulness of having standard units to transfer and communicate measurements to others. They can say the book is 4 inches long and the other person can re-create that length without having to be shown it. The use of standard units is easier for physical quantities such as length, height, area, volume, weight, and mass, but more difficult for nonphysical quantities such as time, temperature, and money (Smith, 1997).

With physical measurements, it is easier for children to make the measurement relate to the quantity of the substance (length, mass, etc.). These children still rely heavily on perception and will relate standard measurements to what they see and sense. In first grade, most children are introduced to two standards of measurement—English units and metric units. In the United States, English units are more widely used and accepted. Most Americans find it very difficult to replace familiar measurements (such as inch, foot, yard, mile, and pound) with metric units.

Even though English units are more familiar, they are more mathematically difficult. There are 12 inches in a foot, 16 ounces in a pound, and 1760 yards in a mile. The metric system was designed using a base-10 system, just like our system of number. It is the standard for most countries in the world and for almost all scientific applications.

First graders can understand that they can use different standards and that there are different ways to transfer measurements. **Transitivity**, or the ability to transfer a measurement of one item to something else, is still developing in first graders and this ability may not fully develop until later elementary years. However, children can begin to use rulers to determine the lengths of items and re-create those lengths. While there may still be some tasks that are confusing or difficult, this can be the basis for discussion or questioning by the teacher.

Nonphysical measurements are harder for children to gauge. For example, here is another exchange with my first-grade son, while on a trip to a nearby town.

Dylan: "How long until we get there?"

G: "About 40 minutes."

Dylan: "How many seconds is that?"

G: "Let's see. I think it is 2400 seconds."

Dylan: "Okay." [He begins to count quickly under his breath.]

G: "Are you counting seconds? If you are, you need to count slower. A second is more like 1 Mississippi, 2 Mississippi."

Dylan: "Those are adult seconds. Kids' seconds are different."

G: "So, are adult minutes different from kid minutes?"

Dylan: "Yeah!"

G: "What about hours?"

Dylan: "Yes. They are different."

G: "So, a minute for you is different than a minute for me?"

Dylan: "Yes. It is different!"

G: "Is it different on our watches? Is a minute longer on my watch than on yours?"

Dylan: "I think so."

Time seems variable based on what we are doing. Time passes at a uniform rate for all, but if you are riding in a car and you are bored, it may seem a lot longer. We also see that instead of using a television show or other known length of time as in kindergarten, Dylan used numbers and his idea of seconds to gauge the passing of time.

Patterns and Algebra. Children in first grade, because of their ability to read and their developing cognitive ability, can understand word problems. Word problems offer children a way to make mathematics relevant to their lives and allow them to use their natural numerical thinking ability to solve them. Word problems, at their best, are more than just problems such as "Susie had three apples and Joe gave her two more. How many apples does she have?" While useful for learning some mathematical computation, a problem such as this does not take advantage of the first grader's ability to actually *solve* a problem. Problems should encourage children to think, not just follow rules. We will discuss what makes a good word problem later in this chapter.

First graders can collect data and find patterns. They can also create and extend patterns, using as many as three factors in their construction of patterns. They can do patterns such as ABBCCABBCC, or any other combination of three factors. They can also use words to describe and explain their patterns to others. They can say, "It is one red and two red and two blues and then it repeats!" They can extend the pattern either through explanation or by placing more blocks in the line (Clements & Sarama, 2004).

They also begin to learn about money. While it may not seem like it, the basic idea that a dollar = 4 quarters = 10 dimes = 20 nickels = 100 pennies is based on algebra. Algebra uses one item or symbol to stand for a quantity. Advanced algebra uses symbols such as X, Y, and Z, for example. But coins also stand for values. Quarters = 25, dimes = 10, and nickels = 5. When I was in first grade, I used to trade my 4-year-old sister all my nickels for her dimes. She thought that because the nickels were bigger, they were worth more. This perception interfered with her judgment of quantity.

Geometry and Spatial Sense. Children in first grade are adept at turning and flipping shapes to make them match other shapes and even pictures. First graders can compose and decompose pictures using other shapes such as triangles, circles, squares, and rhombuses. Geometric puzzles of this nature are of great interest to first graders. Their knowledge of three-dimensional shapes is also developing and blocks in the classroom can support this construction.

Children can copy shapes from memory even when the shapes are not present. Their functional memory is expanding and their long-term memory and memory strategies allow them to recall many geometric shapes and reproduce them. The construction of a **coordinate system** by first graders allows them to make fairly accurate maps of their classrooms, schools, and even neighborhoods. This is an ongoing construction, and turning the map and rotation of shapes can still confuse the child. This coordinate system is not only useful for mapmaking, but for measurement. Using a ruler often requires a coordinate system to plan the measurement activity. As this system strengthens, the ability to use rulers and to understand standard measurement becomes more and more complex (Clements, 2004; Clements & Sarama, 2004).

Data Analysis Probability and Statistics. First graders can not only read and make graphs, they can now collect data using numbers and tally marks. For example, they can flip coins and collect data from the coin flipping by making a column for tails and a column for heads. After 50 throws, they can count the number of heads and tails and make a graph of the results. They can also explain the results to the class and generalize some data from the graph. First graders can also use the graph to make simple predictions about future coin flips. Using this technique, they can create a graph to compare probability of numbers coming up on two number cubes (see Lesson Plans). For example, if they roll the dice 100 times, how many times do the following numbers come up: 1, 2, 3, 4, 5, 6, 7, 8, 9, 10, 11, 12? They usually recognize immediately that one will never come up and, as they graph the data, they notice trends and patterns emerging. There are more tallies for seven than any other number. The children can discuss why this is and, even if they fail to come up with a correct answer, the question will promote solid mathematical thinking and problem solving.

These mathematical developments mean that many new and exciting experiences can be introduced into the classroom at this age. These transitional years are filled with many opportunities and ways to meet young children's standards through experiences, as well as through more traditional teacher-led educational interactions (Geist, 2001).

MEETING STANDARDS WITH K–1 CHILDREN

As children transition into formal mandatory schooling, it becomes more important for teachers to be aware of the standards set by each state. Most states use testing procedures to assess the proficiency of students at different stages in their educational progress, as mandated by the federal government in the No Child Left Behind Act. Over the past 10 years, states have developed ways to hold teachers and schools accountable for the progress that their students make. The standards that each has developed have become the benchmark according to which children, and hence teachers, are judged (National Council of Teachers of Mathematics, 2000; Schoenfeld, 2002).

By the end of each grade, children are expected to be able to demonstrate a certain level of proficiency in mathematics and other subjects. The standards and benchmarks of each state's Department of Education become the measuring stick by which students are compared. Teachers are expected to ensure that the required topics are covered during the academic year. However, as we have stated before, these standards should not dictate to teachers *how* the concepts are taught or *how* they are presented to the students. This allows for some flexibility in the classroom. Examine the NCTM standards for kindergarten and first grade in the Appendix. To understand exactly what your students are expected to know, check with your state's Department of Education for a copy of the K–1 standards.

NCTM Focal Points

As in preschool, NCTM focal points help us to decide which of these standards teachers should focus on in the K–1 years, in order to ensure a focused and coherent mathematics curriculum. While all of the benchmarks are important to cover, NCTM has discerned a few concepts that should be paid special attention in each grade. For kindergarten and first grade, the NCTM focal points emphasize the following (Figures 7.3 and 7.4 list the focal points in their entirety):

Kindergarten
1. Representing, comparing, and ordering whole numbers
2. Describing shapes and space
3. Ordering objects by measurable attributes

Curriculum Focal Points and Connections for Kindergarten

The set of three curriculum focal points and related connections for mathematics in kindergarten follow. These topics are the recommended content emphases for this grade level. It is essential that these focal points be addressed in contexts that promote problem solving, reasoning, communication, making connections, and designing and analyzing representations.

Kindergarten Curriculum Focal Points	Connections to the Focal Points
***Number and Operations:* Representing, comparing, and ordering whole numbers and joining and separating sets** Children use numbers, including written numerals, to represent quantities and to solve quantitative problems, such as counting objects in a set, creating a set with a given number of objects, comparing and ordering sets or numerals by using both cardinal and ordinal meanings, and modeling simple joining and separating situations with objects. They choose, combine, and apply effective strategies for answering quantitative questions, including quickly recognizing the number in a small set, counting and producing sets of given sizes, counting the number in combined sets, and counting backward.	***Data Analysis:*** Children sort objects and use one or more attributes to solve problems. For example, they might sort solids that roll easily from those that do not. Or they might collect data and use counting to answer such questions as: "What is our favorite snack?" They re-sort objects by using new attributes (e.g., after sorting solids according to which ones roll, they might re-sort the solids according to which ones stack easily.
***Geometry:* Describing shapes and space** Children interpret the physical world with geometric ideas (e.g., shape, orientation, spatial relations) and describe it with corresponding vocabulary. They identify, name, and describe a variety of shapes, such as squares, triangles, circles, rectangles, (regular) hexagons, and (isosceles) trapezoids presented in a variety of ways (e.g., with different sizes or orientations), as well as such three-dimensional shapes as spheres, cubes, and cylinders. They use basic shapes and spatial reasoning to model objects in their environment and to construct more complex shapes.	***Geometry:*** Children integrate their understandings of geometry, measurement, and numbers. For example, they understand, discuss, and create simple navigational directions (e.g., "Walk forward 10 steps, turn right, and walk forward 5 steps"). ***Algebra:*** Children identify, duplicate, and extend simple number patterns and sequential and growing patterns (e.g., patterns made with shapes) as preparation for creating rules that describe relationships.
***Measurement:* Ordering objects by measurable attributes** Children use measurable attributes, such as length or weight, to solve problems by comparing and ordering objects. They compare the lengths of two objects both directly (by comparing them with each other) and indirectly (by comparing both with a third object), and they order several objects according to length.	

Figure 7.3 Kindergarten Focal Points.

Source: Reprinted with permission from *Curriculum Focal Points for Prekindergarten through Grade 8 Mathematics: A Quest for Coherence,* copyright 2006 by the National Council of Teachers of Mathematics. All rights reserved. The Curriculum Focal Points identify key mathematical ideas for these grades. They are not discrete topics or a checklist to be mastered; rather, they provide a framework for the majority of instruction at a particular grade level and the foundation for future mathematics study. The complete document may be viewed at *www.nctm.org/focalpoints.*

Curriculum Focal Points and Connections for Grade 1

The set of three curriculum focal points and related connections for mathematics in grade 1 follow. These topics are the recommended content emphases for this grade level. It is essential that these focal points be addressed in contexts that promote problem solving, reasoning, communication, making connections, and designing and analyzing representations.

Grade 1 Curriculum Focal Points	Connections to the Focal Points
Number and Operations and Algebra: Developing understandings of addition and subtraction and strategies for basic addition facts and related subtraction facts Children develop strategies for adding and subtracting whole numbers on the basis of their earlier work with small numbers. They use a variety of models, including discrete objects, length-based models (e.g., lengths of connecting cubes), and number lines, to model "part-whole," "adding to," "taking away from," and "comparing" situations to develop an understanding of the meanings of addition and subtraction and strategies to solve such arithmetic problems. Children understand the connections between counting and the operations of addition and subtraction (e.g., adding two is the same as "counting on" two). They use properties of addition (commutativity and associatively) to add whole numbers, and they create and use increasingly sophisticated strategies based on these properties (e.g., "making tens") to solve addition and subtraction problems involving basic facts. By comparing a variety of solution strategies, children relate addition and subtraction as inverse operations.	**Number and Operations and Algebra:** Children use mathematical reasoning, including ideas such as commutativity and associativity and beginning ideas of tens and ones, to solve two-digit addition and subtraction problems with strategies that they understand and can explain. They solve both routine and nonroutine problems.
Number and Operations: Developing an understanding of whole-number relationships, including grouping in tens and ones Children compare and order whole numbers (at least to 100) to develop an understanding of and solve problems involving the relative sizes of these numbers. They think of whole numbers between 10 and 100 in terms of groups of tens and ones (especially recognizing the numbers 11 to 19 as one group of ten and particular numbers of ones). They understand the sequential order of the counting numbers and their relative magnitudes and represent numbers on a number line.	**Measurement and Data Analysis:** Children strengthen their sense of numbers by solving problems involving measurements and data. Measuring by laying multiple copies of a unit end to end and then counting the units by using groups of terms and ones supports children's understanding of number lines and number relationships. Representing measurements and discrete data in picture and bar graphs involves counting and comparisons that provide another meaningful connection to number relationships.
Geometry: Composing and decomposing geometric shapes Children compose and decompose plane and solid figures (e.g., by putting two congruent isosceles triangles together to make a rhombus), thus building an understanding of part-whole relationships as well as the properties of the original and composite shapes. As they combine figures, they recognize them from different perspectives and orientations, describe their geometric attributes and properties, and determine how they are alike and different, in the process developing a background for measurement and initial understandings of such properties as congruence and symmetry.	**Algebra:** Through identifying, describing, and applying number patterns and properties in developing strategies for basic facts, children learn about other properties of numbers and operations, such as odd and even (e.g., "Even numbers of objects can be paired, with none left over"), and 0 as the identity element for addition.

Figure 7.4 First-Grade Focal Points.

Source: Reprinted with permission from *Curriculum Focal Points for Prekindergarten through Grade 8 Mathematics: A Quest for Coherence,* copyright 2006 by the National Council of Teachers of Mathematics. All rights reserved. The Curriculum Focal Points identify key mathematical ideas for these grades. They are not discrete topics or a checklist to be mastered; rather, they provide a framework for the majority of instruction at a particular grade level and the foundation for future mathematics study. The complete document may be viewed at *www.nctm.org/focalpoints*.

First Grade

1. Addition and subtraction
2. The system of tens and ones (place value)
3. Composing and decomposing geometric shapes

Using the NCTM standards and focal points as a guide to instruction, let's examine developmentally appropriate ways to meet these goals in the kindergarten and first-grade classroom.

WHAT DOES A K–1 MATHEMATICS LEARNING ENVIRONMENT LOOK LIKE?

If you were to examine typical kindergarten and first-grade classrooms, you would notice quite a few differences. Kindergarten classrooms tend to have more play-based activities, such as blocks; more open space in the classroom for group time; and more tables and fewer desks. Given the focal points for kindergarten, this seems appropriate (Figure 7.3). Children in first grade are still very active, learning math through experience as well as through teacher-directed educational activities. Therefore, the environments should contain more similarities than differences. Some concepts are more advanced in first grade, as demonstrated in the NCTM curriculum focal points (Figure 7.4), but the method for learning is basically the same—through interaction with materials and with others.

Discussing, doing, and solving mathematics problems are the central way children in K–1 learn mathematics. Math is best learned in an active, socially interactive environment, not one that is quiet, individual, and sedate. Kindergarten and first-grade classrooms should have tables or desks that allow for children to do individual work and to have a place to store their personal belongings. Sometimes, a child has a "cubby" where he can store items such as his coat, books, and folders. Whichever way your classroom is set up, it is important to their feelings of ownership and defensibility that children have their own space.

The classroom should also have an area for children to work in small groups or play math games. Some children prefer playing on the floor; carpeted areas can make this more comfortable. These should be away from the main traffic areas in the classroom.

There should also be areas set aside as **centers** for specific activities such as math, science, and reading. These should have all the materials that K–1 children need to do the specific task assigned for that space. The curricular activities for these centers will vary depending on the time of the year and the developmental levels of the students. Therefore, the materials will change throughout the year. Although the setup of centers in the kindergarten and first-grade classroom may be different, the goal of independent, individual, and small group work is the same.

In first grade, with the advent of more formal mathematics instruction, the arrangement of desks becomes more of an issue. Many first-grade classrooms come with desks as standard equipment. In a traditional arrangement, children all face the teacher. To support social interaction, children should ideally be arranged so that they can see each other's faces, but the teacher may use one of the other seating arrangements discussed in Chapter 4 to promote an interactive mathematics program.

Whichever arrangement the teacher chooses, it should be the one that works best for his or her teaching style. She may choose, as well, to periodically rearrange the classroom to meet the changing needs of the students. Remember, the goal is to promote learning in ways that are both conscious and unconscious. If the classroom is set up so that children can see each other's faces, it sends the message that they are supposed to talk to each other and discuss. If the desks are arranged so that the teacher's face is the only one seen, the children get the message that she or he is the only one with anything important to say.

DEVELOPMENTALLY APPROPRIATE STRATEGIES AND ACTIVITIES FOR K–1 CHILDREN

A K–1 mathematics program should be built around problem solving. This allows children to use their own natural thinking ability to solve perplexing mathematics problems and to build a conceptual understanding of mathematics. This does not mean that fluency and what Fosnot deemed automaticity are unimportant. These are vitally important for future success in mathematics; however, they must grow out of understanding.

Word Problems

Designing good word problems may seem easy, but it takes more thought than you might think. Marilyn Burns suggests that math problems should be the starting place for mathematical understanding because they establish a "need" and "context" for computation and math skills. However, she also cautions that assigning traditional word problems from textbooks usually accomplishes no more than testing students' abilities to solve problems (Burns, 1992).

She goes on to say that making traditional word problems, such as the one mentioned earlier in this chapter, gives an unrealistic message to children about the way mathematics will serve them as adults. Most daily problems adults deal with that require mathematical reasoning cannot be solved by directly translating the available information into an arithmetic sentence. Let's revisit that problem and see if we can make it a richer problem-solving experience (Burns, 1992; Burns & Silbey, 2000).

"Susie had 3 apples and Joe gave her 2 more. How many does she have?" $3 + 2 = 5$

These types of problems do not reflect real life. Real-life problems do not contain all the information needed to solve them in one easy-to-read sentence. As adults, we often have to collect the data from a variety of sources; there is rarely a situation in which one and only one solution strategy presents itself. There are often many ways to proceed to a solution. As adults, we call on our knowledge, previous experience, and even our intuition to analyze, evaluate, and make predictions (Burns, 1992; Burns & Silbey, 2000).

So, what is a good word problem? Burns proposes four criteria to developing a good word problem and I will add a fifth. These can be implemented in a K–1 math program with little effort.

1. There is a perplexing situation that the student understands
2. The student is interested in finding a solution
3. The student is unable to proceed directly toward a solution
4. The solution requires the use of mathematical ideas (Burns, 1992; Burns & Silbey, 2000)
5. There are many different ways to reach a solution and possibly many different correct answers

These five guidelines might be applied in a problem like this:

On the Monday after Halloween, Mark's mother told him that he could ask for one piece of candy each day after he finished his homework. Mark was very excited and did his homework right away for the rest of the week. On Saturday and Sunday, Mark's mother let him have his candy even though there was no school or homework on those days. After he received his candy on Sunday, he realized he had forgotten to ask for his candy on two days. How many pieces of candy did Mark have and how did he know he missed two days?

In this problem there is a perplexing situation that most students can understand. Most children are familiar with getting candy on Halloween and with doing their daily homework. Kindergarteners are learning the days of the week and can understand the one-to-one correspondence of one piece of candy for one day.

Because the child can relate to the problem, he is interested in finding a solution. The solution will take more time and thought than the previous problem with Suzie and Joe and the apples. The child must first figure out the best strategy for solving the problem. Kindergarteners may use a calendar and blocks to represent candy or act out the scenario. First graders may model the situation or make an arithmetic sentence out of it. Before they can do this, they must determine that there were 7 days when Mark could possibly have received candy and only 5 days when he actually did receive candy.

The solution requires the use of mathematical ideas because children have to use one-to-one correspondence along with addition or subtraction or both to solve the problem. If this problem is too easy for your first graders, you can easily make it more difficult by saying Mark gets two or three pieces of candy each day. This introduces the concepts of multiplication to the solution.

While there is only one correct answer for this problem, there are many different ways to reach a solution. When children are interested and challenged by a problem like this, they will be naturally driven to work on a solution. Human beings crave mental stimulation, which is why crossword puzzles and Sudoku puzzles are so popular. Brainteaser problems and math games are often used as rewards or special "fun" activities in school, whereas they should be the main part of the curriculum.

Problem-Solving Strategies. To become successful problem solvers, children need to have an interest in finding solutions to problems, the confidence to try various strategies, the willingness to be wrong at times, and perseverance. They must also understand that just because the problem is hard and they don't know the answer, they will find it if they keep working (Burns, 1992; Burns & Silbey, 2000). Burns calls this the difference between not knowing the answer and not knowing the answer *yet* (Burns, 1992; Burns & Silbey, 2000).

Teachers can help students become better problem solvers by emphasizing and modeling good problem-solving strategies. Here are some suggestions from Marilyn Burns:

- Look for a pattern
- Construct a table
- Make an organized list
- Act it out
- Draw a picture
- Use objects
- Guess and check
- Work backwards
- Write an equation
- Solve a simpler (or similar) problem
- Make a model (Burns, 2000)

Class discussions are also useful. Children hear others' points of view and other solution strategies. These problem-solving and discussion strategies are also useful for whole-class instruction.

Whole-Class Instruction

During the transitional period of K–1, we begin to see the beginning of teacher-led discussions and whole-class instruction in mathematics. It may not seem like these are present in kindergarten, but with the new proficiency requirements set by No Child Left Behind, it is becoming more and more prevalent. I observed a typical kindergarten class in a school that was engaged in a push to improve its proficiency scores. The teacher sat in a chair with the children in front of her and for 10 minutes went through flash cards as the children chanted the answers.

This is becoming more prevalent in kindergarten classrooms. In first grade, traditionally, teacher-led instruction meant that the teacher would explain the procedure or method of working an arithmetic problem on the board and then hand out worksheets for children to engage in repetition and practice.

Both of these teaching strategies are designed to give children repeated practice to improve fluency. However, there are better and more interactive ways to meet the required goals. The goals of whole-class instruction should be:

1. To allow computation to develop out of word problems
2. To encourage children to invent their own procedures, rather than showing them how to solve problems
3. To encourage the exchange of points of view among children and let the correct answer emerge, rather than simply reinforcing correct answers and correcting wrong ones
4. To encourage children to invent many different ways of solving a given problem
5. To encourage children to *think* rather than write
6. To facilitate the exchange of viewpoints through having children write on the chalkboard
7. The exchange of viewpoints, to encourage and teach place value (Kamii et al., 2003)

Children in K–1 can invent their own procedures for solving problems presented to them by the teacher and then discuss their answers with the whole class. In this model of instruction, only a few problems are presented to them, rather than numerous flash cards or worksheet problems. Fewer problems are presented and more time is spent on each one. Since fluency is not the goal of these activities, the focus can be on conceptual understanding.

Here is an example of a first-grade, whole-class interaction:

Teacher: "Class, I have a problem for you. This is one that I don't think we have seen before. Do you want to give it a try?"

Class: (Enthusiastically): "Yes!"

Teacher: "OK. Here it is." She writes this problem on the board:

$$\begin{array}{r} 13 \\ +\ 9 \\ \hline \end{array}$$

Teacher: "Okay, I want you to think about this problem and, when you have an answer, raise your hand."

(The class works for 5 minutes. When all hands are in the air, she calls on a student to give her answer.)

Teacher: "Lilly, what answer did you get?"

Lilly: "12."

Tonya (as well as some other students): "I disagree."

Teacher: "OK, Tonya, what do you think the answer is?"

Tonya: "22."

Others in the class: "I agree."

Teacher: "Lilly, do you want to explain how you got 12?"

Lilly: "Well, I added three and nine and I got twelve and then . . . um . . . wait a minute. I think I made a mistake."

Teacher: "Okay, Tonya, do you want to tell the class how you got your answer?"

Tonya: "I started with 13 and then (counting on her fingers) 14, 15, 16, 17, 18, 19, 20, 21, 22 so the answer was 22."

Teacher: "Okay, does anyone else want to share their answer? All right, Mario."

Mario: "I knew that 9 plus 3 was 12 and then I added 10 more."

Teacher: (writing what Mario said on the board): "Okay, so you said $9 + 3 = 12$, and then $12 + 10 = 22$. Is that correct?"

Mario: "Yes."

The teacher let this free exchange of ideas continue until all the children who had different ways of solving the problem had a chance to share. The discussion did not end until everyone agreed on an answer.

There are a couple of common questions about this approach to teaching. One is, "What if they never agree on an answer or all agree on the wrong answer?" The teacher can use questioning techniques to help guide them toward the issue that is causing the block. If they still have trouble agreeing on an answer, perhaps the problem was a bit over their heads and the teacher should choose another problem. The other question is, "Don't children get their feelings hurt when others disagree with them in front of the whole class? It seems like it would be stressful." I have not noticed students having a problem with this technique. However, it does mean that you have to set classroom ground rules. These rules should be 1) we listen to everyone respectfully; 2) we can disagree and still be friends; and 3) we focus on the mathematics, not the person (in other words don't make it personal). Children usually have no problems with these rules and adapt to the method easily.

This approach works because they are interacting with fellow students on a level playing field. If they decide to change their answer, it will be because they themselves realize they are wrong, not because another person told them so. In a discussion between equals, either one can be wrong.

When using this technique, teachers need to gauge the comfort level of their class with this interaction. Perhaps the children can explain their answers and discuss different approaches without yelling, "I agree" or "I disagree" after each answer. These are personal classroom decisions each teacher must make.

The importance of this type of approach is the social interaction (Kamii, Piaget, & Federation of North Text Area Universities, 1984; Kamii et al., 2003). Children should discuss and explain their answers and even defend them if necessary. They should be encouraged only to give up if convinced that their answer is not the best one. In the previous vignette, Lilly noticed her own error when she began to explain it to others. This is very common. Since social interaction is so important, it is vital that the teacher does not reinforce correct answers. Instead, she should facilitate discussion through questioning strategies.

Math Games

Math games are important to the construction of mathematics. In K–1, they take on a new purpose—fluency and automaticity (Dolk, 2004; Fosnot, 1989). The repetitive educational tasks that build fluency can be incorporated into math games, freeing up the time traditionally used for worksheets and whole-class instruction.

Card games, such as Double War, can be used for fluency. Children become faster and faster at slapping down two cards, adding the numbers, and determining who has the highest number. This increases speed, automaticity, and memorization of basic addition sums in a way that is enjoyable to the child. Other math games help children understand different numerical relationships. Cover-up games can take on a new dimension with the involvement of addition (see Lesson Plans). Games that involve "making 10" in different ways facilitate the fluency of addition and help the child understand the base-10 system and place value. Group games also facilitate and foster mathematics discussion. Magnetic darts, tossing games, dice games, and outdoor games can be used for mathematical experiences. When teachers see the number of standards that they need to meet in first grade, many feel overwhelmed. Using group math games to meet some of these standards can be a useful approach.

Examples of math games that teach addends of 10 (Kamii et al., 2003):

- Find 10—Cards (1–9) are dealt to each player and one card is placed in the middle of the table. Players place their stacks in front of them without looking at them. Each round the child turns over a card. If he can make 10 using his card and one in the middle, he takes the cards. If not, he discards his card to the center and the next person goes.
- Draw 10—Like Old Maid, except that children use math cards that add to 10 rather than picture cards. If they do not have a match, they can draw from the other person.
- 10s Concentration—Twenty-five cards placed on a table in a 5 × 5 arrangement. At each turn the child turns over two cards. If the cards add up to 10 he takes them, if not, he turns them back over and the next person takes a turn.
- Go 10—Played like "Go Fish" except children are looking to make 10 with two cards instead of matching cards. After they have laid down all the combinations of 10 in their hand they begin to ask other players for cards. For example, "Joe, do you have any 2s?"

Examples of games for other addition and subtraction standards (Kamii et al., 2003):

- Salute!—Cards 1–9 are placed in a deck and divided between three players. One person is the judge for each round. Two children say "Salute!," each picks up the top card, and quickly hold it to his forehead so his opponent can see it, but he cannot. The judge then announces the sum of the two cards. The first player to announce the identity of his card wins.

Projects

As with the previous ages, projects offer a rich mathematical experience to children, allowing them to integrate math and science. Projects in kindergarten and first grade can be more intricate and complex. Children can begin to use projects to explore things happening in the world around them and mathematics can be integrated into this experience. We will discuss this process more in Chapter 9.

A good project for kindergarten and first grade might be a project on construction. In K–1, children can use more sophisticated methods of data collection and presentation. Reading and writing can be used to collect and share data. Children can go to the library to gather data on the topic. For a project on construction, they can invite an architect to their classroom to learn about drawing plans and how to make accurate drawings of the room. They can invite plumbers, carpenters, and electricians into their classroom and ask them questions and record their answers (Geist, 2001).

For mathematics, learning about measurement and the mathematics of building something is a good way to introduce math concepts in a natural and interesting way. The children can use blocks to construct and build their own structures.

For mathematics and other content areas, teachable moments abound when using word problems, social interaction, interactive teaching, math games, and projects. If, as a teacher, you remain flexible and watch and listen to the students, opportunities to promote math will arise around every corner.

SAMPLE KINDERGARTEN AND FIRST-GRADE LESSON PLANS

The following lesson plans are some structured and interactive ways to promote mathematical development in children from, roughly, ages 5 to 7. As in other chapters, these lesson plans should be tried out with children if the opportunity presents itself. Make sure you note any adaptations you needed to make with the group of children you work with, and try out the assessments as well. Note any challenges and think about what you might change the next time you use the lesson.

LESSON PLAN

▼◄ ▲▼◄ ▲▼◄ ▲▼◄ ▲▼◄ ▲▼◄ ▲▼◄ ▲

Lesson Title: Making Number Books

Age: Kindergarten

Subject Area: Mathematics

▼◄ ▲▼◄ ▲▼◄ ▲▼◄ ▲▼◄ ▲▼◄ ▲▼◄ ▲

Objective: Support that numbers have meaning in a child's life and support the child's writing numbers.

Standards: Compare and order whole numbers up to 10. Relate, read, and write numerals for single-digit numbers (0 to 9).

Focal Points: Representing, comparing, and ordering whole numbers.

Lesson Summary: Children will write and explain the numbers important in their lives and make a book out of them. The numbers will be put into sequence before binding it for sharing with the class.

Beginning the Lesson: The teacher should collect a number of counting books appropriate for the level of the children. These should be read to them in the days before the activity commences and the teacher should focus their attention on the counting activities. An excellent resource for this is Jacqueline McDonald's article "Selecting Counting Books" in the May 2007 issue of *Young Children.*

Procedures: The teacher supplies construction paper, crayons, markers, rulers, string, scissors, glue, and any other art supplies the children might need. She explains to the students that they are each going to make a book containing the numbers that are important in their lives. The numbers can be their age, the number of people in their family, the days of the week, their favorite number, or anything else they may choose. The children are to devote one page to each number and can create and decorate it in any way they please. The teacher should try to get each child to create at least three pages for his book. After the book is created, he can put the numbers in sequence from lowest to highest and make a cover. The pages can then be stapled together. During group time, children can share their books and explain why they chose their numbers.

Extension: The teacher can require the children to use all of the numbers 1–9, and come up with something in their lives that relates to each number. If the child can't think of something for nine, the teacher might ask, "Do you think you can hop on one foot nine times?" If he says he can, then that can be suggested for the number "9."

Adaptations: The art portion of this activity can be difficult for children who have limited physical mobility or less advanced fine motor skills. Teachers may need to aid these children in cutting, pasting, and other activities. For children who have limited counting and numerical knowledge, teachers can help them by writing their favorite numbers for the children to illustrate as they like.

Materials: Colored paper or construction paper, scissors, crayons, markers, glue, and yarn.

Assessment: Assessment should be done through observation and recording the children's responses to the experience. The finished product can be collected and put in each child's mathematics portfolio.

LESSON PLAN

▼◄▲▼◄▲▼◄▲▼◄▲▼◄▲▼◄▲▼◄▲

Lesson Title: Measure Me

Age: K–1

Subject Area: Mathematics

▼◄▲▼◄▲▼◄▲▼◄▲▼◄▲▼◄▲▼◄▲

Objective: Use measurement to transfer heights to other medium (transitivity) and compare heights.

Standards:

1. Compare and order objects of different lengths, areas, weights, and capacities; and use relative terms, such as *longer, shorter, bigger, smaller, heavier, lighter, more,* and *less.*
2. Measure length and volume (capacity) using uniform objects in the environment.
3. Estimate and measure lengths using nonstandard and standard units (i.e., centimeters, inches, and feet).

Focal Points: Ordering objects by measurable attributes.

Lesson Summary: Children use the yarn to measure each other's height and length of arms, legs, and feet, then use it to create a self-portrait on butcher paper.

Beginning the Lesson: During group time the teacher can say "I was noticing on the playground how many of you have grown since the beginning of the year. You all seem to be growing so tall. How big do you think you were on your first day in this class?" The teacher can discuss this for a few minutes and get children's responses. "How big do you think you are now?" Again, she should let the children discuss this question. She should then say, "I had an idea. I thought that we could measure ourselves and make life-size drawings of ourselves. That way if you grow anymore between now and the end of the year, we will be able to see it!"

Procedures: Teacher makes scissors, yarn, markers, and masking tape available to the children. She gives each student an instruction sheet with the details of the activity on it (Figure 7.5). Children are to work in pairs or small groups. They are to use the yarn to measure the length of their arms, legs, and feet as well as their height. They cut the yarn to represent that length, then use masking tape to label it with the person's name, and the measurement. Once each child has all four measurements, he is to draw a life-size, proportional self-portrait using the measurements that were taken. He should, with the teacher's help or help from others, use the yarn to determine how tall his self-portrait should be and how long the legs, arms, and feet should be.

Extension: Standard units can be added to the activity. Children can be required to determine how tall they are and the length of each of the other measurements using inches or centimeters. Concepts of symmetry can also be introduced using the body drawings.

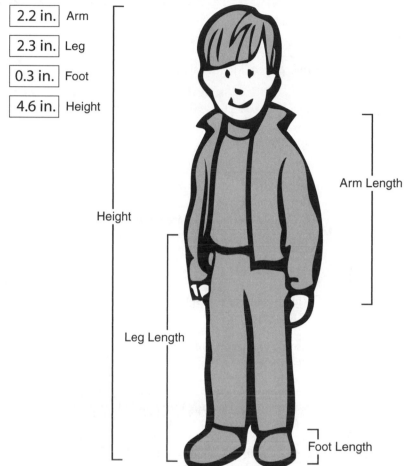

Measure these four parts of your body and
label the yarn. Check the box when
each measurement is complete.

2.2 in.	Arm
2.3 in.	Leg
0.3 in.	Foot
4.6 in.	Height

Height

Arm Length

Leg Length

Foot Length

Figure 7.5 Instruction Sheet for Measure Me Activity.

Adaptations: Children can be asked to draw representations of themselves by lying down and tracing their outlines. They can then use the yarn to compare their height to other drawings. Children with physical disabilities may have trouble lying down and tracing their bodies, so the teacher should find a way that the child can participate. For example, if the child is in a wheelchair, the teacher could encourage the group to make measurements of the wheelchair using the string.

Materials: Yarn, markers or crayons, measuring tapes, butcher paper, scissors, masking tape

Assessment: Assessment should be done through observation and recording the children's responses to the experience.

LESSON PLAN
▼◄▲▼◄▲▼◄▲▼◄▲▼◄▲▼◄▲▼◄▲

Lesson Title: Cover Up 10

Age: K–1

Subject Area: Mathematics

▼◄▲▼◄▲▼◄▲▼◄▲▼◄▲▼◄▲▼◄▲

Objective: To increase fluency of adding and regrouping numbers that add up to 10.

Standards:

1. Represent and use whole numbers in flexible ways, including relating, composing, and decomposing numbers (e.g., five marbles can be two red and three green or one red and four green).
2. Recognize and generate equivalent forms for the same number using physical models, words, and number expressions.
3. Model, represent, and explain addition as combining sets (part + part = whole) and counting on.

Focal Points: 1) Representing, comparing, and ordering whole numbers; 2) addition and subtraction.

Lesson Summary: Children roll two 6-sided number cubes and determine numbers to cover up.

Beginning the Lesson: Math games are introduced to the whole class during a group meeting. During this meeting the basic rules are explained and questions are answered about the game. The teacher can then demonstrate how to play the game by choosing a child from the class to play with. After this the teacher places the game materials in the Math Game Center for children to play during free time or math game time. A 20–40 minute time period should be set aside during the day for children to play math games.

Procedures: Teachers should create a game board with the numbers 1–10 in circles that can be covered by chips (Figure 7.6). Children roll the dice and can do one of the following things:

1. cover up the sum of the two cubes
2. cover up the amount on one of the cubes (for example if three and five are rolled the child could cover a three or a five with a chip) or
3. cover up any combination of numbers that make the sum he rolled (for example, if he rolled a four and a three, and still needs to cover the numbers two and five, he could cover them because they add up to the same sum as the rolled sum. This could also be extended to covering three numbers that add up to the rolled sum). The player who covers all 10 numbers first wins.

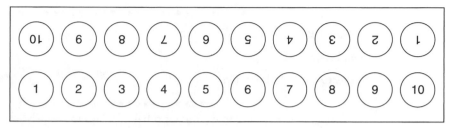

Figure 7.6 Cover up 10 game boards.

Extension: The teacher can suggest more complex ways to play this game to children that are able to understand addition and subtraction or complex regrouping. Kindergarteners will most likely cover up sums and addends.

Adaptations: This game offers a lot of developmental flexibility. The teacher should create number cubes that have the numbers 1–5 on the faces. The sixth face can be designated as either "0" or "wild." You might experiment with leaving it blank just to see what the children decide to do; they may choose just to ignore it.

Materials: Two number cubes with 1–5 on the faces and one blank, "wild," or "0"; a game board numbered 1–10; large chips to cover the numbers.

Assessment: Assessment should be done through observation and recording the children's responses to informal questioning techniques.

LESSON PLAN

▼◄▲▼◄▲▼◄▲▼◄▲▼◄▲▼◄▲▼◄▲

Lesson Title: Probability Graphing

Age: First Grade

Subject Area: Mathematics

▼◄▲▼◄▲▼◄▲▼◄▲▼◄▲▼◄▲▼◄▲

Objective: Use graphing to examine probability and make predictions.

Standards:
1. Answer questions about the number of objects represented in a picture graph, bar graph, or table graph.
2. Describe the likelihood of simple events as possible or impossible and more or less likely.

Focal Points: Addition and subtraction.

Lesson Summary: Children begin by collecting data and graphing the outcomes when they flip two coins (i.e., two heads, one head, one tail, and two tails), three coins (three heads, two heads, one tail, one head, two tails, and three tails), and the sums of two dice (2, 3, 4, 5, 6, 7, 8, 9, 10, 11, 12).

Beginning the Lesson: The teacher should distribute a nickel to each child. A large picture of a nickel would also be helpful. She can ask, "Do you know who this is on the front of the nickel?" Children's discussions should be facilitated. Some representations of Jefferson are different and a comparison can be discussed. The teacher should then ask them to look on the other side of the nickel (obverse). "Does anyone know what is on the other side of a nickel?" Nickels have Monticello, Jefferson's home in Virginia. The teacher should then explain that the front of the coin is often called "heads" and the obverse is called "tails." She can then ask the class what they think would happen if she flipped the nickel. Would it be heads or tails? She can say, "How many think it will be heads?" The children can count and record that number, then the teacher can ask, "How many think it will be tails?" That number can also be recorded, and then she can ask the class to add the numbers to make sure everyone voted. She can flip the coin, then write the result on the board, asking, "What do you think will happen if I do it again? Would I get the same result?" This can be repeated enough times that children understand the difficulty of predicting what will come next.

Procedures: The teacher has the children work in groups of three or four. Children are given two coins to flip, along with a graphing sheet (Figure 7.7). Each group is to toss the coins 10 times and record their results on the sheet. After everyone is done, the teacher facilitates putting each group's data together into one graph. The students then add up the resulting numbers and compare the results. The teacher should lead a discussion of why there are more "one head, one tail" combinations.

Building on this activity the next day or the next week, one more coin is added. Now, children will be graphing four categories and comparing and discussing the results.

2 Heads	1 Head 1 Tail	2 Tails
○	○	○
○	○	○
○	○	○
○	○	○
○	○	○
○	○	○
○	○	○
○	○	○
○	○	○
○	○	○

3 Heads	2 Heads 1 Tail	1 Head 2 Tails	3 Tails
○	○	○	○
○	○	○	○
○	○	○	○
○	○	○	○
○	○	○	○
○	○	○	○
○	○	○	○
○	○	○	○
○	○	○	○
○	○	○	○

Figure 7.7 Recording sheet for flipping two coins. Children color in circles from the bottom up as each combination appears.

Building on the previous experiences, the next day or the next week the teacher explains that many combinations are possible with number cubes. The groups will roll two dice 10 times and record the resulting sum. The results will be tallied and shared as before (Figure 7.8). The discussion of why there are very few 2s and 12s and a lot of 7s may be a long one.

Extension: The teacher can ask the class the best way to aggregate and organize the data before starting the coin flipping or cube rolling. The goal is to make one large class graph and the class may come up with an innovative way of managing the activity. Children can use numbers or tally marks rather than the suggested graphing sheets. Quarters could be used instead of nickels; a geography lesson could be integrated (since newer quarters have state information and depictions on the obverse).

1	2	3	4	5	6	7	8	9	10	11	12
	×	×	×	×	×	×	×	×	×	×	
		×	×	×	×	×	×				
			×	×	×	×	×				
			×		×	×	×				
					×	×					
						×					

Figure 7.8 Recording sheet for rolling two number cubes.

Materials: Paper for tallying or recording results, pencil or marker, coins, number cubes, chart paper for graphing, a couple rolls of nickels or quarters.

Assessment: Assessment should be done through observation and recording the children's responses to informal questioning techniques. Individual work can be collected and put in the child's portfolio.

LESSON PLAN

▼◄ ▲▼◄ ▲▼◄ ▲▼◄ ▲▼◄ ▲▼◄ ▲▼◄ ▲

Lesson Title: Color Train

Age: Kindergarten

Subject Area: Mathematics

▼◄ ▲▼◄ ▲▼◄ ▲▼◄ ▲▼◄ ▲▼◄ ▲▼◄ ▲

Objective: To create and extend patterns in the context of play and everyday activity.

Standards:
1. Sort, classify, and order objects by size, number, and other properties. For example:
   a. Identify how objects are alike and different.
   b. Order three events or objects according to a given attribute, such as time or size.
   c. Recognize and explain how objects can be classified in more than one way.
   d. Identify what attribute was used to sort groups of objects that have already been sorted.
2. Identify, create, extend, and copy sequences of sounds (such as musical notes); shapes (such as buttons, leaves or blocks); motions (such as hops or skips); and numbers from 1 to 10.
3. Describe orally the pattern of a given sequence.

Focal Points: Ordering objects by measurable attributes.

Lesson Summary: Children will make patterns using the attributes of their clothing.

Beginning the Lesson: With the children sitting in a group, the teacher says, "I want everyone to look around and see what everyone else is wearing today. What colors are on the shirts people are wearing?"

Procedures: The teacher writes down on chart paper the different colors that the children notice. She then says, "If you are wearing a green shirt, stand up. How many people are wearing green? Can we count them?" She should repeat this for other colors on the list.

The teacher then introduces the "color train" song. The tune is sung to an old spiritual called "This Train Is Bound for Glory" (a sample can be found here: *http:// maxhunter.missouristate.edu/1273/index.html*).

> Start with a beat and keep it going throughout the experience.
> (have the students clap their hands or tap their knees)
>
> *Here comes the color train, here it comes.*
> *Here comes the color train, here it comes.*
>
> *The color train is here to stay, we line up, line up on the way.*
> *Here comes the color train, here it comes.*

The teacher can make a simple pattern with four children, based on the colors they are wearing (for example, a child wearing blue, a child wearing white, another child wearing blue, and another child wearing white). Have students line up to start making the pattern, while singing the song.

> (Chant in rhythm)
> *Looking for a_____ shirt, come line up.* (keep repeating "come line up" until the student gets in line)
> (next color)
> *Looking for a _____ shirt, come line up.*
> (Repeat until you have the pattern that you want.)
>
> Chant the colors (e.g., *PINK RED) (What's next?) PINK!!!*
>
> *Looking for a_____ shirt, come line up.*
> *PINK, RED, PINK (What's next) RED!!!!!*
> *Looking for a _____shirt, come line up.*
>
> *PINK, RED, PINK, RED*
> Continue singing the song until you've extended the pattern as long as you want.
>
> Finish singing the song while the train chugs around in a circle (led by a teacher).
> Encourage the children sitting to sing with you.
>
> *Here comes the color train, here it comes.*
> *Here comes the color train, here it comes.*
>
> *The color train is here to stay, we line up, line up on the way.*
> *Here comes the color train, here it comes.*
> Repeat experience with a different pattern.

Extension: Children can make patterns based on height or an other measurable attribute. The teacher can develop more complex patterns with children wearing two colors or more. She can create a Venn diagram based on what colors the children are wearing. For example, some children might be wearing blue, others white, and some might have both blue and white. Children can discuss which group the children with both colors should be placed.

Adaptations: Musical experiences help to structure activities for children with special needs, such as autism. With careful attention and by varying the beat, rhythm, and melody the music can be adapted to involve these children in an activity in which they would not otherwise be able to participate. Teachers may need to help the child clap or keep a rhythm during the song. Drums and other instruments can be incorporated as needed.

Materials: Chart paper, markers, drums, or other instruments.

Assessment: Assessment should be done through observation and recording the children's responses to informal questioning techniques. Individual work can be collected and put in the child's portfolio.

Note: Lyrics written and adapted by Kamile Geist MT-BC

LESSON PLAN
▼◄▲▼◄▲▼◄▲▼◄▲▼◄▲▼◄▲▼◄▲

Lesson Title: Venn Diagramming

Age: Kindergarten

Subject Area: Mathematics

▼◄▲▼◄▲▼◄▲▼◄▲▼◄▲▼◄▲▼◄▲

Objective: Use comparison and classification to talk about concepts of same and different.

Standards:

1. Sort, order, and classify objects by one attribute (e.g., size, color, shape, use). Gather, sort, and compare objects by similarities and differences in the context of daily activities and play.
2. Place information about objects or the objects themselves in a floor or table graph according to one attribute (e.g., size, color, shape, or quantity).

Use Algebraic Representations

3. Use play, physical materials, or drawings to model a simple problem (e.g., there are six cookies to be shared by three children. How many cookies can each child receive?).

Focal Points: Identifying shapes and describing spatial relationships; identifying measurable attributes and comparing objects using one or more attributes.

Lesson Summary: Use comparison and classification to talk about concepts of same and different.

Beginning the Lesson: The teacher reads the book *Caps for Sale* and then holds a discussion of the book. She draws the children's attention to the felt board, where there are some different colored caps. The teacher says, "Look! I have some caps here and they are different! Can you tell me how they are different?"

Procedures: Using a felt board or other demonstration medium, the teacher presents the children with four red caps, three blue caps, and two red caps with blue polka dots; she then says, "Can someone tell me how many caps there are all together?" After the counting, the teacher says, "I need to sort these hats by their color. Can you help me?" She then creates two circles out of yarn on a board or table and asks the children to sort the hats. Using questioning techniques, she directs the students to think about the hats that have more than one color and what should be done with them. The yarn circles can be moved to overlap. The teacher can ask guiding questions such as, "Where do these two colored hats go?" and "Are these hats red or blue?" Children may decide that a third circle is needed. The teacher could ask, "Could we overlap the circles? Would that solve our problem?" Early in the year, children may not think this is a good solution and choose the three-circle solution, rather than the overlapping circles. However, with experience and time they will develop the understanding that sometimes items can be part of two groups at once.

The students will be engaged in critical thinking. While this activity contains some counting, it does not directly focus on the development of numbers. Instead, it encourages children to classify objects by their characteristics. Children use their critical thinking abilities to put the caps into relationships of "same" and "different." This task is fairly easy when sorting the red caps and the blue caps, but becomes more challenging when a hat is both red and blue.

Extension: The teacher can introduce hula-hoops to the class and ask the children to sort objects into the hula-hoops based on the objects' attributes. The teacher could demonstrate by using the color of children's shirts and asking children wearing blue shirts to stand in one circle and those wearing white shirts to stand in the other. A child wearing both colors can prompt a discussion of what he should do. One solution might be to stand with one foot in each circle!

Adaptations: Children with developmental delays can be included in this activity. They can be asked to focus more on the difference between red and blue rather than on the "both" category. Children with physical disabilities will need to have the materials adapted to their understanding. Using real colored caps may be an option for children that have difficulty with the felt board. Different textures of felt caps can be used to help the child with poor vision or blindness distinguish between red, blue, and both.

The book used for this activity is available in other languages. If teachers have trouble finding it in a needed language, however, another book can be substituted.

ASSESSING MATHEMATICS IN K–1

Kindergarten is generally the first experience most children have with public school. Even if the child attends private school, state requirements and standards must still be met beginning in this grade. In these first two years (K–1), the process of assessment on a large scale begins. It begins on that very first day in kindergarten with the initial assessment or screening.

This assessment sets a baseline for the child and helps the teacher determine what skills that the child already has. Its purpose is to allow the development of an individualized curriculum; it is a formative assessment that helps teachers and administrators develop goals and curricula that meet the needs of children. Schools should be "ready" for children, rather than children being "ready for school."

Unfortunately, the reality is often different, as shown in this excerpt from the March 5, 2007, *Columbus Dispatch* (Figure 7.9). High-stakes testing is not confined to the upper grades, but begins as early as kindergarten and preschool. The article goes on to report a disturbing trend, in which parents are pressured to hold their children back from starting kindergarten for a year, to ensure that the children are ready for that initial assessment. A test that was meant to be formative in nature is turning into a summative assessment of a child's previous experiences at home or in preschool. It demonstrates the academic pressure that is being "pushed down" into kindergarten.

However, if we are to use a constructivist method of teaching mathematics in K–1, then we need to have a constructivist way of assessing children's accomplishments. Fortunately, we have already discussed many of these methods in previous chapters—Anecdotal and Running Records, Checklists, and Portfolios. In K–1, there is room for more formal summative assessments such as fluency testing; however, we should remember that these are only a few of the tools in our assessment toolbox, and that there are many other ways to assess a child's mathematical accomplishments.

In K–1, children participate in problem-solving activities during math time and large group discussions concerning mathematics. During these times, a teacher can collect assessment data of each child's thought process. In a constructivist classroom children may work on a math problem individually or in small groups for a period of time.

As they are working individually, the teacher can circulate among them discussing the problem and helping them come up with methods of solving it. She can carry a check sheet or note cards to record observations or ideas about individual students.

Reaching the reduced goals set by each state's standards is an important part of teaching mathematics (see Figure 7.10). Observational check sheets help ensure that the teacher is documenting a child's progress toward these goals. Items on a check sheet should be open-ended, allowing for children to meet the requirements in many different ways. Teachers can also add individual goals for each child or add specific goals from standards documents.

Check sheets, however, should never be used as the sole form of assessment and should always be supported with information gathered through other methods, such as observation or portfolios.

Can your preschooler write his name? Read words from her favorite book? Count to 10?

If not, your 5-year-old isn't ready for modern-day kindergarten.

By law, the only requirement to start kindergarten is turning 5.

But with the advent of high-stakes testing and the growing popularity of preschool, kindergarten now has other prerequisites, some educators say.

Some parents have been surprised when kindergarten teachers suggest that their children aren't ready because they haven't started reading or don't sit and listen. And some child-care centers say more kids are returning to preschool after the first few weeks of kindergarten.

"The academic push is being shoved down," said Dianna Lancaster, director of A Place to Grow preschool in Dublin. "What they were learning in first grade, now they're learning in kindergarten."

Figure 7.9 *Columbus Dispatch* article.

First year of school demands more skills. *Monday, March 05, 2007.* Simone Sebastian. *Source: THE COLUMBUS DISPATCH*

Kindergarten: Math
Student Name: _____

CALIFORNIA CONTENT–STANDARD CHECKLIST
Student Number: _____

General Standard	Sub-Standard	Standard Notation	Standard Description	Planned (X)	Date Mastered
NUMBER SENSE (NS)	1.0 Relationships between numbers and quantities	KNS.1.1	Compare two or more sets of objects (up to 10 objects in each group) and identify which set is equal to, more than, or less than the other		
		KNS.1.2	Count, recognize, represent, name, and order a number of objects (up to 30)		
		KNS.1.3	Know that larger numbers describe sets with more objects in them than the smaller numbers have		
	2.0 Simple addition and subtraction	KNS.2.1	Use concrete objects to determine the answers to addition and subtraction problems (for two numbers that are each less than 10)		
	3.0 Estimation	KNS.3.1	Recognize when an estimate is reasonable when computing and solving problems with numbers in the ones and tens places)		
ALGEBRA AND FUNCTIONS (AF)	1.0 Sort and classify objects	K.AF.1.1	Identify, sort, and classify object by attribute and identify objects that do not belong to a particular group (e.g., all these balls are green, those are red)		
MEASUREMENT AND GEOMETRY (MG)	1.0. Concept of time and units to measure it, objects have properties (e.g., length, weight, etc.)	K.MG.1.1	Compare the length, weight, and capacity of objects by making direct comparisons with reference objects (e.g., note which object is shorter, longer, lighter, holds more)		
		K.MG.1.2	Demonstrate an understanding of time (e.g., morning, evening, today, yesterday, tomorrow, week, year) and tools that measure time (e.g., clock, calendar)		
		K.MG.1.3	Name the days of the week		
		K.MG.1.4	Identify the time (to the nearest hour) of everyday events (e.g., lunch time is 12 o'clock; bedtime is 8 o'clock at night)		

			Identify and describe common geometric objects (e.g., circle, triangle, square, rectangle, cube, sphere, cone)			
	2.0 Identify common objects in their environment and describe their geometric features	K.MG.2.1	Identify and describe common geometric objects (e.g., circle, triangle, square, rectangle, cube, sphere, cone)			
		K.MG.2.2	Compare familiar plane and solid objects by common attributes (e.g., position, shape, size, roundness number of corners)			
STATISTICS, DATA ANALYSIS, AND PROBABILITY (SDP)	1.0 Collect information about objects and events in their environment	K.SDP.1.1	Pose information questions; collect data; and record the results using objects, pictures, and picture graphs			
		K.SDP.1.2	Identify, describe, and extend simple patterns (such as circles or triangles) by referring to their shapes, sizes, or colors			
MATHEMATICAL REASONING (MR)	1.0 Make decisions about how to set up a problem	K.MR.1.1	Determine the approach, materials, and strategies to be used			
		K.MR.1.2	Use tools and strategies, such as manipulatives or sketches, to model problems			
	2.0. Solve problems in reasonable ways and justify their reasoning	K.MR.2.1	Explain the reasoning used with concrete objects and/or pictorial representations			
		K.MR.2.1	Make precise calculations and check the validity of the results in the context of the problem			

Figure 7.10 Sample kindergarten math checksheet from California.

Source: Reprinted, by permission, from *California Mathematics Content Standards*, California Department of Education, CDE Press, 1430 N Street, Suite 3207, Sacramento, CA 95814.

285

For example, a first-grade classroom is working on the following problem:

A snack pack has six crackers in each package. If Terrell has five packages, how many crackers does he have?

As the teacher circulates, she notices that three of the children, Santos, Jason, and Amber, all came up with the same answer (30 crackers). Using a check sheet assessment, she could say that these children all achieved a correct solution and they would all receive an "objective met" or a "check" on the check sheet. However, this does not mean that they are all on the same mathematical level. If we use an observational approach and a constructivist philosophy, we can learn more about "how" these children solved the problem.

Santos drew a large number of tally marks on a piece of paper. He then circled six at a time until he had made five circles. He counted all the tally marks he circled and ignored the others. Jason drew five squares and put six tally marks in each. He then went back and counted the tally marks to get 30. Amber wrote the number "6" five times on a piece of paper. Then she added $6 + 6$ twice to get 12 and another 12. She then added $12 + 12$ to get 24 and added the final 6 $(24 + 6)$ to get 30.

The teacher made a note of these different methods of solving the problem and included it in the child's weekly observations. Later, she collected their paperwork to document their process. The teacher saw three children who were on different levels of mathematical understanding, as evidenced by the difference in sophistication of their methods. Now that she knows how each of these children is thinking about mathematics, she can individualize mathematical experiences for each child.

Formal assessments are also part of the school year, especially as children move to first grade. These tests usually assess levels of mastery of mathematical content. For example, a child takes a math test on addition of numbers up to five. If he gets all the problems correct, he has mastered that objective. If not, he needs to work more on it.

Oftentimes these assessments take the form of timed tests. Students are given a specified amount of time to complete a number of problems dealing with addition to five, for example (i.e., $5 + 0 = 5, 5 + 1 = 6, 5 + 2 = 7$, etc.). Once they have mastered the 5s in the time allotted, they can move on to the 6s. This method creates a lot of stress and anxiety in the child.

A way of alleviating possible anxieties about summative evaluations and taking standardized tests is to prepare the children for the process. If they know what to expect, the process will not frighten them. Including them in the testing process will make the tests less stressful and more integrated.

A timed test where the timer counts up instead of down can make the activity much less stressful. Children can focus on improving their own times rather than on meeting an arbitrarily set time limit. Also, children do not consequently "fail" a test if they run out of time. They tend to have more success as they work to set a "personal best" while working on fluency.

Let the children be part of the decision-making process concerning when the test should be given and what they should be tested on. They will then show excitement about the test rather than dread, viewing it as a way to demonstrate their knowledge, rather than a "chance to fail."

SUMMARY

Children in K–1 are in a transitional time. Cognitively, they are still not at their concrete operational stage, but are developing some logical thinking abilities such as conservation. They still rely on perception when challenged, but can use numbers to structure the world.

Children's brains have developed to the point that they can employ selective attention strategies. They are able to work on a task while ignoring other things going on around them. Their attention is developmental, so teachers must ensure that they are not labeling children with "attention problems" in these early grades. Different children may be at different levels of development and it is difficult to diagnose attention problems or other learning disabilities this early in schooling.

Children's motor skills are developed to the point that they are able to write numbers. Children in K–1 begin to prefer writing with a pencil rather than a crayon because it is more precise. They can use writing to express mathematical ideas, to model mathematical problems, and to write number sentences.

K–1 children's memories allow for some degree of memorization and automation, which leads to fluency in mathematics. The best strategy is to allow memorization and fluency to develop from and be based on conceptual understanding. Teaching children to memorize math "facts" in isolation or without conceptual understanding leads to mathematics without thinking; this is not the goal of fluency and automaticity.

Social-emotionally, children are learning to control their emotions in order to reach social goals. Those who have trouble with emotional regulation or are overly aggressive may become neglected or rejected by their peers. This can lead to negative outcomes both socially and academically. Teachers do not identify 80% of neglected and rejected children. When teaching mathematics using social interaction, it is important that teachers keep a gauge on the social welfare of all the children in the class.

In learning mathematics, autonomy should be the main goal of instruction. Teachers should make sure that children are not just parroting answers, but are active thinkers and are self-confidently thinking about mathematics using their own natural abilities. The main goals for kindergarten and first grade are to support numerical regrouping, addition, and subtraction as well as geometric and measurement understandings.

To teach these goals, teachers should employ word problems. These word problems should be more complex than simple number sentences that allow the child to proceed directly to an answer. Word problems should promote the child to think and expand his problem-solving ability. Whole-class instruction using problems and social interaction also help to achieve this goal.

As in preschool, math games and projects are a valuable tool for teachers to employ. In K–1, the goals of math games should be fluency and automaticity of addition, especially combinations of numbers that add up to 10. Projects can be more in depth and involve reading and writing as the children's abilities expand in these areas.

WEB SITES

PBS Parents—Math for Grades 1 and 2
http://www.pbs.org/parents/earlymath/grades_flash.html

Contains developmental information about first- and second-grade mathematics, mathematical development, and suggestions for teachers and parents.

Exploratorium
http://www.exploratorium.edu/

An online science museum that incorporates mathematics into learning about the child's world.

BBC Math Games
http://www.bbc.co.uk/schools/games/

A BBC site of math games for various ages. Games are categorized by age and subject.

Math Games and Activities for Kids
http://www.mathplayground.com/

Math Playground is an action-packed educational site for elementary and middle-school students. Children can practice their math skills, play a logic game, and have some fun!

Math in Daily Life
http://www.learner.org/exhibits/dailymath/

An Annenberg Media web site with lesson plans for integrating mathematics with daily life activities.

Figure This!
http://www.figurethis.org/

Games and resources for supporting family mathematical learning from NCTM.

Math Is Fun
http://www.mathisfun.com/

The main content of the site is aimed at basic math skills. However, you will find some problems that are more complex and some that are easier. Hopefully, there is something for everybody.

DISCUSS AND APPLY WHAT YOU HAVE LEARNED

Reflect

1. What makes the K–1 ages transitional? Discuss development in the physical, cognitive, and social-emotional domains, as well as educational changes.

2. How does your educational experience in kindergarten and first grade differ from today's kindergarten and first grade?

3. Why is social interaction a good way to teach mathematics? How does it compare with how you learned math in K–1?

Discuss

1. What do you think of having children discuss their answers openly and frankly with each other? Do you think it is stressful and damaging to their self-esteem? What could you do to make sure it is not an uncomfortable experience for them?

2. As a group, develop a math problem using the criteria listed in this chapter. Share it with the class. What makes your math word problem a good one?

3. Discuss how using math games to promote fluency and automaticity can be better than using worksheets.

Apply

1. Develop a math lesson and present it to your class. Try to use questioning techniques instead of affirming right answers. Was it difficult not to tell someone they were right or wrong?

2. Teach a math lesson to a group of children. Keep the lesson open-ended and conceptually based. What were the children's responses?

Observe

1. Observe a kindergarten and first-grade classroom. What are the teachers doing to support mathematics? How are the classrooms similar? How are they different?

2. Observe a kindergarten and a first-grade classroom. How is mathematics introduced to children in each grade? Compare the two classrooms. How do the children respond to mathematics?

REFERENCES

Burns, M. (1992). *About teaching mathematics: A K–8 resource*. Sausalito, CA: Marilyn Burns Education Associates.

Burns, M. (2000). *About teaching mathematics: A K-8 resource* (2nd ed.). Sausalito, CA.: Math Solutions Publications.

Burns, M., & Silbey, R. (2000). *So you have to teach math: Sound advice for K–6 teachers*. Sausalito, CA: Math Solutions Publications.

Clements, D. (2004). Geometric and spatial thinking in early childhood education. In D. Clements & J. Sarama (Eds.), *Engaging young children in mathematics*. Mahwah, NJ: Lawrence Erlbaum Associates.

Clements, D., & Sarama, J. (Eds.). (2004). *Engaging young children in mathematics: Standards for early childhood mathematics education*. Mahwah, NJ: Lawrence Erlbaum Associates.

Clements, D., & Stephan, M. (2004). Measurement in pre–k to grade 2 mathematics. In D. Clements & J. Sarama (Eds.), *Engaging young children in mathematics*. Mahwah, NJ: Lawrence Erlbaum Associates.

Fosnot, C. T. (1989). *Enquiring teachers, enquiring learners: A constructivist approach for teaching* New York: Teachers College Press.

Fosnot, C. T., & Dolk, M. (2001). *Young mathematicians at work: Constructing multiplication and division*. Portsmouth, NH: Heinemann.

Geist, E. (2001). Articles: Making math natural and fun; Children are born mathematicians: Promoting the construction of early mathematical concepts in children under five. *Young Children, 56*(4), 8.

Helm, J. H., Katz, L., & Scranton, P. (2000). *A children's journey: Investigating the fire truck* [videorecording]. New York: Teachers College Press.

Inhelder, B., & Piaget, J. (1964). *The early growth of logic in the child classification and seriation.* London: Routledge and Kegan Paul.

Jeynes, W. (2006). Standardized tests and Froebel's original kindergarten model. *Teachers College Record, 108*(10), 1937–1959.

Kamii, C. (1984). Autonomy as the aim of childhood: Education a Piagetian approach. Galesburg, IL: Knox AV.

Kamii, C. (1990). *Achievement testing in the early grades: The games grown-ups play.* Washington, DC: National Association for the Education of Young Children.

Kamii, C., Clark, F. B., & Housman, L. B. (Directors). (2000). *First graders dividing 62 by 5 a teacher uses Piaget's theory.* [Video/DVD] New York: Distributed by Teachers College Press.

Kamii, C., & DeClark, G. (1985). *Young children reinvent arithmetic implications of Piaget's theory.* New York: Teachers College Press.

Kamii, C., Joseph, L. L., & Livingston, S. J. (2003). *Young children continue to reinvent arithmetic: 2nd grade implications of Piaget's theory.* New York: Teachers College Press.

Kamii, C., & National Association for the Education of Young Children. (1982). *Number in preschool and kindergarten: Educational implications of Piaget's theory.* Washington, DC: National Association for the Education of Young Children.

Kamii, C., Piaget, J., & Federation of North Texas Area Universities (Directors). (1984). *First graders invent arithmetic: Implications of Piaget's theory.* [Video/DVD]

Klein, A., Starkey, P., & Wakeley, A. (1998). Supporting pre-kindergarten children's readiness for school mathematics [Electronic Version]. ERIC Document – ED429691, 16.

National Association for the Education of Young Children, & South Carolina Educational Television Network. (1987). *A classroom with blocks* [videorecording]. South Carolina Educational Television Network.

National Council of Teachers of Mathematics. (2000). *Principles and standards for school mathematics.* E–Standards ver. 1.0.

Phelps, P., & Hanline, M. F. (1999). Let's play blocks! Creating effective learning experiences for young children. *Teaching Exceptional Children, 32*(2), 62–67.

Rathbone, C. (1993). *Multiage portraits: Teaching and learning in mixed-age classrooms.* Peterborough, NH: Crystal Springs Books.

Riley, R. (2000). America's kindergarteners. *Teaching Pre K–8, 30*(8), 12.

Santrock, J. W. (2005). *Children* (8th ed.). Boston: McGraw-Hill.

Schoenfeld, A. H. (2002). Making mathematics work for all children: Issues of standards, testing, and equity. *Educational Researcher, 31*(1), 13.

Smith, S. (1997). *Early childhood mathematics.* Needham Heights, MA: Allyn & Bacon.

Thelen, E., & Smith, L. B. (1994). *A dynamic systems approach to the development of cognition and action.* Cambridge, MA: MIT Press.

Thelen, E., & Smith, L. B. (1996). *A dynamic systems approach to the development of cognition and action.* Cambridge, MA: MIT Press.

Tyre, P., Phillips, M., Scelfo, J., Skipp, C., Joseph, N., & Tolme, P. (2006). The new first grade: Too much too soon? (Cover Story). *Newsweek, 148*, 34–44.

CHAPTER 8

Second and Third Grade

CHAPTER OBJECTIVES

After you have read this chapter, you should be able to:

- Describe what eight-, nine-, and ten-year-olds are like physically, cognitively, emotionally, and socially
- Identify what mathematical concepts second and third graders are learning
- Explain how the third "E" (Education) is best implemented in this age group and the importance of a carefully designed mathematics program
- Demonstrate optimal ways of arranging environments to effectively support interactive educational experiences that are both teacher-directed and child-centered
- Discuss how to foster a constructivist educational experience in a second- and third-grade classroom that includes opportunities for problem solving, fluency, and conceptual understanding
- Develop developmentally appropriate mathematics activities for second- and third-grade that includes emphasis on the NCTM focal points for second and third grade (including addition and subtraction with regrouping, multiplication, division, and fractions)
- Explain the uses and misuses of proficiency testing and other assessment strategies

Children in second and third grade are, according to Piaget, able to think logically (Piaget, 1953). Their physical, cognitive, and social-emotional development has reached a level that allows teachers more options in presenting mathematical material. Teacher-led lessons and a focus on directly presenting concepts become more effective methods because of these developments (Eckert, Dunn, Codding, Begeny, & Kleinmann, 2006; Fischbein, Deri, Nello, & Marino, 1985; Fuchs, Fuchs, Finelli et al., 2006). We have reached the third "E" in our age-based mathematics educational model of Environment, Experience, and Education.

Focusing on more formal educational practices does not mean that the basic premise of teaching mathematics has changed. Teachers should still foster the child's own thinking abilities, intellectual autonomy, and conceptual understanding (Borko & Davinroy, 2000; Forman & Ansell, 2001). The teacher remains a facilitator of mathematics construction and will still incorporate environmental and experiential learning into the mathematics program. However, the primary way in which mathematics will be introduced to second and third graders is through the third "E" of Education. She can present more concepts directly to the children but it does not mean a reliance solely on repetitive worksheets, skill and drill, and silent seatwork (Kamii et al., 2003; Kamii, Knight, & Teachers College Press, 1990; Kamii & Livingston, 1994).

Teacher-led mathematics instruction can include opportunities for children to discuss and interact, construct new mathematical knowledge, and develop computational fluency without having to rely on methods that may be uninteresting or even unnecessarily stressful (Drier, 2000). Some traditional high-stress practices can lead to math anxiety. Math anxiety and disparities between boys and girls and minority groups begin to become evident in second and third grade (Gibson, 2004; Gould, 2003; Helwig, Anderson, & Tindal, 2001). As we consider the best way to teach mathematics to second and third graders, we should keep this in mind.

WHAT ARE SECOND AND THIRD GRADERS LIKE?

Physical Development

The child's ability to attend continues to develop in second and third grade. They can sit and attend longer than in first grade. The children's attention levels make it possible to use direct instruction as a central educational strategy. Second and third graders can sit and listen to a lesson and then attend to their individual or group work (Fuchs, Fuchs, Compton et al., 2006; May, 1997).

Their fine motor coordination also produces smaller and more precise writing. By the end of the third grade, many children can begin to use cursive writing. Their improved eye-hand coordination and development of strength in the arms, legs, and trunk, make involvement in sports a popular pasttime for many children (Santrock, 2005). Even though they can sit and attend for longer periods, they still need physical activity and exercise. For children of this age, sitting can cause more fatigue than physical activity. Keeping a child in the classroom during recess for not completing a math assignment could do more harm than good.

Sports and other physical activities can provide for some rich mathematical experiences, which we will discuss later. Whether it is physical playground activity, sports, or classroom mathematics, children should be encouraged to be mentally and physically active rather than passive. A child that is encouraged to participate and actively engage in his physical environment can relate that experience to actively engaging in the mathematical environment (Smith, Thelen, & NetLibrary Inc., 1993). Just as we do not like to see a child sitting on the sideline during play situations, we do not want to promote the situation where he expects to be told every answer or procedure in the mathematics classroom. Active physical engagement and active learning are both important to mathematical development.

Cognitive Development

Concrete Operations. As children progress into second and third grade, they enter the next stage in Piaget's cognitive development. This stage is called concrete operational thought. As mentioned before, this is the beginning of what Piaget considered logical thought. During this stage, thought becomes reversible. Reversible thought, however, does not just mean that children can add three to three to get six and subtract three from six to get three. Reversibility is not just being able to think in two directions, but to be able to think in two directions at the same time.

> . . . An operation is an action which is reversible; that is, it can take place in either direction. It is characteristic for an operation to be part of the total structure. We cannot conceive of a single operation in isolation; rather each operation is an integral part of the whole which in turn consists of many operations. For example, the structure of classification consists of many operations of logical classes (grouping of items with common characteristics) or the structure of seriation consists of the operation of putting things into ascending or descending order. (Piaget, 1952, pp.15–16)

For example, let's revisit our discussion of subtraction in Chapter 8. Many assume that subtraction is just the opposite function to addition and that, if the child can add single-digit numbers, it should be easy for him to reverse that process. However, subtraction requires the child to think in two directions at the same time. He must have reversibility of thought. As children enter the concrete operational stage, their thought becomes reversible and subtraction becomes easier for them to comprehend. They can comprehend the part and the whole at the same time. For example, if the problem is $6 - 3 =$ __ the six is the "whole" and the three is the "part" of that whole. The other part of the "whole" goes on the other side of the "=." The ability to think of both the six and the three is an example of reversible thought.

This new ability allows the child to classify objects in a more complex way. For example, a second- or third-grade child may say that a fly is like a bird because it has wings and is also like a bug because it has six legs. This ability to fit one object into two classes is a characteristic of concrete operational thought. Another more advanced classification scheme is called **hierarchical classification**. Using hierarchical classification, the child understands that while all salmon are fish, not all fish are salmon, and that since all salmon are fish and all fish are animals, all salmon are animals (Piaget, Garcia, Banks, Davidson, & Easley, 1991; Sarama & Clements, 2005).

Another example of hierarchical classification is the construction of a family tree. A preoperational child at a family reunion may have trouble understanding complex family relationships such as uncle, cousin, niece, and so on. It is hard for him to understand that a person can be an uncle, a son, and a brother at the same time. The concrete operational child can navigate this complex series of relationships with little effort.

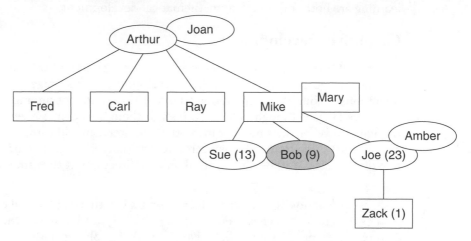

By the age of eight or nine, Bob can understand that Mike is his dad, Joan and Arthur's son, Fred and Carl's brother, and Zack's grandfather. Bob also understands that he can be Mike's son, Zack's uncle, and Fred's nephew all at the same time.

Social-Emotional Development

Second- and third-grade children are in Erikson's *Industry vs. Inferiority* stage. The child's world begins to extend beyond the home environment and becomes more and more school based. Schooling becomes one of the major activities in his life. The emphasis is now on academic performance. Children actually want to work and succeed and, as they make the move from "play" to "work," we can recognize this transition in how they approach school and academics. They begin to focus on the quality of their work and not just enjoyment of the activity. They learn that teachers and parents give recognition for good work and begin to seek this out (Erikson, 1993).

If children are recognized, supported, and encouraged to persevere and finish their work, the result, according to Erikson, is industry. Teachers and parents should be supportive of the child's process even when he arrives at an incorrect solution. For example, a parent might say, "You worked very hard on that problem. Can you explain to me how you got 9 from 5 + 3?" Instead, of telling the child directly that he is wrong, the parent uses questioning techniques to help the child recognize the errors in his process (Erikson, 1963, 1977; Evans, 1967).

Self-esteem grows out of real achievement and perseverance, not from succeeding at easy tasks.

Kenneth P. Davis/PH College

Occasionally pointing out incorrect answers to a child will not lead to inferiority; however, if he is repeatedly told that his work is wrong or lacks worth, he will develop a feeling of inferiority and may be reluctant to attempt work. He may even develop a bad attitude toward mathematics and other school work. This conflict between *industry and inferiority* can have a large impact on second- and third-grade mathematics. Many of the negative feelings toward mathematics and disparities between boys, girls, and minority students begin to become evident in these grades (Beglau, 2005; Cahnmann & Remillard, 2002; Gould, 2003; Helwig et al., 2001).

Self-esteem reflects the child's own global assessment of his self-worth and does not always match reality (Santrock, 2005). Self-esteem can be broken down into domains of competence, called "self-concept." For example, a child may feel good about his ability in sports, but not about his mathematical ability; his athletic self-concept may be high while his self-concept in mathematics may be low. Self-esteem is not highly correlated with academic success. Just because a child has low self-esteem, does not mean he will be a failure in school. However, a poor self-concept in mathematics can lead to the self-fulfilling prophecy we discussed earlier.

If children begin to doubt their ability at mathematics, they will begin to believe they "can't do it." In the mathematical domain, low self-esteem can lead to reduced performance because of lowered expectations. We begin to recognize disparities in children's assessment of their own abilities in mathematics and increased disparities in math scores for minority groups during second and third grade.

Here are a few suggestions to promote good mathematical self-concept:

- *Avoid high-stress activities that involve social comparisons*. Since second- and third-grade children put a large emphasis on comparisons with their peers, teachers should avoid activities that are overly competitive. For example, timed tests put a lot of pressure on a child to perform quickly especially if his results are presented to the class. When I was a child, in my second-grade classroom there was a chart on the front chalkboard with stars showing each child's progress. This made it evident to the whole class who was ahead and who was behind. I do not think I am alone in having such an experience.

- *Avoid comparing children to one another*. Openly acknowledging children who do well on an activity may seem like a nice thing to do but teachers need to be aware how this may affect the rest of the class. It may create resentment rather than encouragement. For example, saying "Patel, Madeline, and Daniel worked very hard and got all the homework problems correct this week" is better than saying "Everyone should be more like Patel, Madeline, and Danny. They got all their answers correct this week." Teachers should find ways to give encouragement to all the children in the class, not just the ones that continually achieve.

- *Avoid empty praise*. Giving rewards or praise, when it is not earned or deserved, can have the opposite effect than the one intended. Children know their abilities and they are very good at comparing their abilities to others. Encourage true achievement in children instead of lowering the standards. This is the difference between praise and encouragement. For example, if Joshua is having trouble remembering his 3X tables and only manages to get halfway through instead of the teacher saying, "You did a great job!" she might say, "You are getting better. You should look them over tonight and you can do them again tomorrow."

- *Avoid criticizing failure*. Failures should be seen as progress toward a correct answer. Teachers should not dwell on failures but on the child's needs in order to succeed. Too often, the child and the teacher focus on the "grade" on a test or assessment and do not address the reasons *why* the child received the grade. An emphasis on mastery, rather on grades, leads to positive outcomes and a good attitude toward mathematics.

WHAT MATHEMATICAL CONCEPTS DO SECOND- AND THIRD-GRADE CHILDREN LEARN?

Second and third graders have reached a level of logical thinking, according to Piaget (1953). Their attention, fine motor, and memory abilities have reached a level where they understand more advanced mathematical concepts and compute more complex problems. However, the emphasis on children's conceptual understanding, problem solving, and critical thinking skills should still be the teacher's focus in these grades (Fuchs et al., 2004; Gibson, 2004; Hutchison, Ellsworth, & Yovich, 2000).

In many states, another controversial aspect of education appears in these grades— the proficiency test (Gould, 2003). Whatever your states call it, it is fundamentally an achievement test to ensure that all children are achieving at a minimum level of competence (Annual Yearly Progress) as required by the No Child Left Behind Act. This is less a test of the students and more a test of the teacher's ability and the individual school's efficacy.

Children in second and third grade are at an especially impressionable time in their educational careers. They are not just learning content knowledge; they are also learning *how* to learn, or the process of learning. If a child's second- and third-grade experience is filled with passive learning such as seat work, rote memorization, skills practice, and fact drills, he will learn that he is to sit and absorb material presented by a teacher or authority figure with little critical thinking or analysis. This can lead to adults who are afraid to voice opinions or synthesize new knowledge. They are unable to hold critical discussions or synthesize important information (Borko & Davinroy, 2000; Chung, 2004).

Taking a Constructivist Approach. Applying what we have learned about Piaget's theories we can now apply them to mathematics education for second and third grade. Elkind & Piaget (1979), Heuwinkel (1996), and Santrock (2006) suggest the following ways:

- Take a constructivist approach—Promote children to be active and seek answers for themselves rather than being passive vessels to be filled up with facts.
- Facilitate rather than direct learning—Promote the child to invent and discover, through interacting with others and "doing." Teachers should listen, watch, and question in order to recognize not only what the child knows, but how he thinks.
- Use ongoing assessment—Standardized tests are not good at assessing individual constructions. Teachers should use individual conferences and portfolios for the major assessment of mathematical progress.
- Promote the student's intellectual health—Children should not be pushed or pressured to move to a higher stage of development. Teachers should respect the child's developmental level and design curriculum to meet that level.
- Turn the classroom into a setting of exploration and discovery—Emphasize children's own discoveries and inventions. Rely less on imposed external structure and more on the requirements of the activity. Promote intrinsic rather than extrinsic (i.e., rewards) motivation.

If a child is exposed to an active learning process where thinking and problem solving are emphasized and the process of getting to an answer is valued as much as the answer itself, he will develop positive learning strategies for life. One of these strategies is critical thinking.

Critical thinking is an ability that most second and third graders are beginning to develop. It requires the student to examine new information in a critical way and not to accept it as fact until they are convinced. They are becoming concerned not just with *what* but also *how* and *why*. They begin to look for evidence to support "facts." This new ability enables children to create new knowledge.

A second-grade class is working on a number of double-column addition problems. The class is familiar with this type of problem and have done similar ones. The teacher presents them with the problem 23 + 16. They work quietly for a few minutes and then discuss the answers as a class. Almost all have the correct answer and, during the course of discussion, those who made errors quickly realize their mistakes. Next, the teacher presents them with another problem.

Teacher: "Here is a problem we have not done before. Are you ready?"

Class: "Yes!"

Teacher: "This is the new problem; 27 plus 14. I want you to think about this problem and work on it alone for 5 minutes. When you think you have an answer, raise your hand and I will come over and take a look."

(After 5 minutes, all the children have their hands up and the teacher circulates around the room discussing their answers.)

Teacher: "OK, who wants to share the way they arrived at their answer. Tony?"

Tony: "Well, I know that 20 plus 10 is 30 and 7 plus 4 is 12. So, I just added 30 to 12 and got 42."

Teacher: "OK, does anyone have a different answer? Kendra?"

Kendra: "I disagree with Tony. I did it the same way but I figured out that 7 plus 4 is 11, so I got 41."

Patrick: "Yes! That is what I got, but I took 3 from 14 and made it 11 and added the 3 to the 27 to make it 30. Then I added 30 and 11 to get 41!"

Teacher: "Tony, would you like to defend your answer?"

Tony: "No, I made a mistake when I added 7 and 4. I agree that 41 is the answer."

Teacher: "Are you sure?"

Tony: "Yes. It's 41."

Here, we see children using critical thinking to address a problem they had not done before and analyzing the answers and methods used to achieve the final solutions. Many children in classrooms where mathematics is taught as a group of rules to be followed and facts to be memorized would say, "We have not yet learned how to do that type of problem." This can be a problem on standardized proficiency tests. Children who cannot remember or do not know the method of solving a problem will not attempt to do it. A child who has been taught to value critical thinking in mathematics will try to find a solution. It may not be the correct one, but it will show a critical thinking process. Unfortunately, one of the disadvantages of standardized tests is that they do not distinguish between a wrong answer due to not trying and a wrong answer that shows critical thinking.

The critical thinking process creates a deep understanding of these concepts and allows children to apply their prior knowledge to new mathematical problems and situations. Five steps to promoting critical thinking can be found in Figure 8.1.

Critical thinking occurs in five basic steps that can be supported in the mathematics classroom:

1. Itemize opinion(s) from all relevant sides of an issue and collect logical argument(s) supporting each.
2. Break the arguments into their constituent statements and draw out various additional implication(s) from these statements.
3. Examine these statements and implications for internal contradictions.
4. Locate opposing claims between the various arguments and assign relative weightings to opposing claims:
   a. Increase the weighting when the claims have strong support, especially distinct chains of reasoning, or different news sources; decrease the weighting when the claims have contradictions.
   b. Adjust weighting depending on relevance of information to central issue.
   c. Require sufficient support to justify any incredible claims; otherwise, ignore these claims when forming a judgment.
5. Assess the weights of the various claims.

Critical thinking is a good basis for teaching other math concepts to second and third graders.

Figure 8.1   Five Steps to Critical Thinking.

Fluency and Recall of Addition and Subtraction. The NCTM focal points cite this as an important mathematical process for this age group. Second and third graders' memories are developed enough to handle remembering the basic mathematical computations that are used for more advanced mathematical concepts. These are traditionally called "math facts" and fluency is usually thought to be through memorization. Research on how the mind processes mathematics demonstrates that each of these "facts" is really a series of interrelated relationships in the child's mind. Ed Labinowicz (1985) depicted it as seen in Figure 8.2.

Addition. Kamii & Anderson, (2003); Kamii & Livingston, (1994) describes this interrelationship as a network of numerical relationships. She states that the goal is not merely getting children to know and recall independent "addition facts" but to construct this network of relationships. "A network of numerical relationships will serve the child throughout life in all other mathematical operations as well" (Kamii & Anderson, 2003; Kamii & Livingston, 1994).

First-grade children may be fluent with addition of doubles such as 4 + 4 and some of the smaller number combinations. However, beginning in second grade, children begin to establish fluency in doubles greater than 6 + 6 and in the harder combinations that make 10 such as 6 + 4 and 7 + 3 (Kamii & Anderson, 2003; Kamii & Livingston, 1994).

Fluency in addition is accomplished not just through memorization of "facts," but by the continued use of the child's network of numerical understanding. Repetition does not mean repeated practice on worksheets, but implementing math games that focus on these numerical relationships (Gibson, 2004). Children develop fluency by using mathematics everyday in many different situations (Fuchs, Fuchs, Finelli et al., 2006). Teachers and parents can look for opportunities to ask children "how many?" For example, if a child says "I see three cows!" a parent might say, "Hey! I see four more! How many cows are there all together?"

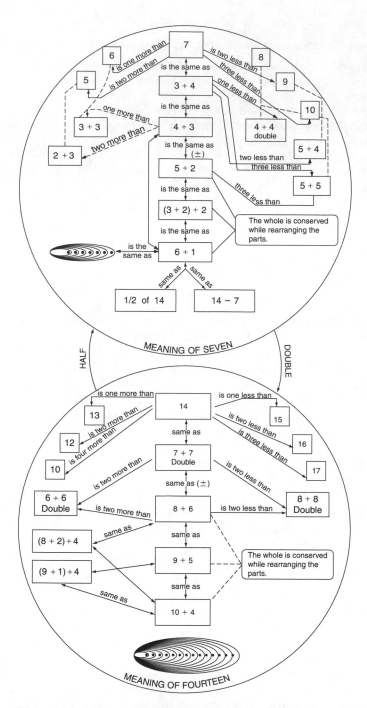

Figure 8.2 Network of Mathematical Understandings.

Source: From *Learning From Children,* by E. Labinowicz, © used by permission of Pearson Education, Inc. All Rights Reserved 1985, p. 99.

Subtraction. As was mentioned in the last chapter, subtraction is a bit more difficult for children to grasp; therefore, fluency in subtraction will likely lag behind fluency in addition. Fluency with differences appear after fluency with sum because children deduce differences from their knowledge of sums (Kamii & Anderson, 2003; Kamii & Lewis, 2003; Kamii & Livingston, 1994). For example, children were asked to solve related addition and subtraction problems such as 4 + 5 and 8 − 4. Through their research they were able to "... conclude that children *deduce* differences from their knowledge of sums. This theory is different from the one that states that children store and retrieve 'subtraction facts' like computers" (Kamii & Anderson, 2003; Kamii & Livingston, 1994).

The best way to strengthen a child's ability in subtraction fluency is to emphasize in addition and understand that fluency in subtraction grows out of fluency in addition.

Base 10 and Place Value

Addition problems that have sums 10 and over include base-10 and place-value concepts. If children construct numerical networks, an understanding of these concepts is integrated into their learning of addition. Kamii (2003) suggests that teachers not conceptualize place value as a separate goal with separate activities, lessons, or units (Kamii & Lewis, 1993b). Instead, she suggests a lesson such as this:

> *Teacher:* (Writes the problem 9 + 6 on the board. "Who can tell me how to solve this problem?"
>
> *Kenesha:* "I know that 9 plus 1 is 10."
>
> *Teacher:* (The teacher erases the 9 and writes 10, then −1 = 5 after the 6.)
>
> *Kenesha:* "10 plus 5 is 15."
>
> *Teacher:* (Erases the 0 of the 10 and replaces it with the 5, then erases everything else except for the answer 15.)

Children construct place value when they see it is useful to them. They will construct the system of tens out of a system of ones, which is the hardest part of double-column addition for second graders (Kamii & Anderson, 2003; Kamii & Livingston, 1994). Instead of separate lessons on place value, addition activities that allow children to use their understanding of addition and numbers to solve problems help this concept develop.

Teaching double-column addition and subtraction with regrouping as a series of rules to be followed, such as carrying and borrowing, teaches children to ignore place value in their computations. This means that they do not construct this concept along with their understanding of addition. Therefore, many textbooks create separate activities for place value because children have "unlearned" (Kamii et al., 2003; Kamii & Lewis, 1993a).

Children in first grade often have difficulty understanding the concept behind the base-10 systems. Through interaction with addition, a more complex understanding develops in second and third grade (Seo & Ginsburg, 2004). In the following example, a first grader and a third grader have both successfully completed the

Lunch time provides many opportunities to do math, like dividing pizza into equal parts (fractions).

Krista Grece/Merrill

addition problem 9 + 5 = 14. The teacher then asks each of them to explain the meaning of the numbers in 14.

> *Gabriel:* "9 plus 5 is 14."
>
> *Teacher:* "Why did you write it with a 1 and then a 4?"
>
> *Gabriel:* "Because that is how you write 14."
>
> *Teacher:* "What does the 1 stand for? How many is it?"
>
> *Gabriel:* "1."
>
> *Teacher:* (indicating the 4) "And this number?"
>
> *Gabriel:* "4."

Gabriel understands the rules of writing the numbers but not the concepts behind a base-10 system of place value (Ginsburg, 1981). An emphasis on just teaching rules will perpetuate this misunderstanding of place value, as Kamii & Anderson (2003); Kamii & Livingston (1994) indicated. However, if children are exposed to true mathematical thinking, they will construct the concept of place value in a more natural way, as demonstrated by this third grader:

> *Teacher:* "Why did you put the 1 before the 4?"
>
> *Dieter:* "Because if I put the 4 followed by the 1, it would be 41."
>
> *Teacher:* "What does the 1 stand for?"
>
> *Dieter:* "It stands for ten and the 4 stands for four. Ten and four is 14. The tens are always on the left side."

Base-10 place value, also known as **decimal system**, is a social convention that we use in mathematics to make understanding and computing with numbers easier. We probably use it because we have 10 fingers, but there are other base systems, such as binary, used by computers and containing only two numerals – 0 and 1. Counting in binary goes 0, 1, 10, 11, 100, 101, 110, 111, 1000. Any number can be used as a "base." Third graders may be able to experiment with other ways of counting, using different base systems such as binary.

Multiplication and Division

Multiplication is a key NCTM focal point for third grade, however, the construction of multiplicative thinking through repeated addition can be introduced as early as first grade. Most mathematics programs introduce multiplication in second grade and treat it merely as a faster way of doing repeated addition (Kamii & Anderson, 2003; Kamii et al., 1990; Lent, Wall, & Fosnot, 2006; Raymond, 1992). While first and second graders can compute multiplication problems and solve word problems that involve multiplication and division, they are usually using repeated addition and subtraction to reach the answer. True multiplication requires **multiplicative thinking** (Clark & Kamii, 1996). Multiplicative thinking is a more complex organization of the child's "system of ones."

As children develop this system, they apply hierarchical inclusion to their counting of objects so that two includes one and three includes two and one and so on (Figure 8.3). This, naturally, leads to addition because counting is adding one each

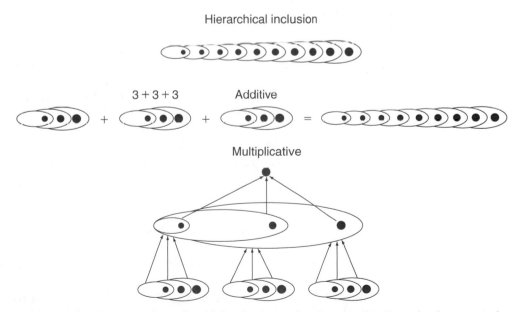

Figure 8.3   The mental act of multiplication is much more complex than simple repeated addition.

time you move up a number. Addition is inherent in the construction of numbers, but multiplication is a more complex operation that is constructed at a higher level of abstraction (Clark & Kamii, 1996).

Clark and Kamii (1996) explain additive thinking as involving only one level of abstraction. In other words, in the example of 3×3, each unit of three that the child adds is made of 3 ones. The groups of three are combined successively or linearly. The child can include one in two and two in three and so on all the way up to nine.

Figure 8.3 shows that in multiplicative thinking the child makes three kinds of relationships not required in addition:

1. The **many-to-one correspondence** between three units of one and one unit of three. One may have three pieces of candy in a bag. The three units of one are the pieces of candy and the one unit of three is the bag that holds the three pieces of candy.
2. The composition of inclusion relationships on more than one level. For example, in Figure 8.3, there are nine pieces of candy (level 1) divided into three bags of candy (level 2) and the third level includes all candy owned.
3. We can also apply hierarchical inclusion relationships to each of the higher levels. We can say that one bag is included in two and two bags are included in three. In other words, we can count the candies and the bags in the same way.

Children's development of multiplicative thinking is at a critical point in second and third grade. Clark and Kamii (1996) conducted an experiment to assess the development of multiplicative thinking in children in first through fifth grade.

The researchers presented each child with three "fish" made out of wooden tongue depressors and painted to look like fish with an eye, mouth, fins, and scales. Fish A was 5 cm, fish B was 10 cm, and Fish C was 15 cm. The three fish were placed in front of the child and the child was told:

> This fish (pointing to fish B) eats 2 times what this fish (pointing to fish A) eats, and this fish (pointing to fish C) eats 3 times what the little one (pointing to fish A) eats. This fish (B) eats 2 times what this fish (A) eats because it is 2 times as big as this one (A) (the interviewer demonstrates by showing that fish A can be placed 2 times on fish B). The big fish (C) eats 3 times what the little fish (A) eats because it (C) is 3 times as big as this one (A). (The interviewer again demonstrated by placing A on C three times.) (Clark & Kamii 1996, p. 45)

The researcher then asked the following questions:

a. If this fish (A) gets one piece of food, how many pieces of food do you feed the other two fish?
b. If this fish (B) gets four pieces of food, how many pieces of food do you feed the other two fish?
c. If this fish (C) gets nine pieces of food, how many pieces of food do you feed the other two fish?

Scott Cunningham/Merrill

An active classroom environment with vibrant exchange of mathematical ideas helps 2nd and 3rd graders develop deep understanding of multiplication and division.

    d. If this fish (A) gets four pieces of food, how many pieces of food do you feed the other two fish?

    e. If this fish (A) gets seven pieces of food, how many pieces of food do you feed the other two fish?

    If a child answered question c incorrectly, the interviewer offered this counter suggestion: "Another student told me that if this fish (C) gets nine pieces of food, the little fish (A) should get three because nine (indicating the nine chips given to the biggest fish) is three times what this is (indicating the three chips given to the small fish). This fish (B) should get six because six is two times what this is (indicating the three chips given to the small fish). What do you think of her idea?" After the child gave an opinion, the interviewer asked for an explanation, such as "Why do you think the other person's way is better?"

    The results indicate four levels of understanding multiplication. At the first level, which correlates with first grade, the children think in terms of more and less and accept any number as long as A < B < C. For example, a child gives one to A, two to B, and three to C, but then quickly changes C to six. When the researcher asks if it is "OK" to take one away from C, the child says, "Yes." When asked if two can be taken away, the child says, "No! That's too many!"

    At the second level, which tends to correlate with second grade, children have an additive sequence of +1 or +2. The child relates A to B and B to C and gives B one or two more than A and C one or two more than B. For example, a child might give three to A, four to B, and five to C.

    At the third level, which tends to correlate with early third grade, we still see some additive thinking involving +2 for B and +3 for C. In this level, the child takes into account the number of "times" indicated by the interviewer (two times for B and three times for C). However, the children add two and three rather than multiplying. For example, when four pieces of food are given to A, six (A+2) is given to B, and nine (A+3) is given to C.

The fourth level, which is multiplicative thinking, also begins to emerge in third grade, however, not always with immediate success. For example, when C was given nine, Abby gave six to B. When asked "why" she said ". . . because C eats three times, so I take away three, and four to A . . . because B eats two times, so I take away two [4, 6, 9]." However, after the counter suggestion she thinks that [3, 6, 9] is a better answer and explains her reasoning multiplicatively. In this early stage of level 4, children may have an understanding of multiplicative thinking, but still rely on additive methods until challenged (Clark & Kamii, 1996).

Doing multiplication is more than just changing the notation. Many mathematics programs assume that if children can do 3+3+3 they can do 3 × 3. Clark and Kamii (1996) found that this was not the case. Premature memorization of multiplication tables can lead to children foregoing the thinking process in lieu of memorization just to please the teacher. Clark and Kamii (1996) found that some children as high as fifth grade, while able to recite the multiplication tables, were, when challenged with the task, actually thinking additively.

The importance of supporting the construction of multiplicative thinking in second and third grade is emphasized by this study. While this thinking begins to develop as early as second grade, it progresses slowly. If children are pushed too quickly to memorize times tables in the name of fluency, they will not construct the concepts so important to understanding multiplication (Young-Loveridge, 2005).

The goals for multiplication in second grade should be modest. Second graders should be given problems that can be solved using repeated addition (Kamii & Anderson, 2003; Kamii & Livingston, 1994). They can also engage in skip counting, such as counting by 3s, 5s, or other numbers. For third graders, multiplication of three-digit numbers by one-digit numbers is the standard level, however, Kamii & Anderson (2003); Kamii & Livingston (1994) found that, using a constructivist approach, many children were capable of multiplying three-digit numbers by two-digit numbers. As mentioned above, memorization of multiplication tables at this early stage of multiplicative thinking can be detrimental to a child's mathematical development.

Using two-dimensional arrays (Figure 8.4) to help children visualize multiplication can be a helpful tool, as they show the two-dimensional multiplicative process and illustrate various number properties, such as associative ($3 \times 27 = 9 \times 9$) and distributive ($24 \times 6 = (20 \times 6) + (4 \times 6)$) by repositioning parts of the array (Young-Loveridge, 2005). The two-dimensional grid system is more advantageous than a number line system because, due to their linear nature, number lines reinforce additive thinking in solving multiplication.

Gradually, children learn that the number of units in a rectangular two-dimensional array can be calculated from the number of units in each row and column. They realize that, if there are eight in each row and three rows, the problem is 8×3. They can then solve the problem using repeated addition or multiplication depending on their level of understanding (Battista, Clements, Arnoff, Battista, & Van Auken Borrow, 1998).

Since children complete multiplication by repeated addition, you might expect to begin division by using repeated subtraction. However, this is not the case

X	0	1	2	3	4	5	6	7	8	9	10
0	0	0	0	0	0	0	0	0	0	0	0
1	0	1	2	3	4	5	6	7	8	9	10
2	0	2	4	6	8	10	12	14	16	18	20
3	0	3	6	9	12	15	18	21	24	27	30
4	0	4	8	12	16	20	24	28	32	36	40
5	0	5	10	15	20	25	30	35	40	45	50
6	0	6	12	18	24	30	36	42	48	54	60
7	0	7	14	21	28	35	42	49	56	63	70
8	0	8	16	24	32	40	48	56	64	72	80
9	0	9	18	27	26	45	54	63	72	81	90
10	0	10	20	30	40	50	60	70	80	90	100

Figure 8.4   Two-Dimensional Array for Multiplication.

(Kamii & Anderson, 2003; Kamii & Livingston, 1994). In these early grades, children avoid using subtraction whenever they can. They approach division problems as repeated addition, much as they do multiplication. However, division has an added aspect. Children must keep track of and count how many iterations of nine they use. For example, if a child is asked to solve the problem 56 divided by 7, he might write "7, 14, 21, 28, 35, 42, 49, 56," and then count the numbers to get an answer of "8."

The thought process for division is similar to that of multiplication and develops from this understanding. When allowed to solve division problems in a way that makes sense to them, children will use repeated addition problems, such as the one just presented, or they may use their understanding of multiplication to achieve the answer.

Traditionally, division has been presented in fourth grade as an algorithm and a set of procedures to be followed and mastered. As with addition algorithms and memorizing multiplication tables, this approach short-cuts the mathematical learning process. Teaching the algorithm should not take place until children understand the concepts behind division. Children often use "tricks" to simplify the problem. The numbers are broken down into smaller numbers and transformed to make the problem easier. This is advantageous for adults who need to compute problems quickly, but for children it is harmful (Kamii & Anderson, 2003; Kamii & Livingston, 1994). Since the numbers are broken down, the child never has to think about the numbers as a whole or the problem in its entirety.

Division in second and third grade should be presented as real-life problems that children can solve using their understanding of addition, multiplication, and even subtraction, rather than as a series of rules to be followed.

Fractions

As children develop reversible thought and the ability to think about "parts" and "wholes" simultaneously, their ability to understand fractions, both in concept and notation, becomes easier. First graders are able to solve problems that deal with situations such as dividing 10 cupcakes between 5 students, but it is not until second or third grade that they begin to understand the concept of having one fifth of the total number of cupcakes.

As with addition, subtraction, multiplication, and division, the understanding of fractions develops with the understanding of basic mathematical concepts and through the child's own natural thinking ability. Using a method like this with fractions leads to a deeper understanding of the concepts (Biddlecomb, 2002).

Martinez and Martinez (2007) give a good example of this. In their first scenario, a fourth-grade teacher is demonstrating the procedure for dividing fractions. She says, "Here's our problem. . . . We have one large pizza that has been cut into 10 pieces but there are 20 students in the class. How can we get enough pieces for all the students?" (Martinez & Martinez, 2007). So far, so good, from a constructivist approach. The teacher has presented the students with a challenging problem that they understand, but they cannot proceed directly toward an answer. Then, she says, "Here is what we do, we take the 10 pieces and we divide them in half." She puts up an overhead transparency that shows the following:

$$\tfrac{10}{1} \div \tfrac{1}{2} \qquad \tfrac{10}{1} \times \tfrac{2}{1} = 20$$

"See, when we divide by ½, we invert the fraction and multiply by 2 so that we get 20 pieces, enough for the whole class" (Martinez & Martinez, 2007, p. 84).

Their next scenario shows a teacher presenting a similar problem to a group of second graders. She begins with an overhead projection of a large pizza, then says,

Learning math is an interactive process with a great deal of talking; not a solitary one with lots of worksheets.

Silver Burdett Ginn

"Let's divide this pizza up so that all 16 of us can have a piece." Some children use construction paper, some use fraction circles, and some use paper and pencil. They are encouraged to solve the problem anyway they want. One student has trouble making 16 pieces out of one pizza and decides she needs 2 pizzas. Another child uses 16 square blocks to make her pizza and proudly announces, "I am making a square pizza!" (Martinez & Martinez, 2007). With square pizza, children can even use the multiplication arrays (Figure 8.4), in this case, to solve a fraction problem the child invented himself.

In second grade, fractions should be taught from real-life situations and hands-on explorations. Allowing children to represent quantities and parts of whole quantities using multiple representations including drawing, models, and words, helps them to construct an understanding of fractions.

Many students learn to dislike fractions because they learn representation and computation before they have a solid foundation in the concept of parts and wholes. In third grade, using fraction notation becomes another way to represent fractions. Children can also begin to think about fractions as ratios, such as 3 to 1.

Linear Measurement

With the advent of concrete operations, the ability to think logically, reverse operations, and relate the part to the whole, second and third graders can use measurement to achieve larger goals such as drawing scale plans and constructing maps and models. However, the sequence of developmental aspects of teaching measurement is under debate. Many researchers feel that children should learn nonstandard units before moving on to using rulers and standard units. Others feel that children may be incapable of using a ruler until they have constructed unit iteration and conservation of length. Clements & Sarama (2004), on the other hand, suggests that while children are constructing many of these ideas, they can successfully use rulers and standard units and suggests the following sequence that can be applied in second and third grade.

1. Children should be given the opportunity to compare sizes of objects in many different types of activities.
2. Children should engage in activities that allow them to connect length with number.
3. Children should have the opportunity to use conventional rulers (English and metric) and manipulative units such as inches and centimeters.
4. Concepts such as unit iteration (for example, not leaving a space between successive units) and zero-point alignment with a ruler can be facilitated in the classroom environment.
5. Children should be exposed to the need for standard units and the relationship between the size of the unit and the number of units needed to measure an object (for example, it takes more centimeters than inches to measure the same length).
6. Introduction of various measuring devices used to measure length (for example, distance wheels or lasers).

Clements and Stephan (2004) suggest that children develop a "measurement sense." A measurement sense requires that teachers present problems involving drawing, estimating lengths, and problem solving using measurement. They suggest using computer programs that use Turtle geometry. Turtle geometry grew out of Seymour Papert's research and his book *Mindstorms* (Papert, 1993). The original turtles were little robots controlled by a computer. A child used the computer to give instructions to the robot about how far to move, the angles to turn, and other length and geometric instructions. As computer graphics developed, the need for a robot diminished. Most Turtle geometry programs today use computer graphics. Children can draw pictures by giving instructions to the turtle. We will discuss Turtle geometry more in the next sections of this chapter (Papert, 1997).

Whatever methods you choose to teach measurement, remember that it is not a simple "skill," but rather a complex combination of concepts and skills that develop slowly over the years. In second and third grade, these concepts begin to come together, allowing for many different types of measurement explorations that children were incapable of in earlier grades. Emphasis on solving real measurement problems and including informal activities that help children develop these concepts and skills are more beneficial than direct instruction and memorization. Finally, teachers should help facilitate the child's ability to link manipulative units and rulers (Clements & Stephan, 2004). Using standard measuring devices is a standard for second and third grade.

Sides and Angles That Make Up Two-Dimensional Shapes

As with length and area, children need to understand concepts such as partitioning and unit iteration to understand angle and turn measure. Due to the nature of this domain of measurement, and our focus on young children, we emphasize basic concepts of understanding of what is being measured (Clements & Stephan, 2004).

The understanding of angles and sides are difficult concepts for second and third graders to grasp. An angle is usually defined as a figure created by intersecting rays and measured using the division of a circle. Since a circle is divided into 360 degrees, it is superimposed over an angle and where the sides intersect the circle is the measure of the angle.

Unfortunately, for children in second and third grades, these concepts can be very difficult to comprehend. They may have different concepts about what is an angle and often do not recognize angles as important parts of figures. When looking at the sizes of angles, children often focus on the length of the line or the distance between end points as the important measure. Introducing the concepts of parallel and perpendicular lines in first grade can help overcome some of these difficulties. Children in first grade can identify parallel and nonparallel lines (Clements & Stephan, 2004). Sensory experiences that allow children to feel the angles or corners of shapes using pattern blocks or tangrams also help them understand the concepts of angles and intersecting lines.

To be successful in the early stages this idea should be introduced in an informal way, with links to real-life uses and situations. Again, the use of Turtle geometry in second and third grade may help with understanding angles, turns, and sides.

Children not only have to instruct the turtle how far to move, but at what angle to turn. With experimentation, a child can learn that repeating certain length movements and angle turns can make interesting shapes and designs.

Children's intellects are expanding mathematically during second and third grade. Their new ability to think logically opens up a new world of opportunities for mathematical thinking and problem solving. However, teachers need to be aware of several types of learning disabilities that can interfere with the teaching and learning of mathematics. The sooner these are recognized and addressed, the better the long-term outcome for the students.

LEARNING DISABILITIES—ADHD, DYSLEXIA, AND DYSCALCULIA

During these first years of formal schooling, there are a few learning disabilities that can manifest themselves. Attention Deficit/Hyperactive Disorder, dyslexia, and dyscalculia are three that can have an impact on how children learn mathematics. The growing emphasis on formal education requires close attention to the teacher, or to the educational task or activity (Rosselli, Matute, Pinto, & Ardila, 2006). These learning disabilities can make this difficult for the affected child.

Attention Deficit/Hyperactive Disorder (ADHD) results when the portion of the brain that processes attention and self-control is less active than it should be. Therefore, these children can exhibit hyperactive behavior, inattention, poor impulse control, or any combination or these factors (Monuteaux, Fraone, Herzig, Navsaria, & Biederman, 2005). ADHD is most often diagnosed in boys, but recent evidence suggests that the incidence in girls may be underreported, as girls tend to exhibit mainly inattention, without hyperactive or impulsive characteristics (Gurian, Henley, & Trueman, 2002; Gurian & Stevens, 2005; Pollack, 1999). Children with any form of ADHD will have trouble staying on task or paying attention. The more demands on their attention that are made, the more this problem becomes evident.

While the primary treatment for ADHD is medication to stimulate the portion of the brain that is underfunctioning this is usually only a partial solution; there are a number of things teachers can do to help children with ADHD during mathematics lessons.

- Individual attention—ADHD children benefit from having a teacher to keep them on task. This may not be possible for the entire mathematics activity, but the teacher should know which children may need special help.
- Games—Many ADHD children do well with games due to the fast-paced nature of the activity. Incorporating math games as much as possible will help give these children an active way to achieve mathematics goals.
- Computers—For many ADHD children, computer activities and games can be a great benefit. As with math games, the changing graphics and fast-paced nature of many of these games help keep children on task and attending to the mathematics concepts.

- To-Do lists—To help keep them on task, it is sometimes helpful to make lists of tasks these children need to complete within a specific time limit. Timers can be very helpful during these activities.

- Limit distractions—The more distractions there are, the harder it is for the ADHD child to work. Many times, the very things that make the classroom more appealing to students are the things that make it hard for the ADHD child to focus. Find a quiet place in the room that has limited visual and auditory distractions for the child to do his mathematics work. The teacher should be careful not to make this seem like punishment.

- Play to the child's strengths—The ADHD child may have trouble attending in the classroom, but may have other skills that can be linked to mathematics. Try to find ways to use his strengths to teach mathematics concepts. (Monuteaux et al., 2005)

Dyslexia and dyscalculia (Birsh, Potts, Potts, & Vineyard Video, 1997) are learning disabilities that result in difficulty understanding and decoding words or numbers. Children with dyslexia have trouble with the automaticity of reading. When most people learn to read, they don't have to read or sound out each word. Our brains develop an automatic recognition that allows normal readers to develop speed and fluency (Chinn et al., 2001). Children with dyslexia find this fluency difficult to achieve and end up having to read and sound out each word, often leading to letter reversals and mistakes. This disability may be evidenced in reading delays and the child's dislike or avoidance of reading. Dyslexia worsens as the child gets older and stricter reading demands are placed him, so the reading problems it causes are best addressed when it is caught early (Mazzocco & Myers, 2003).

These reading problems can affect mathematics learning, because children may have trouble understanding word problems or directions for assignments (Malmer, 2000; Miles, Wheeler, & Haslum, 2003). However, one of the "red flags" for dyslexia is a child that is poor in reading skills, but excels in mathematics. Poor reading skills are often attributed to the child being developmentally delayed or even "lazy." However, if the child excels in mathematics or other areas, and has a specific deficiency just in reading, this can be an indicator of dyslexia (D'Arcangelo, 2001).

Dyscalculia is a similar problem except that it affects mathematical functioning. The cause of dyscalculia is less defined, but results from a combination of poor visual processing and a deficiency in mathematical memory. The slightest misunderstanding or break in logic can overwhelm the student and cause emotional distress. It is typical for these students to study until they know the material well; then, get every problem wrong on the test. A few minutes later, they can perform the test with just the teacher, using the chalkboard, and get all problems correct (Birsh et al., 1997).

Some of the "red flags" for dyscalculia are:

- Students might have spatial problems and difficulty aligning numbers (Fortescue-Hubbard, 2006).

- Have trouble with sequence, including left/right orientation. They may read numbers out of sequence and do operations backwards. They may also become confused over the sequences of past or future events.

- Students typically have problems with mathematics concepts in word problems and confuse similar numbers (e.g., 7 and 9; 3 and 8).
- It is common for students with dyscalculia to have normal or accelerated language acquisition: verbal, reading, writing, and good visual memory for the printed word. They are typically good in the areas of science (until a level requiring higher mathematics skills is reached), geometry (figures with logic not formulas), and creative arts (Helland & Asbjornsen, 2004).
- Students may have difficulty with the abstract concepts of time and direction (e.g., inability to recall schedules, and unable to keep track of time). They may be chronically late.
- Students may have inconsistent results in addition and may have poor mental mathematics ability. They are poor with money and credit and cannot do financial planning or budgeting (e.g., balancing a checkbook). They have short-term, not long-term financial thinking. They may have a fear of money and cash transactions and may be unable to mentally figure change due back, the amounts to pay for tips, taxes, and so on.
- When writing, reading, and recalling numbers, these common mistakes are made: number additions, substitutions, transpositions, omissions, and reversals.
- Difficulty grasping and remembering mathematics concepts, rules, formulas, sequence (order of operations), and basic addition, subtraction, multiplication, and division facts.
- Poor long-term memory (retention and retrieval) of concept mastery. Students understand the material as it is being presented, but when they must retrieve this information, they become confused and are unable to do so. They may be able to perform mathematics operations one day, but draw a blank the next. They may be able to do book work but fail all tests and quizzes (George, 2005).
- Poor ability to "visualize or picture" the location of the numbers on the face of a clock and the geographical locations of states, countries, oceans, streets, and so on.
- Difficulty keeping score or remembering how to keep score during games. Often lose track of whose turn it is during card and board games. Limited strategic planning ability for games like chess (Ruth, Orly, & Varda, 2005).

Figure 8.5 suggests some things that can be done to help children with dyscalculia or trouble learning mathematics (Vaidya, 2004). Most importantly, be patient. Realize that mathematics can be a traumatic experience and is highly emotional because of past and future failures. (Adapted from *http://www.as.wvu.edu/~scidis/dyscalcula.html*.)

It is important to keep in mind that all children are different and have their own unique learning styles. Children's minds are very active and constantly questioning and it is important not to underestimate these unique abilities. To address differences in learning styles, teachers can use questioning techniques to assess what they know about these concepts. They may find that a child knows much more than has been presented here. Teachers should use their observations and authentic assessments to understand each student's unique abilities, and how to support him or her mathematically.

- Encourage students to work extra hard to "visualize" mathematics problems. Draw, or have them draw, a picture to help them understand the problem, and make sure that they take the time to look at any visual information that is provided (picture, chart, graph, etc.).
- Have children read problems out loud and listen very carefully. This allows them to use their auditory skills.
- Have children role-play instructions to aid in understanding.
- Provide examples and try to relate problems to real-life situations (Taverner, 2006).
- Provide children with graph paper and encourage them to use it in order to keep numbers in line.
- When using worksheets, be sure they are uncluttered so that the student is not overwhelmed by too much visual information. Keep instructions brief and concise.
- Use rhythm or music to help them remember critical concepts.
- Many students need one-on-one attention to fully grasp certain concepts. Have students work with a tutor, a parent, or a teacher in a one-on-one environment.
- Allow ample time to complete problems and check to see that the student is not panicking.

Figure 8.5   Suggestions for Helping Children with Dyscalculia.

MEETING STANDARDS FOR SECOND- AND THIRD-GRADE CHILDREN

Second and third grade are those grades in which proficiency testing becomes a factor in educational decisions. The requirements of No Child Left Behind are reaching a critical point in these grades as most states have some sort of proficiency test in fourth grade. As a teacher, you are responsible for preparing your students for these tests and to meet "Annual Yearly Progress" or AYP standards as defined by No Child Left Behind. We can debate the efficacy of these testing procedures (and will do so later, in the assessment section), but the reality is that, as a teacher, you need to make sure that your students are well prepared for this testing. As has been said before in this book, this does not mean you have to use boring drill and skill practice to meet these standards and goals. You can use interactive and active teaching to introduce the necessary concepts. Standards do not dictate how to teach, just what needs to be taught.

A sample of one state's standards can be found in the Appendix. As mentioned earlier, the standards for each state are based to some degree on the *NCTM Principles and Standards for School Mathematics*. Recently, the "NCTM Curriculum Focal Points" were also released, in an attempt to give coherence to the mathematics curriculum. A great number of concepts are covered in second and third grade, as can be seen in Figures 8.6 and 8.7. The focal points are meant to help teachers know which concepts are most important. For second grade, understanding a base-10 system, fluency with addition and subtraction, and an understanding of linear measurement are singled out as being the important concepts. For third grade, the focus is on understanding multiplication, division, and fractions, and describing and analyzing properties of two-dimensional shapes.

Curriculum Focal Points and Connections for Grade 2

The set of three curriculum focal points and related connections for mathematics in grade 2 follow. These topics are the recommended content emphases for this grade level. It is essential that these focal points be addressed in contexts that promote problem solving, reasoning, communication, making connections, and designing and analyzing representations.

Grade 2 Curriculum Focal Points	Connection to the Focal Points
Number and Operations: Developing an understanding of the base 10 numeration systems and place-value concepts Children develop an understanding of the base 10 numeration system and place-value concepts (at least to 1000). Their understanding of base 10 numeration includes ideas of counting in units and multiples of hundreds, tens, and ones, as well as grasp of number relationships, which they demonstrate in a variety of ways including comparing and ordering numbers. They understand multidigit numbers in terms of place value, recognizing that place-value notation is a shorthand for the sums of multiples of powers of 10 (e.g., 853 is 8 hundreds + 5 tens + 3 ones). ***Number and Operations and Algebra: Developing quick recall of addition facts and related subtraction facts and fluency with multidigit addition and subtraction*** Children use their understanding of addition to develop quick recall of basic addition facts and related subtraction facts. They solve arithmetic problems by applying their understanding of models of addition and subtraction (such as combining or separating sets of using number lines), relationships, and properties of numbers (such as place value), and properties of addition (commutativity and associativity). Children develop, discuss, and use efficient, accurate, and generalizable methods to add and subtract multidigit whole numbers. They select and apply appropriate methods to estimate sums and differences or calculate them mentally, depending on the context and numbers involved. They develop fluency with efficient procedures, including standing algorithms, the adding and subtracting of whole numbers, understanding why the procedures work (on the basis of place value and properties of operations), and use them to solve problems. ***Measurement: Developing an understanding of linear measurement and facility in measuring lengths*** Children develop an understanding of the meaning and processes of measurement, including such underlying concepts as partitioning (the mental activity of slicing the length of an object into equal-sized units) and transitivity (e.g., if object A is longer than object B and object B is longer than object C, then object A is longer than object C). They understand linear measure as an iteration of units and use rulers and other measurement tools with that understanding. They understand the need for equal-length units, the use of standard units of measure (centimeter and inch), and the inverse relationship between the size of a unit and the number of units used in a particular measurement (i.e., children recognize that the smaller the unit, the more iterations they need to cover a given length).	***Number and Operations:*** Children use place value and properties of operations to create equivalent representations of given numbers (such as 35 represented by 35 ones, 3 tens and 5 ones, or 2 tens and 15 ones) and to write, compare, and order multidigit numbers. There are these ideas to compose and decompose multidigit numbers. Children add and subtract to solve a variety of problems, including applications involving measurement, geometry, and data, as well as nonroutine problems. In preparation for grade 3, they solve problems involving multiplications situations and developing initial understandings of multiplication as repeated addition. ***Geometry and Measurement:*** Children estimate, measure, and compute lengths as they solve problems involving data, space, and movement through space. By composing and decomposing two-dimensional shapes (intentionally substituting arrangements of smaller shapes for larger shapes or substituting larger shapes for many smaller shapes), they use geometric knowledge and spatial reasoning to develop foundations for understanding area, fractions, and proportions. ***Algebra:*** Children use number patterns to extend their knowledge of properties of numbers and operations. For example, when skip counting, they build foundations for understanding multiples and factors.

Figure 8.6 Second-Grade Focal Points.

Curriculum Focal Points and Connections for Grade 3

The set of three curriculum focal points and related connections for mathematics in grade 3 follow. These topics are the recommended content emphases for this grade level. It is essential that these focal points be addressed in contexts that promote problem solving, reasoning, communication, making connections, and designing and analyzing representations.

Grade 3 Curriculum Focal Points	Connections to the Focal Points
Number and Operations and Algebra: Developing understandings of multiplication and division and strategies for basic multiplication facts and related division facts	**Algebra:** Understanding properties of multiplication and the relationship between multiplication and division is a part of algebra readiness that develops at grade 3. The creation and analysis of patterns and relationships involving multiplication and division should occur at this grade level. Students build a foundation for later understanding of functional relationships by describing relationships in context with such statements as, "The number of legs is four times the number of chairs."
Students understand the meanings of multiplication and division of whole numbers through the use of representations (e.g., equal-sized groups, arrays, area models, and equal "jumps" on number lines for multiplication, and successive subtraction, partitioning, and sharing for division). They use properties of addition and multiplication (e.g., commutativity, associativity, and the distributive property) to multiply whole numbers and apply increasingly sophisticated strategies based on these properties to solve multiplication and division problems involving basic facts. By comparing a variety of solution strategies, students relate multiplication and division as inverse operations.	**Measurement:** Students in grade 3 strengthen their understanding of fractions as they confront problems in linear measurement that call for more precision than the whole unit allowed them in their work in grade 2. They develop their facility in measuring with fractional parts of linear units. Students develop measurement concepts and skills through experiences in analyzing attributes and properties of two-dimensional objects. They form an understanding of perimeter as a measurable attribute and select appropriate units, strategies, and tools to solve problems involving perimeter.
Number and Operations: Developing an understanding of fractions and fraction equivalence	**Data Analysis:** Addition, subtraction, multiplication, and division of whole numbers come into play as students construct and analyze frequency tables, bar graphs, picture graphs, and line plots and use them to solve problems.
Students develop an understanding of the meanings and uses of fractions to represent parts of a whole, parts of a set, or points or distances on a number line. They understand that the size of a fractional part is relative to the size of the whole, and they use fractions to represent numbers that are equal to, less than, or greater than one. They solve problems that involve comparing and ordering fractions by using models, benchmark fractions, or common numerators or denominators. They understand and use models, including the number line, to identify equivalent fractions.	**Number and Operations:** Building on their work in grade 2, students extend their understanding of place value to numbers up to 10,000 in various contexts. Students also apply this understanding to the task of representing numbers in different equivalent forms (e.g., expanded notation). They develop their understanding of numbers by building their facility with mental computation (addition and subtraction in special cases, such as $2500 + 6000$ and $9000 − 5000$), by using computational estimation, and by performing paper-and-pencil computations.
Geometry: Describing and analyzing properties of two-dimensional shapes	
Students describe, analyze, compare, and classify two-dimensional shapes by their sides and angles and connect these attributes to definitions of shapes. Students investigate, describe, and reason about decomposing, combining, and transforming polygons to make other polygons. Through building, drawing, and analyzing two-dimensional shapes, students understand attributes and properties of two-dimensional space and the use of those attributes and properties in solving problems, including applications involving congruence and symmetry.	

Figure 8.7 Third-Grade Focal Points.

Source: Reprinted with permission from *Curriculum Focal Points for Prekindergarten through Grade 8 Mathematics: A Quest for Coherence*, copyright 2006 by the National Council of Teachers of Mathematics. All rights reserved. The Curriculum Focal Points identify key mathematical ideas for these grades. They are not discrete topics or a checklist to be mastered; rather, they provide a framework for the majority of instruction at a particular grade level and the foundation for future mathematics study. The complete document may be viewed at *www.nctm.org/focalpoints*.

WHAT DOES A SECOND- AND THIRD-GRADE MATHEMATICS LEARNING ENVIRONMENT LOOK LIKE?

As has been mentioned, children in second and third grade are in the "education" phase of the "3E" approach to learning mathematics and classrooms should begin to reflect that change, with a stronger emphasis on instruction and less emphasis on a play-based approach. The environment for second- and third-grade mathematics classrooms needs to be more "homelike" than what we traditionally think of as a traditional classroom. A focus on standards, proficiency, and fluency means that children will be doing the "work" of learning mathematics. The goal of the teacher is to make that "work" engaging and enjoyable rather than boring drudgery (Buschman, 2005). Children, as mentioned earlier, are in the industry vs. inferiority stage of emotional development. If they feel successful at their work, they will enjoy their work.

However, just because they are focusing on "work," does not mean that the environment cannot be comfortable and pleasant. Plants and comfortable places to sit are welcome respites in the adult workplace and they are just as important in the classroom. Allow children to take part in decorating the room; bring in plants and other items of psychological comfort. Physically comfortable places to work, such as chairs and couches, are also useful if space permits (Curtis & Carter, 2003).

Most important to teaching mathematics in second and third grade is setting up an interactive classroom. As we discussed in the K–1 chapter, arranging desks so that children can see each other's faces is important and encourages interaction. A space front of a chalkboard should be reserved for whole-class discussions. Children can congregate there as groups to work on and discuss problems, or the teacher can convene the class there to review answers to problems or to discuss and review independent work.

Environments should foster interaction between teacher and student, as well as student and student.

Barbara Schwartz/Merrill

Setting up the classroom is a personal task. It should reflect the nature of your teaching philosophy and the goals you wish to achieve with your students. It should reflect your personality and that of your class. When a guest walks into your room, they should be able to feel the presence of you and your class. As they walk around your classroom, they should get an understanding of what your class is learning and the work they are doing. Having their work presented in this way also helps build industry. Imagine a child giving a tour of the classroom to a parent or another adult. Think of the pride that child will exhibit when explaining his work and the work of the class. If children feel ownership of the classroom and it is relevant to their lives, this is exactly what can happen (Curtis & Carter, 2003).

DEVELOPMENTALLY APPROPRIATE STRATEGIES AND ACTIVITIES FOR SECOND- AND THIRD-GRADE CHILDREN

Teaching Lessons and Problem Solving

As was discussed in the last chapter, classroom lessons are composed of individual problem-solving time, group interaction and sharing of ideas and solutions, and invention of multiple ways of reaching a solution. The process is no different in second and third grade. The difference is the level of the problems. In second grade, children are working on double-column addition with regrouping, multiplication, division, and fractions. Third-grade developments and concepts are based on the foundation laid in first and second grade.

While children are becoming more accustomed to the traditional schooling environment and are constructing and learning new concepts through "education," this does not mean that the teacher should become a "transmitter" of knowledge. Her role is as a facilitator, helping children use their critical thinking skills to develop mathematically (Lent et al., 2006). She sets up problems and situations that allow children to investigate mathematics. The best investigations grow out of children's experiences and the world around them. Another factor in good mathematical investigations is that they last for an extended period of time—days and sometimes weeks. Lent et al. (2006) describe a second-grade classroom algebra investigation that grew out of a class field trip to Central Park in New York, where the school is located. This is how the teacher introduced the problem:

> Remember when we took our birding trip to Central Park? We rode the subway and it was really crowded. None of us had seats. At the first stop, a few of us got seats. Then at the next stop, a few more of us got seats. The car kept getting emptier and emptier, until, by the time we got to the park, every one of us had a seat. In fact, we were practically the only people in the car. During our subway ride, a lot of people got off the car, but people also got on the car at nearly every stop. I wonder how our subway car kept getting emptier if there were people getting on at every stop? (Lent et al., 2006, p. 4)

The teacher then said that on her way home she counted 10 people at the Chambers Street stop. At the next stop, Franklin Street, some people got on and some people got off and when the train left Franklin Street there were 15 people in the car. She then asked the class, "What could have happened? How many people could have gotten off? How many people could have gotten on?"

This problem is an example of an open-ended question because it has a number of different correct answers. Children of different mathematical abilities approach this question differently. Lent et al. (2006) found that some children thought of this as a "one-solution" problem while the more advanced students were able to understand that there were a finite number of solutions. Some of the children made patterns and others used more random methods of determining a solution. Some represented their solutions as diagrams, some as number lines, some as equations, and others chose to write out the solution using words.

As children begin to formulate solutions and present and discuss them in class, the teacher presents new, but similar, problems to the class to help them generalize their findings, or use their patterns on a new situation. Most children use a pattern of first jumping backward then forward. For example, the problem can be written $10 - \underline{A} + \underline{B} = 15$. Through experimentation, the children discover that there is a correspondence between A and B. In this case, when A gets *one bigger* so does B. They also realize that A can't be more than 10 because you can't have "negative people" and they may even recognize that A and B are functions of each other. In other words, $A + 5 = B$.

> At first children do not use a systematic approach to generate possibilities . . . The production of a systematic approach allows them to see and explore patterns regarding the functional relations—*the more that get off, the higher the number that get on.*" (Lent et al., 2006, p. 7)

Lessons that require children to investigate problems and use their logic to solve problems strengthen their understanding of mathematics. Second and third graders become logical thinkers with the advent of concrete operations. This should be used in developing lessons and problems.

In these types of classrooms, most of the talking is done by the children, not the teacher. It is often difficult for teachers to give up this control. We need to see learning as a social activity as opposed to an acquisition model of education (Forman & Ansell, 2001). An acquisition model assumes that children learn by being told or instructed, whereas viewing education as a social activity means that the teacher's role is to facilitate discussion. As teachers learn to start setting educational goals based more on a social activity model, they tend to focus on conceptual understanding in their students and have higher expectations for them. They "let go of control" and begin to better facilitate learning in the classroom (Wood, 1999).

Teachers should let children do the thinking, as active participants in the classroom, rather than just sitting passively while being told the information. The more a child is involved mentally, physically, and emotionally in the classroom, the better the learning and discipline outcomes (Drier, 2000).

Technology

Technology, such as computers and software programs, calculators, overhead projectors, and other high-tech gadgets, can be a valuable tool in the teaching of mathematics. The computer fascinates many children (Eunsook & Davis, 2005). Second and third graders have often had experience with computer games at home, so using one can be a natural extension of their play activities (Sinclair & Crespo, 2006). However, computers can hinder a child's construction of mathematics if overused or misused. Computer software to teach mathematics concepts and skills are prevalent in any computer store. However, they do not always achieve the goals that we have proposed in this book, and usually end up being electronic versions of worksheets or flashcards.

These activities can sometimes be useful because children often find doing math on the computer with interesting graphics engaging. If used as an activity that they choose themselves and if they are actively engaged, computers can be a good way to encourage fluency (McClure, 2006; Orme & Monroe, 2005). Teachers, however, need to choose computer activities that are more than just worksheets or electronic flash cards; they need to become good consumers of classroom software. Engaging software has deeper levels of understanding built into the activity. A good example of this is Logo.

Logo

Logo is a programming language based on the constructivist ideas of Seymour Papert (Siaw & Winbourne, 2005). It was designed to be a computer programming language accessible to children, and has been around and under development for almost 30 years. In the early years, teachers and children used it to develop geometric patterns by programming the "turtle" to make repeated lines and turns. In

Computers can engage second- and third-grader's interest, but remember there is no substitute for a well-prepared teacher.

Anthony Magnacca/Merrill

Mindstorms (Papert, 1993), Papert proposed that children learn mathematics by teaching a computer to draw shapes.

Today, Logo programs have many other uses besides drawing geometric designs (although this is still a useful function). Programs such as MicroWorlds EX and Terrapin Logo allow children to build their own activities and video games using the Logo language.

Micro Worlds EX is more than just a Logo program. It is a collection of tools designed to help support investigations in mathematics and other subject areas. The tools are designed to encourage children to think about their questions, ideas, and strategies for finding answers and constructing deeper understandings (Ball, 2004). This type of software is more open-ended than the usual mathematics software. It allows the children to design their own experiences and to build their own games and programs. It can also aid in project work and mathematical investigations. One project used it to develop a program to roll three dice and record the results for later analysis.

Terrapin Logo was one of the first logo software companies. While not as all-inclusive as MicroWorlds EX, Terrapin Logo used turtle graphics to teach children about concepts such as patterns, functions, multiplicative arrays, and geometric principles. Using Logo to program a "turtle," children learn about angles, turns, linear geometry, the relations of sides and angles, and many other geometric and mathematical concepts.

There are many other Logo programs on the market and some of them are free. There are, additionally, books, web sites, and support groups for teachers that use Logo-based software programs. I have included a few links to web sites devoted to Logo so you can examine some of the projects that children have engaged in when using the Logo language and related programs (Sutherland, 1993).

Calculators

The goal of mathematics, during this time, is to promote mathematical thinking and fluency. Calculators can be helpful if children choose to use them. There are instances in second and third grade when a calculator may prove useful and help to meet mathematical goals. When the goal of the mathematical activity is larger problem solving and logic and the numbers become too large for the students to efficiently handle, using a calculator might be appropriate. For example, if children are trying to determine the measurement of the perimeter of an oddly shaped playground, they might find they need to add eight numbers such as 143, 213, 78, 23, 30, 23, 35, and 213. If your focus is on the measurement activity, the time spent doing the computation could get in the way of your main educational objective. In this case, using a calculator could be justified.

Using the calculator for a problem such as this, children can begin recognizing the ways multiplication can be used to make large tasks easier. They may use the calculator to compute 213×2, then add the sum of 23×2 and the other numbers to get their answer. Overall, calculators and other computational crutches should be kept to a minimum. They can hinder the development of automaticity and fluency (Dolk, 2004).

Timed and Fluency Activities

Fluency in addition and multiplication is a vital focus for second and third grade. However, teachers should avoid using activities that overemphasize rote memorization and skill practice. Fluency in mathematics means that the child can quickly and easily produce solutions to basic mathematics problems, such as sums of numbers 0–20 and multiplication products 0–10. This can be accomplished through means that focus on developing conceptual understanding (Labinowicz, 1985).

Even when focusing on fluency, children should be thinking about the interrelatedness of the numbers. Memorizing multiplication tables may help them recall the answer to a multiplication problem, but does not help the child develop multiplicative thinking.

Traditionally, fluency has been linked to the amount of time a child needs to retrieve an answer. In an effort to improve this recall, **timed tests** are often employed (Burns, 1995; Cates & Rhymer, 2003). The timed test usually includes a paper test sheet with a number of math problems, such as "four times" multiplication facts, and children are given a very limited time in which to complete them. The children may move on to the "five times" test, once they have successfully answered all the "four times" problems in the allotted time. If the child fails to get all the "four times" facts correct or runs out of time, he must repeat that test until he completes it successfully.

The problem with this type of test is twofold. First, the goal of the test is to teach the child to recall without thinking. This goes counter to everything we know about teaching children mathematics (Burns, 1995; Cates & Rhymer, 2003). The second problem is the pressure and stress this puts on a child. If one of the problems we are trying to combat in teaching children mathematics is math anxiety, then we should avoid activities and tests that produce a high level of anxiety. Have you ever tried to think or solve a problem when you were under stress or anxious about something?

Children in second and third grade are emotionally susceptible to the negative aspects of such testing procedures. Remember, they are becoming much more reliant on social comparisons to gauge their abilities. Even if the teacher does not announce the results of the test, children know who is doing well and who is behind. Tests such as this can lead to inferiority feelings among the children that are behind, according to Erikson (1958).

Speed and mindless recall without thinking are really not mathematical objectives. The true goal is fluency. **Fluency** is recall of mathematical computations quickly and with understanding. Instead of tying recall of facts to a timer, fluency means that children can quickly and efficiently remember and produce answers to basic mathematics problems without the help of fingers for counting or other computational aids. Fluency is not about mindless recall; it is about a child being so familiar with the network of numbers, that he simply knows the answers (Davis, 2006).

High-stress tests can be replaced with math games similar to the ones we discussed in earlier chapters. During math games, children use basic addition and multiplication to repeatedly solve problems within the game. The friendly competition of a game is much less stressful than a timed test situation and the social comparison becomes about playing games rather than academic performance (Davis, 2006).

For example, children can play multiplication war. We have discussed War (in which each child lays down one card and the highest number wins) and Double War (in which each child puts down two cards and the highest sum wins). These games help to increase fluency in "greater than and less than" and basic addition. Multiplication war is played the same way, except that children multiply the two numbers and the highest product wins. Because each child wants to be the first to say the answer, speed is important, but it is not the main goal of the game. To play the game and keep it moving along, the children must become fluent at coming up with the answers. They construct the methods of achieving this fluency themselves and for reasons that are real and meaningful to them—to keep the game interesting (Kamii & Anderson, 2003; Kamii & Livingston, 1994).

This type of activity achieves the goals we want without the detrimental effects of high-stakes testing. There is room for testing and teachers need to assess the child's fluency level periodically, but there are better ways than timed tests (Kamii & Anderson, 2003).

Worksheets and Homework

If you ask most second- and third-grade children what math means to them, they will respond that it means a bunch of worksheets and a lot of homework. In these grades, these items become very common and can be very useful to teaching mathematics if used correctly (Baker & LeTendre, 2005). The trick is to find ways to make the use of these activities engaging and interactive (Hartweg, 2005). The problem with worksheets and homework is that they tend to be premade by a textbook series, copied, and distributed to students as silent, individual work. Sometimes, this is a good goal for a mathematics activity. However, many times the silent and individual nature of these generic worksheets is overused in the classroom (Gibson, 2004).

With a bit of creativity, teachers can use premade worksheets as tools for interaction and exploration. For example, let the children work on the worksheets in pairs or in groups, or let them develop their own worksheets that will be given to another group to do. Worksheets can be used in many different and creative ways (Milbourne, Haury, & ERIC Clearinghouse for Science, Mathematics, and Environmental Education, 1999).

The same is true for homework assignments. Too often, homework assignments are just worksheets similar to the ones done in class. For second and third graders, homework is acceptable and developmentally appropriate as long as it is not designed to take more than 15–30 minutes to complete. Also, it should be more than just repeated practice (Samples, 2004). We need to ask ourselves, what is the real benefit of homework? Why is it important?

The most compelling answer is that it allows parents and the rest of the family to help in mathematics instruction (Schumm, 2005), making mathematics something that the child can engage in at home and other places, as well as at school. Homework should take advantage of things the child has access to in his home. Kitchen items, toys, and other everyday objects in the home can be used to support mathematics homework. For example, a homework activity could be to keep a journal of the amount of time spent on certain weekly activities the child engages in, such as watching TV, playing outside, playing inside, and eating dinner. At the end of the week, the child adds up the totals and reports them. In class, the teacher can make a chart and the students can add up the totals for the whole class.

Here are some suggestions for using and developing worksheets and homework assignments.

1. You do not need to use the worksheet or homework assignment given to you. Make modifications to fit your goals for the lesson.
2. Let the children move around the classroom. There is no rule that says worksheets have to be done at a desk.
3. Make sure that homework engages the whole family when possible. An activity that encourages the child to ask questions or explain a concept to another family member helps to contextualize the importance of the homework activity.
4. Allow the children to talk about and to discuss the worksheet with others. There is a time for silence when doing mathematics and a time to talk and interact. Let the child choose which he needs. Have areas for children to talk and discuss and a place for them to work silently.
5. Keep the worksheet or homework relevant. Whenever possible, link the work being done to activities children are engaged in or working on.
6. Worksheets and homework can be more than just a series of similar problems to solve. Worksheets with 50 addition problems that are only different because of the numbers used can become boring to a child. Develop worksheets that allow the child to think and investigate mathematical concepts. Use word problems and brainteasers on worksheets.
7. Think about your goal when designing the worksheet or homework assignment. Is there a better way to achieve your goal using a classroom discussion or a math game? Avoid using worksheets to buy time. Never assign them just so you can have time to grade papers or catch up on work. While teachers often have more work than they can finish during the day, using a "make work" activity in order to find more time is not what is best for the students.

Hands-On Materials and Manipulative

Earlier in this book we mentioned that math is not "in" the manipulative. Using manipulatives, however, supports mathematics (Burns & Cuisenaire Company of America, 1987). Manipulatives and real-life situations help children to contextualize concepts that may be abstract to them (Research and Education Association, 1999). When using manipulatives, remember that it is not the manipulative itself that is important, but the mathematical thinking that it encourages (Alexander & Robinson, 2001; Burns, Burns, & Math, 2003; Creative Wonders, 1997).

For example, fractions tend to be an abstract concept for many second and third graders. Teaching about ½, ¼, and so on can be hard for these children to understand without some sort of concrete representation to link it to (National Council of Teachers of Mathematics, 2006). Here is an interaction with a second grader.

G: Do you know what fractions are?

D: No, but I know what 3 × 3 is.

G: Great, what is it?

D: Nine.

G: Wow, that's great. Do you know what, ⅓ of 9 is?

D: No.

G: Well ⅓ of 9 is 3. One third is a fraction.

D: No! Three 3s make 9, not ⅓.

G: What if we had a pizza and it was cut into 9 pieces?

D: Wait! Let me draw it.

D: (Draws a circle then divides it in half then in 4, then 6 then 8.) It has to be even! I can't get 9.

G: Well, if we had to divide it up between 9 people, what would you do?

D: (Divides one of the pieces in half so that there are now 9 pieces) But the pieces are not the same size. Two people are going to get smaller pieces.

G: What can we do about that?

D: (Divides all the pieces in half) Now we have enough for everyone to have one piece and some leftover if people want extra.

G: (Draws a new circle pizza) What if your mom and I wanted to share this pizza with you and we wanted to split it up? Can you show me how you would do that?

D: I will use the red marker for you, the blue marker for mommy, and the green marker for me. (D splits the pizza up into three pieces and then colors one section green, one blue, and one red.)

G: How many pieces will each of us get?

D: One.

G: That's a big piece of pizza. Can you divide up each of the pieces into three pieces?

D: Yes! (Draws two lines in each piece, making roughly equal sizes).

G: How many pieces are there in the whole pizza?

D: Nine.

G: Did we all get a whole pizza?

D: No! We all got three pieces of the pizza. We each got three pieces and 3 × 3 is 9!

G: Guess what. You just did fractions!

D: Um . . . I don't think so.

This child can understand the basic concepts of fractions from his new understanding of multiplication. He can also use his familiarity with pizza and how to divide one up between friends to actually use fractions, but the abstract concept of ⅓ is still hard for him.

The math is not in the pizza, but the pizza activity helped to scaffold his learning (Sinclair & Kamii, 1994). It allowed him to use his prior knowledge and a concrete representation to think about something new and more abstract. This is how manipulatives can be used best in the classroom.

There are many manipulatives that can be used in second- and third-grade classrooms to help children understand fractions, multiplication and larger addition concepts (Olkun, 2003). Base-10 blocks (Goodnow, 1994b), board games, blocks (Goodnow, 1994a), puzzles, tangrams (Goodnow, 1994c), fraction boards, and many other tools can help a child organize his thinking and visualize more abstract concepts. The manipulative supports the thinking; it does not supplant it.

Teaching mathematics to second and third graders is an exciting experience. Developing interactive lessons and activities that allow the child to discuss and explore using his mind and senses will open up the world of mathematics to him. Mathematics can be exciting and fun if presented in an engaging manner. Most games, puzzles, and diversions that adults engage in include mathematics in some form. Developing good lessons during these vital formative years is of paramount importance (Gibson, 2004).

SAMPLE SECOND- AND THIRD-GRADE LESSON PLANS

The following lessons give you suggestions for ways to begin to understand second- and third-graders' capabilities in math activities. They focus on fluency and recall of addition and multiplication, measuring length and experimenting with angles and other geometric shapes, practicing regrouping and length measurement, using addition, subtraction, multiplication and division and understanding values of coins and money, and representing fractions. As with all math activities, consider the individual children, and remember to observe, assess as you go, listen, adapt, and reflect on how to make it more appropriate or effective next time.

LESSON PLAN

▼◄▲▼◄▲▼◄▲▼◄▲▼◄▲▼◄▲▼◄▲

Lesson Title: Addition/Multiplication Take-Em

Age: Second and Third Grade

Subject Area: Mathematics

▼◄▲▼◄▲▼◄▲▼◄▲▼◄▲▼◄▲▼◄▲

Objective: Fluency and quick recall of multidigit addition and/or fluency in basic multiplication tables 0–9.

Standards: 1) Model, represent, and explain multiplication as repeated addition, rectangular arrays, and skip counting. 2) Understand that, unlike addition and subtraction, the factors in multiplication and division may have different units (e.g., three boxes of five cookies each). 3) Model and use the commutative and associative properties for addition and multiplication. 4) Demonstrate fluency in addition facts with addends through nine and corresponding subtractions (e.g., $9 + 9 = 18$, $18 - 9 = 9$).

Focal Points: 1) Develop an understanding of multiplication and division and strategies for basic multiplication facts and related division facts. 2) Develop quick recall of addition facts and related subtraction facts and fluency with multidigit addition and subtraction.

Lesson Summary: Children play this math game in pairs or 3s. Students add or multiply the numbers on the cards to determine the winner.

Beginning the Lesson: Math games are introduced to the whole class during a group meeting. During this meeting the basic rules are explained and questions are answered about the game. The teacher can demonstrate how to play by choosing a child from the class to play with while the class observes. After this she can place the game materials in the Math Game Center for children to play with during free time or math game time. A 20–40-minute period should be set aside during the day for games.

Procedures: This math game can be set up for either addition or multiplication using the same rules. The teacher may change the numbers on the cards to set the level of instruction. Students put down two cards with numbers on them (0–20 for addition or 0–9 for multiplication). They add or multiply the numbers and the child with the highest sum or product gets to take both cards. If the sum product is equal, each student puts down two more cards and adds or multiplies those. This continues until one student has a higher sum or product; he then takes all the cards. The child with the most cards at the end of the game wins.

Extension: The teacher changes the quantities on the cards to adjust the level. If using addition, begin with numbers 0–6 to focus on fluency, adding larger numbers up to 10 (or higher if not using standard cards) as the children become more capable. For multiplication (third grade usually) begin with numbers up to five and then add higher number as children's abilities progress.

Adaptations: This game can easily be adapted for children of lower mathematical ability. Teachers can adjust the rules of the game so that one card is laid down by each child; the winner is determined by comparing the numbers on each card. For children who are visually impaired, large numbers or Braille cards can be purchased or created.

Materials: A deck of cards (playing cards work fine for numbers 1–10, but lack a 0). For numbers above 10, or if you would like children to not be able to count the markings, 3 × 5 cards can be used for the War deck.

Assessment: Assessment should be done through observation and recording the children's responses to the experience. The teacher should use formative assessment to determine when to increase the difficulty or add numbers.

LESSON PLAN

▼◀ ▲▼◀ ▲▼◀ ▲▼◀ ▲▼◀ ▲▼◀ ▲▼◀ ▲

Lesson Title: Logo

Age: Second and Third Grade

Subject Area: Mathematics

▼◀ ▲▼◀ ▲▼◀ ▲▼◀ ▲▼◀ ▲▼◀ ▲▼◀ ▲

Objective: Use measurement to transfer heights to another medium (transitivity) and compare them.

Standards: 1) Draw lines of symmetry to verify symmetrical two-dimensional shapes. 2) Identify and describe the relative size of angles with respect to right angles as follows: A. Use physical models, like straws, to make different-sized angles by opening and closing the sides, not by changing the side lengths. B. Identify, classify, and draw right, acute, obtuse, and straight angles. 3) Estimate and measure lengths using nonstandard and standard units (i.e., centimeters, inches, and feet).

Focal Points: 1) Describe and analyze properties of two-dimensional shapes. 2) Develop an understanding of linear measurement and facility in measuring lengths.

Lesson Summary: Children will use a turtle graphics program (examples include Star-Logo—free at *http://education.mit.edu/starlogo/*, MicroWorlds Jr.—PreK-second grade, Microworlds EX—3rd and up, and Terrapin Logo) to draw shapes and designs using instructions of length of sides and turn angles.

Beginning the Lesson: Logo is a computer graphics program that uses a computer and commands to draw pictures. To introduce this activity, teachers can start by having children study and draw geometry shapes such as squares, rectangles, and triangles on paper using a ruler. The teacher can use questioning techniques to focus the child on concepts such as length of sides, degrees of angles, and symmetry. She may introduce a drawing set such as Hasbro's Deluxe Spirograph to demonstrate the ability of repeating shapes to make visual patterns.

Procedures: On the large display or computer projector, demonstrate how to tell the computer to move forward 25 steps—FD 25. Repeat this action to make a longer side, then tell the turtle to turn right 90 degrees—RT 90. Ask the students the following questions: What would happen if we entered FD 25 again?

How can we make the turtle go back to the start? (Remember, the turn has to be determined from the turtle's viewpoint.) Alternatively, students could tell it to retrace its steps.

The teacher can take this opportunity to introduce functions of back—BK and left—LT.

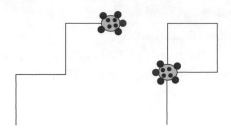

Select pupils to work on available computers. Others will work on paper. Ask them to draw a "staircase" and "flag." Record the turtle commands.

Bring the class together again to try their suggestions. Look at the flag. What is its shape? How was it drawn? Is there a quicker way? Show how to draw a square with REPEAT.

Triangles: Ask the students "How are we going to tell the turtle to draw an equilateral triangle?" The turtle is facing the top of the screen. Draw the possibilities suggested by the students with a marker:

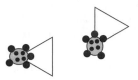

Focus on the turtle facing a particular direction. The screen display enables the whole class to see this. Children need to identify the angle that the turtle has to turn through, seeing it from the turtle's viewpoint.

The class works on plain paper, drawing the triangle with the help of a protractor and writing the commands below. Get the class together to try out some of their "programs." It's very likely that 60-degree turns will look like the following:

It's important to establish an atmosphere where children are not afraid to make mistakes, but see that feedback from the computer is helpful in planning the next step.

Other Polygons: Ask the children, "How are we going to tell the turtle to draw a hexagon?" Start with the turtle facing the top of the screen. Draw the first side. Questions you might ask are, "The turtle now has to face which direction?" and "What angle does it turn through?"

When the hexagon is complete, check that the turtle is facing in its original direction. What is the total number of turns it has made?

Individual students can work on paper grids, with a table to record their findings. First, they investigate a regular octagon. Can they see the connection between the number of sides and the number of turtle turns?

If the turtle repeatedly moves forward the same distance, then moves RT 30, what polygon will it draw? (Dodecagon, 12 sides).

Extension: Students can predict other shapes using this table:

Name	Number of sides	Turn (degrees)	Total turn
equilateral triangle	3	120	360
square	4	90	360
hexagon	6	60	360
octagon	8	45	360

What is the rule for telling the turtle to draw a regular polygon? How do we draw a pentagon? Test some of the children's suggestions.

Adaptations: The software is very adaptable to differing abilities and lessons can be modified to meet the level of each child. Children with physical disabilities who have trouble with computer keyboards may need extra help or special equipment to make the computer more accessible.

Materials: A Logo program. MicroWorlds Jr. is very easy for children to use and understand. Many of the commands can be entered graphically; turns and angles are completed using the graphic of a ship's wheel. Text-based programs work well with older children who are more experienced with the computer.

Assessment: Collection of student's work in a portfolio. Interviews with individual students to assess their understanding of angles and turns work for formative assessment of the activity. Paper-and-pencil assessments can be used as a summative evaluation of content learned with this activity.

LESSON PLAN
▾◂▴▾◂▴▾◂▴▾◂▴▾◂▴▾◂▴▾◂▴

Lesson Title: Floor Plans

Age: Second and Third Grade

Subject Area: Mathematics

▾◂▴▾◂▴▾◂▴▾◂▴▾◂▴▾◂▴▾◂▴

Objective: To increase fluency of adding and regrouping numbers that add up to 10.

Standards: 1) Find and name locations on a labeled grid or coordinate system (e.g., a map or graph). 2) Make estimates for perimeter, area, and volume using links, tiles, cubes, and other models. 3) Build a three-dimensional model of an object composed of cubes; e.g., construct a model based on an illustration or actual object.

Focal Points: 1) Describe and analyze properties of two-dimensional shapes. 2) Develop an understanding of linear measurement and facility in measuring lengths.

Lesson Summary: Children will measure, draw and build 3D representations of classroom and school spaces.

Beginning the Lesson: The teacher can begin this lesson by discussing with the children how they could rearrange the classroom. Using a questioning technique, he can focus the children's attention on making a scale drawing of the classroom. Discussions of what an architect does, along with blueprints and books on these topics, can be introduced into the classroom.

Procedures: The teacher might begin this investigation by asking an architect to visit the classroom and talk about blueprints and floor plans. The class can then examine existing blueprints of buildings to investigate concepts of scale, use of coordinates, and locating and orienting objects using a grid system. If time permits, the teacher may lead an investigation to find the actual blueprints of their school building (these may be on file at county planning offices).

Children are then instructed to make a blueprint or floor plan of the classroom in groups. They can investigate different ways to measure the perimeter of the classroom, the angles of corners, and the room's dimensions. They will need to decide on what scale to draw their results.

Extension: Children can continue to make blueprints of other spaces in the school, if appropriate. They can also make blueprints of their rooms at home.

Adaptations: Children with physical limitations may have difficulty with the drawing tasks. The teacher should be sure to include alternate methods for these children to represent what they know. For example, they may be able use a computer to assist with drawing.

Materials: Yardsticks, tape measures, or other measurement tools; paper (preferably blue), pencils, rulers, or other straight edges. Access to blueprints of other buildings should be available to students.

Assessment: Assessment can be done in the form of an open house in which findings are presented to the principal, other teachers, and parents. Portfolios of students' group and individual work can be collected. Mathematical concepts such as measurement, scale, and angles can be assessed using a formal paper-and-pencil assessment if the teacher desires.

LESSON PLAN
▼◄▲▼◄▲▼◄▲▼◄▲▼◄▲▼◄▲▼◄▲

Lesson Title: Money Sense

Age: Second and Third Grade

Subject Area: Mathematics

▼◄▲▼◄▲▼◄▲▼◄▲▼◄▲▼◄▲▼◄▲

Objective: Recognize relative values of a penny, nickel, dime, quarter, and dollar; show how different combinations of coins equal the same amounts of money; and add and subtract different amounts of money to make change.

Standards: 1) Count money and make change using coins and paper bills to 10 dollars. 2) Write, solve, and explain simple mathematical statements, such as $7 + \_ > 8$ or $\_ + 8 = 10$. 3) Model problem situations using objects, pictures, tables, numbers, letters, and other symbols. 4) Extend multiplicative and growing patterns, and describe the pattern or rule in words. Other standards could be met depending on the questions developed from this lesson.

Focal Points: Develop an understanding of multiplication and division and strategies for basic multiplication facts and related division facts. 2) Develop quick recall of addition facts and related subtraction facts and fluency with multidigit addition and subtraction.

Lesson Summary: Children will use money to solve problems and learn about using money in everyday life. Children will use algebra to determine if they have enough money for certain items.

Beginning the Lesson: The teacher can begin this lesson with a discussion of money. Children can be prompted to talk about how much things cost, what they spend money on, and if they have a "piggy bank." The teacher then asks them how they could find out what things cost in the cafeteria. Their ideas should be written down and the most efficient ones selected by student vote.

Procedures: Once the children have a list of items sold in the cafeteria and how much each item costs, they should make a "menu" that can be referred to during the lesson. An example might look like this:

Grilled Cheese Sandwich	$1.25
Slice of Pizza	$1.35
Hot Dog	$1.00
Hot Pretzel	$0.70
Chips	$0.75
Milk	$0.45
Water	$0.85

The teacher can then develop questions based on this menu. For example:

You have $4.75 to spend in the cafeteria. You are very hungry so you want to get as much food as you can. What combinations of food allow you to spend the most money?

Or:

Jose is trying to figure out if he got all the food that he paid for. He paid $4.25 and has two slices of pizza and a hot pretzel. Is he missing something? If so, what is he missing?

Or:

Jose buys the same things every day: a hot dog, a bag of chips, and a bottle of water. How much money does he need for a week of lunches?

Teachers can develop other questions as needed to achieve other goals and meet other standards. Teachers could have a daily question based on this (or any other) data, using the guidelines for developing good word problems discussed in this book.

At the conclusion of this activity, the teacher can have the children from small groups to develop their own word problems for the class to solve. These problems can be written on a sheet of paper, along with the questions from other groups, illustrated, and bound into a small book to be placed in the math center for children to work with during free time or math game time.

Extension: Children can visit a grocery store and develop a price list of familiar items such as cereal, meat by the pound, and bologna. While there they can also investigate the concept of coupons, looking for sales and bargains and prices per pound or ounce, to make sure they are getting the most for their money.

Adaptations: For children who are less advanced, simpler questions can be introduced, such as, "Raj purchased a bottle of water and a soft pretzel and paid with a $5 bill. How much did his food cost and how much change did he get?" Foreign currency can also be introduced, such as the euro and the peso. Discussions about why different countries use different kinds of money may lead to new activities and cross-cultural experiences.

Materials: Paper, pencils, play money, real coins and dollar bills for demonstrations, chart paper.

Assessment: Assessment can be done by collecting the children's work and through the production of the word problem book. Teachers may also choose to give a paper-and-pencil test of children's understanding of money and money concepts.

LESSON PLAN
▼◄ ▲▼◄ ▲▼◄ ▲▼◄ ▲▼◄ ▲▼◄ ▲▼◄ ▲

Lesson Title: Dividing Candy Fractions

Age: Second and Third Grade

Subject Area: Mathematics

▼◄ ▲▼◄ ▲▼◄ ▲▼◄ ▲▼◄ ▲▼◄ ▲▼◄ ▲

Objective: Use fractions to solve the problem of distributing a special snack. Children will develop many concepts related to fractions, including an understanding of the basis of dividing fractions, using representations familiar to them.

Standards: Represent fractions (halves, thirds, fourths, sixths, and eighths), using words, numerals, and physical models. For example:

  a. Recognize that a fractional part can mean different amounts depending on the original quantity.
  b. Recognize that a fractional part of a rectangle does not have to be shaded with contiguous parts.
  c. Identify and illustrate parts of a whole and parts of sets of objects.
  d. Compare and order physical models of halves, thirds, and fourths in relation to 0 and 1.

Focal Points: Develop an understanding of fractions and fraction equivalence.

Lesson Summary: Small groups of children will be provided with graham crackers that have four crackers on each "sheet." Children will problem solve how to distribute the crackers evenly among the people in their group.

Beginning the Lesson: The teacher can begin this lesson with a discussion of fractions, writing ¼ on the board and asking the children if they know what it means. In this manner, the teacher can gauge some prior knowledge. She then tells the class that they are going to use fractions to solve some problems regarding a snack that she has brought for them. The teacher shows them the graham crackers and explains how each sheet is serrated so it can easily be broken into four smaller crackers. She may ask a student to come up and show how the cracker can be broken to make two halves. She can then write ½ + ½ = 1 on the board. She can then ask a student to come up and show how to divide the two halves into fourths. Another student can be asked to demonstrate ¾.

Procedures: Once the teacher has determined their level of understanding, she presents the class with a problem. In groups of five, children need to divide up four sheets of crackers as evenly as possible, using fractions. This would mean that each group of five receives four sheets of crackers or 16 crackers. Each child therefore gets three crackers or ¾ of a sheet of crackers.

　　While the groups are working on this problem, the teacher should rotate around the room giving guidance and asking questions to aid in the problem solving. This time can also be used to assess the level of understanding of each child. After ample time to work on the problem in small groups, the class as a whole can discuss the different ways of solving the problem. Each group presents its solution and method. The teacher should be sure to focus the children on using fractional notation and wording to emphasize that the sheets were the "wholes" and the individual crackers the "parts."

Extension: Children could be asked what to do with the leftover cracker. One cracker will likely be treated as a "remainder" as in division. However, the teacher could ask, "Is there a way to divide this cracker between five people, to make sure that all the crackers are eaten?" Dividing the actual cracker may be difficult because of its size, but children could be encouraged to draw their solutions.

Adaptations: Teachers must be careful to create groups that allow for different learning styles and levels. Children less advanced in their understanding of fractions and mathematics can still contribute to the problem-solving process by relying on their drawing or spatial skills. The group activity should contain elements that let children with different modalities excel. Allow for use of manipulatives, drawing materials, physical movement, writing, and other activities to allow all children in a group to contribute.

Materials: Graham crackers that come in sheets of four, napkins, other materials as needed by the groups to solve the problems, such as manipulatives and drawing or writing instruments.

Assessment: Assessment can be done by documenting the children's use of the problem-solving process. Running records, photos, interviews with children, and collecting artifacts are also good ways to assess the efficacy of this type of activity. Teachers may also choose to give a paper-and-pencil test of children's understanding of fractions and fraction concepts.

ASSESSING MATHEMATICS IN SECOND AND THIRD GRADE

Many of the assessment practices used from infancy through first grade work equally well with second- and third-grade children. However, a new development in second and third grade that changes the way most teachers view assessment of their students is the requirement for more standardized proficiency testing. The emphasis on ensuring "Adequate Yearly Progress" becomes of paramount concern in many teachers' minds. Teachers and administrators are required to prove that the children in their charge are progressing adequately and meeting the standards set by each state.

Because of this, in second- and third-grade formal assessments that can be recorded as numbers are emphasized over observations and portfolios. One reason is the presence of standardized proficiency testing in most states in the USA. There is a lot of pressure on teachers to ensure that their students are meeting the requirements set by the No Child Left Behind Act (NCLB). According to NCLB, schools are required to assess and document "Annual Yearly Progress," or AYP. The goal of AYP is to set clear goals and time frames, to give parents information on academic achievement, and to provide choices if their child's school continues to be identified as needing improvement. Under No Child Left Behind, the federal government is trying to ensure that every child learns by setting measurable goals and standards for every school.

- States will establish academic achievement goals by setting academic standards in core subjects and measuring progress using tests aligned to state standards.
- States will set annual progress goals for school improvement, so all students can reach proficiency and no child is left behind.
- Schools will be identified as needing improvement if they are not meeting these goals.

This federal involvement in education is rather new. The Constitution of the United States does not give the power of controlling educational issues to the federal government. It leaves that responsibility to local and state governments, in order to ensure local control of schools. However, many are concerned that this local control can lead to an uneven educational experience for children.

The United States Department of Education discusses NCLB and testing in this way:

The Challenge: For too long, America's education system has not been accountable for results and too many children have been locked in underachieving schools and left behind.

The Solution: Information is power; testing and gathering independent data are the ways to get information into the hands of parents, educators, and taxpayers.

WHY TESTING WILL WORK

Testing provides information. Until teachers and parents recognize what their students know and can do, they can't help them improve. Testing will raise expectations for all students and ensure that no child slips through the cracks.

- Under No Child Left Behind, every state must set clear and high standards for what students in each grade should know and be able to do in the core academic subjects of reading, math, and science.
- States will measure each student's progress toward those standards with tests aligned with those higher standards.
- Testing is not new to education. Good teachers and excellent schools and districts have always used tests to provide objective and up-to-date information on how their students are performing.

Testing allows teachers, parents, and principals to follow each child's progress.

- Every student should make substantial academic progress every year in every class. Good instruction will ensure that they meet this goal.
- Annual testing tells parents and teachers how much progress students have made toward meeting the academic standards.
- Annual tests show principals exactly how much progress students at each grade level have made so that principals and teachers can make good decisions about teacher training and curriculum.
- Accountability systems gather specific, objective data through tests aligned to standards and use that data to identify strengths and weaknesses in the system.

No Child Left Behind will test every child in grades three through eight and give parents report cards for every school—highlighting success and shining a light on failure.

- The law requires that all schools be held accountable for making sure that every student learns.
- Test scores will be broken out by economic background, race and ethnicity, English proficiency, and disability. That way parents and teachers will know the academic achievement of each group of students and can work to ensure that no child will be left behind.
- Testing tells parents, communities, educators, and school boards which schools are doing well. If a school takes a challenging population and achieves great results, testing will show that. If a school is allowing certain groups to fall behind year after year, testing will expose that, too. Cheryl Krehbiel, a fourth-grade teacher at Broad Acres Elementary School in Silver Spring, Md., said, "Clearly students can't learn what I don't teach them. Having the courage to learn about my own professional needs from the [testing] data is a lesson that I can't afford to miss."

From *http://www.ed.gov/nclb/accountability/ayp/edpicks.jhtml?src=ln*

This standardized testing, required beginning in third grade, does not so much test children, as it does teachers and schools. This process is not used for either of the two purposes of assessment that we have discussed. Although it can be used to adapt educational practice in the classroom, it is not really a formative assessment and, even though children can be held back if they don't meet proficiency goals, it is not really a summative test either.

These tests, for better or worse, are part of the educational landscape, for at least the foreseeable future. As teachers, we need to know their weaknesses as well as their strengths. You have already read about why the federal government feels that testing will work, but others are not so sure.

While federal involvement in testing is new, this type of achievement testing is not, and there are many educators concerned about its effects on children and schools. Kamii (1990) had this to say:

> Authors of textbooks and achievement tests think about mathematics as knowledge of mathematical symbols, rules and conventions. Test makers therefore state objectives such as knowing the names of geometric shapes, the value of coins, time as shown by a clock, and the conventional units used to measure length . . . These are all examples of social knowledge that constitutes the most superficial aspects of mathematics. . . Paper and pencil tests cannot tap young children's logico-mathematical knowledge. (Kamii, 1990)

Another negative outcome of this type of standardized testing is that it stunts the growth of innovative ideas in the classroom. There are three main reasons it has this effect. First, there are so many requirements and objectives that teachers feel they must meet during the year, in order to prepare a child for "the test," that they do not have time for interactive or innovative approaches to teaching mathematics. Second, teachers are reluctant to try approaches that do not have specific measurable outcomes on numerical tests. The requirement to document children's work becomes so strong that it leads to only one type of assessment procedure—formal testing with numerical scores. Finally, teachers are often required or feel the need to follow a didactic mathematics program. In other words, mathematics is taught using a direct-teaching model in which children memorize bits of information to reproduce on a test. The emphasis is on children being able to produce correct answers on this test, rather than on their ability to think mathematically.

The bottom line is that, in second and third grade, much of the children's best mathematical thinking cannot be assessed by simply counting right or wrong answers. While preparing children for proficiency tests and AYP is important, teachers also need to use portfolios, interactive check sheets, and direct observation of children to understand how the child is truly thinking and progressing in mathematics. Formal tests, whether standardized or in the form of paper-and-pencil "unit tests," only tell part of the story.

SUMMARY

Second- and third-grade children are entering Piaget's concrete operational stage of development. They can think logically about mathematics and other subjects. Because of this development, they are better equipped to handle more teacher-led lessons and educational activities. These teacher-led educational experiences do not need to be dry and one-sided. Children can still be actively engaged in solving mathematics problems and investigating mathematical concepts.

Physically, children of this age can produce finer and more precise writing, but sitting still for long periods of time is more fatiguing for them than physical activity. Cognitively, they can handle more complex hierarchical classifications, such as a family tree, in which there are multiple relationships. In third grade, the development of multiplicative thinking enables the child to better understand the use of multiplication as a more complex numerical organization, rather than just repeated addition.

Social-emotionally, children are becoming better at social comparisons. They are gauging their abilities by comparing themselves to others. Erik Erikson showed that these children are in the **industry versus inferiority** stage. This means that if a child is supported and feels successful in his explorations, he will develop a sense of industry. Academic performance becomes a large part of how children gauge their industry. If they are ridiculed or made to feel "inferior," they can develop negative attitudes to mathematics or other academic subjects.

Supporting critical thinking about mathematics should be one of the main goals of instruction in these grades. This is a lifelong learning strategy that will benefit the child as much as learning specific concepts. Fluency in addition and multiplication is also an important goal. Most state standards documents and the NCTM Curriculum Focal Points all support the importance of fluency. This does not simply mean memorization. These skills should be taught in a way that requires the use of a numerical network so that children do not disassociate the answers from the concepts, no matter how quickly they learn to produce answers. Math games are a good way to develop fluency and automaticity.

Place value and base-10 systems are another important concept that children in this stage learn. It is important that this not be taught as an isolated concept. Place value and base-10 should be taught as an integrated part of number and by teaching addition with regrouping without the standard algorithm. Teaching the addition algorithm before children understand the basic concepts of double-column addition with regrouping, "unteaches" place value (Kamii, 2003). In third grade, fractions begin to show up in the state standards documents. Using hands-on, representational materials can help children to visualize and understand fractions. Finally, NCTM's Curriculum Focal Points designate linear measurement as an important concept for second graders.

There are many interactive ways that teachers can introduce these topics to children. They need to be sure to make lessons explorative and interactive even when developing fluency and automacity. Technology tools such as the computer programming language called Logo can be helpful in teaching many of the mathe-matical and geometric concepts required in second and third grade. Worksheets and homework are a big part of education in these grades. While these are helpful tools, there are creative ways the teacher can modify a worksheet or homework activity to make it more engaging and interactive.

WEB SITES

The Math Forum: Problems of the Week
http://www.mathforum.org/pow/

Puzzles and problems from the Math Forum at Drexel University. It poses weekly prob-lems and contains other resources for teaching math in the classroom.

Visual Fractions
http://www.visualfractions.com/

A site dedicated to helping children visualize fractions and the operations on them such as addition, multiplication, and division.

Brain Boosters
http://school.discovery.com/brainboosters/index.html

This site from the Discovery Channel contains a number of "brain boosters" puzzles and problem-solving activities.

Cosmeo
http://www.cosmeo.com/welcome/math.html

Cosmeo is the Discovery Channel's online homework help site. Children can logon to ac-cess help with their homework as well as math puzzles.

Guide to Math Night
http://orion.math.iastate.edu/mathnight/guide/

Information on how to start and conduct family math nights at your school.

AIMS Puzzles
http://www.aimsedu.org/Puzzle/index.html

Puzzles from AIMS (Activities Integrating Math and Science). The AIMS Puzzle Corner provides over 100 interesting math puzzles that can help students learn to enjoy puzzles and the mathematics behind them.

Set Daily Puzzle
http://www.setgame.com/set/puzzle_frame.htm

This site offers puzzles related to the card game Set, which can be purchased in most toy stores.

DISCUSS AND APPLY WHAT YOU HAVE LEARNED

Reflect

1. What makes the second and third grades better suited to teacher-led instruction? Discuss development in the physical, cognitive, and social-emotional domains as well as educational changes.

2. Why are the requirements for environments in second and third grade different from kindergarten and first grade?

3. Why do we need to worry about second- and third-graders' social-emotional development when learning mathematics?

Discuss

1. What are some ways to support industry in second and third graders using mathematics? What are some negative practices that may lead to inferiority?

2. How is additive thinking different from multiplicative thinking? Why is this important to know?

3. Discuss how to promote fluency in multiplication and double- and triple-column addition in a way that is engaging and interactive for second and third graders.

Apply

1. Develop a math lesson for your class and present it to them. Try to use questioning techniques instead of affirming right answers. Was it difficult not to tell someone they were right or wrong?

2. Teach a math lesson to a group of second- and third-grade children. Keep the lesson open-ended and focus on multiplication. What were the children's responses to your math lesson?

Observe

1. Observe second- and third-grade classes. What are the teachers doing to support mathematics? How are the classrooms alike? How are they different from K–1?

2. Observe second- and third-grade classes. How is mathematics introduced to children in each grade? Compare the two classrooms. How do the children respond to mathematics?

REFERENCES

Alexander, R. B., & Robinson, T. (2001). *Fraction jugglers: A math gamebook for kids + their parents*. New York: Workman Pub.

Baker, D., & LeTendre, G. K. (2005). *National differences, global similarities: World culture and the future of schooling*. Stanford, CA: Stanford Social Sciences.

Ball, D. (2004). Micromath—The early years. *Micro Math, 20*(1), 31–34.

Battista, M. T., Clements, D. H., Arnoff, J., Battista, K., & Van Auken Borrow, C. (1998). Students' spatial structuring of 2D arrays of squares. *Journal for Research in Mathematics Education, 29*(5), 503.

Beglau, M. M. (2005). Can technology narrow the black-white achievement gap? *T H E Journal, 32*(12), 13–17.

Biddlecomb, B. D. (2002). Numerical knowledge as enabling and constraining fraction knowledge: An example of the reorganization hypothesis. *Journal of Mathematical Behavior, 21*(2), 167.

Birsh, J. R., Potts, M., Potts, R., & Vineyard Video Productions. (1997). *LD—LA, learning disabilities, learning abilities*. West Tisbury, MA: Vineyard Video Productions.

Borko, H., & Davinroy, K. H. (2000). Exploring and supporting teacher change: Two third-grade teachers' experiences in mathematics. *Elementary School Journal, 100*(4), 273.

Burns, M. (1995). Timed tests. *Teaching Children Mathematics, 1*(7), 408.

Burns, M., Burns, M., & Math, S. P. (2003). The Marilyn Burns fraction kit grades 4–6. *EAI Education, http://www.eaieducation.com/530900.html*

Burns, M., & Cuisenaire Company of America. (1987). *Mathematics with manipulatives*. New Rochelle, NY: Cuisenaire Co. of America.

Buschman, L. E. (2005). Isn't that interesting! *Teaching Children Mathematics, 12*(1), 34–40.

Cahnmann, M. S., & Remillard, J. T. (2002). What counts and how: Mathematics teaching in culturally, linguistically, and socioeconomically diverse urban settings. *Urban Review, 34*(3), 179.

Cates, G. L., & Rhymer, K. N. (2003). Examining the relationship between mathematics anxiety and mathematics performance: An instructional hierarchy perspective. *Journal of Behavioral Education, 12*(1), 23–34.

Chinn, S., McDonagh, D., Elswijk, R. V., Harmsen, H., Kay, J., McPhillips, T., et al. (2001). Classroom studies into cognitive style in mathematics for pupils with dyslexia in special education in the Netherlands, Ireland and the UK. *British Journal of Special Education, 28*(2), 80.

Chung, I. (2004). A comparative assessment of constructivist and traditionalist approaches to establishing mathematical connections in learning multiplication. *Education, 125*(2), 271–278.

Clark, F. B., & Kamii, C. (1996). Identification of multiplicative thinking in children in grades 1–5. *Journal for Research in Mathematics Education, 27*(1), 41.

Clements, D. H., & Sarama, J. (Eds.). (2004). *Engaging young children in mathematics: Standards for early childhood mathematics education*. Mahwah, N.J: Lawrence Erlbaum Associates.

Clements, D., & Stephan, M. (2004). Measurement in pre-k to grade 2 mathematics. In D. Clements & J. Sarama (Eds.), *Engaging young children in mathematics*. Mahwah, NJ: Lawrence Erlbaum Associates.

Creative Wonders (1997). *3rd & 4th grade essentials*. Redwood City, CA: Creative Wonders.

Curtis, D., & Carter, M. (2003). *Designs for living and learning: Transforming early childhood environments*. St. Paul, MN: Redleaf Press.

D'Arcangelo, M. (2001). Wired for mathematics: A conversation with Brian Butterworth. *Educational Leadership, 59*(3), 14.

Davis, E. J. (2006). A model for understanding: Understanding in mathematics. *Mathematics Teaching in the Middle School, 12*(4), 190–197.

Dolk, M. L. A. M. (2004). *Young mathematicians at work [electronic resource]: Constructing number sense, addition, and subtraction: Taking inventory grades, K–1: The role of context / Maarten Dolk and Catherine Twomey Fosnot [facilitator's guide and overview manual by Antonia Cameron, Sherrin B. Hersch, Catherine Twomey Fosnot]*. Portsmouth, NH: Heinemann.

Drier, H. S. (2000). Investigating mathematics as a community of learners. *Teaching Children Mathematics, 6*(6), 358.

Eckert, T. L., Dunn, E. K., Codding, R. S., Begeny, J. C., & Kleinmann, A. E. (2006). Assessment of mathematics and reading performance: An examination of the correspondence between direct assessment of student performance and teacher report. *Psychology in the Schools, 43*(3), 247–265.

Elkind, D., & Piaget, J. (1979). *Child development and education a piagetian perspective.* New York: Oxford University Press.

Erikson, E. H. (1963). *Youth: Change and challenge.* New York: Basic Books.

Erikson, E. H. (1977). *Toys and reasons: Stages in the ritualization of experience.* New York: Norton.

Erikson, E. H. (1993). *Childhood and society.* New York: Norton.

Eunsook, H., & Davis, G. (2005). Kindergartners' conversations in a computer-based technology classroom. *Communication Education, 54*(2), 118–135.

Evans, R. I. (1967). *Dialogue with Erik Erikson.* New York: Harper & Row.

Fischbein, E., Deri, M., Nello, M. S., & Marino, M. S. (1985). The role of implicit models in solving verbal problems in multiplication and division. *Journal for Research in Mathematics Education, 16*(1), 3–17.

Forman, E., & Ansell, E. (2001). The multiple voices of a mathematics classroom community. *Educational Studies in Mathematics, 46*(1–3), 115–142.

Fortescue-Hubbard, W. (2006). Getting numbers the write way round. *Times Educational Supplement,* (4684), 31–31.

Fuchs, L. S., Fuchs, D., Compton, D. L., Powell, S. R., Seethaler, P. M., Capizzi, A. M., et al. (2006). The cognitive correlates of third-grade skill in arithmetic, algorithmic computation, and arithmetic word problems. *Journal of Educational Psychology, 98*(1), 29–43.

Fuchs, L. S., Fuchs, D., Finelli, R., Courey, S. J., Hamlett, C. L., Sones, E. M., et al. (2006). Teaching third graders about real-life mathematical problem solving: A randomized controlled study. *Elementary School Journal, 106*(4), 293–311.

Fuchs, L. S., Fuchs, D., Prentice, K., Harnlett, C. L., Finelli, R., & Courey, S. J. (2004). Enhancing mathematical problem solving among third-grade students with schema-based instruction. *Journal of Educational Psychology, 96*(4), 635–647.

George, R. (2005). Dyslexia, dyspraxia and mathematics. *Child & Adolescent Mental Health, 10*(1), 48–48.

Gibson, K. (2004). Math doesn't always have to be taught as math! *Technology & Children, 9*(1), 16–17.

Ginsburg, H. (1981). *Social class and racial influences on early mathematical thinking.* Herbert P. Ginsburg, Robert L. Russell. Chicago, IL: Society for Research in Child Development.

Goodnow, J. (1994a). *Math discoveries with attribute blocks* [illustrations by Frank Cirocco]. Oak Lawn, IL: Ideal School Supply Co.

Goodnow, J. (1994b). *Math discoveries with base-ten blocks.* Oak Lawn, IL: Ideal School Supply Co.

Goodnow, J. (1994c). *Math discoveries with tangrams.* Oak Lawn, IL: Ideal School Supply Co.

Gould, F. (2003). Testing third-graders in New Hampshire. *Phi Delta Kappan, 84*(7), 507.

Gurian, M., Henley, P., & Trueman, T. (2002). *Boys and girls learn differently: A guide for teachers and parents.* San Francisco, CA: Jossey-Bass.

Gurian, M., & Stevens, K. (2005). *The minds of boys: Saving our sons from falling behind in school and life.* San Francisco, CA: Jossey-Bass.

Hartweg, K. (2005). Solutions to the catching growing night crawlers problem. *Teaching Children Mathematics, 11*(7), 362–367.

Helland, T., & Asbjornsen, A. (2004). Digit span in dyslexia: Variations according to language comprehension and mathematics skills. *Journal of Clinical & Experimental Neuropsychology, 26*(1), 31–42.

Helwig, R., Anderson, L., & Tindal, G. (2001). Influence of elementary student gender on teachers' perceptions of mathematics achievement. *Journal of Educational Research, 95*(2), 93.

Heuwinkel, M. K. (1996). New ways of learning = new ways of teaching. *Childhood Education, 73*(1), 27.

Hutchison, L., Ellsworth, J., & Yovich, S. (2000). Third-grade students investigate and represent data. *Early Childhood Education Journal, 27*(4), 213.

Kamii, C., & Anderson, C. (2003). Multiplication games: How we made and used them. *Teaching Children Mathematics, 10*(3), 135–141.

Kamii, C., Joseph, L. L., & Livingston, S. J. (2003). *Young children continue to reinvent arithmetic—2nd grade implications of Piaget's theory.* New York: Teachers College Press.

Kamii, C., Knight, M., & Teachers College Press (1990). Multiplication of 2 digit numbers: Two teachers using Piaget's theory. New York: Teachers College Press.

Kamii, C., & Lewis, B. A. (1993a). Primary arithmetic: Children inventing their own procedures. *Arithmetic Teacher, 41*(4), 200.

Kamii, C., & Lewis, B. A. (1993b). The harmful effects of algorithms . . . in primary arithmetic. *Teaching PreK–8, 23*(4), 36.

Kamii, C., & Lewis, B. A. (2003). Single-digit subtraction with fluency. *Teaching Children Mathematics, 10*(4), 230.

Kamii, C., & Livingston, S. J. (1994). *Young children continue to reinvent arithmetic—3rd grade implications of Piaget's theory.* New York: Teachers College Press.

Labinowicz, E. (1985). *Learning from children: New beginnings for teaching numerical thinking.* Menlo Park, NJ: Addison-Wesley.

Lent, P., Wall, E., & Fosnot, C. T. (2006). Young mathematicians at work: Constructing algebra in grade two. *Connect Magazine, 19*(3), 4–7.

Malmer, G. (2000). Mathematics and dyslexia, an overlooked connection. *Dyslexia (10769242), 6*(4), 223–230.

Martinez, J., & Martinez, N. (2007). *Activities for mathematical thinking: Exploring, inventing, and discovering mathematics.* Upper Saddle River, NJ: Prentice Hall.

May, L. (1997). Developing logical reasoning. *Teaching PreK–8, 28*(2), 22.

Mazzocco, M. M. M., & Myers, G. F. (2003). Complexities in identifying and defining mathematics learning disability in the primary school-age years. *Annals of Dyslexia, 53,* 218–253.

McClure, A. (2006). Enhanced math. *District Administration, 42*(9), 76.

Milbourne, L. A., Haury, D. L., & ERIC Clearinghouse for Science, Mathematics and Environmental Education, (1999). *Helping students with homework in science and math.* Columbus, OH: ERIC Clearinghouse for Science, Mathematics and Environmental Education.

Miles, T. R., Wheeler, T. J., & Haslum, M. N. (2003). The existence of dyslexia without severe literacy problems. *Annals of Dyslexia, 53,* 340–354.

Monuteaux, M. C., Fraone, S. V., Herzig, K., Navsaria, N., & Biederman, J. (2005). ADHD and dyscalculia: Evidence for independent familial transmission. *Journal of Learning Disabilities, 38*(1), 86–93.

National Council for Teachers of Mathematics. (2006). *Curriculum focal points for prekindergarten through grade 8 mathematics: A quest for coherence.* Reston Va.: NCTM.

Olkun, S. (2003). Comparing computer versus concrete manipulatives in learning 2D geometry. *The Journal of Computers in Mathematics and Science Teaching, 22*(1), 43.

Orme, M. P., & Monroe, E. E. (2005). The nature of discourse as students collaborate on a mathematics WebQuest. *Computers in the Schools, 22*(1/2), 135–146.

Papert, S. (1993). *Mindstorms: Children, computers, and powerful ideas* (2nd ed.). New York: Basic Books.

Papert, S. (1997). Educational computing: How are we doing? *T.H.E. Journal, 24*(11), 78.

Piaget, J. (1952). *The child's conception of number*. London: Routledge & Paul.

Piaget, J. (1953). *The origin of intelligence in the child*. London: Routledge & Paul.

Pollack, W. S. (1999). *Real boys: Rescuing our sons from the myths of boyhood*. New York: Henry Holt & Company.

Raymond, A. (1992). Linda Joseph embraces "constructivist math" (cover story). *Teaching PreK–8, 22*(4), 34.

Research and Education Association. (1999). *The ESSENTIALS: Math made nice-n-easy*. Piscataway, NJ: Author.

Rosselli, M., Matute, E., Pinto, N., & Ardila, A. (2006). Memory abilities in children with subtypes of dyscalculia. *Developmental Neuropsychology, 30*(3), 801–818.

Ruth, S. S., Orly, M., & Varda, G.-T. (2005). Developmental dyscalculia: A prospective six-year follow-up. *Developmental Medicine & Child Neurology, 47*(2), 121–125.

Samples, J. (2004). *Taking the guesswork out of school success: A standards approach*. Lanham, MD: Scarecrow Education.

Santrock, J. W. (2005). *Children* (8th ed.). Boston: McGraw-Hill.

Sarama, J., & Clements, D. H. (2005). *Encouraging mathematical thinking: How to help children explore and expand math skills*. Early Childhood Today, 20(2), 11.

Schumm, J. S. (2005). *How to help your child with homework: The complete guide to encouraging good study habits and ending the homework wars*. Minneapolis, MN: Free Spirit Pub.

Seo, K.-H., & Ginsburg, H. (2004). What is developmentally appropriate in early childhood mathematics education? Lessons from new research. In D. Clements & J. Sarama (Eds.), *Engaging Young Children in Mathematics*. Mahwah, NJ: Lawrence Erlbaum Associates.

Siaw, L., & Winbourne, P. (2005). Logo—Still the potential for imagination. *Micro Math, 21*(1), 17–21.

Sinclair, H. & Kamii, C. (Directors). (1994). *Piaget and Vygotsky on collaboration, argumentation, and coherent reasoning*. [Video/DVD] Birmingham, AL: University of Alabama at Birmingham.

Sinclair, N., & Crespo, S. (2006). Learning mathematics in dynamic computer environments. *Teaching Children Mathematics, 12*(9), 437–444.

Smith, L. B., Thelen, E., & NetLibrary Inc. (1993). *A dynamic systems approach to development*, from *http://www.netlibrary.com/urlapi.asp?action=summary&v=1&bookid=1772* An electronic book accessible through the Internet.

Sutherland, R. (1993). Connecting theory and practice: Results from the teaching of Logo. *Educational Studies in Mathematics, 24*(1), 95.

Taverner, S. (2006). Dyscalculia action plans for successful learning in mathematics. *British Journal of Special Education, 33*(2), 102–103.

Vaidya, S. R. (2004). Understanding dyscalculia for teaching. *Education, 124*(4), 717–720.

Wood, T. (1999). Creating a context for argument in mathematics class. *Journal for Research in Mathematics Education, 30*(2), 171.

Young-Loveridge, J. (2005). Fostering multiplicative thinking using array-based materials. *Australian Mathematics Teacher, 61*(3), 34–40.

CHAPTER 9

Integrating Mathematics

CHAPTER OBJECTIVES

When you have read this chapter, you should be able to:
- Discuss the importance of teaching mathematics as an integrated subject rather than as isolated skills
- Explain the three phases in project-based education
- Describe the benefit that using projects in the classroom has on learning mathematics
- Explain how mathematics can be integrated into reading, science, social studies, music, art, and physical activity
- Be familiar with a number of books and other resources to integrate mathematics into the everyday activity of the classroom and other subject areas

Integrating the curriculum is often used as a buzzword in curriculum guides and other curriculum resources. It is used so much that it has become a cliché. However, integration of the curriculum is vitally important for teaching mathematics in the way that we have discussed in this book. In real life, mathematics is not used in isolation, but in the context of solving real-life problems, such as dealing with personal finance issues, figuring a tip at a restaurant, or cooking a family dinner.

Even with the repeated use of the term *integration* in curriculum guides, the reality is that mathematics and other subjects are still taught mostly as separate subjects. Teachers are required to document that a certain amount of time is spent on a specific subject each day. The simplest way to accomplish this is to set aside time during the day to do each one separately.

While this can help to establish a routine, teachers still need to find ways to integrate other subjects into the lessons. It is also valuable to have time during the day where children can work on a project that demonstrates the integrated knowledge that they have learned and to explore new knowledge using subjects, such as math, as a tool.

THE IMPORTANCE OF INTEGRATION

The traditional method of learning subjects in isolation does not reflect how mathematics is used in real-life situations. Finding time during lessons or the school day to show how subjects overlap and support each other is vital to developing students that learn how to apply knowledge, not just repeat information by rote.

For example, a child can learn a collection of names and dates such as Christopher Columbus, the Nina, the Pinta, and the Santa Maria, and 1492. However, without mathematics, he can't understand how much time it actually took to sail across the Atlantic in 1492, how fast the ship sailed, how big the ship was, how much food was needed to feed the crew, or any of the other problems that had to be dealt with on such a treacherous and momentous voyage.

Lillian Katz (Katz & Chard, 2000) in *Engaging Children's Minds: The Project Approach*, calls this difference **vertical** and **horizontal relevance**. **Vertical relevance** refers to instruction that prepares children for the next level of instruction, such as the next level of a worksheet. This instruction is usually unrelated to real-life experience and is only important in how well it prepares students for the next lesson. There is little emphasis on integration or real-life application. **Horizontal relevance** refers to learning that equips the child to solve problems both in and out of the classroom. This is what integration can help to achieve.

In order to achieve this horizontal relevance, there are a number of things that we can do in the classroom to integrate curricular areas. The first and easiest thing a teacher can do is to find and point out the math in the other subjects they teach. For example, when reading a book during circle time, a teacher might ask, "How many yellow ducks do you see on this page?" For older children, she may emphasize the mathematical computation needed when doing a science investigation. Let's examine the main subject areas and explore a few ways in which mathematics can be integrated into each.

Integrating Math with Reading

According to Whitin and Wilde (1992), children begin to see mathematics as a "common human activity" through books. It breaks down the artificial dichotomy between *learning* mathematics and *living* mathematics. Through books and literature, children learn to communicate mathematically. They see mathematics as a natural way to communicate in everyday conversation.

There are many ways in which children's literature can be used in the classroom (Loveless & Ebrary, 2001). Teachers are limited only by their imaginations. Figure 9.1 contains a list of available books that directly link math and reading. Check with your school district to see if curriculum specialists have compiled a similar list. If not, you may try making one yourself. Each year, update it with new books that are released.

Let's take two of these books and see how they can be used in the classroom to integrate mathematics into reading instruction or group reading time. *One Hundred Hungry Ants* by Elinor J. Pinczes has always been one of my favorite mathematics books for younger children. Although it deals with multiplication and division principles, it is appropriate for children as young as preschool and kindergarten. In the book, a line of 100 hungry ants is trying to get to a picnic as soon as possible. The smallest ant (and the smartest, it seems) suggests to the leaders that in order to get there faster, they should arrange the lines into different configurations. First, he suggests two lines of 50, then four lines of 25, then five lines of 20.

> "Stop!" screamed the littlest ant.
> "We're moving way too slow.
> Lots of food will long be gone
> Unless we hurry up. So. . .
> With 5 lines of 20,
> We'd get there soon I know."*

The teacher can ask the children to write about their favorite part of the book or which configuration they thought was best. When the children form their own lines, they can be asked how many people would be in each one if they decided to form two. Would the number be equal in each line?

Another important aspect of this book, and one that is common in many others written for young children, is that it is a "predictable" book. A predictable book has elements that help the child to predict what words are coming next. Predictable books make use of rhyme, repetition of words, phrases, sentences, and patterns to help children guess what words, phrases, sentences, events, and characters could come next in the story.

Many of the elements that make a book predictable are mathematically based—patterns, sequence, and structure. For example, as you read the excerpt from *100 Hungry Ants*, you will see a rhythmic pattern. If you clap the rhythm while reading it, it becomes

---

*Excerpt from ONE HUNDRED HUNGRY ANTS by Elinor J. Pinczes. Text copyright (c) 1993 by Bonnie MacKain. Reprinted by permission of Houghton Mifflin Company. All rights reserved.

Addition

Anno, Mitsumasa. (1982). *Anno's Counting Book*. New York: Philomel.
Carle, Eric. (1979). *The Very Hungry Caterpillar*. New York: Collins.
Giganti, Paul. (1992). *Each Orange Had Eight Slices*. New York: Greenwillow.
Hong, Lily Toy. (1993). *Two of Everything*. Morton Grove, IL: A. Whitman.
Merriam, Eve. (1993). *12 Ways to Get to 11*. New York: Simon and Schuster.

Counting

Aardema, Vera. (1981). *Bringing the Rain to Kapiti Plain*. New York: Dial.
Aker, Suzanne. (1990). *What Comes in 2's, 3's, and 4's?* New York: Simon and Schuster.
Anno, Mitsumasa. (1982). *Anno's Counting Book*. New York: Philomel.
Aylesworth, Jim. (1988). *One Crow: A Counting Rhyme*. Philadelphia: HarperCollins.
Bang, Molly. (1983). *Ten, Nine, Eight*. New York: Greenwillow.
Bertrand, Lynne. (1992). *One Day, Two Dragons*. New York: C.N. Potter.
Boon, Emilie. (1987). *1, 2, 3, How Many Animals Can You See?* New York: Greenwillow.
Burningham, John. (1980). *The Shopping Basket*. New York: Crowell.
Carle, Eric. (1984). *The Very Busy Spider*. New York: Philomel.
Clifton, Lucille. (1992). *Everett Anderson's 1-2-3*. New York: Holt.
Crews, Donald. (1986). *Ten Black Dots*. New York: Greenwillow.
Dee, Ruby. (1988). *Two Ways to Count to Ten*. New York: Holt.
De Regniers, Beatrice Schenk. (1985). *So Many Cats!* New York: Clarion.
Dunbar, Joyce. (1990). *Ten Little Mice*. San Diego, CA: Harcourt, Brace, Jovanovich.
Fleming, Denise. (1992). *Count*. New York: Holt.
Fowler, Richard. (1987). *Mr. Little's Noisy 1 2 3*. New York: Grosset and Dunlap.
Hague, Kathleen. (1986). *Numbers*. New York: Holt.
Hoban, Tana. (1972). *Count & See*. New York: Mackillan.
Hoban, Tana. (1985). *1, 2, 3*. New York: Greenwillow.
Hutchins, Pat. (1982). *1 Hunter*. New York: Greenwillow.
Inkpen, Mick. (1987). *One Bear at Bedtime*. New York: Dial.
Kitchen, Bert. (1987). *Animal Numbers*. New York: Dial.
Mack, Stan. (1974). *10 Bears in My Bed*. New York: Pantheon.
Nikola, Lisa. (1991). *One, Two, Three Thanksgiving*. Morton Grove, IL: A. Whitman.
Peek, Merle. (1981). *Roll Over*. New York: Clarion.
Potter, Beatrix. (1988). *Peter Rabbit's 1 2 3*. New York: Warne.
Sendak, Maurice. (1962). *One Was Johnny*. New York: Harper and Row.
Sheppard, Jeff. (1990). *The Right Number of Elephants*. New York: Harper and Row.
Stobbs, William. (1984). *1, 2 Buckle My Shoe*. Oxford, UK: Oxford University Press.
Tafuri, Nancy. (1986). *Who's Counting?* New York: GreenWillow.
Wadsworth, Olive. (1985). *Over in the Meadow: A Counting Out Rhyme*. New York: Viking.
Wahl, John, & Wahl, Stacy. (1976). *I Can Count the Petals on a Flower*. Reston, VA: National Council of Teachers of Mathematics.

Estimating

Clement, Rod. (1991). *Counting on Frank*. Milwaukee, WI: G. Stevens Books.
Giff, Patricia Reilly. (1984). *The Candy Corn Contest*. New York: Dell.
Podendorf, Illa. (1970). *Many Is How Many?* Chicago: Children's Press.
Polacco, Patricia. (1990). *Thunder Cake*. New York: Philomel.

Figure 9.1   Children's Literature That Supports Mathematics.

Sheppard, Jeff. (1990). *The Right Number of Elephants*. New York: Harper and Row.
Williams, Karen. (1990). *Galimoto*. New York: Lothrop, Lee, & Shepard.
Williams, Vera. (1982). *A Chair for My Mother*. New York: Greenwillow.

Fractions

Dragonwagon, Crescent. (1986). *Half a Moon and One Whole Star*. New York: Macmillan.
Emberly, Ed. (1984). *Picture Pie*. Boston: Little, Brown.
Giganti, Paul. (1988). *How Many Snails*. New York: Greenwillow.
Golub, Matthew. (1993). *The Twenty-Five Mixtec Cats*. New York: Tambourine.
Hutchins, Pat. (1986). *The Doorbell Rang*. New York: Greenwillow.
Matthews, Louise. (1979). *Gator Pie*. New York: Dodd, Mead.
McMillan, Bruce. (1991). *Eating Fractions*. New York: Scholastic.
Pomerantz, Charlotte. (1984). *The Half Birthday Party*. New York: Clarion.
Watson, Clyde. (1972). *Tom Fox and the Apple Pie*. New York: Crowell.

Geometry

Alder, David. (1975). *3D 2D 1D*. New York: Crowell.
Emberly, Ed. (1961). *The Wing on a Flea*. Boston: Little Brown.
Goble, Paul. (1983). *Star Boy*. New York: Bradbury.
Hoban, Tana. (1971). *Look Again*. New York: Macmillan.
Hoban, Tana. (1981). *Take Another Look*. New York: Greenwillow.
Hoban, Tana. (1986). *Shapes, Shapes, Shapes*. New York: Greenwillow.
Hoban, Tana. (1988). *Look, Look, Look*. New York: Greenwillow.
Jonas, Ann. (1984). *The Quilt*. New York: Greenwillow.
McMillan, Bruce. (1993). *Mouse Views What the Class Pet Saw*. New York: Holiday House.
Podendorf, Illa. (1970). *Shapes, Sides, Curves, and Corners*. Chicago: Children's Press.
Testa, Fulvio. (1983). *If You Look Around You*. New York: Dial.
Tonpert, Ann. (1990). *Grandfather Tang's Story*. New York: Crown.

Graphing

Anno, Mitsumasa. (1982). *Anno's Counting Book*. New York: Philomel.
Kasza, Keiko. (1987). *The Wolf's Chicken Stew*. New York: Putnam.

Measurement

Briggs, Raymond. (1970). *Jim and the Beanstalk*. New York: Coward-McCann.
Carrick, Carol. (1983). *Patrick's Dinosaurs*. New York: Clarion.
Kellogg, Steve. (1976). *Much Bigger Than Martin*. New York: Dial.
Lionni, Leo. (1960). *Inch by Inch*. New York: Aston-Honor.
Low, Joseph. (1980). *Mice Twice*. New York: Atheneum.
Morimoto, Junko. (1988). *The Inch Boy*. New York: Puffin.
Myller, Rolf. (1991). *How Big Is a Foot?* New York: Dell.
Porte, Barbara Ann. (1993). *Leave That Cricket Be, Alan Lee*. New York: Greenwillow.
Russo, Marisabina. (1986). *The Line Up Book*. New York: Greenwillow.

Figure 9.1 Children's Literature That Supports Mathematics (*continued*).

Money

Adams, Barbara. (1992). *The Go-Around Dollar*. New York: Four Winds Press.
Axelrod, Amy. (1994). *Pigs Will Be Pigs*. New York: Four Winds Press.
Brown, Mare. (1990). *Arthur's Pet Business*. Boston: Joy Street.
Hoban, Lillian. (1981). *Arthur's Funny Money*. New York: Harper & Row.
Hoban, Tana. (1987). *26 Letters and 99 Cents*. New York: Greenwillow.
Maestro, Betsy. (1988). *Dollars and Cents for Harriet*. New York: Crown.
Modell, Frank. (1981). *One Zillion Valentines*. New York: Greenwillow.
Schwartz, David. (1985). *How Much Is a Million?* New York: Lothrop, Lee, & Shepard.
Schwartz, David. (1989). *If You Made a Million*. New York: Lothrop, Lee, & Shepard.
Viorst, Judith. (1978). *Alexander, Who Used to Be Rich Last Sunday*. New York: Atheneum.

Multiplication and Division

Anno, Masichiro. (183). *Anno's Mysterious Multiplying Jar*. New York: Philomel.
Froman, Robert. (1978). *The Greatest Guessing Game*. New York: Crowell.
Giganti, Paul. (1992). *Each Orange Had Eight Slices*. New York: Greenwillow.
Hoban, Tana. (1972). *Count and See*. New York: Macmillan.
Hulme, Joy. (1991). *Sea Squares*. New York: Hyperion.
Hutchins, Pat. (1986). *The Doorbell Rang*. New York: Greenwillow.
Matthews, Louise. (1978). *Bunches and Bunches of Bunnies*. New York: Dodd, Mead.
Pinczes, Elinor. (1993). *One Hundred Hungry Ants*. Boston: Houghton Mifflin.
Pittman, Helena Clare. (1986). *A Grain of Rice*. New York: Hastings.
Srivastavia, Jane Jonas. (1979). *Number Families*. New York: Crowell.

Number Sense

Anno, Mitsumasa. (1982). *Anno's Counting Book*. New York: Philomel.
Crews, Donald. (1986). *Ten Black Dots*. New York: Greenwillow.
Giganti, Paul. (1988). *How Many Snails?* New York: Greenwillow.
Hoban, Tana. (1981). *More Than One*. New York: Greenwillow.
Hort, Lenny, (1991). *How Many Stars in the Sky?* New York: Tambourine.
Kuskin, Karla. (1986). *The Philharmonic Gets Dressed*. New York: Harper & Row.
Medearis, Angela Shelf. (1990). *Picking Peas for a Day*. Austin, TX: State House Press.
Nesbit, E. (1989). *Melisande*. San Diego: Harcourt, Brace, Jovanovich.
O'Keefe, Susan. (1989). *One Hungry Monster*. Boston: Joy Street Books.
Pinczes, Elinor. (1993). *One Hundred Hungry Ants*. Boston: Houghton Mifflin.
Pittman, Helena Clare. (1986). *A Grain of Rice*. New York: Hastings.
Schwartz, David. (1985). *How Much Is a Million?* New York: Lothrop, Lee, & Shepard.
Shepard, Jeff. (1990). *The Right Number of Elephants*. New York: Harper & Row.

Figure 9.1   Children's Literature That Supports Mathematics (*continued*).
Source: Reprinted by permission of the Ohio Literacy Resource Center, *http://literacy.kent.edu/Oasis/Resc/Educ/ mathkidslit.html*

much clearer (Schumm, 1999). Children recognize patterns like this in books and music and learn to anticipate them. We will discuss music and math later in the chapter.

Another of my favorite mathematics-based children's book is the irreverent tale of a child who spends the day seeing math everywhere. *Math Curse,* by Jon Scieszka and Lane Smith includes page after page of mathematics problems and questions. For example, a teacher could read portions of the

Literacy and math are a natural combination.

David Mager/Pearson Learning Photo Studio

book on Monday and each day after that for about 2 weeks. She could take one page of the book and discuss the mathematics problem or concept on that page. Children can be encouraged to write their own thoughts or solutions each day. After the teacher has gone through the entire book, children could be assigned to write their own math curse problem, then collect them all together to make their own book that can be read to the class and worked on during the day.

Whitin and Wilde (1992) and McDonald (2007) developed some suggestions for selecting and using books in your classroom.

- Enjoy the story. As you read aloud, don't destroy the magic of a story by interrupting it with mathematical questions. Allow the book to speak and the children to interact with the story. Later, there will be time to discuss the mathematics in the book.
- Read the book aloud more than once. There is a lot to absorb in a story and it often takes more than one reading to make the mathematical connections.
- Keep the book experiences open-ended to encourage multiple interpretations. Ask questions such as "What did you like about the story?" or "What math did you see in the story?"
- Select books that have quantities more than 10 for children to count.
- Select books that give children the opportunity to use their developing ability to conserve number.

- Encourage children to respond mathematically to these stories through poetry, drama, art, written narrative, or oral discourse. Each form of expression affords the learner a way to view mathematics from a different perspective.
- Integrate these books into current topics of study in the classroom (both in your mathematics curriculum and in other areas). Learners make more connections, ask deeper questions, and add more detail to their writing when teachers use books in a context that is familiar or that arises from the students' own concerns.
- Select books that allow children to explore number quantity in other cultures and languages.
- Provide books that include skip counting experiences.
- Use the illustrations in the book to help children use counting-on strategies, place value, and compare "more," "less," and other non-numerical mathematical concepts.
- Use your students as a guide for deciding what to read. You know best the level your students are on and what their interests are and how to link those to mathematics.
- Consider the ages of your students and your intended use of a book to decide whether oral reading to the class or silent individual reading would work best for introducing mathematics through literature.

Reading and children's literature allows mathematics to be integrated into other subject areas. Whitin and Wild (1992) use the example of the classic children's book *The Carrot Seed* (1945) to show how math can be integrated with science. In their example, children read the book with their teacher and then began to think about how the carrot might grow. They also discussed reasons why it might not grow. They planned experiments to see which seeds would grow the best, then wrote stories about their experiences that included math and science. One little girl wrote, "8 seeds in all, 4 rotting in the dark. But, the girl was happy because the plants were living." (Whitin & Wilde, 1992, p. 12).

When integrating the curriculum, books are a great place to start. Reading is a prerequisite for almost all other content areas (Smith, & Wills, 1994). As we saw with *The Carrot Seed*, integrating math with science using reading is a snap. Many books contain topics for scientific investigation, from the ants in *One Hundred Hungry Ants* to *Cloudy with a Chance of Meatballs*. Using a project approach, which we will talk about later in this chapter, makes these investigations rich and rewarding and integrates all of these content areas.

Social studies requires reading books that can be integrated with mathematics. The National Council of Social Studies publishes a yearly list of notable trade books for young children on their web site (*http://www.socialstudies.org/resources/notable/*). One of the books from the 2005 list is *Gargoyles, Girders & Glass Houses: Magnificent Master Builders* written by Bo Zaunders and Illustrated by Roxie Munro. It concerns the building of domes, mosques, bridges, towers, and skyscrapers, and the master builders that are behind the creation of the world's most stunning structures. It doesn't take a lot of planning to see how mathematics could be integrated into a topic like building.

Integrating Math with Science

Integrating math with science is almost second nature. It is very difficult to interact with science without using mathematics. While in our current environment of standardized tests and curriculum, science, like math, is sometimes taught through memorization from a textbook rather than as an interactive subject (Hansen-Powell, 2007), it should not be too difficult for teachers to design science experiences that allow children to explore math and science as active and integrated subjects (Hillen et al., 1986).

A University of Illinois at Chicago initiative called TIMS: Teaching Integrated Math and Science Education supports the integration of math and science using the following goals as a guideline for developing curriculum (TIMS-Project, 2004):

- learn to carry out quantitative experiments using the Scientific Method;
- master basic variables that are fundamental to scientific study—length, area, volume, mass, time, velocity, density, force, work, and energy;
- learn mathematics by using it as a tool in scientific investigations;
- become proficient in using the tools of science, such as meter sticks, balances, graduated cylinders, and force gauges while using them in engaging activities that involve carts, balloons, bouncing balls, bubbles, and other materials;
- develop their quantitative thinking skills;
- become masters at graphing data;
- truly understand how to set up and carry out controlled scientific investigations.

Science is usually the easiest subject to integrate with math.

Anthony Magnacca/Merrill

(from *http://www.math.uic.edu/~imse/IMSE/LAB/labcdrom.html*). Using these goals as a guideline, teachers can easily develop science experiences that integrate rich mathematical experience.

Rockets. One of my favorite resources for integrating mathematics with science is NASA. NASA, or the National Aeronautics and Space Administration, has a large number of resources available to teachers on space flight, astronomy, and the earth. Their web site at *www.nasa.gov* contains links for students and teachers to learn about earth and space science. They produce an especially good activity booklet about rockets called the *Rocket Educators Guide. (http://www.nasa.gov/audience/foreducators/topnav/ materials/listbytype/Rockets.html*). This book contains a number of activities for children as young as kindergarten to learn about rockets and rocket power. These activities include a great deal of mathematics; for example, the X-35 project requires children to budget, weigh, measure, draw scale models, and make graphs as they go through the process of building their own water-powered rocket. More information on the X-35 project can be found at *http://quest.nasa.gov/space/teachers/rockets/act12.html*.

Food and Cooking. Another example and resource of integration of math and science is the FoodMaster initiative (*http://www.foodmaster.org/index.html*) (Phillips & Eugene, 2004). This project, developed with funding from the National Institute of Health, was initially designed to help children learn mathematics and science while learning about food and cooking. Current projects include ways to help in slowing the rising incidence of childhood obesity in the United States. These links to real-life problems make integration of curricula vitally important. The FoodMaster web site explains their program this way:

> It is our theory that if food is used as a tool to teach math and science, that students will be better prepared to demonstrate and apply mathematic and scientific knowledge.

Cooking requires a great deal of mathematics.

Ken Karp/PH College

Because students encounter food on a daily basis, we believe that they have preexisting contextual experience that will have already prepared them for learning new and relevant math and science material. Food is also conducive to hands-on, inquiry-based, active learning that is likely to use multiple senses to engage students in the learning process. Additionally, food allows for an interdisciplinary approach to learning concepts and ideas in a variety of scientific subjects like microbiology, chemistry, biology, nutrition, and health along with math and other subjects. The knowledge and skill development that can be inspired by the FoodMaster approach is limitless. Proper use of measurement tools, and data collection, application and generalization, classification and organization, comparative analysis, and interpretation of data, chemical and physical changes, observing the functions of ingredients and controlling variables, critical thinking, self-directing learning, and team building are only a few of the potential knowledge and skill development areas for students experiencing FoodMaster's learning labs!

As the FoodMaster initiative states, learning about food can be an excellent way to integrate math, science, and real-life situations. An investigation of food can offer rich science and math explorations for students. Some ideas and a sample schedule can be found in Figure 9.2 (Phillips, Duffrin, & Geist, 2004).

These curriculum ideas are just the beginning. Teachers are not restricted to teaching math and science from a textbook. Food offers a rich basis for integrating mathematics and science. The FoodMaster program is just one attempt to achieve the goal of teaching mathematics and science through a topical, project-based approach.

When this program was implemented and tested with second- and third-grade children, their enjoyment and excitement about the experience was evident. The students would come to class excited and ready to work. Oftentimes they would present stories about what they had made at home and how they interacted with their families during the food preparation process (Phillips, Duffrin, & Geist, 2004).

Students were engaged in the learning process; food, math, and science educational experience were enhanced. They not only interacted and shared common experiences with other students but also with their families, friends, and teachers.

This experience provides tremendous insight into the potential for using food as a tool to integrate math and science concepts. The use of food also opens up the possibility of collaborations with area businesses such as restaurants and bakeries. Think of all the rich learning that can take place in a bakery. Children could learn about the exact measurements needed to ensure bread turns out the same every time. They could learn how to price items to ensure that the cost to profit ratio leads to making money on the transaction. They could learn about the role yeast plays in making bread and how it multiplies and grows. Learning about bread opens a plethora of possibilities for integration of math and science. If you add the history and the social implications of bread to the learning activity, you can easily begin to integrate social studies into the lesson.

Integrating Math with Social Studies

Whereas math and science go together like "milk and cookies," social studies is not usually thought of as integrated with mathematics (Stodolsky, 1988). However, there are just as many rich mathematical experiences in social studies as in other subject

"Kitchen Wizards: Food Science for Kids"

This unit is a 14 week adventure for fourth- and fifth-grade students into the world of food preparation, cooking chemistry, and consumer science. Students will learn basics about measuring, as well as the chemical reason why foods need to be prepared and cooked the way they do. Exciting labs in vegetable, fruits, and egg cookery teach concepts about acids and bases, fats and emulsifiers, and the role of carbohydrates in food. Students will practice scientific processes that require observational research to make predictions and design sound measurable experimentation. Student-created products will introduce ideas about product testing and marketing.

Food Science Inquiry Lessons

Week One: Weighing In! Students will learn three concepts: the importance of using appropriate measuring tools; the differences between packing, leveling, and sifting; and two ways that fats can be measured.

Week Two: Application, Let the Chips Fall! Using measuring concepts learned last week, students will make chocolate chip cookies and taste test the results.

Week Three: Application, Let the Chips Fall! Continued.

Week Four: Hard Candy, Easy Recipe! Observing and noting temperature changes in hard candy sugar mixture through four different cooking states (thread, soft ball, hard ball, and soft cracked stages)

Week Five: Fruit Follies. Using the chemistry of acids and bases to manipulate the browning processes in fresh apples and bananas and making taste test comparisons between canned, fresh, and frozen fruits.

Week Six: Apple Analysis. Using rubric-style evaluations to compare a variety of apples both fresh and cooked in apple crisp.

Week Seven: Scientific Salad. Comparing fresh, frozen, and canned carrots, and observing the effects of broccoli boiled in a soda and cream of tartar solution.

Week Eight: Good Eggs Fry Hard. Discovering effects of acids and bases on poached eggs; Venn diagramming real and substitute egg dishes.

Consumer Science Lessons

Week Nine: Cola Wars. Determine the amount of sugar needed to attract consumers to a cola product. Using ingredients provided, create and taste test designer colas and name the product.

Week Ten: Mad Marketing. Surveying magazines for persuasive language and marketing strategies that could be used to sell a designer cola, designing packaging, and performing a jingle or commercial for a designer cola.

Week Eleven: Toothpaste Testing. Following test processes to compare the effectiveness of several aspects of three brands of toothpaste, foam volume, taste, and cleaning strength.

Week Twelve: Original Toothpaste Recipes. Selecting predicted amounts of glycerin, soap, bicarbonate, and flavoring to make the best tasting and most effective toothpaste (based on tile tests).

Week Thirteen: Super Cereal Consumers Product Lab. Using steps in the scientific process (question, prediction, experimentation, summarize, generalize) to test a variety of cereal for class-determined rubric characteristics using student-designed tests, planning the application of this process to another product of their choosing.

Week Fourteen: Battle of the Ads! Presenting tests that provide evidence that would support or refute product claims for videotaping.

Figure 9.2 FoodMaster Sample Lessons.

areas, for the teacher who is willing to look for them. Books on historical, cultural, community, governmental, and social issues are a good place to start when looking for ways to include mathematics into social studies investigations (Restivo, 1993).

Maps. Maps help to develop children's understanding of coordinate systems and location in space. They can also be integrated into social studies activities. Applying the mathematical skill of using coordinates on geopolitical maps can help children find out more about their world.

For example, a lesson on the pony express can incorporate history, geography, map reading, and mathematics. First, students can learn about the pony express either from their history textbooks or from a web site such as *http://www.xphomestation.com/*. Then, students or teachers can download a copy of a United States map from a web site that has a free collection of maps, such as *http://www.eduplace.com/ss/maps/*. Students can then trace the route of the pony express (generally regarded as the current route of US 50), and investigate solutions to the following math questions (McClelland, 1996).

- What was the maximum the rider was allowed to weigh? How much could his supplies weigh? How much could the mail he carried weigh? What was the total weight that horses were allowed to carry?
- How many legs of the journey did it take to cover the whole route from Missouri to California? (Total miles approximately 2000, average leg was 10 to 15 miles; answer could be 133 to 200.)
- If the average rider rode 75 miles, how many riders did the entire route need?
- If it cost $2 per ounce to mail a letter, how much money could a rider make if he was carrying the maximum amount of mail on his trip? ($2 \times 16 \times 20 = $640)

Easier or harder questions can be constructed depending on the ages and developmental level of the students. Children could label the names of oceans, states, cities, and landmarks on the map, as well as geological formations such as the Rocky Mountains.

Government. Local government, elections, and voting can be used as topics to integrate social studies with mathematics. Children can study the workings of local government by visiting the office of the mayor or another local community leader. Children should be encouraged to ask questions about city or local community operations. They can learn about taxes and budgets, voting in elections, and the benefits of governments. In an election year, the opportunities are even more abundant.

Mathematically, teachers can incorporate voting and vote counting into the classroom. Lessons on taxes and budgets can be implemented for the higher grades using graphs and charts and data collection. Students might even be able to set up their own classroom budget. For younger children, the teacher may want to use the book *Katy and the Snowman* by Virginia Lee Burton to discuss government services in more detail. Katy, a snowplow, helps her community by clearing paths for the town workers. This could serve as a springboard for writing about or discussing the services that are needed in a city.

Black History Month

Not long ago, I had a teaching student come to me with a problem. The teacher she was working with wanted her to do a unit for Black History Month, but she was perplexed as to how to integrate this subject with mathematics. My first question to her was, "What prior knowledge do your children have on this topic?" Her answer was, "None." She indicated that the children were white, upper-middle-class students and that there was very little diversity in the school. She wanted to know how to make a topic like Black History Month relevant to these children's lives and integrate it with mathematics.

It has been over 50 years since integration of schools became the law of the land, yet in reality there is still a great deal of "defacto segregation." There are few incidences of truly integrated schools in this country. Whatever the reason, the phenomenon of teachers teaching in nondiverse settings is not unique. How can topics such as Black History Month be made relevant to students in these settings?

The first thing I suggested was that she ask her students to make a list of all the famous African-American people they could recall. After she had done this, she found that her students actually had a good deal of knowledge about African-American

Tempo, meter, measure, rhythmic patterns, and many other musical elements have mathematical underpinnings.

Anthony Magnacca/Merrill

leaders, musicians, scientists, and sports figures. Names such as Martin Luther King Jr., Jessie Jackson, Ken Griffey Jr., Michael Jackson, Maya Angelou, Oprah Winfrey, Michael Jordan, Colin Powell, Ella Fitzgerald, and George Washington Carver were on the list.

Using this list, the students put the people into categories based on what they knew about them. One child said that she knew George Washington Carver invented peanut butter, so the students made a category for inventors and scientists. When they were done, they had a web that included scientists and inventors; musicians and political leaders; and famous people from sports, TV, and movies.

The problem now was where to go next, in order to link this assignment with mathematics. Since the children were most interested in musicians, she started with music. Speaking with African-American musicians and music teachers in the area, she found that most popular musical styles in the United States had African-American influences. Jazz, blues, gospel, rap, and even rock and roll and pop can be traced back to African-American experiences and rhythms. She began to introduce different music to her students, discussing the artists and the history of the musical style. She began to notice that music contained a lot of mathematics.

Integrating Math with Music

Music is a good way to introduce math not just to older children, through projects such as the one described previously, but to younger children as well. A child's first mathematical experience is often being rocked as an infant gently while being sung to and patted rhythmically. Music and mathematics have been hypothesized to have a link in the brain (Begley, 2000; Burack, 2005; Weinberger, 1998). Some even claim that playing Mozart music in the background while children do mathematical and spatial tasks, improves performance. While the jury is still out on that, other research is more convincing.

A child does not need to have formal musical instruction, such as piano lessons, to get the benefit of improved mathematical ability and understanding from music. Simply interacting with music stimulates development of mathematical understanding. Children can be exposed to and interact with music in many ways that stimulate the brain and incorporate mathematical concepts.

Research also suggests that math and music may be related in the brain from very early in life (Begley, 2000; Burack, 2005; Weinberger, 1998). We know, for instance, that music contains numerous mathematical constructs within its basic structure. Musical elements such as steady beat, rhythm, tempo, volume, melody, and harmony possess inherent mathematical principals such as spatial properties, sequencing, counting, patterning, and one-to-one correspondence. Also, music seems to be related to very primal parts of the brain (Holden, 1999). Our bodies cannot help but react physiologically to musical input (Hasan & Thaut, 2004; Thaut & Kenyon, 2003). This indicates that even very young children inherently respond to music and the mathematical constructs it contains.

If math and music share similar inherent characteristics, how convenient and helpful it would be to utilize musical elements as support for learning mathematics when teaching infants, toddlers, and preschoolers. As a teacher, you may already be using some of the elements of music and mathematics in your classroom. For example, rhythm can be used to make books predictable. Children's anticipation of the rhythmic pattern helps them remember the words to a familiar story. The challenge is to recognize the effect that musical elements can have on the development of emergent mathematics. Let's look at some basic elements of music and how they relate to mathematics, especially for infants, toddlers, and preschoolers.

Steady Beat. A steady-beat is what you have a physical response to when you hear music. If you tap your foot while listening to music, you are tapping the steady beat. It is repetitive and evenly spaced. Using a steady beat as part of teaching young children can support the construction of "one" and the development of patterns.

Steady-beat activities such as clapping or marching help children understand numerical relationships such as "more" and one-to-one correspondence. Toddlers may not know numbers but they understand "more." For example, if you clap once and then you say, "Can you clap more than I clapped?" a toddler will most likely clap more than once.

Rhythm. Rhythm is not always the same as a steady beat. An illustration of this can be done by using "Old MacDonald Had a Farm." Although the rhythm varies, the steady beat is constant, allowing the child to notice more complex and distinct patterns. The child can also make one-to-one correspondence relationships between the rhythm, beat, and words to a song. The words represent the rhythm and the clapping represents the beat. Clapping and singing together keeps them synchronized and creates a natural one-to-one correspondence experience.

Rhythm helps children develop patterning abilities. They can easily repeat, predict, and extend rhythmic patterns. For example, in "Old MacDonald Had a Farm," when the teacher sings "with a moo, moo here," the child can repeat and extend the pattern with little effort by singing "and a moo, moo there."

Melody. Consider the melody of "Old MacDonald Had a Farm," focusing on the repetitive pattern "EIEIO." When sung, you may notice that you sing from a higher note to a lower note. The first "EI" is repeated on a higher note. The next "EI" is repeated on a lower note, and O is sung on an even lower note. Moving from one note to another creates the melody, or tune, of the song.

With a basic understanding of steady beat, rhythm, and melody, teachers and parents can incorporate these musical elements into the "normal" teaching strategies they use to promote emergent mathematics. Children can create, reproduce, and extend patterns, and explore one-to-one correspondence using these elements. They can be used alone or in combination to create simple and complex patterns for children to explore and interact with in a developmentally appropriate manner.

Tempo, Dynamics, Timbre, and Style. Other musical elements include tempo, dynamics, timbre, and style. Tempo refers to speed, dynamics refers to volume, and timbre is another word for the quality of the sound. For example, when listening to someone playing a tambourine, a person might say that the timbre has a "shrill sound" when played fast. Descriptor words such as "shrill" or "dry" are used to describe the timbre or tone quality of the music.

A trip to the museum can be filled with mathematical wonder.

The style of a song usually refers to an established genre of music such as jazz, country, rock and roll, blues, spiritual, American folk, and so on. Children may enjoy listening to different styles. Older children even begin comparing different styles of music. Can you describe what makes rock and roll and country music different? Is it the steady beat? The rhythm? The melody? Is there a specific pattern in the rhythm that makes the style distinctive? What about the timbre? Think about these elements the next time you listen to your favorite music.

Let's look at how these elements apply when using music to interact with children. How can these elements of music promote mathematical thinking?

Music Experiences to Promote Emergent Mathematics

Teachers can use drums with infants and toddlers. Other musical activities with regular steady beats that the teacher can emphasize during movement activities include tapping cymbals, shaking bells, and marching to music. Even a novice or "untrained" musician can use elements of steady beat, rhythm, melody, tempo, dynamics, style, and timbre when interacting with children. These techniques can be used in the classroom or at home, making the world of learning much more enjoyable and effective for the parent, teacher, and child. Any activity can be made musical.

Research on emergent mathematics is beginning to show that even infants can interact with and understand mathematics. Music can be employed as an important tool in facilitating the construction and support of emergent mathematics (Geist, 2003). Even the youngest children can interact with music, therefore it is an exciting means for engaging them in mathematics. The structure of musical elements such as steady beat, rhythm, and melody can be used to support many different activities in the classroom. Mathematical activities such as patterning and one-to-one correspondence are especially easy to link to music. However, other early mathematics concepts can also be supported by integration with the visual arts.

Integrating Math with Art

Visual arts such as drawing, painting, and sculpture, just to name a few, can offer opportunities to introduce shape, symmetry, patterning, scale, three-dimensionality, and numerous other mathematical concepts. Art, like music, is a great medium for teaching these concepts because of its interactive nature. Art activities should emphasize creativity. In other words, teachers are discouraged from telling children what to draw, how to draw it, or what color it should be. Mathematics and art are similar due to 1) their creative nature, 2) the personal construction of meaning in each child, and 3) the danger of teachers stifling these aspects by overcontrolling the process.

Museums and Weaving. Art can be incorporated into math through both studying and creating it. For example, I accompanied my first-grade son on a class field trip to a local museum to examine Native American weavings and rugs. Before the children embarked on the trip, their teacher had quickly gone over concepts of symmetry, so the children were on the lookout for patterns and symmetry in the weavings. I overheard excited young voices discussing the different shapes in the weavings and talking about the symmetry and the patterns. I asked my son what symmetry was and he was able to tell me the definition, using the weavings as examples. He showed me a woven rug and pointed out the symmetry and patterns while he explained the concept.

We went into a workroom where Native American docents explained how the rugs were woven and how each shape was created. When they asked for questions, I was amazed at the number of hands that were raised. However, the question that struck me most (as it was one I also had) was, "Why are there no circles in the weaving patterns?" The docents explained they are very hard and time consuming to weave and gave an example of what is involved in weaving one.

Next, the children were provided with precut shapes and a piece of paper. They were instructed to make their own rug design on the paper using pattern and symmetry. They worked on their creations for about 15 minutes with help from the docents, parents, and teachers. The next activity was the actual weaving. The children were provided with small plastic weaving frames and yarn. Using the basic techniques they had learned during their visit, they made their own weavings that incorporated pattern and symmetry.

Leonardo DaVinci

Most art activities contain some sort of mathematics. Leonardo DaVinci's art is almost entirely based on studies of scale and geometry. He studied nature, looking for its mathematical and geometric underpinnings and used art to show his results. Children can study DaVinci's drawings and paintings and look for the mathematical and geometric features. A good way to start is with one of DaVinci's

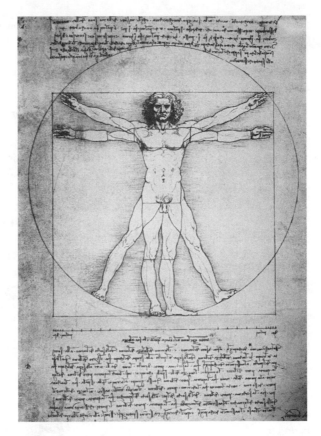

Figure 9.3 Vitruvian Man.

most ubiquitous works: **Vitruvian Man** (Figure 9.3). (Note: You may want to edit out the genitalia before presenting this to younger children to avoid parental concerns. A fig leaf usually works, but putting shorts on him always produces a chuckle from the children.) The drawing shows a square inscribed inside a circle. Inside the circle is a man with two sets of outstretched arms and legs, which touch both the circumference of the circle and the vertices of the square. The drawing indicates that the length of the man's arm span is equal to his height (MathForum, 2005).

Children can determine if this is true, using rulers, measuring tape, string, or any other media to measure the length of their arm span and compare it to their height, then recording their data on a chart. For younger children, the chart may simply record if the length is equal or not. For older children, actual measurements can be recorded. They can then perform the experiment at home on adults to see if the proportions are the same for adults. What about older siblings? Children can examine a number of questions in this way.

As a final activity, children can use large pieces of paper to trace their own outlines in poses similar to that of Vitruvian Man and then draw circles and squares around it. They can decorate the pictures however they wish, and the pictures can be displayed in the schoolroom for parents and other children to see.

Integrating Math with Physical Activity

There are many ways math can be used with physical activity. Most children use mathematics to structure their play activities. Their play may include taking turns, creating a sequence of who is next, creating two equal teams, keeping score, and many other tasks.

When I was in grade school and the weather began to get warm, the whole school would take a day to do outside sporting activities. There was kickball, tee-ball, 50-yard dash, the high jump, the long jump, distance running (the distance varied depending on the age of the children), and many other activities.

This "field day" idea can be used to integrate physical and mathematics activities into the classroom. Children rotate through different activities that each class is responsible for planning and running for part of the day. During the time children are participating in the activity, they keep a record of their achievements. For long and high jumps, they measure their distances and heights; for running activities, they record times; for team events, they keep score.

In play activities children use math often without even recognizing it.

John Paul Endress/Moder Curriculum Press/Pearson Learning

Distance	Frequency
17	0
18	0
19	1
20	2
21	2
22	1
23	5
24	4
25	2
26	4
27	1
28	1
More	0

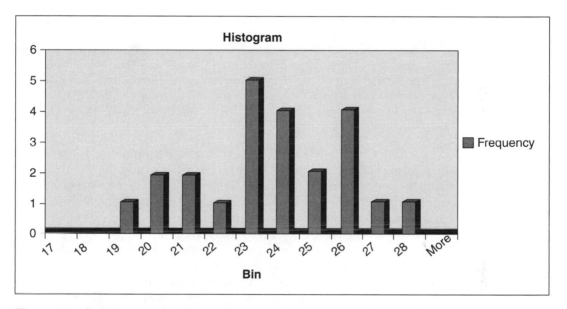

Figure 9.4   Sample Field Day Data Chart and Graph.

Back in the classroom, this data can be recorded on charts and graphs and examined. For example, the teacher can make a bar graph of the long jump results, following a discussion about "rounding up or down" so the data does not contain decimals (with younger children, the teacher might just round the numbers for them; for older children, rounding may not be necessary at all). Then, the teacher can enter the different distances onto the chart so that the children can see that most of the results will bunch around an "average" (Figure 9.4).

This type of measuring and "number crunching" can be done with any physical activity. Teachers can keep charts and graphs of children's physical growth and their improvements in physical accomplishments. Children can see the improvements they make over time. For example, a teacher can have a weekly height measurement. Children pick a partner, measure each other's heights, and record the numbers on their height charts each week, then record the reading on graph paper and draw a line connecting the dots.

Taking this idea one step further, what if we could integrate the entire learning process in such a way as to make it relevant to the child? This is the goal of the Project Approach (Helm & Katz, 2001; Katz, Chard, & ERIC Clearinghouse on Elementary and Early Childhood Education, 1998).

USING THE PROJECT APPROACH

The project approach refers to a set of teaching strategies for guiding children through in-depth studies of real-world topics within their environment. While structured, it also allows for a great deal of flexibility. Lillian Katz has researched the project approach as a method of integrating subjects in classrooms. According to Katz (Katz & Chard, 2000):

> A project is an in-depth study of a particular topic that one or more children undertake. It consists of exploring a topic or theme such as "going to the hospital," "building a house," or "the bus that brings us to school." Work on a project should extend over a period of days or weeks depending on the children's ages and the nature of the topic . . . It encourages them to pose questions, pursue puzzles and increases their awareness of the significant phenomenon around them. (p. 2–3)

Katz goes on to say that the project approach emphasizes the teacher's role in encouraging children to interact with people, objects, and the environment in ways that have personal meaning to them. Some teachers integrate the project work into learning centers while others (mostly preschool teachers) may devote most of their curriculum to it (Helm & Katz, 2001).

Children engaging in projects tend to be highly motivated. They are actively involved in their own learning and produce high-quality work. It enables them to do firsthand research and to incorporate learning into all aspects of their school and home activity, including play. Children have substantial control over their work. By fourth grade, students who had these experiences generally showed higher grades in all subjects (Helm & Katz, 2001).

With the project approach, children use a variety of resources to find answers to their questions, such as interviewing experts, making their own plans, and engaging in problem solving. They record what they learn by making posters, graphs, charts, and journals. They take responsibility for their learning process and are self-motivated because they are learning about topics that interest them.

Topic Selection

"What topics make for the most interesting projects?" "Who decides the topic for the project?" These are questions that are often asked. The first question depends on several things: the age and experience of the children, the locale, the natural and man-made environments near the school, the amount of expertise the teacher can draw on in the neighborhood, and the children's and teacher's experience with and interest in the topic.

It is a good idea to choose a topic that is within the children's experience, and to use the language children would normally use to describe it. For example, teachers should consider topics such as *food* rather than *nutrition* or *buses* rather than *transportation*. The topic is a starting point and, in order to access the children's prior knowledge, it is a good idea to use words that they can grasp. A topic should be focused enough to allow for an in-depth investigation. While the topic of transportation can encompass many different modes of travel; narrowing it to buses allows children to focus their investigation.

Choosing the topic depends on the children's ages of and the teachers' comfort level. It is important that the teacher select a topic with the cooperation of the students, keeping in mind the children's interests as well as the curriculum goals for the grade, both within the school district and nationwide.

The younger the children the more important it is for them to be able to handle objects; observe processes; and appreciate sounds, textures, smells, and tastes associated with the chosen topic. Fantasy play most frequently mirrors what goes on in the kitchen, the home, the car, the store, or the doctor's office. Young children have a serious interest in and desire to understand the things they see going on around them.

Good topics take advantage of local resources and things that children can readily investigate. For example, studying snow in Miami, Florida, is probably not the best choice because most children do not have firsthand experience with snow. These types of topics may be good for teacher-directed units but are not the best choices for child-centered investigations, which require hands-on exploration. A good topic should ensure understanding through firsthand experience and include information that is important in the daily lives of most children, parents, and families. For example, choosing "the grocery store" as a topic meets these requirements and is a topic that is rich with mathematical opportunities.

Using the Project Approach

The project approach is divided into three phases. There are no time limits to these phases and it is important to be flexible and to listen to the children. Sometimes the best ideas and the most rewarding activities come from a small question that a child asks that the teacher had never considered.

Phase One: Getting Started—The goal of phase one is to assess students prior knowledge of the topic. They can engage in an initial discussion of the topic and share their experiences with the class through writing, dramatic play, painting, or any other way they feel comfortable. A letter can be sent home to parents informing them of the topic and inviting them to share any expertise they may have. A KWL chart can be constructed in which children share with the class what they know about the topic (K); what they want to know (W); and later in Phase Three, what they learned (L) (Chard, 1998).

Other characteristics of Phase One include:

- Initial starting point—There should be an opening event that stimulates the class's interest, such as an object to pass around or a guest speaker. This may be something that children see while on the playground, like a fire truck speeding by. This activity is discussed during group time and the teacher can create a project around the experience (Chard, 1998).
- Topic web plan—The teacher can begin to map out the topic with the class using a topic web, which can be expanded on in her planning time. The teacher should brainstorm ideas about the topic and possible experiences and lessons that can be developed from those ideas, then present the ideas to her students in order to gauge their interest.
- Listing questions—When the teacher presents the topic web to the class, she should begin to collect questions about what the children would like to investigate. These questions will be developed into experiences for the students.

Phase Two: Fieldwork—Phase two is the fieldwork phase. Planning field trips, inviting experts into the classroom, and conducting experiments are the children's work during this phase. Real objects and processes are investigated, questions answered, more questions posed, and explanations sought. From a mathematical standpoint, this is where children will gather data, compute, and represent many different findings and reactions to their experiences (Chard, 1998).

- Preparation for fieldwork—One or more field trips can be planned. Before the trip, children should have a good idea of what they hope to see and learn. What data do they need to collect? What questions do they need to have answered?
- Field Trip—The class goes to a site that affords opportunities to see things related to their topic. Museums, parks, community spaces, retail outlets, government facilities, and any other relevant establishment can be used for field trips.
- Fieldwork follow-up—The children discuss the trip and record and share what happened, discussing the questions that were answered and asking new ones. Information books may be consulted to enhance the learning.
- Visiting experts—People who have expertise in the topic can be invited to further explore the questions that children have (Chard, 1998).

Phase Three: The Culminating Event—The focus of phase three is presenting and sharing what has been learned with others, such as parents and fellow classmates. The work is reviewed and evaluated and particular items are selected for presentation (Chard, 1998; Helm & Beneke, 2003). Children should be an integral part of this assessment and selection process. They should have a major say in the form this culminating activity takes.

It can take the form of an open house, where children invite friends, family, principals, and community members to see an exhibit of what they have done. They can show visitors around and explain the work that is presented around the room. The culminating activity could also take the form of a video about their topic. Children can decide who will direct and act in various parts of the movie and write the script. There are numerous ways they represent their knowledge. Let them be as creative as possible during this part of the project.

- Debriefing—This is the time for students to communicate and share the work with others in the class or in the community. Different groups may have been working on separate parts of the project; this can be the time to bring everything together to prepare for the culminating activity.
- Personalizing new knowledge—Children need time to reflect on new knowledge in order to understand what it means to them. They may want to represent their knowledge using writing, dramatic play, art, music, or some other medium.
- Presentation of the project—The culminating activity should be a celebration of the topic as well as a way to demonstrate knowledge. Children should take pride in their accomplishments as they show friends or family members what they have been doing at school for the past few weeks.

Integrating mathematics using the project approach just takes a bit of planning. As you progress through these phases, think to yourself, "Where is the math?" Using the suggestions and examples given in this chapter should help answer that question.

SUMMARY

Math can be integrated into just about every aspect of a child's day at school and at home. At school, math can easily be integrated with subject areas such as reading, science, social studies, music, art, and physical activity. Reading is a subject that over-arches the school day and mathematics can be a big part of this breaking down the artificial dichotomy between *learning* mathematics and *living* mathematics. Books and literature help children learn to communicate mathematically. Some books have specific mathematical themes that can be extended and discussed as mathematics problems, while others have rhythmic patterns that children can recognize and that help scaffold the reading experience.

Science is full of mathematical opportunities. It is hard to do science without mathematics. Measurement, data collection, and reporting data all require the application of math and mathematical concepts. Social studies likewise contains many rich mathematical experiences. Integrating math with social studies helps children to see the everyday, practical uses of mathematics, and how it is involved in their government, their history, and their lives.

Art and music rely on mathematics for some of their inherent structure. Music is based on mathematical principles and patterns that can be utilized with the very young as their first patterning experience. Even as children get older, research suggests that music can aid in mathematical learning. Visual art contains shapes, patterns, and other more advanced mathematical concepts such as scale and perspective that can be integrated into its creation and appreciation.

Using the project approach, all of these subject areas can be integrated in the investigation of a topic that is of interest to the child. Child and teacher collaborate in choosing a topic and investigating it in depth. The three phases of a project are 1) getting started, 2) fieldwork, and 3) a culminating activity. During all of these phases, integrating mathematics enables children to learn about their world in a more natural way than they could by learning each subject in isolation. Children use mathematics in their life every day, and should learn about it in the same way.

WEB SITES

Ask Dr. Math
http://www.mathforum.org/dr.math/

A question and answer site maintained by the Math Forum at Drexel University, containing answers to many common mathematical questions. If you can't find one, you can "Ask Dr. Math."

Young Investor
http://www.younginvestor.com/

A site that helps kids build sound-saving habits and reap the benefits in the future. Children can invest, plan, and earn income with online games and activities.

FoodMaster Initiative
http://www.foodmaster.org/index.html

Site dedicated to teaching mathematics and science through food and nutrition.

Science and Math at Kids.gov
http://www.kids.gov/k_science.htm

A site with a wealth of links to information on lots of possible project topics.

Kidsgardening
http://www.kidsgardening.com/

A site about helping children learn to garden. This can be used to support a project on gardening that integrates mathematics.

Science.gov resources
http://www.science.gov/

Resources on just about every science topic imaginable and methods for integrating them with math and other subjects.

Smithsonian: Kids

http://www.si.edu/kids/

The kids' page for the Smithsonian institute. It has information about all the museums at the Smithsonian.

NASA - Kids' Club Home Page

http://www.nasa.gov/audience/forkids/kidsclub/flash/index.html

The National Aeronautics and Space Administrations' site for kids. This can be a good resource for projects dealing with space, rockets, planets, or the earth.

Central Intelligence Agency Homepage for Kids

https://www.cia.gov/cia/ciakids/index_2.shtml

The Central Intelligence Agency's Kids site. It contains information about the CIA and what it does, as well as activities for budding spies. The site is secure, so be sure to start with https://

United Nations Cyberschoolbus

http://cyberschoolbus.un.org/

The kid's site for the United Nations. It contains information on the U.N. and model U.N. program as well as links to information on children from around the world.

DISCUSS AND APPLY WHAT YOU HAVE LEARNED

Reflect

1. Why is it important to integrate mathematics into other curricular areas?
2. Why do you think math is usually taught as an isolated subject?
3. Why do children learn and retain information better when it is presented in the context of what they already know?

Discuss

1. Discuss a nonmath activity that you have seen a teacher present to students. How could you have integrated math into the activity?
2. As a group, discuss and compile a list of the benefits and difficulties involved with integrating the curriculum. How many of the problems can you solve?

Apply

1. Develop a topic for a project that can be done in a second-grade classroom. Include a web for the activity and for the mathematics concepts. Include how it integrates mathematics with science, social studies, reading, music, art, and physical activity.
2. Develop a set of guidelines for teachers on how to incorporate mathematics into other areas of the classroom. What are some questions teachers might ask?

Observe

1. Observe in a third-grade classroom. What are the teachers doing to support integration of mathematics? What opportunities are they missing?

2. Observe a teacher's classroom and ask about her planning process. How are topics, units, or themes planned? How does this compare with integrating the curriculum using the project approach?

REFERENCES

Begley, S. (2000). Music on the mind. *Newsweek, 136*(4), 50.

Burack, J. (2005). Uniting mind and music. *American Music Teacher, 55*(1), 84–84.

Chard, S. (1998). *The project approach: Developing the basic framework.* New York: Scholastic.

Geist, E. (2003). Children are born mathematicians. *Young Children.*

Hansen-Powell, P. (2007). Constructing knowledge. *Connect Magazine, 20*(3), 1–4.

Hasan, M. A., & Thaut, M. H. (2004). Statistical analysis for finger tapping with a periodic external stimulus. *Perceptual & Motor Skills, 99*(2), 643–661.

Helm, J. H., & Beneke, S. (Eds.). (2003). *The power of projects: Meeting contemporary challenges in early childhood classrooms—Strategies and solutions.* New York: Teachers College Press.

Helm, J. H., & Katz, L. (2001). *Young investigators: The project approach in the early years.* New York: Teachers College Press.

Hillen, J., Mercier, S., Wiebe, A. J., & Ecklund, L. (1986). *Pieces and patterns: A patchwork in math and science.* Fresno, CA: AIMS Education Foundation.

Holden, C. (1999). Music as brain builder. *Science, 283*(5410), 2007.

Katz, L., & Chard, S. C. (2000). *Engaging children's minds: The project approach* (2nd ed.). Stamford, CT: Ablex Pub. Corp.

Loveless, T., & Ebrary, I. (2001). *The great curriculum debate: How should we teach reading and math?* Washington, DC: Brookings Institution Press.

MathForum. (2005). From *http://mathforum.org/geometry/rugs/symmetry/whatis.html*

McClelland, R. (1996). Math/social studies activity—The Pony Express at *http://score.kings.k12.ca.us/lessons/ponyexp.htm*

McDonald, J. (2007). Selecting counting books: Mathematical perspectives. *Young Children* (May), 38–42.

Phillips, S. K., Duffrin, M. W., & Geist, E.A. (2004). Be a food scientist. *Science and Children, 41*(4), 24–29.

Restivo, S. (1993). *Math worlds: Philosophical and social studies of mathematics and mathematics education.* Albany, NY: State University of New York Press.

Schumm, J. S. (1999). *Adapting reading and math materials for the inclusive classroom.* Reston, VA: Council for Exceptional Children.

Smith, C. B., & Wills, H. (Directors). (1994). *Writing to learn across the curriculum strategies for math, science, social studies, and language arts.* [Video/DVD] Bloomington, IN: ERIC/EDINFO Press.

Stodolsky, S. S. (1988). *The subject matters: Classroom activity in math and social studies.* Chicago: University of Chicago Press.

Thaut, M. H., & Kenyon, G. P. (2003). Rapid motor adaptations to subliminal frequency shifts during syncopated rhythmic sensorimotor synchronization. *Human Movement Science, 22*(3), 321.

TIMS-Project. (2004). *Math trailblazers teacher implementation guide* (2nd ed.). Dubuque, IA: Kendall-Hunt.

Weinberger, N. M. (1998). The music in our minds. *Educational Leadership, 56*(3), 36.

Whitin, D. J., & Wilde, S. (1992). *Read any good math lately? Children's books for mathematical learning, K–6.* Portsmouth, NH: Heinemann.

APPENDIX

Sample State Standards

PRESCHOOL

Number and Number Sense

1. Count to 10 in the context of daily activities and play (e.g., number songs).
2. Touch objects and say the number names when counting in the context of daily activities and play (e.g., cookies on a plate, steps on a set of stairs).
3. Demonstrate one-to-one correspondence when counting objects (e.g., give one cookie to each child in group).
4. Determine "how many" in sets of five or fewer objects.
5. Construct two sets of objects, each containing the same number of objects (e.g., five crayons and five blocks).
6. Compare sets of equal, more, and fewer and use the language of comparison (e.g., equal, more, and fewer).
7. Group and regroup a given set in the context of daily activities and play (e.g., five blocks can be two blue and three green or one blue and four green).

Source: Adapted from the Ohio State Content Standards

8. Represent quantity using invented forms (e.g., child's marks to represent a quantity of objects).
9. Write numerical representations (e.g., scribbles, reversals) or numerals in meaningful contexts (e.g., play situations).
10. Identify and name numerals 0–9.
11. Compare and order whole numbers up to five.
12. Identify penny, nickel, dime, and quarter and recognize that coins have different values.

Meaning of Operations

13. Construct sets with more or fewer objects than a given set.
14. Count on (forward) using objects such as cards, number cubes, or dominoes that have familiar dot patterns (e.g., when selecting five apples from a bag, take out two and continue counting 3, 4, 5).
15. Join two sets of objects to make one large set in the context of daily routines and play (e.g., combining two bags of raisins, each containing three pieces; combining two groups of blocks, each containing three blocks).
16. Equally distribute a set of objects into two or more smaller sets (e.g., share six crackers with three friends equally).

Measurement

Measurement Units

1. Begin to identify and use the language of units of time. For example:
   a. Day, night, week
   b. Yesterday, today, tomorrow

Use Measurement Techniques and Tools

2. Recognize that various devices measure time (e.g., clock, timer, calendar).
3. Sequence or order events in the context of daily activities and play (e.g., washing hands before and after snacks, which student is next in line for the computer).
4. Begin to use terms to compare the attributes of objects (e.g., bigger, smaller, lighter, heavier, taller, shorter, more, and less).
5. Order a set of objects according to size, weight, or length (e.g., cups of different sizes).
6. Measure length and volume (capacity) using nonstandard, units of measure (e.g., how many paper clips long a pencil is; how many small containers are needed to fill one big container using sand, rice, or beans).

Geometry and Spatial Sense for Preschool

Characteristics and Properties

1. Match identical two- and three-dimensional objects found in the environment in play situations (e.g., two squares of same size, two stop signs).

2. Sort and classify similar two- and three-dimensional objects in the environment and in play situations (e.g., paper shapes, two balls of different size).
3. Identify, name, create, and describe common two-dimensional shapes in the environment and in play situations (e.g., circles, triangles, rectangles, and squares).
4. Identify, name, and describe three-dimensional objects using the child's own vocabulary (e.g., sphere—"ball," cube—"box," cylinder—"can" or "tube," and cone—"ice cream cone").

Spatial Relationships

5. Demonstrate and begin to use the language of the relative position of objects in the environment and in play situations (e.g., up, down, over, under, top, bottom, inside, outside, in front, behind, between, next to, right side up, and upside-down).

Patterns, Functions, and Algebra for Preschool

Use Patterns Relations and Functions

1. Sort, order, and classify objects by one attribute (e.g., size, color, shape, use).
2. Identify, copy, extend, and create simple patterns or sequences of sounds, shapes, and motions in the context of daily activities and play (e.g., creates red, blue, red, blue pattern with blocks).

Use Algebraic Representations

3. Use play, physical materials, or drawings to model a simple problem (e.g., There are six cookies to be shared by three children. How many cookies can each child receive?).

Data Analysis and Probability in Preschool

Data Collection

1. Gather, sort, and compare objects by similarities and differences in the context of daily activities and play (e.g., leaves, nuts, socks).
2. Place information or objects in a floor or table graph according to one attribute (e.g., size, color, shape, or quantity).

Statistical Methods

3. Select the category or categories that have the most or fewest objects in a floor or table graph (e.g., favorite ice cream).

KINDERGARTEN

Number, Number Sense, and Operations

Numbers and Number Systems

1. Compare and order whole numbers up to 10.
2. Explain the rules of counting, such as that each object should be counted once and that order does not change the number.
3. Count to 20 (e.g., in play situations or while reading number books).
4. Determine "how many" in sets (groups) of 10 or fewer objects.
5. Relate reading and writing of numerals for single-digit numbers (0 to 9).
6. Construct multiple sets of objects each containing the same number of objects.
7. Compare the number of objects in two or more sets when one set has one or two more, or one or two fewer objects.
8. Represent and use whole numbers in flexible ways, including relating, composing and decomposing numbers (e.g., five marbles can be two red and three green or one red and four green).
9. Identify and state the value of a penny, nickel, and dime.

Meaning of Operations

10. Model and represent addition as combining sets and counting on, and subtraction as take-away and comparison. For example:
    a. Combine and separate small sets of objects in contextual situations (e.g., add or subtract one, two, or another small amount).
    b. Count on (forward) and count back (backward) on a number line between 0 and 10.
11. Demonstrate joining multiple groups of objects, each containing the same number of objects (e.g., combining three bags of candy, each containing two pieces).
12. Partition or share a small set of objects into groups of equal size (e.g., sharing six stickers equally among three children).

Computation and Estimation

13. Recognize the number or quantity of sets up to five without counting (e.g., recognize without counting the dot arrangement on a domino as five).

Measurement

Measurement Units

1. Identify units of time (day, week, month, and year) and compare calendar elements (e.g., weeks are longer than days).

Use Measurement Techniques and Tools

2. Compare and order objects of different lengths, areas, weights, and capacities; and use relative terms, such as *longer, shorter, bigger, smaller, heavier, lighter, more,* and *less.*
3. Measure length and volume (capacity) using uniform objects in the environment. For example, find:
    a. How many paper clips long a pencil is;
    b. How many small containers are needed to fill one big container using sand, rice, or beans.

4. Order events based on time. For example:
   a. Activities that take a long or short time;
   b. Review what to do first, next, last;
   c. Recall what we did or plan to do yesterday, today, tomorrow.

Geometry and Spatial Sense

Characteristics and Principles

1. Identify and sort two-dimensional shapes and three-dimensional objects. For example:
   a. Identify and describe two-dimensional figures and three-dimensional objects from the environment using the child's own vocabulary.
   b. Sort shapes and objects into groups based on student-defined categories.
   c. Select all shapes or objects of one type from a group.
   d. Build two-dimensional figures using paper shapes or tangrams; build simple three-dimensional objects using blocks.

Spatial Relationships

2. Name and demonstrate the relative position of objects as follows:
   a. Place objects over, under, inside, outside, on, beside, between, above, below, on top of, upside-down, behind, in back of, in front of;
   b. Describe placement of objects with terms, such as *on, inside, outside, above, below, over, under, beside, between, in front of, behind.*

Patterns, Functions, and Algebra

Use Patterns, Relations, and Functions

1. Sort, classify, and order objects by size, number, and other properties. For example:
   a. Identify how objects are alike and different.
   b. Order three events or objects according to a given attribute, such as time or size.
   c. Recognize and explain how objects can be classified in more than one way.
   d. Identify what attribute was used to sort groups of objects that have already been sorted.
2. Identify, create, extend, and copy sequences of sounds (such as musical notes), shapes (such as buttons, leaves, or blocks), motions (such as hops or skips), and numbers from 1 to 10.
3. Describe orally the pattern of a given sequence.

Use Algebraic Representations

4. Model a problem situation using physical materials.

Data Analysis and Probability Standard

Data Collection

1. Gather and sort data in response to questions posed by teacher and students (e.g., how many sisters and brothers, what color shoes).
2. Arrange objects in a floor or table graph according to attributes, such as use, size, color, or shape.

Statistical Model

3. Select the category or categories that have the most or fewest objects in a floor or table graph.

FIRST GRADE

Number, Number Sense, and Operations

Number and Number Systems

1. Use ordinal numbers to order objects (e.g., first, second, third).
2. Recognize and generate equivalent forms for the same number using physical models, words, and number expressions (e.g., concept of 10 is described by "10 blocks," full tens frame, numeral 10, 5 + 5, 15 − 5, one less than 11, my brother's age).
3. Read and write the numerals for numbers to 100.
4. Count forward to 100, count backwards from 100, count forward or backwards starting at any number between 1 and 100.
5. Use place-value concepts to represent whole numbers using numerals, words, expanded notation, and physical models with ones and tens. For example:
   a. Develop a system to group and count by 2s, 5s and 10s.
   b. Identify patterns and groupings in a 100s chart and relate to place-value concepts.
   c. Recognize the first digit of a two-digit number as the most important indication of number, size, and its nearness to 10 or 100.
6. Identify and state the value of a penny, nickel, dime, quarter, and dollar.
7. Determine the value of a small collection of coins (with a total value up to one dollar) using one or two different types of coins, including pennies, nickels, dimes, and quarters.
8. Show different combinations of coins that have the same value.
9. Represent commonly used fractions using words and physical models for halves, thirds, and fourths, recognizing that fractions are represented by equal-sized parts of a whole and of an object set.

Meaning of Operations

10. Model, represent, and explain addition as combining sets (part + part = whole) and counting on. For example:
    a. Model and explain addition using physical materials in contextual situations.

b. Draw pictures to model addition.
c. Write number sentences to represent addition.
d. Explain that adding two whole numbers yields a larger whole number.

11. Model, represent, and explain subtraction as take-away and comparison. For example:
    a. Model and explain subtraction using physical materials in contextual situations.
    b. Draw pictures to model subtraction.
    c. Write number sentences to represent subtraction.
    d. Explain that subtraction of whole numbers yields an answer smaller than the original number.

12. Use conventional symbols to represent the operations of addition and subtraction.

13. Model and represent multiplication as repeated addition and rectangular arrays in contextual situations (e.g., Four people will be at my party. If I want to give three balloons to each person, how many balloons will I need to buy?).

14. Model and represent division as sharing equally in contextual situations (e.g., sharing cookies).

15. Demonstrate that equal means "the same as" using visual representations.

Computation and Estimation

16. Develop strategies for basic addition facts, such as:
    a. counting all;
    b. counting on;
    c. one more, two more;
    d. doubles;
    e. doubles plus or minus one;
    f. make 10;
    g. using tens frames;
    h. identity property (adding zero).

17. Develop strategies for basic subtraction facts, such as:
    a. relating to addition (for example, think of $7 - 3 = ?$ as "3 plus ? equals 7");
    b. one less, two less;
    c. all but one (for example, $8 - 7, 5 - 4$);
    d. using tens frames;
    e. missing addends.

Measurement

Measurement Units

1. Recognize and explain the need for fixed units and tools for measuring length and weight (e.g., rulers and balance scales).
2. Tell time to the hour and half hour on digital and analog (dial) timepieces.
3. Order a sequence of events with respect to time (e.g., summer, fall, winter, and spring; morning, afternoon, and night).

Use Measurement Techniques and Tools

4. Estimate and measure weight using nonstandard units (e.g., blocks of uniform size).
5. Estimate and measure lengths using nonstandard and standard units (i.e., centimeters, inches, and feet).

Geometry and Spatial Sense

Characteristics and Principles

1. Identify, compare, and sort two-dimensional shapes (i.e., square, circle, ellipse, triangle, rectangle, rhombus, trapezoid, parallelogram, pentagon, and hexagon). For example:
   a. Recognize and identify triangles and rhombuses independent of position, shape, or size;
   b. Describe two-dimensional shapes using attributes such as number of sides and number of vertices (corners or angles).
2. Create new shapes by combining or cutting apart existing shapes.
3. Identify the shapes of the faces of three-dimensional objects.

Spatial Relationships

4. Extend the use of location words to include distance (near, far, close to) and directional words (left, right).
5. Copy figures and draw simple two-dimensional shapes from memory.

Patterns, Functions, and Algebra

Use Patterns, Relations, and Functions

1. Sort, classify, and order objects by two or more attributes, such as color and shape, and explain how objects were sorted.
2. Extend sequences of sounds, shapes, or simple number patterns, and create and record similar patterns. For example:
   a. Analyze and describe patterns with multiple attributes using numbers and shapes (e.g., AA, B, aa, b, AA, B, aa, b, . . .).
   b. Continue repeating and growing patterns with materials, pictures, and geometric items (e.g., XO, XOO, XOOO, XOOOO).
3. Describe orally the basic unit or general plan of a repeating or growing pattern.

Use Algebraic Representations

4. Solve open sentences by representing an expression in more than one way using the commutative property (e.g., $4 + 5 = 5 + 4$ or the number of blue balls plus red balls is the same as the number of red balls plus blue balls ($R + B = B + R$)).
5. Describe orally and model a problem situation using words, objects, or number phrase or sentence.

Data Analysis and Probability Standard

Data Collection

1. Identify multiple categories for sorting data.
2. Collect and organize data into charts using tally marks.

3. Display data in picture graphs with units of one and bar graphs with intervals of one.
4. Read and interpret charts, picture graphs, and bar graphs as sources of information to identify main ideas, draw conclusions, and make predictions.
5. Construct a question that can be answered by using information from a graph.

Statistical Model

6. Arrange five objects by an attribute, such as size or weight, and identify the ordinal position of each object.
7. Answer questions about the number of objects represented in a picture graph, bar graph, or table graph (e.g., category with most, how many more in a category compared to another, how many altogether in two categories).

Probability

8. Describe the likelihood of simple events as possible/impossible and more likely/less likely (e.g., when using spinners or number cubes in classroom activities).

SECOND GRADE

Number, Number Sense, and Operations Standard

Number and Number Systems

1. Use place-value concepts to represent, compare, and order whole numbers using physical models, numerals, and words, with 1s, 10s, and 100s. For example:
   a. Recognize 10 can mean "10 ones" or a single entity (1 ten) through physical models and trading games.
   b. Read and write three-digit numerals (e.g., 243 as two hundred forty three, 24 tens and 3 ones, or 2 hundreds and 43 ones, etc.) and construct models to represent each.
2. Recognize and classify numbers as even or odd.
3. Count money and make change using coins and a dollar bill.
4. Represent and write the value of money using the ¢ sign and in decimal form when using the $ sign.
5. Represent fractions (halves, thirds, fourths, sixths and eighths), using words, numerals, and physical models. For example:
   a. Recognize that a fractional part can mean different amounts depending on the original quantity.
   b. Recognize that a fractional part of a rectangle does not have to be shaded with contiguous parts.

c. Identify and illustrate parts of a whole and parts of sets of objects.

d. Compare and order physical models of halves, thirds, and fourths in relation to 0 and 1.

Meaning of Operations

6. Model, represent, and explain subtraction as comparison, take-away, and part-to-whole (e.g., solve missing addend problems by counting up or subtracting, such as "I had six baseball cards, my sister gave me more, and I now have 10. How many did she give me?" can be represented as $6 + ? = 10$ or $10 − 6 = ?$).

7. Model, represent, and explain multiplication as repeated addition, rectangular arrays, and skip counting.

8. Model, represent, and explain division as sharing equally and repeated subtraction.

9. Model and use the commutative property for addition.

Computation and Estimation

10. Demonstrate fluency in addition facts with addends through nine and corresponding subtractions (e.g., $9 + 9 = 18$, $18 − 9 = 9$).

11. Add and subtract multiples of 10.

12. Demonstrate multiple strategies for adding and subtracting two- or three-digit whole numbers, such as:

    a. compatible numbers;

    b. compensatory numbers;

    c. informal use of commutative and associative properties of addition.

13. Estimate the results of whole number addition and subtraction problems using front-end estimation, and judge the reasonableness of the answers.

Measurement

Measurement Units

1. Identify and select appropriate units of measure for:

    a. length – centimeters, meters, inches, feet, or yards;

    b. volume (capacity) – liters, cups, pints, or quarts;

    c. weight – grams, ounces, or pounds;

    d. time – hours, half-hours, quarter-hours, or minutes and time designations, a.m. or p.m.

2. Establish personal or common referents for units of measure to make estimates and comparisons (e.g., the width of a finger is a centimeter, a large bottle of soda pop is 2 liters, a small paper clip weighs about 1 gram).

3. Describe and compare the relationships among units of measure, such as centimeters and meters; inches, feet, and yards; cups, pints, and quarts; ounces and pounds; and hours, half-hours, and quarter-hours (e.g., how many inches in a foot?).

4. Tell time to the nearest minute interval on digital and to the nearest 5-minute interval on analog (dial) timepieces.

Use Measurement Techniques and Tools

5. Estimate and measure length and weight using metric and U.S. customary units.
6. Select and use appropriate measurement tools; a segment 3 inches long, a measuring cup to bowl, a scale to weigh 50 grams of candy.
7. Make and test predictions about measurements, to measure the same length or volume.

Geometry and Spatial Sense

Characteristics and Properties

1. Identify, describe, compare, and sort three-dimensional objects (i.e., cubes, spheres, prisms, cones, cylinders, and pyramids) according to the shape of faces or number of faces, edges, or vertices.
2. Predict what new shapes combining or cutting apart existing shapes will form.
3. Recognize two-dimensional shapes and three-dimensional objects from different positions.

Spatial Relationships

4. Identify and determine whether two-dimensional shapes are congruent (same shape and size) or similar (same shape, different size) by copying or using superposition (laying one thing on top of another).

Transformations and Symmetry

1. Create and identify two-dimensional figures with line symmetry (e.g., what letter shapes, logos, polygons are symmetrical?).

Patterns, Functions, and Algebra

Use Patterns, Relations, and Functions

1. Extend simple number patterns (both repeating and growing patterns), and create similar patterns using different objects, such as using physical materials or shapes to represent numerical patterns.
2. Use patterns to make generalizations and predictions (e.g., determine a missing element in a pattern).
3. Create new patterns with consistent rules or plans, and describe the rule or general plan of existing patterns.

Use Algebraic Representations

4. Use objects, pictures, numbers, and other symbols to represent a problem situation.
5. Understand equivalence and extend the concept to situations involving symbols (e.g., $4 + 5 = 9$ and $9 = 4 + 5$, and $4 + 5 = 3 + 6 = + \ldots$).
6. Use symbols to represent unknown quantities and identify values for symbols in an expression or equation using addition and subtraction (e.g., $+ = 10, - 2 = 4$).

Analyze Change

7. Describe qualitative and quantitative changes, especially those involving addition and subtraction (e.g., a student).

Data Analysis and Probability

Data Collection

1. Pose questions, use observations, interviews, and surveys to collect data, and organize data in charts, picture graphs, and bar graphs.
2. Read, interpret, and make comparisons and predictions from data represented in charts, line plots, picture graphs, and bar graphs.
3. Read and construct simple time lines to sequence events.

Statistical Methods

4. Write a few sentences to describe and compare categories of data represented in a chart or graph, and make statements about the data as a whole.
5. Identify untrue or inappropriate statements about a given set of data.

THIRD GRADE

Number, Number Sense, and Operations Standard

Number and Number Systems

1. Identify and generate equivalent forms of whole numbers (e.g., 36, 30 + 6, 9 × 4, 46 − 10, number of inches in a yard).
2. Use place-value concepts to represent whole numbers and decimals using numerals, words, expanded notation, and physical models. For example:
   a. Recognize 100 means "10 tens" as well as a single entity (1 hundred) through physical models and trading games.
   b. Describe the multiplicative nature of the number system (e.g., the structure of 3205 as 3 × 1000 plus 2 × 100 plus 5 × 1).
   c. Model the size of 1000 in multiple ways (e.g., packaging 1000 objects into 10 boxes of 100, modeling a meter with centimeter and decimeter strips, or gathering 1000 pop-can tabs).
   d. Explain the concept of tenths and hundredths using physical models, such as metric pieces, base-10, blocks) decimal squares, or money.
3. Use mathematical language and symbols to compare and order (e.g., less than, greater than, at most, at least, <, >, =, ≤, ≥).
4. Count money and make change using coins and paper bills, to 10 dollars.
5. Represent fractions and mixed numbers using words, numerals, and physical models.

6. Compare and order commonly used fractions and mixed numbers using number lines, models (such as fraction circles or bars), points of reference (such as more or less than $\frac{1}{2}$), and equivalent forms using physical or visual models.

7. Recognize and use decimal and fraction concepts and notations as related ways of representing parts of a whole or a set (e.g., three of ten marbles are red can also be described as $\frac{3}{10}$ and 3 tenths are red).

Meaning of Operations

8. Model, represent, and explain multiplication (e.g., repeated addition, skip counting, rectangular arrays, and area model). For example:
   a. Use conventional mathematical symbols to write equations for word problems involving multiplication.
   b. Understand that, unlike addition and subtraction, the factors in multiplication and division may have different units (e.g., three boxes of five cookies each).

9. Model, represent, and explain division, (e.g., sharing equally, repeated subtraction, rectangular arrays, and area model). For example:
   a. Translate contextual situations involving division into conventional mathematical symbols.
   b. Explain how a remainder may impact an answer in a real-world situation (e.g., 14 cookies being shared by four children).

10. Explain and use relationships between operations, such as:
    a. relates addition and subtraction as inverse operations;
    b. relates multiplication and division as inverse operations;
    c. relates addition to multiplication (repeated addition);
    d. relates subtraction to division (repeated subtraction).

11. Model and use the commutative and associative properties for addition and multiplication.

Computation and Estimation

12. Add and subtract whole numbers with and without regrouping.

13. Demonstrate fluency in multiplication facts through 10 and corresponding division facts.

14. Multiply and divide two- and three-digit numbers by a single-digit number, without remainders for division.

15. Evaluate the reasonableness of computations based upon operations and the numbers involved (e.g., considering relative size, place value, and estimates).

Measurement

Measurement Units

1. Identify and select appropriate units for measuring:
   a. length – miles, kilometers, and other units of measure as appropriate;
   b. volume (capacity) – gallons;

c. weight – ounces, pounds, grams, or kilograms;

d. temperature – degrees (Fahrenheit or Celsius).

2. Establish personal or common referents to include additional units (e.g., a gallon container of milk; a postage stamp is about a square inch).

3. Tell time to the nearest minute and find elapsed time using a calendar or a clock.

4. Read thermometers in both Fahrenheit and Celsius scales.

Use Measurement Techniques and Tools

5. Estimate and measure length, weight, and volume (capacity), using metric and U.S. customary units, accurate to the nearest $\frac{1}{2}$ or $\frac{1}{4}$ unit as appropriate.

6. Use appropriate measurement tools and techniques to construct a figure or approximate an amount of specified length, weight, or volume (capacity) (e.g., construct a rectangle with length $2\frac{1}{2}$ inches and width 3 inches; fill a measuring cup to the $\frac{3}{4}$-cup mark).

7. Make estimates for perimeter, area, and volume using links, tiles, cubes, and other models.

Geometry and Spatial Sense

Characteristics and Properties

1. Analyze and describe properties of two-dimensional shapes and three-dimensional objects using terms such as *vertex, edge, angle, side,* and *face.*

2. Identify and describe the relative size of angles with respect to right angles as follows:

   a. Use physical models, like straws, to make different-sized angles by opening and closing the sides, not by changing the side lengths.

   b. Identify, classify, and draw right, acute, obtuse, and straight angles.

Spatial Relationships

3. Find and name locations on a labeled grid or coordinate system (e.g., a map or graph).

Transformations and Symmetry

4. Draw lines of symmetry to verify symmetrical two-dimensional shapes.

Visualization and Geometric Models

5. Build a three-dimensional model of an object composed of cubes (e.g., construct a model based on an illustration or actual object).

Patterns Functions and Algebra

Use Patterns Relations and Functions

1. Extend multiplicative and growing patterns, and describe the pattern or rule in words.

2. Analyze and replicate arithmetic sequences with and without a calculator.

3. Use patterns to make predictions, identify relationships, and solve problems.

Use Algebraic Representations

4. Model problem situations using objects, pictures, tables, numbers, letters, and other symbols.
5. Write, solve, and explain simple mathematical statements, such as: $7 + \_\_\_\_ > 8$ or $\_\_\_\_ + 8 = 10$.
6. Express mathematical relationships as equations and inequalities.

Analyze Change

7. Create tables to record, organize, and analyze data to discover patterns and rules.
8. Identify and describe quantitative changes, especially those involving addition and subtraction (e.g., the height of water in a glass becoming 1 centimeter lower each week due to evaporation).

Data Analysis and Probability

Data Collection

1. Collect and organize data from an experiment, such as recording and classifying observations or measurements, in response to a question posed.
2. Draw and interpret picture graphs in which a symbol or picture represents more than one object.
3. Read, interpret, and construct bar graphs with intervals greater than one.
4. Support a conclusion or prediction orally and in writing, using information in a table or graph.
5. Match a set of data with a graphical representation of the data.
6. Translate information freely among charts, tables, line plots, picture graphs, and bar graphs (e.g., create a bar graph from the information in a chart).
7. Analyze and interpret information represented on a time line.

Statistical Methods

8. Identify the mode of a data set and describe the information it gives about a data set.

Probability

9. Conduct a simple experiment or simulation of a simple event, record the results in a chart, table, or graph, and use the results to draw conclusions about the likelihood of possible outcomes.
10. Use physical models, pictures, diagrams, and lists to solve problems involving possible arrangements or combinations of two to four objects.

Index

Abstract stage, 49
Addition
    advancement, 250–251
    fluency/recall, 299–301
    principles, understanding, 251–252
Age-appropriate responses, 155
Anecdotal record
    example, 176f
    usage, 175
Angles, usage, 310–311
Animism, 54
Answers, logical certainty derivation, 4
Area, measurement, 200
Art materials, usage, 216
Association for Childhood Education
        International
        (ACEI), Play (position
        paper), 188–189
Associative property, 254
Attention Deficit/Hyperactive
        Disorder (ADHD),
        311–312
Authentic assessment, components, 114

Base 10, 301–303
    system, understanding, 314
Behavioral problems, reduction, 110
Behaviorism, mathematics
        (relationship), 45
Black history month, 362–363
Blocks
    shapes, mathematical relationship,
        162–163
    usage, 120–121, 211–212
Board games, usage, 121
Books, selection (suggestions),
        355–356
Boys/girls
    differences, 93t
    learning styles, differences
        (accommodation), 93–94

Calculators, usage, 321
California Content-Standard Checklist,
        284f–285f
Cardinal number, 195
Cards, decks (usage), 120
Causality, 138

Centration, 186–187
Chaining, involvement, 37
Charting, usage, 216
Charts, examples, 214f, 369f
Child-centered approach, objections,
        107–114
Child-centered curriculum, 104–114
    impact, 110
Child-centered environment,
        preparation, 115–118
Child-centered practices,
        implementation,
        113–114
Child-centered strategies, discussion,
        108
Child-initiated activities, benefits, 109
Children
    backgrounds/interests,
        understanding, 86
    behaviorist approach, 44–45
    characteristics, 75f
    constructivist approach, 49–57
    desks, arrangement, 117
    development, understanding, 43–57
    experience/knowledge,
        enhancement, 153
    learning, support, 157
    mathematicians, treatment, 4,
        11–15
        discussion, 104–105
    mathematics, combination, 1
        web sites, 31
    Montessori method, 46–47
    social nature, 189
    thinking ability, reliance
        (reduction), 3–4
Children with special needs, 82–89
    instruction, individualization
        (guidelines), 85f
Chips, usage, 120
Classification, 196, 242–244
Class inclusion, definition, 162
Classroom pod arrangement, 118f
Cognitive development, stages
        (Piaget), 52
Commercial curriculum, presence, 7–8
Commutative property, 254
Comparing words, usage, 198
Compose, action (initiation), 247

Concrete operational stage
        (Piaget), 52, 54
Concrete operations, usage, 293
Concrete stage, 48
Conservation, 54, 186, 200, 242–244
Consolidation stage, 127–128
Constructive play, 190
Constructivism, 42
    mathematics, relationship, 56
Constructivist classroom
    creation, 103
        web sites, 129–130
    guidance techniques, 111f
    lesson plans, standard items
        (inclusion), 126–127
    limitations/experience, education,
        127–128
    materials, usage, 118–123
    math series, 122–123
    parents, concerns (addressing), 113
    preparation, 123–128
    principal/administrator,
        communication, 124–125
    teachers, communication, 125
    textbooks
        review, 124
        usage, 122–123
Content areas, instruction, 28
Content standards, 16
Coordinate system, construction,
        198, 258
Counters, usage, 120
Counting all, 247
Counting on, 247
Counting skills, 194–195
Critical thinking, 297–299
    steps, 299f
Culturally appropriate responses, 155
Curriculum
    coherence, ensuring, 155
    focal points, rationale, 27f
    practices, usage, 154–155

Data analysis, 250, 258–259
Da Vinci, Leonardo, 366–368
Decimal system, 303
Decompose, action (initiation), 247
Disequilibrium, 55
Distance, accumulation, 201

Diversity, 65
    web sites, 96–97
Division, 303–305
Double Horseshoe classroom
            arrangement, 117f
Drawing, usage, 216
Dynamics, usage, 364–365
Dyscalculia, 83–84, 311, 312–313
Dyslexia, 83, 311, 312

Early childhood education,
            mathematics
            implications, 15
Education of All Handicapped
            Children
            Act (1975), 82
Egocentric characteristic, 185
Emergent mathematics, 4–6, 160
    definition, 4
    promotion, 6–7
        music experiences, usage,
            365–366
    support, 166
English language learners, 90–91
Environment Experience and Education
            (3E) approach, 28–29
    ages, appropriateness, 28f
Equality, transitivity, 255
Equity, 65
    web sites, 96–97
Ethnicity, home environment
            differences, 72

Families, characteristics, 75f
First grade, 239
    lesson plans, 270–282
    mathematical concepts, 250–259
    mathematics
        assessment, 282–286
        games, 268–269
        learning environment,
            appearance, 262–263
    NCTM focal points, 259, 261f, 262
    projects, 269
    web sites, 288
First grade children
    brain development/attention, 241
    characteristics, 240–245
    cognitive development, 242–244
    conservation/classification/pattern-
            ing, 242–244
    developmentally appropriate
            strategies/activities,
            263–269

linguistic development, 244
mathematical concepts, learning,
            245–259
memory/automation, 244
motor skills, 241–242
physical development, 241–242
social emotional development,
            244–245
standards, meeting, 259–262
Fluency, definition, 322
Food/cooking, resource, 358–359
FoodMaster
    initiative, 359
    lessons, samples, 360f
Formal assessment, informal assessment
            (contrast), 174
Formal operational stage (Piaget), 52,
            55
Formative assessment, summative
            assessment (contrast),
            175
Fractions, 308–309
Functions, usage, 196–197

Games, rules (usage), 54–55, 190
Gardner, Howard, 57
    Multiple Intelligences, 57f 58f
Gender differences, 91–95
Geometric concepts, 198–203
Geometry, spatial sense (relationship),
            250, 258
Gifted students, 89
Government, resource (usage), 361
Graphing, usage, 216
Graphs, examples, 369f
Group time, usage, 209
Growing pattern, 196

Hierarchical classification, 293–294
Hierarchical inclusion, 195, 303f
    relationships, application, 304
Homework, usage/development
            (suggestions), 324
Horizontal relevance, 350

Identity property, 255
Imaginative play, 216
Inclusion relationships, composition, 304
Inclusive classroom, description, 87f
Inclusive environments, creation, 86
Individual Family Service Plan
            (IFSP), 83
Individualized Education Plan (IEP),
            82–83

components, 83
services, 84
Individualized instruction, 65, 67–72
    definition, 67
    guidelines, 70f
    web sites, 96–97
Individually appropriate responses, 156
Individuals with Disabilities Education
            Act (IDEA), 82
Industry versus inferiority stage
            (Erikson), 294
Infants, 135
    activities, 163–165
    assessment, 174–177
        usage, 175–177
    characteristics, 136–144
    developmentally appropriate
            strategies/activities,
            159–166
    developmental milestones,
            139t–144t
    environments, characteristics, 158
    learning environment, 157–159
    lesson plans, 168, 169–173
    mathematical concepts, 150t–152t
        impact, 145–152
    mathematical games, 165
    mathematics, support, 166t–168t
    standards, meeting, 152–157
    web sites, 178
Initiative versus guilt stage, 188
Instructional repertoire, development
            (guidelines), 8–9
Integration, importance, 350–370
Intellectual autonomy, 245–247
Intellectual heteronomy, 246
Intuitive thinking, 53
Intuitive thought substage, 185

Kindergarten, 239
    lesson plans, 270–282
    mathematical concepts, 247–250
    mathematics
        assessment, 282–286
        checksheet, sample, 284f–285f
        games, 268–269
        learning environment,
            appearance, 262–263
    NCTM focal points, 259, 261f
    projects, 269
    web sites, 288
Kindergarten children
    brain development/attention, 241
    characteristics, 240–245

cognitive development, 242–244
conservation/classification/pattern-
        ing, 242–244
developmentally appropriate
        strategies/activities,
        263–269
linguistic development, 244
mathematical concepts, learning,
        245–259
memory/automation, 244
motor skills, 241–242
physical development, 241–242
social emotional development,
        244–245
standards, meeting, 259–262
Knowledge base
construction, 35
inclusion, 40
usage, 37
web sites, 61–62
Knowledge construction, 51

Language barrier, overcoming, 90
        suggestions, 91f
Learning disabilities, 83–84, 311–314
Learning styles, 59–60
Least restrictive environment (LRE), 82
Length, concepts, 201
Linear measurement, 309–310
Line symmetry, 200
Linguistic diversity, 89–90
Literature, usage, 351
Logico–mathematical knowledge, 146
Logo (programming language), usage,
        320–321
Looping program, incorporation, 112

Manipulatives, 120–122
        usage, 164–165, 210
Many-to-one correspondence, 304
Map making, usage, 215
Maps, usage, 361
Mathematical concepts/
        methods/language,
        introduction, 156–157
Mathematical learning/achievement,
        children with special
        needs (impact), 83–84
Mathematical self-concept, promotion
        (suggestions), 296
Mathematical understanding
        network, 300f
        perspective, 5
Mathematicians

attempts, usage, 14–15
colleagues, collaboration, 12–13
problems, complexity, 13–14
problem solving process,
        satisfaction/pride, 14
single problem, analysis, 12
solution, correctness (proof), 13
Mathematics
anxiety, control, 38–39
art, integration, 366–368
children, natural interest
        (enhancement), 152–153
classroom
        gifted students, interaction
                guidelines, 88f
        nature/nurture, impact, 66–67
curriculum/teaching practices,
        basis, 154–155
games, 212–213
integration, 156, 350
        web sites, 374–375
learning, visual approach, 48–49
lessons, 41–42
        planning, 125–126
Piaget, importance, 55
problem, design criteria, 14
standards, usage, 126–127
support, children's literature
        (usage), 352f–354f
teacher, necessities, 36
teaching
        findings, 9–11
        NCTM principles, 17f
web apples, example, 220f
Mathematics acquisition device
        (MAD), 5
Maturity stage, 128
Meaningful counting, 193
Measurement
concepts, 198, 200–203
iterated units, 248–249
understanding, 256–257
Melody, usage, 364
Memory, automation (relationship), 244
Mind, qualitative/quantitative
        changes, 51
Minority enrollment, test scores, 81f
Minority students, achievement, 78–82
Montessori, materials/mathematics
        (relationship), 47–48
More, concept, 149
Multi–age program, incorporation, 112
Multiple classifications,
        example, 162–163

Multiplication, 303–307
        two-dimensional array, 307f
Multiplicative thinking, 303
        construction, support, 306
Museums, usage, 366
Music
        art/physical education, integration,
                119f
        mathematics, integration, 363–365

National Aeronautics and Space
        Administration (NASA),
        resource, 358
National Assessment of Education
        Progress (NAEP), 79
National Association for the Education
        of Young Children
        (NAEYC)
        Code of Ethical Conduct, 71, 79
        mathematics, joint statement, 18–27
National Council for Social Studies
        (NCSS), 108
National Council of Teachers of
        Mathematics (NCTM)
        focal points, 15, 259–262
        mathematics
                joint statement, 18–27
                theoretical basis, 56–57
        Principles for School Mathematics,
                204–205
        principles/standards/curriculum,
                16–28
National Science Teachers Association
        (NSTA), 108
Neurons, efficiency, 137
No Child Left Behind, testing, 339
Non-physical measurements, gauging
        (difficulty), 257
Number
        nature, 55
        relationship, 149–150, 201
Number cubes, usage, 121

Object
        habituation, 145
        permanence, 52
                importance, 137–138
        physical knowledge, construction,
                146
One, concept, 149
Order, concepts, 195
Ordinal number, 195
        understanding, 198
Organizing behaviors, progression, 147

Papet, Seymour, 320
Parental attainment level, scores, 73f
Parents, constructivist classroom letter, 124
Partitioning, 200
Patterning, 196, 242–244
Patterns, algebra (relationship), 249, 257–258
Physical activity, 368–370
Place value, 301–303
    understanding, 252–256
Positional words, usage, 198
Practice play, 189
PreK-5th grades, NCTM
            standards/indicators, 20t–26t
PreK-8th grades, curriculum focal
            points, 27–28
Pre-operational stage (Piaget), 52, 53–54
Preschool age, 183
    children, developmentally
            appropriate
            strategies/activities, 208–230
    web sites, 234
Preschool children
    assessment, 230–233
    centration, 186–187
    characteristics, 184–191
    cognitive development, 185
    conservation, 186
    emotional development, 188
    lesson plans, 218–230
    mathematical concepts, learning, 191–203
    physical development, 184
    play, 188–190
    standards, meeting, 204–205
    symbolic/intuitive thought, 185–186
    thought, reversibility, 187–188
Preschool focal points, 206f
Preschool mathematics
    concepts, 192–193, 202f–203f
    developmental milestones, 190–191
        list, 192t
    learning environment, appearance, 207
    mathematics standards/
            benchmarks, 204–205
    numerical concepts, 193–198

Pretence play, 190
Probability, 250, 258–259
Problem
    consideration, importance, 2–3
    introduction, rules, 2
Problem solving
    strategies, 266
    usage, 197–198
Process
    product, contrast, 3–4
    standards, 16
Project Approach, 108–109
    usage, 213–215, 370–373
Puzzles, usage, 122

Reading, mathematics (integration), 350–357
Recycled materials, usage, 122
Reflection
    definition, 37
    learning, 35
    process, 37–38
    web sites, 61–62
Relationship pattern, 196
Relationships, making, 149–150
Renewal stage, 128
Repeating patterns, 196
Representation, 185
Representational thought, 147
Rhythm
    music, mathematical relationship, 160–161
    usage, 364–365
Rockets, resource, 358
Rotational symmetry, 199
Rote counting, 193
Running record, 176–177
    example, 177f

Scaffolding, 50
Schemas (Piaget), 147
    assimilation, 55
Schemes, 52
School mathematics
    NCTM principles, 16
    NCTM standards, 16
Schools, poverty (characteristics), 75f
Science, mathematics (integration), 357–359
Second grade, 291
    constructivist approach, 297–298
    division, presentation, 307
    focal points, 315f

hands-on materials/manipulatives, usage, 324–326
lesson plans, 327–337
mathematics
    assessment, 338–340
    learning environment, appearance, 317–318
    teaching lessons/problem solving, 318–319
    technology, usage, 320
    timed/fluency activities, 322–323
    web sites, 342
    worksheets/homework, usage, 323–324
Second grade children
    characteristics, 292–296
    cognitive development, 293–294
    developmentally appropriate
            strategies/activities, 318–326
    mathematical concepts, learning, 296–311
    physical development, 292–293
    rulers/standard units, usage, 309
    social emotional development, 294–296
    standards, meeting, 314–316
    Selective attention, 241
    Self-esteem, reflection, 295
Self-fulfilling prophecy (Pygmalion effect), 69–71
Self-understanding, 36–39
Semi-concrete stage, 49
Sensorimotor play, 189
Sensorimotor stage (Piaget), 52–53
Sequence words, usage, 198
Seriation, concepts, 195
Shape concepts, 198–203
Shape words, usage, 198–199
Sides, usage, 310–311
Social knowledge, 146
Social studies, mathematics
            (integration), 359–362
Socio-constructivist, 49
Socioeconomic factors, 72–78
    Socio-economic status (SES), 72
obstacles, overcoming, 75–78
Spatial awareness, 138
Standardized assessment, authentic
            assessment (contrast), 174
Standardized testing, gender differences
            (relationship), 94–95
Standard unit, understanding, 256–257

Statistics, 250, 258–259
Steady beat, usage, 364
Stimulus, introduction, 145
Students
    expectations, holding, 69–72
    historical scores, 80t
    understanding, 57–60
Subtraction, fluency/recall, 299–301
Survival stage, 127
Symbolic function substage, 185
Symbolic play, 190
Symbols, usage, 52–53
Symmetry
    idea, understanding, 198–199
    usage, 199
System of ones, 195

Talented students, 89
Tangrams, usage, 210–211
Teachable moments, 106–107
Teachers
    decision makers, 40–42
    desk, placement, 116–118
    impact, 7–9
    math games, usage, 212–213
    NAEYC/NCTM recommendations,
        19f
Teaching
    child–centered approach, 114
    practices, usage, 154–155
Tempo, usage, 364–365
Theory of Multiple Intelligences (MI),
    57
Third grade, 291
    constructivist approach, 297
    division, presentation, 307
    focal points, 316f
    hands-on materials/manipulatives,
        usage, 324–326
    lesson plans, 327–337
    mathematics
        assessment, 338–340

learning environment,
        appearance, 317–318
    teaching lessons/problem solving,
        318–319
    technology, usage, 320
    timed/fluency activities, 322–323
    web sites, 342
    worksheets/homework, usage,
        323–324
Third grade children
    characteristics, 292–296
    cognitive development, 293–294
    developmentally appropriate
        strategies/activities,
        318–326
    mathematical concepts, learning,
        296–311
    physical development, 292–293
    rulers/standard units, usage, 309
    social emotional development,
        294–296
    standards, meeting, 314–316
Trends in Mathematics
        and Science Study
        (TIMSS), 9
    data, usage, 11
    findings, 10f
Thought, reversibility, 187–188
Three-dimensional shapes, attributes,
    198–199
Timbre, usage, 364–365
Time
    concepts, 199–200
    units, 249
Timed tests, usage, 322
Time Sample, 176–177
Toddlers, 135
    activities, 163–165
    assessment, 174–177
        usage, 175–177
    characteristics, 136–144

developmentally appropriate
        strategies/activities,
        159–166
    developmental milestones,
        139t–144t
    learning environment, 157–159
    lesson plans, 166, 169–173
    mathematical concepts, 150t–152t
        impact, 145–152
    mathematical games, 165
    mathematics, support, 166t–168t
    standards, meeting, 152–157
    web sites, 178
Topic selection, usage, 370–371
Transformations, idea (understanding),
    199
Transitivity, 200, 257
Trial and error thinking, 54
Two-dimensional shapes
    attributes, 198–199
    sides/angles, usage, 310–311

Unit iteration, 200, 201

Venn diagram, example, 197f
Vertical relevance, 350
Visual perception, usage, 6
Vitruvian Man, 367
Vygotsky, Lev, 49

Weavings, usage, 366
Weight, measurement, 200
Whole-class instruction, 265–268
Word problems, usage, 263–265
Words, writing/saying, 193–194
Worksheets, usage/development
        (suggestions), 324

Zone of Proximal Development
        (ZPD), 49–50